DRAMATIC CONSTRUCTION

Edward
Mabley

DRAMATIC
CONSTRUCTION
An Outline of
Basic Principles

Followed by technical analyses of significant
plays by Sophocles, Shakespeare, Molière, Sheridan,
Ibsen, Wilde, Chekov, Shaw, O'Casey, O'Neill,
Brecht, Sartre, Williams, Miller,
Beckett, Pinter, Ionesco, Weiss, and others

CHILTON BOOK COMPANY
Philadelphia · New York

Copyright © 1972 by Edward Mabley

First Edition

All Rights Reserved

*Published in Philadelphia by Chilton Book Company
and simultaneously in Ontario, Canada,
by Thomas Nelson & Sons, Ltd.*

Library of Congress Cataloguing in Publication Data

Mabley, Edward Howe, date.
  Dramatic construction.

  Includes bibliographical references.
  1. Drama—History and criticism. 2. Drama—
Technique. I. Title.
PN1691.M3   808.2   72–3964
ISBN 0–8019–5680–3

Manufactured in the United States of America

Designed by Adrianne Onderdonk Dudden

Chief credit for the founding and success of the New Dramatists Committee, which has nurtured so many of America's finest playwrights, must go to

MICHAELA O'HARRA

a lady of vision, persistence, and common sense, and to her this book is affectionately dedicated.

FOREWORD

Playwriting is often thought, by those with no experience of it, to be the telling of a story by means of dialogue. Hence the craft, it would seem, is to devise things for the actors to say to one another consistent with their characterizations. If it were as simple as this nearly everyone could be a dramatist. It is infinitely more complex than this, and the amateur can no more hope to practice it successfully without a period of training than he can medicine, the law, or architecture.

It is the aim of this work to explain problems of craft that the inexperienced writer will face, problems that he might solve intuitively, or by trial and error, or by actual experience and observation in the theatre, but for which answers already exist. Dramatists have been facing these problems from the time of Aeschylus to the present day, and the solutions are to be found in their plays.

Of course, a fine play is far more than a piece of good engineering. It will reflect the understanding, the humor and compassion, the breadth of vision of the writer—qualities not to be developed by textbook or classroom instruction. But the engineering is important too—even essential.

In attempting to set down what I and many others believe to be the basic principles of dramatic construction (which, incidentally, are the same for film and television as for the stage), I have thought it best to rely on illustration rather than long and involved explanations. Hence the principles are discussed somewhat briefly, while the bulk of the work is devoted to analyses of some well-known and easily accessible plays, most of which can be found in any library or purchased in paperback. Although the analysis of each play contains a synopsis, this must not be thought of as a substitute for reading and studying the full text. Even though the reader may have recently seen or read the play in question, total familiarity is essential, and the serious student should not approach the analyses without copies of the plays in hand.

Ideally he should see the play, then read it. Seeing it is not quite enough for the present purpose. A good play well produced and performed is such an exhilarating experience that it is difficult to maintain an objectively analytical attitude during the performance. One is far less apt to be overwhelmed by the printed text—after all, the work was not written for this medium—and the printed play can be studied slowly and carefully. The synopses in this book should be regarded merely as a sort of bird's-eye view of each play's text. Their purpose is to make the basic structural movements of the plays more readily identifiable.

For additional comment on most of the plays and their significance in the wider spectrum of dramatic history, John Gassner's *Masters of the Drama* is highly recommended. Other works of Mr. Gassner's—*Directions in Modern Theatre and Drama* (also published under the title *Form and Idea in Modern Theatre*), *Theatre at the Crossroads, The Theatre in Our Times,* and *Dramatic Soundings*—are also helpful. Walter Kerr has written an extremely perceptive book, *Tragedy and Comedy,* in which he discusses the development and meaning of these two enduring forms. A. C. Bradley's *Shakespearean Tragedy* examines *Hamlet, Othello, King Lear,* and *Macbeth* in some very penetrating character analyses. *The Peopled Wound,* by Martin Esslin, analyzes the plays of Harold Pinter. *Creative Theatre,* an important work by Roy Mitchell, written in 1929, has been privately reprinted and, like the others, may be secured at the Drama Book Shop, 150 West 52nd Street, New York 10019.

Edward Mabley
February 1972

ACKNOWLEDGMENTS

As I studied with the late John Gassner, I got into the habit of making notes at his lectures and copying from his books statements that particularly interested me. I have quoted Mr. Gassner a number of times in this volume, with the gracious permission of Mrs. Mollie Gassner. Unfortunately, I no longer know the exact source of most of the statements. John Gassner's major critical works, listed in the Foreword, seem to me indispensable to a comprehensive study of the drama and invaluable to the playwright.

Quotations from Brooks Atkinson, Marian Gallaway, Walter Kerr, Gian Carlo Menotti, and John Russell Taylor are made with the courteous permission of the writers themselves. Dr. Gallaway is author of a splendid book, *Constructing a Play*, now unfortunately out of print and hard to find; *The Rise and Fall of the Well-Made Play*, by Mr. Taylor, the English critic, is exceptionally interesting.

The quotation from Friedrich Duerrenmatt is made with permission of his representative, Kurt Hellmer. It appeared in the Tulane Drama Review, October 1958. The quotation from Thornton Wilder is made with permission of his representative, Brandt & Brandt. It appears under the title "Some Thoughts on Playwriting" in *The Intent of the Artist*, edited by Augusto Centeno, published by Russell and Russell (copyright 1941). Both articles are reprinted in Toby Cole's *Playwrights on Playwriting*.

Dialogue from *Juno and the Paycock* and *The Plough and the Stars*, by Sean O'Casey, is quoted with the kind permission of Mrs.

Eileen O'Casey and the publishers, Macmillan and Co., Ltd., of London.

Lines from Samuel Beckett's *Waiting for Godot* are reprinted by permission of Grove Press, Inc., translated from the original French text by the author (copyright © 1954 by Grove Press).

Dialogue from *Mr. Roberts,* by Thomas Heggen and Joshua Logan, is quoted with permission of the publishers, Random House, Inc. (copyright 1948).

The quotation from *Mr. Abbott,* by George Abbott, is made with permission of the publishers, Random House, Inc. (copyright 1963).

The quotation from *The American Musical Theatre,* by Lehman Engel, is made with the permission of the publishers, The Macmillan Company (copyright © CBS Records 1967).

The quotation from *Theory and Technique of Playwriting,* by John Howard Lawson, is made with permission of the publishers, G. P. Putnam's Sons (copyright 1936, 1949, 1960).

The quotations from Margaret Webster are reprinted by permission of the World Publishing Company, from *Shakespeare Without Tears,* by Margaret Webster (copyright 1942 by McGraw-Hill, Inc.; revised edition copyright © 1955 by the World Publishing Company).

I am grateful to Little, Brown and Company for their courtesy in sending me, long in advance of publication, proofs of *The Citizen Kane Book,* which made it possible to include an analysis of this important film.

And I am especially indebted to Richard Mansfield for his penetrating and lucid analysis of Samuel Beckett's *Waiting for Godot.*

E. M.

THE FULL TEXTS

Nearly all the plays (except *Citizen Kane*), since they are so well known, may be found both in paperback and in various anthologies, such as those edited by John Gassner. However, the following list may help a reader to find inexpensive copies. All may be secured at the Drama Book Shop, 150 West 52nd Street, New York 10019, and may be ordered by mail.

Oedipus the King, in a translation by David Grene, may be found in *Greek Tragedies*, Volume One, Phoenix Books, The University of Chicago Press (copyright 1942 by the University of Chicago).

The Folger Library *General Reader's Shakespeare* is recommended for *Hamlet* (and all Shakespeare's plays). This series of very inexpensive paperbacks is splendidly edited, with the notes conveniently placed opposite the text.

One of the best translations of *Tartuffe* is that made by Richard Wilbur. It is published as a Harvest Book by Harcourt, Brace and World, Inc. (copyright 1961, 1962, 1963 by Richard Wilbur).

The School for Scandal is in the Reader's Enrichment Series, published by the Washington Square Press.

Ibsen's *Ghosts,* in a translation by Kai Jurgensen and Robert Schenkkan, is in the Bard Theatre Library, published by Avon.

Samuel French now publishes an acting edition of *Charley's Aunt* as first performed in 1892. This is superior to the modernization of the play which they published in 1935.

The Importance of Being Earnest is in the Bard Theatre Library, published by Avon.

The Cherry Orchard, translated by Stark Young, is issued in a Samuel French acting edition. A translation by Avrahm Yarmolinsky is issued by the Avon Theatre Library.

The full text of *Pygmalion,* including Shaw's preface and the scenes he later interpolated, may be found in a Penguin paperback; also in the Reader's Enrichment Series, published by the Washington Square Press.

An Acting edition of *Juno and the Paycock* is published by Samuel French (copyright 1925 by Macmillan; acting edition copyright 1932 by Samuel French, Ltd.).

Desire Under the Elms is published in a Signet paperback; also in *Eight Great Tragedies,* a Mentor Book from the New American Library (copyright 1924, 1952 by Eugene O'Neill).

An acting edition of *Life with Father* is published by Dramatists Play Service, Inc. (copyright 1939, 1940 by Howard Lindsay, Russel Crouse, and Katharine B. Day; copyright renewed 1967).

The Citizen Kane Book, an Atlantic Monthly Press Book published by Little, Brown and Company, contains both the shooting script and the cutting continuity of *Citizen Kane,* as well as Pauline Kael's critical article *Raising Kane* (copyright 1971 by Bantam Books).

Maurice Valency's translation of *The Madwoman of Chaillot* is issued in an acting edition by the Dramatists Play Service, Inc. (copyright 1947 by Maurice Valency, under the title *La Folle de Chaillot* by Jean Giraudoux).

The Caucasian Chalk Circle, in an original English version by Eric Bentley and Maja Apelman, may be found in *Parables for the Theatre,* published by Grove Press, Inc. It is also published separately by Grove Press, Inc. (copyright by Eric Bentley, 1947, as an unpublished ms., and in 1948 as a published book).

No Exit, in a collection of Sartre's plays, is published by Vintage Books, a Division of Random House. An acting edition has also been published by Samuel French (*No Exit* as *Huis Clos,* copyright by Librarie Gallimard, 1945).

A Streetcar Named Desire is published in a Signet paperback, from the New American Library (copyright 1947 by Tennessee Williams).

Death of a Salesman is published in an acting edition by Dramatists Play Service, Inc. (copyright 1948, 1949, 1951, and 1952 by Arthur Miller).

Waiting for Godot is published by Grove Press, Inc. (copyright 1954 by Grove Press).

The book and lyrics of *My Fair Lady* may be found in a Signet paperback from the New American Library (copyright 1956 by Alan Jay Lerner and Frederick Loewe).

The Birthday Party is published by Grove Press, Inc. (copyright 1959, 1960, and 1965 by Harold Pinter).

Rhinoceros, translated by Derek Prouse, is published by Grove Press, Inc. An acting edition is also published by Samuel French (copyright by John Calder [Publishers] Ltd., 1960).

An acting edition of *A Man for All Seasons* is published by Samuel French (copyright 1960, 1962 by Robert Bolt).

Marat/Sade, in an English version by Geoffrey Skelton, with an introduction by Peter Brook, originally published by Atheneum, is available in a Pocket Books paperback. The Dramatic Publishing Company of Chicago also issues an edition (copyright 1965 by John Calder Ltd.).

CONTENTS

APPENDICES

THE TOOLS

Competence in literary composition is not enough. Many great men of letters, like Tennyson, Browning, and Henry James, wrote for the theatre in forms that were acceptable to their times, but their plays fell flat on the stage. Pinero was no match for any one of them intellectually or artistically, but what he wrote came to life in the theatre of his day. Ponderous as he was as a thinker and craftsman, he had the rhythm of the theatre in his blood.

—*Brooks Atkinson*

There are as well-established rules for the theatre as there are for painting and music. The only ones who can successfully break the rules are the people who know them. —*Eugene O'Neill*

The principles I speak of are not rules; they are merely the expressions of the usable practices that can be derived from the work of our best practitioners. It is quite possible and perhaps even desirable for a talented writer who fully understands the principles, as they have come down to us, to depart from them provided he is *aware* of his departure and has knowingly substituted some other (perhaps now undreamed of) workable element to replace what he chooses to reject from the past. This practice is, in itself, the very history of all the arts. But the "new" has been authentically new when it has consciously descended from a knowledge of everything good that has preceded it. —*Lehman Engel*

The Playwright's Task

The creation of a play is certainly one of the most difficult forms of writing in all literature. Indeed, it is because the end result, if successful, is so much more than literature that the writer finds his path strewn with pitfalls and problems that don't arise in the creation of an essay, a novel, a poem. It is significant that many of the greatest playwrights, notably Shakespeare and Molière, were identified with particular theatres and were thoroughly conversant with theatre problems and aware of audience psychology.

But playwriting is an ancient art that has been successfully practiced by all kinds of men for different kinds of audiences in attendance under widely varying circumstances. And if we examine successful plays (and by this I mean simply plays that have held the interest of large audiences over a period of time) we find that they seem to share certain features, that the technique employed to hold audience interest is strikingly similar in a comedy by Plautus and one by Neil Simon, a Greek tragedy and a drama by Ibsen, a Shakespearean play and today's trail-blazing work of Ionesco, Beckett, Sartre, or Weiss. In other words, there is a technique of focusing audience interest that can be observed, and it can be learned. (Not that mastery of the technique will automatically assure the creation of a viable play, but certainly the lack of a deliberate or instinctive technique is almost certain to insure failure.)

The printed play is no more the drama than the score of a symphony is the symphony or the dancer's notes the dance, or the architect's blueprint the cathedral. Indeed, the manuscript is precisely a score or blueprint of the actual drama.   —*Marian Gallaway*

The playwright's task is far more than the setting down of dialogue. Indeed, this part of the task may turn out to be the least of his problems. The concept to which the dramatist must address himself is the creative vision of an event to take place before a large number of people gathered together for the purpose of experiencing that event. It is a vision of a story being enacted not only by means of dialogue spoken by actors, but by their physical activity, by their surroundings (in modern times usually a setting designed from a description furnished by the writer), by lighting, by music perhaps, and dancing and costumes, by the whole pace and rhythm of the play and its production. All these matters are the concern of the dramatist, for though others must be called upon to help interpret his vision (he cannot be a specialist in all the elements that go to make up a theatrical performance), the vision is his, and he had better be clear in his own mind as to what he wants the audience to see and hear and experience when his play is finally mounted and performed.

We can be sure that the author of every great and successful play imagined the activity of the actors as well as their dialogue, that he envisioned where as well as when they would be making their entrances and exits, what the effect of settings and costumes would be, the effect of music and dancing if they were to be employed, the subtle changes of rhythm and pace that good direction would bring to the production. This is not to suggest that the playwright has to be a composer, choreographer, set designer, or electrician any more than he has to be his own director or leading actor; but he must know how the various arts of the theatre can be utilized to make real in the playhouse what was born in his head. His vision is contained in the playscript, a sort of blueprint of what is to follow. And what follows is an extremely complex art form, existing not only in three dimensions, like sculpture and architecture, but in the extra dimension of time, which also enters into the arts of music, poetry, and dance.

Unless he is very fortunate, the playwright can hardly anticipate a total fulfillment of his vision. Shakespeare was well acquainted with actors' failings, as is apparent in Hamlet's advice to the players, and his awareness of the limited resources of his playhouse led him to call it an "unworthy scaffold," and warn us to "piece-out our imperfections with your thoughts." But he was master of his actors' performances and their surroundings so far as that was possible. He undoubtedly served as his own director when he could. The point is simply that all the elements were in his mind as parts of his scheme for the production. His dialogue, magnificent as it is, was only one of those elements.

So in all that follows it should be borne in mind that, in considering dramatic construction, we are dealing with plans for a physical representation of the story on a stage, in four dimensions— the dimension of time being the one that introduces the elements of pace and rhythm as part of the pattern.

A Cautionary Note

One of the great difficulties in play analysis is the confusion of its vocabulary. When a doctor uses the word "appendicitis," or a lawyer "subpoena," or an architect "fenestration," others in the same profession know exactly what he is talking about. When a teacher or dramatist or critic uses the following words (all of them taken from chapter headings in books on playwriting)—continuity, progression, premise, theme, forestalling, finger-posts, preparation, anticlimax, complication, scene, catastrophe, resolution, representation, crisis, antagonist, impressionism, adjustment, peripety, irony, attack, focus, suspense, action, recognition, balance, movement, orchestration, unity of opposites, static, jumping, transition, incident—only he can be sure of what he means, for most of the terms have no precise definitions in the context of the subject matter. They are used to mean different things by different writers. Reading half a dozen books on playwriting in succession is apt to leave the student quite bewildered, unless he can ignore the terminology and think in terms of concepts.

And anyone venturing another book on the subject must perforce choose his own vocabulary, and indicate what every imprecise term means to him. The reader, to avoid confusion, had best ignore for the moment what others have meant by "premise" and "crisis" and "unity" and so on, and concentrate on the meaning in the context of the work in hand. Unfortunately, there seems to be no other way around this difficulty.

Conflict

Drama is the representation of the will of man in conflict with the mysterious powers or natural forces which limit or belittle us. It is one of us thrown living upon the stage, there to struggle against fatality, against social law, against one of his fellow mortals, against himself if need be, against the ambitions, the interests, the prejudices, the folly, the malevolence of those who surround him.

—*Ferdinand Brunetière*

Conflict is one element that seems to be an essential ingredient, the *sine qua non*, of every forceful dramatic work. It may be taken as axiomatic to say that without conflict we are not going to have a play to which an audience will pay much heed. A play depicts a contest, in which the conscious will is employed to accomplish some specific goal, a goal that is hard to reach, and whose accomplishment is actively resisted.

The Premise and the Opening

Shakespeare, however startling it may be to remind ourselves of the fact, started with the story. In *Hamlet* and in *Lear*, he had an old play upon which to work, in *Othello* an Italian romance, in *Macbeth* the chronicles of his old friend Holinshed, who had seen him through so many medieval battles. The amazing poetic and dramatic genius which enabled him to transform his story material into the essentials of pity and terror is a commonplace of critical praise. But let us remember that he never lost the story.

—*Margaret Webster*

I place construction, or story line, first, and words second. A playwright seems to me like an architect—he must know what the whole building is like before he begins, and he must put up the iron girders first and then, after the unadorned frame is standing, begin to add the things that show. —*George Abbott*

The beginning of a play is necessarily an arbitrary point, selected by the playwright, in a larger story. The circumstances that have brought about the conflict with which the play deals can usually be ascribed to things that happened long before the point at which the curtain rises. (Lillian Hellman even fashioned another full evening's drama, *Another Part of the Forest,* from material antecedent to *The Little Foxes.* And Percy MacKaye managed to write a cycle of four plays, *The Mystery of Hamlet, King of Denmark,* all of which are prelude to Shakespeare's work.)

The premise, as the term is used here, is simply the entire situation, including the pertinent background material, that exists as the principal character, the protagonist, starts moving toward his goal, the objective. The opening, as distinguished from the premise, is that spot in the extended story selected by the playwright to begin his play—specifically, that part of the larger story that he intends to put upon the stage.

Here are the premises and openings of five famous plays:

Athens has been at war for eighteen years, and the women are heartily tired of the interminable fighting. Aristophanes chose as his opening Lysistrata's attempt to persuade the women of Athens, some of whom are reluctant to co-operate, that by denying their favors to their husbands and lovers they can force the men to stop making war.

The Capulets and the Montagues have for years been bitter enemies. Romeo, an impulsive young man and scion of the Montagues, and Juliet, the sensitive daughter of the Capulets, fall deeply in love. Shakespeare chose to open the play with a street brawl dramatizing the enmity of the two families, then moved soon to a ball given by the Capulets at which Romeo, an unbidden guest, first encounters Juliet.

Anna Christie has been brought up by relatives on a Minnesota farm. There she had been ill-treated and seduced; eventually she left the farm to earn her own way. After an absence of fifteen years she comes to live with her father, who idolizes her. It is apparent to everyone but him that she is a prostitute. O'Neill chose as his opening the father's break with the woman with whom he has been sharing his quarters on the barge, so that Anna, when she arrives, may find a decent home.

Elizabeth Barrett has been bullied and made an invalid by her father years before Robert Browning appears on the scene in *The Barretts of Wimpole Street*. He is already well acquainted with her poems, and has been importuning her, by mail, to let him call. Rudolf Besier selected as his opening the day before Browning's first meeting with Elizabeth. In that first scene he establishes her invalidism, the tyranny of her father, and the atmosphere of the Barrett household. Browning's arrival seems like a breath of fresh air in a tomb, and clearly foreshadows the coming conflict.

Tony's interest in Alice Sycamore, in *You Can't Take It With You*, starts before the play begins, and what his parents find when he brings them to meet Alice's family has its roots in many years of a pleasantly unconventional life style. Kaufman and Hart found it necessary to establish the unusual behavior of the Sycamores at the opening of the play; then they bring on Alice, the daughter, who reveals her romantic interest in Tony, her boss's son, and informs them that he is about to call.

Many plays are conceived, in the writer's mind, with a situation that is essentially the premise. A satisfactory premise always contains the potential of conflict. Once the opening has been selected, the start of that conflict should not be long delayed.

The Protagonist and Objective

Drama does not occur because a character thinks something right or wrong; it occurs because he wants something intolerably. The protagonist must feel passionately even more than he must think clearly. . . . The common denominator, the universal factor which moves audiences, is not thought, not unpurposive activity, not the mere writhing of passion, but *will*. —*Marian Gallaway*

The protagonist of a play is usually the leading character. But this is by no means a definition, nor does it indicate his function in the structure of a play. The chief characteristic of the protagonist is a desire, usually intense, to achieve a certain goal, and it is the interest of the audience in watching him move toward that objective that constitutes its absorption in the play. Indeed, it is the movement toward the objective that determines where the play shall begin and end.

Near the beginning of every well-constructed play the author directs our attention strongly toward one of his characters. He does this principally by showing this person, the protagonist, in the grip of some strong desire, some intense need, bent on a course of action from which he is not to be deflected. He wants something—power, revenge, a lady's hand, bread, peace of mind, glory, escape from a pursuer. Whatever it may be, some kind of intense desire is always present.

Antigone is determined, in spite of Creon's edict, that her brother shall be buried with appropriate funeral rites. Othello, a man of unimpeachable rectitude, desperately needs to believe in the faithfulness of his beloved wife, whose honor has been attacked. Monsieur Jourdain, of *The Would-Be Gentleman*, a *nouveau riche*, longs to be accepted by the fashionable world as a cultivated gentleman. In *An Enemy of the People* Dr. Stockmann insists, against the opposition of an entire town, on disclosing that the waters of a proposed spa are polluted. Regina Giddons, of *The Little Foxes*, disregarding every ethical and moral scruple, is determined to exploit a business opportunity that will make her rich. In *Fiddler on the Roof*, Tevye, the milkman, living precariously, wants merely to provide decently for his family and to see his five daughters properly married.

It is the protagonist's pursuit of his objective that we follow during the course of the play. The importance of this fact can hardly be overestimated, for when we are shown whether he has achieved or failed to achieve his objective, the play is over. It is the protagonist's pursuit of his goal that is the real subject matter of the play.

A good protagonist is one that arouses some kind of emotional response from the audience. He can be sympathetic, like Antigone or Tevye. He can arouse our pity, like Othello, or amusement, like M. Jourdain, or admiration, like Dr. Stockmann, or antagonism, like Regina. The important thing is that the audience not be indifferent to him. We must care, one way or another, whether he achieves his goal. A protagonist incapable of arousing some kind of emotional response is almost certain to bore the audience and sink the play.

It should be noted too that our interest in whether the protagonist achieves his desire is just about proportionate to *his* interest in the same subject. The more intensely he desires, the greater our concern. It isn't a question of whether he's pursuing a socially desirable objective, whether he's moral or immoral, just or unjust, generous or selfish; it's how fiercely he wants something that determines the degree of our interest in him. *What* he wants determines our emotional attitude toward him—but that's another matter. A protagonist who doesn't know what he wants, or knows but doesn't greatly care whether he gets it or not, is poor dramatic material indeed. Imagine how concerned we would be for Hamlet if somewhere along the line he decided the path he was pursuing was much too dangerous and that he'd better let bygones be bygones.

In the commercial theatre the role of the protagonist is nearly always the starring part. It is usually the most interesting role (not always), and it is certainly the character most often in focus, for the simple reason that it is his fortune we are following. Dramatists often give their plays the name of the protagonist: *Medea, Lysistrata, King Lear, Volpone, Phaedra, Peer Gynt, Cyrano de Bergerac, Candida, Galileo*—the list is endless. Once in a while we encounter a double protagonist—that is, two people who want the same thing and strive equally hard to achieve the same goal. Shakespeare very properly named such a play after the two protagonists, *Romeo and Juliet.*

Only in the light of the protagonist's objective can the play be plotted, for the pursuit of that objective is the course of the action, however straightforward or devious the path may be.

There are three main points to be made about the objective:

1. There can be but one main objective if the play is to have unity. A play whose protagonist has more than one ultimate aim must invariably dramatize the success or failure of one effort before going on to the other, and this breaks the spine of the work and dissipates our interest. A play is like a suspension bridge, with one end anchored in a statement or indication of what the protagonist wants, and the other to the disclosure of whether he gets it. A bridge that forks in the middle, with branches leading to two different destinations, can never be an aesthetically satisfying structure. (The fact that other characters also have desires, or objectives, must not obscure the fact that the story we are following is the pursuit of the main, or protagonist's, objective.)

2. The objective must be capable of arousing opposition, in order to produce conflict.

3. The nature of the objective is a leading factor in determining the attitude of the audience toward the protagonist and his opposition. If the objective is a heroic one, we will probably admire the protagonist; if a quixotic one, he may amuse us; a detestable objective will arouse our hatred or contempt for the leading character; and so

on. Protagonist and objective are so closely identified in our minds that it is impossible to consider one without the other.

The Obstacles

Every part of a play has to be alive at every moment. Although every line has to say something coherent in itself, it also has to contribute to the interior life of the play. That's the elusive quality. For the life of the play is in a state of flux from scene to scene.

—Brooks Atkinson

If the protagonist and his objective may be said to constitute the first two important elements in the construction of a play, the various obstacles, collectively, comprise the third. Without impediments to the attainment of the protagonist's desire there would be no conflict and no play. He would simply accomplish his objective without difficulty. Delightful as this situation is in real life, it is fatal to drama, for without a struggle to attain a desired goal, audience attention cannot be held.

There may be but one obstacle, and it may be simple and easily identified—the stubborn refusal of Creon, until too late, to permit the burial of Polyneices, or the ambition and malevolence of Iago. (The term for such an opposing character is, of course, the antagonist.)

On the other hand, there may be more than one obstacle. Browning's pursuit of Elizabeth Barrett is impeded not only by the tyranny of her father, but by the doubts and uncertainties in Elizabeth's own mind.

There may be several obstacles, arising one after another. Romeo and Juliet cannot openly declare their love because of the enmity of their families. But they also face a series of complications: Romeo is exiled for killing Tybalt; Juliet's parents, unaware of her marriage to Romeo, insist that she wed Paris; Friar Lawrence's message to Romeo that Juliet has taken a potion fails to reach him; supposing her dead, Romeo tries to reach Juliet in her tomb, but must fight a duel with Paris; Juliet, awakening, finds Romeo a suicide. Only by Juliet's killing herself can the lovers be reunited.

Finally, the obstacles may be very subtle and complex indeed, as the analyses of *Hamlet* and *Death of a Salesman* will indicate.

The protagonist and the obstacles he encounters must be fairly evenly matched. If the obstacle is weak, then the achievement of the objective is too easy, and the play is weak. Neither should the obstacle be so overwhelming that the protagonist has no chance of overcoming it.

This latter point may seem to be contradicted by such plays as *Oedipus the King, Ghosts,* and *Death of a Salesman,* where the element of a past action poses overwhelming odds against the achievement of the objective. It should be noted that the protagonists do not acknowledge the inevitability of failure until that failure stares them in the face and they must bow to it. They fight against the odds, believing they have a chance of succeeding.

One last point, and an important one: while the unity of a play depends on there being but one main objective, there appears to be no threat to unity by the use of multiple obstacles.

Major Crisis and Climax

The climax is the concrete realization of the theme in terms of an event. In practical playwriting, this means that the climax is the point of reference by which the validity of every element of the structure can be determined. —*John Howard Lawson*

The average play contains a number of minor crises and climaxes, but here we are concerned only with the crisis and climax in which the major and controlling conflict of the play is resolved.

Since the achievement of the objective is impeded by obstacles, every play poses the dramatic question, "Does the protagonist succeed in reaching his goal?" As the struggle between the opposing forces reaches the degree of maximum effort, the point at which the issue can swing one way or the other, we have come to the crisis. At this moment the answer to the dramatic question may be either "yes" or "no."

The crisis is usually followed by the climax, immediately or after a short interval. At the climax the issue of the conflict is determined and the dramatic question answered. In other words, the crisis is a fluid situation that is resolved by the climax, a stable one.

Will Macbeth succeed in remaining on the throne of Scotland? The crisis occurs when Macbeth, lulled into a false sense of security by the peculiar prophecy of the witches, determines to fight the army that has come to dethrone him (V-3). The climax, a rather extended one, comes when he learns that trees in Birnam wood are moving toward Dunsinane (V-5) and his encounter with Macduff, who was not, in one sense, "of woman born" (V-8). Macbeth is defeated, though he goes down fighting. The answer to the dramatic question is "No, Macbeth will not remain on the throne of Scotland."

Will Nora, of *A Doll's House*, awaken to the true nature of her marriage to Torvald? The crisis is the arrival of Krogstad's letter with the return of Nora's bond, which removes the threat of scandal that her husband so greatly fears. The climax is her decision, when she sees Torvald's abrupt about-face from condemnation to forgiveness, to leave him. The answer is "yes."

Will Harry Brock, of *Born Yesterday*, succeed, with the connivance of a corrupt politician, in expanding his junk business contrary to the intent of existing laws? There is an extended crisis in Act Three, when Harry and his cohorts hold Billie, his mistress, and Paul, Billie's tutor and admirer, captive in Harry's hotel suite. For legal reasons control of Brock's enterprises has been put in Billie's name, and, having turned against him and all he stands for, she refuses to surrender her authority. The climax occurs when Billie tells Brock that she will turn back control of the junk yards to him, but one at a time, provided he acts responsibly over the years. Brock has to capitulate. The answer to the dramatic question is "no."

Occasionally the answer to the question is not quite so clear-cut. In Sidney Howard's *The Silver Cord*, for instance, the protagonist is Mrs. Phelps, a selfish mother whose objective is the complete possession of her two sons. The obstacle is the resistance of both the elder son's wife and the fiancée of the younger one. At the climax she loses the elder son to his wife, but succeeds in driving off the fiancée. The answer to the dramatic question "Will Mrs. Phelps succeed in hanging on to her sons?" must be answered, "One of them." (This is not a case of a double objective. Her motivation in the case of both her sons is identical, and her actions would be the same whether she had one son or a dozen.)

The climax is the high point of the play, the event toward which all that precedes it is driving. Hence it is extremely wasteful of the writer's time and energy to begin work on a play until the climax is clearly in mind. A play started without knowing the climax invariably wanders into endless revisions and such frustration that the play is often abandoned before it is finished. The climax is the lighthouse toward which the dramatist steers his ship.

Given the protagonist, objective, and obstacles, the writer should have no difficulty in establishing what his climax should be. The climactic scene answers the question posed near the beginning of the play—the question that has formed the thread to which all the other events have somehow been related. In deciding on his climax, the writer will instinctively choose one that correctly interprets his attitude toward his subject matter. If we try to envision opposite answers to the climaxes already mentioned, the plays will be seen to be wholly different in meaning.

Knowing the climax is useful to the playwright in another way, for it can help him to determine the pertinence and validity of the various scenes in his play. If he imagines the play without the scene he has in mind, and the climax is damaged or altered by the omission, then that scene is probably an essential one and should be kept. On the other hand, if dropping the scene makes no difference at the climax, the playwright had better regard that scene with a skeptical eye.

A characteristic of the climax is the disappearance of the will to struggle. Perhaps the protagonist acknowledges defeat and gives up the struggle, or he may achieve his objective and have no further need to struggle. In any case, the conflict subsides, and with it so does drama. (A fluid situation has become a stable one.) The major climax of most plays occurs near the end, for interest cannot long be sustained without conflict.

Theme

I do not want the emotion that arises out of thought, but thought that arises out of emotion.   —*Arthur Hopkins*

Shakespeare is too good a showman to force a sermon down our throats, and too experienced a theatre man to do less than provide us with entrancing entertainment, leaving us to draw the moral for ourselves.   —*Margaret Webster*

If you *are* going to write what is called a propaganda play, don't let any character in the play know what the propaganda is.
                                —*Howard Lindsay*

A good way to destroy a play is to force it to prove something.
                                —*Walter Kerr*

The theme might be defined as the playwright's point of view toward his material. Since it hardly seems possible to write a play, even the most frivolous, without an attitude toward the people and the situations one has created, every play has a theme of some kind. And there is one spot in the play where it can invariably be discerned

—the climax. For here the author reveals, perhaps even unconsciously, what interpretation he puts on the material.

The principle is well illustrated by comparing two modern comedies, Somerset Maugham's *The Constant Wife* and Philip Barry's *Paris Bound*. Both plays deal with the same situation—a successful marriage threatened by a bit of philandering on the part of the husband. At the climax of *Paris Bound* the wife forgives her mate and the marriage is stabilized. In *The Constant Wife* the wife arranges to go off to the continent for a fling with a lover before returning to her husband. Barry's ending says, quite plainly, that a sexual lapse shouldn't be permitted to destroy a good marriage. Maugham seems to be telling us that what's sauce for the gander is also sauce for the goose. The climaxes chosen by these two skillful writers disclose their respective attitudes toward the situation, and, if you will, establish the themes of the plays.

The experienced dramatist seldom begins with a theme, or attempts to fashion a story in order to present a philosophical position. This method can lead to clichés, propaganda, and lifeless characters. Instead, he creates characters and situations, and then chooses a climax that seems right and satisfactory to him. He lets the theme take care of itself. It probably won't be very original, but this won't matter, so long as it is the truth as the author interprets it.

Neither is the seasoned playwright apt to put into the mouths of his characters statements that spell out the theme. I remember George Kaufman's words to me, when I was less experienced and considerably younger: "You really ought to cut some of these speeches that reflect your own attitude. They're too explicit. They make the character sound as if he were on a soapbox." I was horrified. "But that's what the play's about. That's what it means." "Listen, if I took a blue pencil and crossed out every single line that says what the play means, the audience would still know what it means. You can't conceal your own attitude. It's built right into the play, in your treatment of it." He was right, of course.

The author of *Ghosts* had something to say on this subject too:

They try to make me responsible for the opinions certain of the characters express. And yet there is not in the whole work a single opinion, a single utterance, which can be laid to the account of the author. I took good care to avoid this. The very method, the order of technique that imposes its form on the play, forbids the author to appear in the speeches of his characters. My object was to make the reader feel that he was going through a piece of real experience; and nothing could more effectually prevent such an impression than the intrusion of the author's private opinions in the dialogue. Do they imagine at home that I am so inexpert in the theory of drama as not to know this? —*Henrik Ibsen*

I doubt very much that Shakespeare was trying to prove anything about jealousy in *Othello*, or about ambition in *Macbeth*. Molière was undoubtedly far more concerned with the character of Alceste than he was with proving anything about the insincerity of French society. A play can have somewhat different meanings for different people, for each of us brings his own attitudes and experiences to bear on the interpretation of the work. But we find the clue in the way the play ends.

The Resolution

All that follows the major climax of a play may usually be classified as the resolution. Since the conflict is over, the resolution is normally built on a relatively stable situation. It serves primarily as a transition for the audience from the high emotional peak of the climax back to the reality of their own lives outside the theatre. In modern times the resolution has tended to become briefer.

Material for the resolution is extremely variable. It can suggest what may happen to characters in the future (as exposition in the beginning of the play has informed us of events in the past). Often it seems to reflect, in the mouth of one of the characters, the author's point of view toward the protagonist or the material of the play. After Brutus' suicide Anthony says of him:

This was the noblest Roman of them all:
All the conspirators, save only he,
Did that they did in envy of great Caesar;
He only, in a general honest thought,
And common good to all, made one of them.
His life was gentle; and the elements
So mixt in him, that Nature might stand up
And say to all the world, "This was a man!"

Octavius Caesar then orders a soldier's burial for Brutus, and the play ends.

In *The Little Foxes*, Regina Giddons, after her triumph, asks her daughter if she wouldn't like to sleep in the same room with her tonight; Alexandra's only response is to ask her mother if she's afraid.

Dead End brings down its curtain on a note of irony, with the kids singing a ditty one of them has learned in reform school, "If I Had the Wings of an Angel." And Nora, at the end of *A Doll's House*, goes out and shuts the door with a slam heard round the civilized world.

Unity

The structural unity of the parts is such that, if any one of them is displaced or removed, the whole will be disjointed and disturbed. For a thing whose presence or absence makes no visible difference is not an organic part of the whole. —*Aristotle*

Many good plays are diffuse, but the big hits have unity.
—*George Abbott*

The stage action condenses an event to the extent to which Aristotle's unities are fulfilled; the closer a playwright adheres to the three unities, the more important is the background history of the action.
—*Friedrich Duerrenmatt*

Due perhaps to the physical form of their theatre, the Greeks set the entire action of their plays in a single locale, usually the entrance to a royal palace. They also limited the supposed passage of time to a single day. These practices came to be known as the unities of place and time.

Aristotle laid down the rule for unity of action, quoted above. Material unessential to the development of the plot was to be eliminated. Today all three unities may be disregarded, though the last with caution, for irrelevant story material can very quickly weaken audience interest. Usually, when not all the elements of a play bear directly on the main plot line, there is a compensating unity of mood, of social environment, perhaps of character relationship— something besides the plot line to hold the play together and make it seem "all of a piece."

The Lower Depths, the Chekov plays, Elmer Rice's *Street Scene*, all achieve unity in this manner in spite of their discursiveness. *Anthony and Cleopatra* and *Peer Gynt*, on the other hand, suffer from trying to cover too much territory, both literally and figuratively.

Every play with but one specific setting may be said to observe the unity of place. Many also observe the unity of time, with continuous action, though this is usually interrupted by an intermission or two. (*Who's Afraid of Virginia Woolf?* is a recent example.) Few modern plays of full evening length attempt to dispense with an intermission. It has been tried—Shaw's *Getting Married* and Barry's *Hotel Universe*. But even these, when produced, usually have intermissions arbitrarily inserted.

Exposition

In the greatest of his plays, especially the tragedies, Shakespeare spends little time on exposition. The Prologue to *Troilus and Cressida* frankly announces that the author proposes to "leap o'er the vaults and firstlings of these broils, Beginning in the middle"; and in *Macbeth* he fairly hurls his characters at the crisis of the action.

—*Margaret Webster*

Facts not evident to the audience from the events on stage, but facts of which they must be made aware, are handled by the device called exposition. These may be things that have happened in the past, before the action of the play begins (including much of the play's premise), or events that have occurred between acts or off-stage.

Exposition is to be used sparingly, as a rule, for, being a narrative device rather than a dramatic one, it can be tedious on the stage. It is surprising how little exposition is needed in many plays, and how quickly an audience grasps the essentials of a situation without a lot of preliminary background material.

However, most plays require at least some expository information in order to get moving, and dramatists have been supplying this, over the centuries, in a number of ways. The Greek plays often open with a formal chorus in which the historical events antecedent to the play are reviewed. Shakespeare's prologue to *Troilus and Cressida* serves the same purpose, as does Gloucester's soliloquy that opens *Richard III*. That Shakespeare recognized the danger of narrative exposition, however, seems clear from the second scene of *The Tempest*, when Prospero's long-winded speeches to his daughter, informing her of facts with which she should be deeply concerned, put the poor girl to sleep. The prologue or chorus has survived in recent plays in the form of a narrator or character who talks directly to the audience, as in Wilder's *Our Town*, Van Druten's *I Remember Mama*, Williams' *The Glass Menagerie*, and Patrick's *The Teahouse of the August Moon*.

A clumsy convention that flourished for many years was the introduction of gossipy servants at the opening of a play, who told one another facts with which they must have already been perfectly well acquainted. The practice is amusingly satirized in the opening of Wilder's *The Skin of Our Teeth*. Slightly less transparent, but still inept, is the device of the confidant, the friend who has been away, perhaps, and must be brought up to date, or the newcomer in town, who has to be briefed on the local situation.

But exposition need not be dull if handled correctly. An early scene in *Anna Christie* finds old Chris sitting in a saloon with Marthy, who lives with him on the barge. Chris is handed a letter from his daughter, telling him of her imminent arrival. Chris talks of Anna and how she was left on a Minnesota farm fifteen years before when her mother died—pure exposition, but vitalized by our wondering, along with Chris, what effect all this is having on Marthy, who will have to find another home.

Exposition can usually be made engrossing if it is revealed in conflict, and this is the most widely practiced method of handling it. The necessary information then becomes a sort of by-product of a scene that is dramatically interesting in itself. Shaw, with his usual skill, handles a great deal of expository material at the opening of *The Devil's Disciple* without our realizing how much information he is feeding us. He does it by using Mrs. Dudgeon's ill temper and angry outbursts to provoke discussion and conflict with the Reverend Anderson.

As Synge's *Riders to the Sea* opens, Maurya's two daughters have a package containing clothing taken from a drowned man and sent there for possible identification, for one of their brothers is missing. But the girls hesitate to open the package, for their mother may enter at any moment, and they fear the effect on her if it is her son's clothing. Meanwhile, a storm is brewing, and they know that a second brother, Bartley, plans a boat trip to a nearby fair. Our concern if Maurya should come in and recognize the clothing, plus the danger to Bartley, turn this expository material into the stuff of drama.

Chekov eschews the methods used by most dramatists in handling exposition. We find his highly emotional people pursuing a self-examination, often almost talking to themselves, or perhaps reminiscing, without conflict, on events that bring them to the verge of tears or laughter. It is Chekov's extraordinary skill in characterization that makes this kind of exposition possible.

The inexperienced playwright often tries to crowd a lot of exposition into the beginning of a play. This can result in a static opening that bores the audience before the play itself begins to move. Television drama characteristically avoids expository openings, for the viewer can so easily switch to another program if his interest isn't caught immediately.

A few rough rules of thumb might be kept in mind when one is confronted with the need for exposition: 1. Eliminate exposition that isn't essential or that would soon become clear in the natural course of the play. 2. Present necessary exposition in the form of conflict, or at least let it be told to someone to whom the information is important, someone it will move to action. 3. Postpone using expository material whenever possible until later in the play, and reveal it then at its moment of maximum dramatic impact. (In this connection *Oedipus the King* especially repays study. This play is nearly all exposition, but handled in such a way that it drives the play forward relentlessly at the same time.)

Characterization

Characterization and story are interdependent on the stage, and the tie that binds them together is the objective, for that is the foundation on which the writer builds and fleshes out each of his characters; it is the objectives that determine the course of events. They are the key, not only to character and behavior, but to the actual plot line, as the people involved try various means of attaining their goals.

King Lear's objective is clearly stated: "to shake all cares and business from our age; Conferring them on younger strengths, while we Unburden'd crawl toward death." Lear is proud and full of majesty, but he is also gullible, susceptible to sycophantic flattery, and far too trusting. Shakespeare gives us a complete picture of the man, but all in the light, of course, of his retirement and its consequences. Monsieur Jourdain, who longs to be thought a cultivated gentleman, is credulous, crude, ignorant, and something of a fool; all these qualities are an inseparable part of his ambition, and are disclosed to us in his pursuit of his goal. Greed is what moves Regina Giddons of *The Little Foxes*. As we watch her in action we see that she can be gracious and charming, but also that she is utterly calculating and ruthless.

There are superficial traits that help to depict character—language, manner of speaking, dress, gesture, physical condition, mannerisms, and so on. But the key factor is still the objective and the means employed to attain it. Many of the less important facets of a personality flow from this central and controlling element, and can be determined to some degree by the actor in his interpretation of the role. But only the playwright can be responsible for the mainspring of a character's behavior. Hence the importance of having the objectives clearly in mind.

It is not only the protagonist of a play who has an objective. Other major characters have their own desires, and conflicting desires are the stuff of drama. Juliet's nurse wants what she believes is practical and best for her beloved charge, even if this means forgetting the banished Romeo and taking another husband, Paris, bigamously. Nils Krogstad, of *A Doll's House*, is determined that he will not be discharged from his position at the bank, and will blackmail Nora to keep it. Edward Barrett of Wimpole Street wishes to isolate his family from emotional involvements, from the experience of love that he himself so mistrusts and fears.

Personalities can be depicted on the foundation of such desires, and on conflicting desires scenes can be built. The conflict may be no more than a slight friction of temperaments that grate upon each other, or it may depict an overwhelming clash of willpower; but without at least some measure of conflict a scene is apt to be lifeless.

Obviously, differing personalities set these conflicts in motion, and the playwright must thoroughly understand his characters—all about them, as though they were close acquaintances. In fact, he should know a great deal more about them than he is ever apt to use in his play. For only by understanding the deeply rooted desires of his people can he plausibly depict their motives. Only thus can he make his characters believable, their behavior natural and consistent.

Development

Dialogue is so easy to write that many people with a knack for catching the flavor of conversation happily regard themselves as born dramatists. But dialogue itself is valueless. In a play there is an element of meaningful motion that dialogue has to sustain while it is also apparently reproducing human speech. Something has to be growing at the core of a play. The growth, in turn, has to acquire a momentum that carries the play on to a climax where the motion is either stopped or interrupted. —*Brooks Atkinson*

The protagonist's progress toward his goal is traced in a series of scenes, each of which, even though he may not be present in the scene at all, moves him toward or away from his objective.

The scene is, in a sense, a one-act play that is also a part of the longer play. Conventionally constructed (as many of the best ones are), the scene has a protagonist, just as the full play does, an objective, obstacles, a climax, and a resolution. It should be emphasized that the scene's protagonist isn't necessarily the same as the play's.

The scene gives us one aspect of the larger conflict, but at the end it leaves the larger conflict still unresolved. The play's protagonist is either closer to or farther from his goal. The next scene will be another development in the encompassing story, and will again alter the position of the protagonist in relation to his objective.

Shaw's fourth scene in *Saint Joan* will repay study. Joan is the protagonist of the entire play, but she does not appear in this scene at all, which takes place in the tent of the Earl of Warwick. He is the protagonist of the scene. With Warwick is his clerk, the bigoted and chauvinistic chaplain, Stogumber. The opening of the scene is expository—England is losing the war. We are unaware of this information as exposition, however, for the friction between the cool and worldly warrior and his fatuous priest not only characterizes the two men but disguises the fact that we are being brought up to date on the military situation. Warwick is waiting to receive the French Bishop of Beauvais, Cauchon, who has been turned out of his diocese by Joan's sympathizers. Warwick states his objective early: he wants to "arrange the burning" of the maid. To do this he must first of all come to an understanding with Cauchon.

As he and the bishop talk, it becomes clear that while Warwick views Joan as a political threat, that is, a threat to the feudal system and the authority of the lords, Cauchon regards her as a danger to the Catholic Church. Cauchon conceives it his first duty to save the girl's soul. Failing this, the Church will turn her over to the secular authorities. The differences in their points of view pose an obstacle to the understanding that Warwick seeks. The crisis is their nearly open quarrel. The climax comes when Cauchon finally proposes to "sink our differences in the face of a common enemy." Warwick will pursue the Maid to stem the movement toward "nationalism," while Cauchon will battle to save Joan's soul and to save the Church from "Protestantism" (both terms being invented on the spot). The resolution of the scene brilliantly contrasts the earl and the bishop, on the one hand, two shrewd and perceptive men who have finally reached an understanding, with the narrow-minded Stogumber, who would burn Joan because she is a rebel, a nonconformist, and an enemy of England.

While this example is an isolated unit in *Saint Joan*, that is, separated from the rest of the play by the rise and fall of the curtain and by a different stage setting, most scenes are not so formally set apart. They follow one after another without a break in time or locale and without dropping the curtain. Although the beginning or the end of a scene is often signaled by the exit of one character or the arrival of another, the determining factor is the structural pattern. One of the characters, the scene's protagonist, is under pressure. Does he achieve his objective or doesn't he (climax)? And how does the situation now stand in regard to the larger pattern of the play (resolution)? This pattern, which is simply a miniature of the larger pattern on which the entire play is built, can be observed repeatedly in scene after scene and play after play if one is aware of it and observing analytically.

Dramatic Irony

Sitting in the theatre, we taste, for a moment, the glory of omniscience. With vision unsealed, we watch the groping of purblind mortals after happiness, and smile at their stumblings, their blunders, their futile quests, their misplaced exaltations, their groundless panics. To keep secret from us is to reduce us to their level, and deprive us of our clairvoyant aloofness. There may be a pleasure in that, too; we may join with zest in the game of blind-man's-buff; but the theatre is in its essence a place where we are privileged to take off the bandage we wear in daily life, and to contemplate, with laughter or with tears, the blindfold gambols of our neighbors.
—*William Archer*

Suppose one sees a man walking toward the edge of a cliff. There is nothing dramatic about this. Doubtless he has a reason for going that way. But suppose we learn that the man is blind. Instantly the situation is charged with drama, and we shout a warning. In the theatre we don't shout warnings to the actors, but if we know something the characters on stage don't know, the situation is intrinsically dramatic.

Charlie Chaplin confidently walks a high wire in the circus. He doesn't know, as we do, that his safety belt isn't operative. If this were real life we'd shout a warning. As it is, we are held in comic suspense.

When Romeo takes poison in Juliet's tomb, we know that her death is only feigned, that she will waken, and we weep for what Romeo doesn't know.

The pathos of *Cyrano de Bergerac* is built on the fact that we know what Roxanne doesn't know—that ugly Cyrano, and not the handsome Christian, is the author of the verses by which Roxanne is wooed, that it is Cyrano who truly loves her.

Much of the fun in Molière's *The School for Wives* derives from the fact that Horace, the young blade trying to seduce Arnolphe's intended bride, confides his successes and all his plans to Arnolphe himself, unaware, as we are, of the latter's identity. If the audience weren't in possession of all the facts, the situation wouldn't be funny. The dramatic irony ends (in this case near the end of the play) when Horace learns with whom he has been sharing his secrets.

Oscar Wilde, in *Lady Windermere's Fan*, ends the play with a double dramatic irony, each one balanced against the other. Mrs. Erlynne, a notorious woman, is the mother of Lady Windermere. Lord Windermere knows this, but his wife does not. When Lady Windermere commits a serious indiscretion, Mrs. Erlynne pretends that it was she who was caught in the compromising situation, thus saving Lady Windermere's reputation, and indeed her marriage. Lord Windermere doesn't know that it was his wife who was actually involved in the scandal, and Lady Windermere still doesn't know that the woman who saved her was really her mother. The final lines of the play are addressed to a man Mrs. Erlynne has consented to wed. Lord Windermere: "Well, you are certainly marrying a very clever woman." Lady Windermere: "Ah! You're marrying a very good woman." Only the audience is aware of the entire truth.

Every playwright uses the device of dramatic irony, often several times in a play, sometimes throughout the entire play. Kaufman and Hart, in *Merrily We Roll Along*, tell the story of Richard Niles, an idealistic young man, who attains fame and wealth as a fashionable playwright, but in climbing to the top so compromises his ethics and his morals that he ends up a worthless human being. This hackneyed material was given theatrical vitality and excitement by playing its nine scenes in chronologically reverse order. We first meet Richard in 1934, famous, wealthy, and degraded, his personal life a shambles. The next scene, in 1927, presents him well advanced on the path he has chosen, everything that occurs in the scene being made significant by the fact that the audience knows, as he doesn't, what happens later. We see every mistake he makes, and know the consequences. We wish he could be warned. And so it goes, back through the years, with Richard growing more innocent, less corrupt, as the play continues. The final scene, in 1916, presents him as the valedictorian of his class at college, delivering an address of pure idealism, ending with the quotation, "This above all, to thine own self be true. . . ."

John van Druten, in *Bell, Book and Candle*, poses the situation of an extremely attractive New York woman, Gillian, with whom Shep, an eligible publisher, falls precipitately in love. What the audience knows, and Shep does not, is that Gillian is a witch, that she has snared him by witchcraft. We are eager to see what happens when he finally learns what we know. Van Druten has set up an "obligatory scene," one the audience anticipates and is entitled to see.

Most uses of dramatic irony similarly require the staging of the scene wherein the people on stage who don't know what we know are given that information. This is not true of *Lady Windermere's Fan* nor, because of the form of the play, of *Merrily We Roll Along*. But Charlie Chaplin must find out that his safety belt doesn't protect him, Roxanne must learn of Cyrano's love, and Shep must be made aware that he is under a witch's spell.

Frequently the playwright will have to choose between the device of dramatic irony and the use of surprise; that is, between letting the audience in on the secret, or startling them with it later. Surprise can be very effective dramatically. In fact, it can be the whole point of a mystery play (as distinct from a suspense play). But consider which is better—our knowing that Chaplin's safety belt isn't functioning, or our finding this out when he does; our knowing that Cyrano loves Roxanne, or coming to the realization, as she does, late in the play; our knowing that Gillian used witchcraft on Shep, or our sharing his surprise when he learns of Gillian's powers. The answer is obvious.

Preparation

A "plant" is a preparatory device that helps to weave the fabric of a play together, in the sense that it arouses curiosity and anticipation of a coming event, or prepares the audience to accept an event when it does occur. Examples can be found in most well-constructed plays.

An expert use of the device is the potted palm tree in *Mister Roberts*. The container is labeled "Prop.t of Captain, Keep Away." The first piece of business after the curtain rises is a petty officer surreptitiously spitting in the container, thus calling our attention to the tree and incidentally indicating his own attitude toward the captain. Moments later Roberts, after telling Doc about the naval task force he has seen gliding by in the night, says: "And then I looked down from our bridge and saw our captain's palm tree! Our trophy for superior achievement! The Admiral John J. Finchley Award for delivering more toothpaste and toilet paper than any other Navy cargo ship in the safe area of the Pacific."

During the play we are never permitted for long to forget the palm tree or the tyrannical captain's pride in it. We see him watering it; we see how the crew detests it. Late in the play Roberts, in exuberant rebellion, jerks the palm tree from the container and throws it over the side. And when the angry captain is trying to learn who did it, he remarks that it couldn't have been Pulver. "He hasn't the guts." In the next scene the captain has dug up two small palms and brought them aboard ship to replace the missing one. In the final moments of the play, after Roberts has been killed, Pulver suddenly throws the two palms overboard and confronts the captain. In this symbolic gesture Pulver has replaced Roberts, and the audience roars with pleasure. It is the careful preparation all through the play, of course, that makes the gesture so effective.

In the first act of *Bell, Book and Candle* there is a scene between the lovely Gillian and her eccentric aunt (both of them witches), in which the aunt reveals what she knows about Shep's fiancée, thus making possible Gillian's and our identification of the young woman later. At the same time the aunt remarks that Gillian could use her supernatural powers to make Shep forget his fiancée and love her instead. Gillian's pride leads her to reject so underhanded a method of attracting a man, but we are prepared for her to do just that when she learns that Shep and the fiancée intend to announce their engagement that very evening.

Plants are useful in building suspense and in establishing the credibility of characters and action. Unlike pure exposition, a plant has a pay-off—the reason for using it appears later.

Activity

The father of the dramatist was the dancer.   *—Gordon Craig*

The skeleton of a good play is a pantomime.   *—Brander Matthews*

It is instructive to find that all through theatre history the writers whose comments are preserved for us have cherished most keenly the things their eyes remembered.   *—Margaret Webster*

Nothing could be truer than the comments just quoted, and no truth about the theatre is so often overlooked by the neophyte, who thinks of a play as an arrangement of words instead of a plan of action.

Alfred Jarry, author of the early surrealist play *Ubu Roi*, remarked that the amateur or literary dramatist thinks in terms of what has happened (that is, in terms of narrative), whereas the true dramatist thinks of what is happening on the stage.

Speech is an activity, and thus part of a play's action, but it is the total action that must concern the playwright. Sometimes the activity will consist of speech alone, but more often the most effective treatment of a scene will be found to consist of some form of physical activity combined with speech. Truly significant activities must first be determined before the words are attached, activity that expresses the emotion and the desire of the speaker. (The term "activity" as used hereinafter will refer to physical movement and business on the stage.)

The experienced dramatist, using his visual imagination, tries first of all to determine what the characters are doing, what activity he can devise that will reveal character and carry the story forward. The degree of hostility between the Capulets and the Montagues is shown by dueling and street brawling. Lady Macbeth's guilty conscience is seared in our minds by the image of her sleepwalking and rubbing her hands. Peer Gynt's mischievous nature is evident at once when he playfully perches his mother on the millhouse roof. Edward Barrett's tyranny over his daughter Elizabeth is exemplified by his forcing her to drink the porter that she detests, when milk would do as well. Jeeter Lester's greed, hunger, and indolence are all dramatized by his repeated attempts to steal a sack of turnips belonging to his son-in-law. Kaufman and Hart don't talk about the unconventional behavior of the Sycamores in *You Can't Take It With You;* they show it to us. Penny types while the cat serves as a paperweight; Essie dances as Ed plays the xylophone, then sets type on a printing press in the living room; and so on.

Robert Anderson, in a brilliantly conceived scene in *Tea and Sympathy,* shows us Al trying to teach his roommate, Tom, how to walk in a more masculine way. The scene is not only touching and funny, but, without being explicit in the dialogue, it demonstrates that there is no sexual relationship between the boys, that Tom is unhappy about the suspicion he is under and wants to do something to prove his masculinity, that Al likes Tom and wants to help him.

Examples of this kind could be repeated endlessly. It must be clear, however, that the dialogue for any of these particular scenes could not have been written unless the activity had been invented first.

Of course, effective pieces of business will often occur to the author while he is writing the dialogue (or to the director during rehearsals), but such stage business tends to be illustrative and is seldom the kind of activity that moves the drama forward by itself.

The best procedure for the dramatist is to find, if he can, an activity that would be natural in the given situation, that helps to reveal character, if possible, and that moves the story forward. Once this has been found, whatever words are necessary and appropriate can be added. If there appears to be no satisfactory physical activity, then dialogue alone will have to carry the scene. But the playwright should never forget that people are reached more quickly and forcefully by what they see than by what they hear. As Roy Mitchell put it in *Creative Theatre*, "Literature crosses the threshold of the theatre only as the servant of motion."

Dialogue

A play is an exercise in time and motion. The man who creates it has to control it, like a man who has hooked a powerful fish but still faces the problem of boating it. The word is useless unless it also transmits motion to the next line of dialogue and unless it is spoken at a particular moment in time.   —*Brooks Atkinson*

Dramatic dialogue can afford to drop a lot of what would be necessary in something meant just to be read. The actors are there, and their tone of voice, their comportment towards each other, even their facial expressions can convey a lot which therefore does not need to be spelt out in words.   —*John Russell Taylor*

There is endless variety in the dialogue of different periods and different writers. There are the magnificent cadences of the Greeks, the Elizabethans, and the French classicists, the witty artificialities of the Restoration dramatists, or Sheridan and Wilde, the brilliant discussions of Bernard Shaw, the "realism" of Ibsen and the hundreds who have followed the trail he blazed, the romantic verse of Rostand and Maxwell Anderson, the regional speech that O'Casey, Odets, and some of our black writers have turned into prose-poetry, the gutter realism of Kingsley's *Dead End*, the bold directness of Brecht, the ellipses and tangential dialogue of Beckett, Albee, and Pinter.

No two playwrights write exactly the same kind of dialogue, though obviously the differences are not always so wide as those listed above. But there are certain characteristics that are common to good dialogue of whatever kind. Such dialogue arises out of character, situation, and conflict; it reveals character and moves the story forward. The speaker on stage is usually more articulate than he would be in life, even when a naturally inarticulate character is being presented, for good dialogue is an intensification of normal speech. So-called realistic speech is hardly real at all, for though it may create that illusion, the confusion, excesses, fumblings, and backtracking of ordinary conversation have been trimmed away, and the speeches given direction and a pattern.

Dialogue carries a tremendous burden. Consider all it must accomplish for the playwright:

1. It must characterize the speaker, and perhaps the person addressed.

2. It must reflect the relationship of the speaker to other characters.

3. It must reflect the speaker's mood, convey his emotion.

4. It must be connective, that is, grow out of a preceding speech or action and lead into another.

5. It must advance the action.

6. It must be idiomatic, maintaining the individuality of the speaker, yet still blend into the style of the play as a whole.

7. It must be clear and comprehensible to the audience.

8. It must often reveal the speaker's motivation.

9. It must often carry information or exposition.

10. It must often foreshadow what is to come.

In addition to fulfilling these functions some other characteristics of good dialogue are:

1. Actors must be able to speak it without stumbling over the words. It must avoid tongue twisters, and too much alliteration unless for effect. In long speeches it must provide natural spots for the actors to breathe.

2. Speeches should build toward the end, with the strongest idea saved for the last. The most emphatic position in a speech is at the end, the second strongest at the beginning. Putting a modifying clause at the end of a speech, or the name of the character being addressed, is invariably weakening.

3. The concrete image, one that can be visualized, is generally more effective than an abstract one. Mountain is a more vivid word than grandeur, storm than turmoil, rose than beauty.

Consider this speech of Bessie's, from *The Plough and the Stars*, Act One. Although it has been chosen almost at random, it illustrates every point listed above.

Puttin' a new lock on her door . . . afraid her poor neighbors ud break through and steal . . . (*In a loud tone*) Maybe, now, they're a damn sight more honest than your ladyship . . . checkin' th' children playin' on th' stairs . . . gettin' on th' nerves of your ladyship . . . Complainin' about Bessie Burgess singin' her hymns at night, when she has a few up . . . (*She comes in half-way on the threshold, and screams*) Bessie Burgess'll sing whenever she damn well likes! (*Nora tries to shut the door, but Bessie violently shoves it in, and, gripping Nora by the shoulders, shakes her*) You little overdressed throllop, you, for one pin I'd paste th' white face of you!

This is dialogue writing at its most skillful, for with the greatest economy of means it is accomplishing everything O'Casey wants to do. (And note the activity—the struggle with the door and Bessie shaking Nora.)

One of the major problems inexperienced playwrights run into is overwriting. Their plays move too slowly and they are too long. A principal reason for this is that they haven't yet learned the secret of compressing the dialogue, of making it do several things at once.

In writing dialogue it is well to remember not only that activity is going to carry part of the burden, but the actors themselves, with their physical presence and their voices, will also make an immense contribution. Even a single speech can be spoken in a score of ways—with indifference or with passion, with respect or suspicion, with hope, with anger, or any other possible interpretation. A skillful actor supports and reinforces the playwright's intent and illuminates the lines with his own understanding. Good dialogue leaves room for him to do so. In other words, the lines are not so explicit as to put the actor in an interpretive strait jacket.

In the long run, though, as William Archer says of dialogue in *Playmaking*, the dramatist "must rely on his instinct, not numb and bewilder it by constantly subjecting it to the dictates of hard-and-fast aesthetic theory."

Effects

The history of the theatre shows us that in its greatest ages the stage employed the greatest number of conventions. The stage is fundamental pretense, and it thrives on the acceptance of that fact and in the multiplication of additional pretenses.

—*Thornton Wilder*

The theatre has a multitude of resources to help the writer and producer create a work of maximum effectiveness in production. Some are as old as the theatre itself—music, dance, poetry, and heightened speech, for example. In modern times we have precise control of lighting and sound effects, both of which can be used superbly.

It is the musical theatre that has most consistently taken advantage of these resources. One has only to recall the light and color and spectacle, the technical imagination displayed in such shows as *West Side Story, Carousel, Brigadoon,* or *Man of La Mancha* to realize what instruments lie at hand for the playwright who can use them.

As Thornton Wilder has pointed out in *Some Thoughts on Playwriting,* departures from strictly realistic staging, by stimulating the spectator's imagination, make him more of a collaborator in the performance; and, even more important, a nonrealistic presentation moves the subject from the specific to the general. This, depending on the play, can be distinctly advantageous.

A brief discussion of realism and theatricalism will be found in Appendices A and B. It may simply be noted here that Brecht and the plays his Epic Theatre style has influenced employ theatrical effects extensively. John Patrick's *The Teahouse of the August Moon* and Wilder's own *The Skin of Our Teeth* both benefit by abandoning a realistic approach in favor of more theatricality. In fact, it is impossible to conceive of the Wilder play at all in terms of conventional realistic writing and staging.

Plausibility

Drama must be a constant balance, weighted one way or another, between the need for contrivance and the need to suggest that nothing has been contrived.   —*John Russell Taylor*

There is only one kind of bad theatre: when the author's imagination steps outside the very area of illusion he has created. But as long as the dramatist creates within that area, almost no action on the stage is too violent or implausible.   —*Gian Carlo Menotti*

Deus ex machina, the Latin words for "the god from the machine," identifies a Greek invention. Frequently a Greek play ended with the intercession of a god, who was lowered to the acting area, the *proskenion,* by means of a crane above and behind the *skene.* Readers of Mary Renault's *The Mask of Apollo* will recall the incident in the theatre at Delphi when another player tries to kill the actor playing Apollo by cutting through the rope that is lowering him to the stage. (Incidentally, this skillfully researched novel is throughout a vivid portrayal of the Greek theatre and the conditions under which its actors performed.)

But the *deus ex machina* is of little use to modern playwrights, for we no longer accept the notion that a supernatural being will intercede in human affairs. The Greek dramatist could disentangle the knotted threads of his plot by introducing a god to take charge of the action, or, in the case of *Medea,* by permitting her to escape mortal consequences "in a chariot drawn by dragons." But the gods of the Greeks were much closer to them than any similar beings are to us.

We have modern equivalents for the device, but they must still be avoided. The unexpected arrival of a powerful figure, the conveniently timed heart attack, the sudden inheritance, anything introduced by the writer from outside the boundaries of the play to help him resolve his plot is to be shunned. Audiences recognize shoddy craftsmanship and refuse to accept a solution that doesn't evolve naturally from the circumstances.

Molière had a tendency to end his plays in the easiest possible way (for him)—an extravagant coincidence, perhaps, or the introduction of a higher power. His undisguised buttering-up of his patron, Louis XIV, near the end of *Tartuffe,* is not the only thing that makes us smile. We are equally disdainful of the dramatist's lack of ingenuity in solving his dramatic problem.

A Broadway comedy some years ago presented a family of refugees from central Europe who were in America illegally. With the threat of deportation imminent they were saved at the last moment by the intercession of Barney Baruch, with whom, we were told, the father of the family had recently struck up an entirely fortuitous acquaintance on a bench in Central Park. It seems hardly necessary to add that the play failed. And a major motion picture, based on a Broadway play, found itself in difficulty with the production code of the time, which provided that sinners must be punished for their transgressions. So the film killed off its villain, a murderess, by having her struck by a bolt of lightning. Audiences howled with laughter.

Horace, in Hellman's *The Little Foxes,* dies of a heart attack, but he is suffering from a bad heart before the play opens. Regina brings him home from the hospital at considerable risk to his life, goads him to anger, and lets him climb the stairs in an effort to reach his medicine during an attack. It might be said that Horace really dies of murder. Certainly the heart attack is part of the forward movement of the play, and not a *deus ex machina.*

Dramatic effect derives from what is probable, and not from what is possible.   —*Aristotle*

A dramatist may postulate any situation he has the means to interpret, if he will abide by the logic of it after.
                                                              —*Harley Granville-Barker*

Many years ago the great German playwright and critic Gotthold Lessing wrote that the dramatist must so arrange his story that "with every step we see his personages take, we must acknowledge that we should have taken it under the same circumstances and with the same degree of passion. We suddenly find ourselves filled with profound pity for those whom a fatal stream has carried so far, and full of terror at the consciousness that a similar stream might also thus have borne ourselves."

A characteristic of the finest plays is the effect of inevitability the writer has been able to achieve. The course of events he set in motion has not only followed the plausible path; there could not possibly have been any other outcome. This feeling of inevitability—a combination of characters moving along a course from which there is no possible turning—is perhaps a playwright's finest achievement.

The Scenario

Inexperienced playwrights often say: "Oh, I couldn't work from an outline. My writing would lose its spontaneity." The experienced writer knows that whether he has committed his scenario to paper or whether it is all in his head, he is following a preconceived framework on which the play will be built. To begin writing without knowing where one is going is to head for the wilderness, with normally little prospect of finding one's way out again. Such writing is almost always wasted effort, abandoned long before the project nears a conclusion, for the playwright has lost his way.

For the lucky dramatist who can formulate his plan in his head and keep it there without going to the trouble of putting it on paper, working without a formal outline may be possible. Most play-wrights find a scenario essential. For one thing, it permits a critical scrutiny of the skeleton before the flesh of activity and dialogue are applied. In fact, the very act of putting the structure down on paper reveals things about it that may not be evident without such discipline. It is obvious that changes are easier to make in outline than in a first draft, when a lot of work must be discarded. Once the play-wright is satisfied that he has a sound structure on which to build, his creative faculties are free to concentrate on the fine points of characterization, activity, and dialogue.

Many playwrights, in order to keep the entire structure of a play in mind at all times, carry the scenario method considerably farther. They have found they can best maintain this perspective by starting with a brief outline, perhaps a single page indicating the general movement of each act, then expanding the outline again and again, each time encompassing the entire play. This encourages a kind of organic growth of the work, and helps to achieve the balance and unity so essential if the play is to be successfully completed.

As the scenario grows more detailed with each writing, the playwright finds himself gradually slipping into activity and dialogue. And with a scenario he can begin writing any scene at all that he feels is ready for dialogue. He needn't start with Act One, Scene One; he can just as well do the climax or any other scene he feels the urge to write, and slip it into place in the scenario. In fact, it is an excellent idea to write the most important scenes first. It clarifies the movement of the play in the author's mind, and allows the maximum time to consider revisions of the major scenes.

Whether the playwright chooses to develop a scenario first and work from that is, of course, up to him, but I would suggest that the beginner skips this important step at his peril.

ANALYSES

SOPHOCLES

Oedipus the King

Ca. 427 B.C.

This is a play of shattering power that in a good performance can leave its audience limp with emotion. Part of its force, it seems fair to say, is due to its technical excellence. It is generally recognized as a masterpiece of dramatic construction.

The play was written for outdoor theatres of enormous size, each with an unchangeable background simulating the entrance to a large building. The Theatre of Dionysus in Athens (of which only a portion of the stage, orchestra, and the first few rows of seats remain) apparently seated about 17,000, perhaps more. The theatre at Epidaurus seats over 14,000. The actors—all men, as in Shakespeare's theatre—wore masks. These helped to identify the characters from a distance, permitted the actors to double in more than one role, and may have served still a third purpose as megaphones. They also wore high-soled boots, or *cothurni,* to increase their stature. Many highly theatrical elements were employed in the performance—vivid color and action, music, solo and choral singing, rhythmic poetry, and dancing.

In form the play is similar to many others of the period. It is not long, and was presented without intermission. The course of the action is punctuated by choral odes, spoken or sung by the chorus, and these divide the play into episodes that correspond roughly to acts or scenes in the modern theatre. There are six such episodes in *Oedipus the King,* each followed by the comment or interpretation of the chorus. This group apparently numbered about fifteen, and represents, for the most part, people of the city.

Premise

The city of Thebes is ruled by a revered king, Oedipus, who some years before, as a young prince of Corinth, had earned the gratitude of the citizens by solving the riddle of a sphinx that was preying on them. He had married their widowed queen, Jocasta, and had four children by her. Now the city is in the grip of a devastating plague, whose cause is unknown. Oedipus is the kind of man who will try to alleviate his people's suffering.

The following facts, also antecedent to the play, are unknown both to Oedipus and, it must be assumed, to the audience. Oedipus is actually the son of the former king, Laius, and as a baby had been exposed to die because of a prophecy that he would kill his father and marry his mother. Both parts of the prophecy have been fulfilled, and this is the reason for the plague.

Synopsis

FIRST EPISODE

A crowd of townspeople, led by a priest of Zeus, beseech Oedipus, before his palace, to learn the cause of the pestilence and put an end to it. The king replies that he has already sent Creon, Queen Jocasta's brother, to Delphi for advice.

Creon returns with word from the oracle that the city harbors the slayer of Laius, the former king, and that only by finding and driving out the murderer can the pestilence be conquered. Oedipus is told that Laius and all of his party save one man, who fled in terror, were killed by a band of robbers. Oedipus vows to discover the slayer and cleanse the city of pollution.

SECOND EPISODE

Oedipus issues an appeal to any citizens with knowledge of Laius' slayer to come forward with information, and restates his determination to find the murderer and lift the curse from the city.

Creon has suggested consulting a blind seer, Teiresias, who is now led in. It appears that the aged prophet knows more than he is willing to divulge, and Oedipus is angered by his reluctance to speak. As the king's fury mounts, he accuses Teiresias himself of being the slayer. At this the old man turns on the king with the statement that he, Oedipus, is the killer. Aghast at this effrontery, Oedipus sees in it a plot by Creon to drive him from Thebes and usurp the throne. Teiresias denies that he is in league with Creon, predicts the blindness and exile of Oedipus, and states that he is both son and husband to the queen, father and brother to his children.

THIRD EPISODE

Creon, having learned that he has been accused of treason, confronts the king. Oedipus repeats the charge, which Creon denies, along with any ambition to occupy the throne himself. Oedipus is not convinced, and orders Creon's death. Queen Jocasta arrives and tries to make peace between the two men. Oedipus reluctantly permits Creon to leave unharmed.

Jocasta then tries to allay her husband's fears by demonstrating that the predictions of oracles are not always fulfilled. She tells him that although it was foretold that Laius would be slain by his own son, he was killed by a band of robbers. His son, furthermore, as a baby had been left to die on a hillside, his feet pierced and staked. But her words fill Oedipus with foreboding. He tells the queen of the rumor in Corinth that he was not the son of his supposed parents, and that he had consulted the Delphic oracle on this matter. Instead of being enlightened, he had been told that he would one day slay his father and marry his mother. He had fled Corinth, that the prophecy might not be fulfilled. Then Oedipus describes to Jocasta an encounter on a highway in which he slew a man in a carriage, together with his coachman and attendants. He is sick with fear that the man in the carriage may have been Laius. He asks the queen to send for the man in the king's party, now a shepherd, who survived the crossroads encounter. If the shepherd confirms that it was a band of robbers and not a single individual who killed Laius, then Oedipus was not the slayer.

FOURTH EPISODE

A messenger, meanwhile, arrives from Corinth to report the death there of the king, whom Oedipus still presumes to be his father. This news, apparently disproving at least half of the dreadful prophecy, greatly relieves Oedipus and Jocasta. The messenger tells them that the people of Corinth want Oedipus to come back and be their king. But Oedipus is still fearful about the other half of the prophecy—that he may defile his mother. As to this, the messenger bids him to have no fear, for the rulers of Corinth were not his true parents. The messenger relates that he himself had taken a babe with wounded feet from a Theban shepherd and carried it to the Corinthian court, whereupon the childless king had brought up the boy as his own son. A citizen states his belief that the Theban shepherd is the same man that escaped from the crossroads when Laius was slain.

By now Jocasta has realized the full and terrible truth, and she begs Oedipus to pursue the inquiry no farther. When he insists on questioning the shepherd, she retires in despair. Oedipus thinks that Jocasta is merely afraid he may be proved of lowly birth, that it is her pride that makes her reluctant to hear what the shepherd knows about the baby's parents.

FIFTH EPISODE

The shepherd is brought before Oedipus and identified by the Corinthian messenger as the man from whom he received the baby. When the shepherd is told that Oedipus is the same child, now grown, he is terrified and begs the messenger to be silent. Under threat of torture, however, he reveals that the baby was a son of Laius. Because of a prophecy the baby's mother, Jocasta, had given him the infant to be exposed to die. But he had taken pity on the babe and given it to a man from Corinth. In utter dismay and horror Oedipus goes into the palace.

SIXTH EPISODE

A messenger from the palace appears to tell the citizens that Jocasta has hanged herself, and that Oedipus, breaking into her chamber, had cut her down, then had seized the brooches from her robe and torn out his eyes. (The Greeks preferred that scenes of violence be described, not staged.)

Oedipus appears, in agony of body and spirit, cursing the shepherd who did not let him die. He pleads for someone to lead him away from Thebes or kill him.

Creon enters, and Oedipus begs him to care for his two young and innocent daughters, Antigone and Ismene. Creon has sent for the children, and Oedipus bids them farewell. He is then led into the palace to await Creon's decision on banishment.

Protagonist and Objective

The protagonist is, of course, Oedipus himself. He clearly states his objective early in the play—to remove the cause of the pestilence afflicting Thebes. It is his implacable determination to accomplish this end that motivates the rest of the play. Had his will faltered anywhere along the way, the play would have collapsed. He succeeds in his objective, for the plague will be over after he has left the city.

Obstacles

Factors hindering Oedipus in his effort to end the pestilence are, first, his own ignorance as to the cause of it. But ignorance of the cause will not propel the play very far dramatically, as there exists as yet no active opposition to his objective. But the search for the cause of the plague quickly turns into a search for the slayer of Laius, and this brings about a conflict of will and greatly heightened dramatic interest. The first such conflict is the reluctance of the seer, Teiresias, to tell what he knows and his accusation, which Oedipus rejects. Creon provides the second conflict, which grows out of the first. (It is true that the king's anger is directed at Creon not because he believes Creon to be hindering his search for the slayer of Laius, but because he thinks Creon is conspiring to seize the throne. Thus this scene does not bear directly on the search for the slayer. It is pertinent, however, and it is extremely revealing of Oedipus' hot temper and his present state of mind.)

The third conflict develops as Jocasta tries to calm the king's fears. Instead of being reassured, he is further alarmed, and determined to ferret out the truth, no matter where it leads. By this time the original objective has come to embrace the question of Oedipus' own identity, a matter that is even more emotionally charged for him than the fact of the plague. And the major obstacle that begins to emerge is inexorable Fate, the will of the gods. (We of a very different age and culture cannot accept the ancient Greeks' concept of a man's fate being controlled by capricious gods. This may have a bearing on the fact that few plays since then have scaled the heights reached by the Greek dramatists. But that is not the subject of the present inquiry.)

The news that Oedipus is not the natural child of the king and queen of Corinth indicates that Fate, willful and vindictive, has begun to close in, as Jocasta clearly sees when she begs the king to abandon the search for the slayer. But Oedipus sticks to his resolve.

The last obstacle to the search is the shepherd's fear of revealing that Oedipus and the baby he sent to Corinth are the same person.

Major Crisis and Climax, Theme

As with many later dramas in which the outcome is foreordained and inevitable, the crisis (which often presents the protagonist with a choice between two courses of action) occurs long before the play itself begins. Given the kind of man that Oedipus is, we never have any question as to the catastrophe toward which he is moving. (Cf. *Ghosts, Desire Under the Elms, Death of a Salesman.*) Oedipus was set upon this road at birth.

The climax occurs when the shepherd finally tells what he knows, and Oedipus has all the facts in his possession.

We have seen a great and noble man pursue a moral action (the search for the cause of the plague) even though it brought him to his own destruction. The genius of Sophocles imbued the story of these legendary characters with this exalted theme.

Resolution

Theoretically Oedipus could now claim that he was the innocent victim of Fate, and refuse to give up the throne and go into exile, plague or no plague, vow or no vow. But Oedipus is not that kind of man. He assumes the responsibility for his actions. What remains of the play, therefore, is the effect upon him of the dreadful knowledge, and the implicit fulfillment of his vow to end the pestilence. All of episode six is resolution.

Opening and Unity

The play observes the typical Greek unities of time, place, and action—that is, it is continuous, it unfolds in a single locale, and concerns itself with one problem.

The unity of time and its relation to the opening is worth

examining in some detail, for unity of time imposed a discipline upon the Greek playwrights that greatly increased the power of their plays. By obliging the dramatist to begin his play so close to the climax (in order that the action might be supposed to have taken place all in one day), the story had to be compressed, and only those events dramatized that led directly to the climax. Naturally, this kind of construction is apt to show the characters in a more critical situation and more highly charged with emotion than a work that traces the development of an action over a long period of time. One can conceive of a play about Oedipus beginning with, say, his encounter with the sphinx, his being welcomed as the deliverer of Thebes, and his marriage to the widow Jocasta. But can anyone imagine that this would be a more absorbing play than the one Sophocles has given us?

Ibsen often raised the curtain on his realistic plays very late in the story, too, and thus achieved the same kind of compression and intensity. But plays that cover a wide time span can also build up tremendous force—*Hamlet* and *King Lear,* for example.

Exposition

The facts generally known to the Theban people at the beginning of *Oedipus the King* are conveyed to the audience in fairly conventional exposition early in the play, mainly in the conversation between Oedipus and the priest. Revelation of facts unknown to Oedipus, however, become the actual mechanism of the play, for it is his determination to learn the truth that ultimately destroys him. Here is exposition handled with a technical dexterity unequalled in all dramatic literature, even to the point where the final disclosure of fact provides the climax of the play.

Characterization

Characterization is varied, balanced, and convincing. It is accomplished both through dialogue and behavior. Oedipus himself is shown to be brave and intelligent (his encounter with the sphinx), a compassionate and responsible ruler (his determination to relieve his people's suffering), a man of unshakeable will, but also a man of rash judgment and fiery temper (the scene with Teiresias and the second scene with Creon). The final scene, in which he bids farewell to his daughters, is convincing evidence, should there still be any question, that we have witnessed the destruction of a very human creature.

Creon is presented as an attractive and responsible man. He will defend himself against a false charge, but he is reasonable, slow to anger, and at the end, after his sister's suicide and Oedipus' downfall, he is gentle, firm, and without recrimination. Jocasta has dignity and warmth, and her behavior throughout is that of a loyal and loving wife.

Development

Most of the major scenes are constructed in the conventional way. Oedipus is the protagonist of the scene with Teiresias; his goal, to learn who slew Laius; obstacle, the seer's reluctance to speak; climax, the accusation that Oedipus himself is the slayer; resolution, Oedipus' opinion that the accusation is part of a plot hatched by Creon, and Teiresias' further disclosures. It may be noted that Oedipus is successful at this point in learning the identity of Laius' slayer, but since he doesn't believe it, the effect is similar to a failure to achieve his objective. If he did believe the accusation the play would reach its climax right here.

Jocasta is the protagonist of her long scene with Oedipus in the third episode; her objective, to allay her husband's fears by citing the fallibility of oracles; obstacle, the fact that her examples do not fully exclude Oedipus as the culprit; climax, she fails to convince him; resolution, his order to send for the shepherd, the only surviving witness of the slaying of Laius.

The scene with the shepherd in the fifth episode is similar in structure, except for the resolution, to the earlier scene with Teiresias. (Note that the climax of this scene is also the climax of the entire play.)

Dramatic Irony

Dramatic irony is used extensively in a very subtle and skillful way. We, the audience, are told by Teiresias early in the play that Oedipus is the slayer of his father and the husband of his mother. Since we, unlike Oedipus, are probably impressed by the old man's sincerity and honesty, we are less skeptical of his statements than the king. The effect dramatically is that we know more than Oedipus does, that we are in possession of knowledge that he still seeks. Thus we wait for Oedipus to "catch up with us," and we watch in fascination as he pieces together the damning evidence, the facts that will convince him of what we are already sure of. Dramatic irony has probably never been put to more effective use in a play. (A dramatist must presume that his audience has no prior knowledge of his story. Thus though the Greek audience may have been familiar with the Oedipus legend before coming to the theatre, Sophocles had to assume that the tale was new to them and construct his play accordingly. The same holds true for playwrights today.)

Preparation

In one sense the various bits of information disclosed as the play progresses, which Oedipus will piece together until he sees the whole truth about himself, are all preparation for the climactic scene. (As pointed out above, it is our acceptance of the preparatory facts before Oedipus accepts them that creates the dramatic irony.) In the narrower sense of the word, however, the play does not contain what we are accustomed to think of as "plants."

Activity

There is comparatively little physical activity on the stage during the dialogue of this very formal tragedy. The dancing of the chorus, however, relieves what would otherwise be a somewhat static visual presentation.

Dialogue

The Greek dramatists were poets, and their dialogue was formal in the extreme. Modern translations that attempt to capture and reinforce this formality with archaic forms and language merely set up a barrier between the play and its audience. Good straightforward English translations, without colloquialisms or awkward constructions, bring us closer to the originals.

Plausibility

Oedipus the King is a prime example of the fact that an audience will accept an improbable, illogical, or fanciful situation so long as the play itself is logical and the unfolding action consistent with its premise. Consider: Oedipus, though he was brought up to believe himself the son of the rulers of Corinth, was by his own admission aware of the rumor that he was not their natural child. He also knew the fate that had been foretold for him—that he murder his father and marry his mother. Yet we are asked to believe that this supposedly sensible man would be so rash as to kill a stranger on a highway and soon afterward marry a woman twice his age. The folly of such actions under the circumstances is not a factor in the play. Presumably the audience is uninterested in this aspect of the matter simply because it occurred before the action of the play begins. (We might here repeat the words of Granville-Barker, quoted earlier. He was speaking of *King Lear*, but the statement applies with equal pertinence to *Oedipus the King*: "Its probabilities are neither here nor there. A dramatist may postulate any situation he has the means to interpret, if he will abide by the logic of it after.")

Finally, we may note the complete acceptance by a modern audience of even more basic factors implicit in the premise of this ancient play—namely, that a man can be cursed and pursued by the gods, acting as Fate, and that there is no escape for him. We would be extremely skeptical of such a premise in a modern work, to say the least, but we here "suspend disbelief" for the sake of the play and put ourselves in the place of the Greek audience. Fortunately for ourselves, we are able to extend the same courtesy to dramatists of any place or period.

WILLIAM SHAKESPEARE

Hamlet

Ca. 1600

Hamlet is, of course, at once a theatrical masterpiece, great literature, and one of the most popular plays ever written. The work has been subject to so much interpretation and analysis, however, that it is well to remind ourselves that as Shakespeare conceived him Hamlet was an Elizabethan, the central figure in a play designed for audiences accustomed to suspense melodramas and the lurid trappings of regicide, vengeance, madness, and assorted violence. The play was written to be performed, and its success in performance all these years testifies to its validity as a theatre work. Incidentally, it is usually more effective when the complete or nearly complete text is used than when it is cut down to two or two and a half hours. Condensations of the text concentrate too heavily on Hamlet alone. In full the play is seen to be a colossal and furious drama of an entire court, moving inexorably and with increasing momentum toward its tragic climax.

    Hamlet is better adapted to the kind of thrust stage for which it was written than to the proscenium stage where we usually see it today. It has many scenes, and today these are customarily grouped into five acts. The action covers a wide range of time and various locations at Elsinore.

Premise

Prince Hamlet—intelligent, sensitive, introspective, and already mourning the death of his father—is profoundly shocked by his mother's hasty remarriage to his detested uncle, Claudius, who has assumed the throne.

Antecedent action, unknown to Hamlet, includes the fact that Claudius and his mother were adulterers, and that Claudius murdered the king.

Synopsis

ACT ONE

[]   *Scene One*

A ghost resembling the late king has been walking the battlements of Elsinore. Horatio, a trusted friend of Hamlet's, has been summoned by the watch to confront the spectre. While waiting for it to appear, Horatio speaks of the recent conflict between Denmark and Norway. Young Fortinbras, whose father the elder Hamlet had slain in battle, is, according to Horatio, preparing to retake Norwegian lands lost to Denmark.

The ghost appears, but it will not speak, and it disappears as the cock crows. Horatio decides that Hamlet must be informed.

[]   *Scene Two*

Claudius sends two ambassadors to the king of Norway to persuade him to restrain Fortinbras in the latter's warlike preparations against Denmark. Then he grants permission to Laertes, son of his counselor, Polonius, to return to his studies in France. Seconded by the queen, he next urges Hamlet to bring to an end his prolonged and excessive mourning for his father.

Alone, Hamlet, in the first of the soliloquies, expresses his revulsion at his mother's quick remarriage, especially to a man so far inferior to his father. (Such a marriage was also regarded, in Shakespeare's time, as incestuous.) Hamlet's outrage is so intense that he has become bitter and disgusted with life itself.

Horatio and the two soldiers of the watch tell Hamlet of the apparition on the battlements. Deeply disturbed, Hamlet agrees to watch with them that night and to address the ghost.

[]   *Scene Three*

Laertes bids farewell to Ophelia. He warns his sister that Hamlet's attentions should not be taken too seriously. Polonius enters and with some ponderous advice on behavior speeds Laertes on his way to France. He then turns to his daughter and insists that she see no more of Hamlet. Ophelia agrees.

[]   *Scene Four*

Hamlet and Horatio keep the watch with Marcellus, one of the soldiers who had first reported the apparition. The ghost appears and beckons Hamlet to follow him. Horatio and Marcellus try to hold him back, but Hamlet breaks away.

[]   *Scene Five*

On another part of the ramparts the ghost speaks, saying that he is indeed the spirit of the elder Hamlet. He commands his son to avenge his murder, stating that Claudius had seduced Gertrude, then poured poison into his ear as he slept. He urges leniency for Gertrude. Hamlet swears vengeance on Claudius, and the ghost disappears.

Horatio and Marcellus find Hamlet, but he refuses to tell them what has passed. He does, however, swear both men to secrecy as to what they do know, no matter how strange and puzzling his actions may be in the future.

[]   *In Brief*

Hamlet, already grieving over the death of an adored father, mistrustful of his uncle, and deeply disturbed by his mother's hasty remarriage, is suddenly confronted by a version of events that requires him to take action not only contrary to his nature and on doubtful evidence (for the ghost may or may not have been his father's spirit), but at a time when he himself is suffering a profound disgust and disillusionment.

ACT TWO

[] *Scene One*

Polonius suspects that his son Laertes may be leading a profligate life in France, and dispatches a servant to spy on him.

Then Ophelia reports to her father a distressing and frightening encounter with Hamlet, at which he did not behave rationally. (Shakespeare chose to omit the scene that Ophelia describes. Some commentators assume that Hamlet, coming to Ophelia for solace and affection, sensed her withdrawal, decided that he could not trust her, and realized that he must bear his responsibility alone. On the other hand, his visit may have been part of a deliberate plan to give a false impression of lunacy. It has also been suggested that the author is deliberately whetting our curiosity about Hamlet's madness, making us anxious to see him again so that we may judge for ourselves whether his malady is feigned or real. If this is so, then Shakespeare could hardly have chosen a better means than Ophelia's report of her encounter with the prince.)

Polonius interprets Hamlet's behavior as madness due to un-requited love. He determines to inform the king.

[] *Scene Two*

Rosencrantz and Guildenstern, two old friends of Hamlet, have been summoned to the court and are welcomed by the king and queen. They are instructed to try to learn the cause of Hamlet's strange disposition and behavior.

The ambassadors sent to Norway report that the Norwegian king has restrained his nephew Fortinbras in his preparations to attack Denmark. He will make war on "the Polack" instead. For this purpose permission is requested for Fortinbras' troops to cross Denmark. Claudius is delighted with the success of the mission.

Polonius now tells the king that Hamlet's love for Ophelia, which he says she does not return, has unquestionably driven Hamlet mad. Claudius is skeptical, but agrees to a plan to spy upon an arranged meeting between the prince and Ophelia.

Polonius encounters Hamlet. The young man's behavior, compounded of disgust and contempt, convinces Polonius more than ever that Hamlet has lost his reason.

As Polonius leaves, Rosencrantz and Guildenstern enter. Hamlet is at first glad to see them, but almost immediately suspects the truth—that they have been summoned to engage his confidence and report back to the king. The two young men cannot deny it. They tell Hamlet that a traveling company of actors is coming to Elsinore.

Moments later Polonius arrives with the same news, and then the players themselves. Hamlet welcomes them warmly. A long speech delivered by one of the players from *Dido and Aeneas* starts Hamlet's mind working on a plan to prove Claudius' guilt. He asks the leading player if they can perform a work called *The Murder of Gonzago,* and if they can insert some lines that Hamlet will write for them. The player agrees to do so.

Shakespeare ends the scene, and the act, with Hamlet's second soliloquy. It is built on Hamlet's exasperation that the players can express emotion in a fictitious situation that means nothing to them personally, while he must dissemble and bottle up his own feelings. But he has found a way at last to test the truth of the ghost's charge of murder. If Claudius is truly guilty, it is implied, then Hamlet can summon up the courage and the will to act.

(How far Hamlet's doubts about the authenticity of the ghost account for his delay in carrying out the burden of vengeance placed upon him, and how far these doubts are merely an excuse for further delay and inaction brought on by his melancholia, is subject to debate and wide interpretation. Both reasons could be operative, for neither excludes the other. It seems to be mainly a question of emphasis and, of course, interpretation.)

[]   *In Brief*

Hamlet fails to avenge his father's murder, as he has sworn to do. This can be accounted for by the fact that he is still not certain the ghost was telling the truth, by the melancholy that robs him of the will to act, and by his own nature, which shrinks from ill-considered violence. This inner struggle leaves him moody, irritable, and often so hostile and contemptuous in manner and speech that there is even a question of his sanity. But with the arrival of the players he devises a plan to resolve his doubts, and there is a promise of action.

ACT THREE

[]   *Scene One*

The only thing that Rosencrantz and Guildenstern are able to tell the king is that Hamlet has arranged to have a play performed that evening. Claudius is pleased that Hamlet is interested in something besides his own mysterious concerns.

Ophelia is told to walk where Hamlet will come upon her, presumably by chance. Polonius and the king will spy on the encounter. In an aside Claudius reveals his guilty conscience. He and Polonius hide.

Hamlet enters. In the third of the soliloquies he ponders suicide as a possible escape from earthly trials and responsibilities. What deters him is not the fact that he hasn't fulfilled the task laid upon him, but the thought that perhaps death might not end his misery.

Ophelia greets him and he answers courteously. But then she returns gifts that he had given her, and, sensing her betrayal of him and knowing their relationship is foredoomed by the business at hand, he tells her that he doesn't love her, and in venomous and insulting language bursts forth against the perfidy of women. He goes on to insult Polonius and hints a threat against the king. Ophelia then too believes that he has lost his reason.

Claudius and Polonius discuss what they have overheard. The king decides that in his present frame of mind Hamlet is too dangerous a man to have at court, and determines to send him to England. Polonius still holds to the theory of unrequited love, and suggests that after the play the queen question her son.

[]   *Scene Two*

Hamlet advises the players on acting (in what could well be Shakespeare's own sentiments). He then turns to Horatio, whom he trusts implicitly, and asks him to observe carefully the king's reaction to the play.

The court assembles and the play begins with a pantomime that adumbrates the plot, then moves on to dialogue with a story paralleling Claudius' murder of his brother. Claudius is greatly perturbed, and runs out of the hall. Hamlet and Horatio know that the king has betrayed his guilt. The ghost was telling the truth.

Rosencrantz and Guildenstern come to report the king's intense anger, and the queen's desire to see Hamlet in her chamber. Hamlet is utterly contemptuous of the efforts of these two young men to "play upon him." Polonius enters and urges Hamlet to visit his mother at once. He agrees to do so, vowing, in a fourth soliloquy, not to allow his emotions so to overwhelm him that he will kill her.

[]   *Scene Three*

Rosencrantz and Guildenstern are ordered by the king to accompany Hamlet to England. Polonius tells Claudius that Hamlet is on his way to the queen, and that he himself will hide behind an arras to eavesdrop. Alone, Claudius tries to ease his conscience by prayer, and Hamlet comes upon him. This is an opportunity to take vengeance, but Hamlet will not kill him during a moment of repentance, for this could send Claudius to heaven instead of hell. Ironically, at the end of the scene, we learn that the king has been unable to pray.

(It is widely held that, his melancholy having nearly immobilized his will to act, Hamlet's reason for his failure to kill the king at this point is a mere rationalization.)

[]   *Scene Four*

Hamlet confronts the queen. His manner so alarms her that she calls for help, and Polonius, behind the arras, echoes the cry. Believing it to be the king, Hamlet stabs him. Pulling the arras aside, he sees that he has slain the meddling counselor. He turns back to his mother and upbraids her for her marriage to Claudius. Gertrude is overwhelmed with shame and terror. Hamlet seems almost on the point of revealing that Claudius is a murderer when the ghost reappears, blunting the edge of the prince's fury toward his mother, but reminding him that vengeance has not yet been taken. Since the apparition can be seen and heard only by Hamlet, Gertrude interprets his behavior as proof of lunacy. (Popular belief held that spirits could make themselves visible to whom they wished, remaining unseen by others.)

Hamlet urges the queen to continence and repentance, his whole effort now concentrated on redeeming her from the degradation of her marriage. He then says that he has been ordered to England with Rosencrantz and Guildenstern. He suspects that he is to be slain there, and resolves to turn the tables on the two young men. He leaves, dragging out Polonius' body.

[]   *In Brief*

Hamlet breaks with Ophelia, blaming her for what he considers her perfidy. He is unaware that she is simply obeying her father, and that from her point of view her action is not a betrayal at all, but part of an effort to discover the cause of his indisposition.

Hamlet carries out his plan to test the king's guilt, and this is spectacularly proven. But Claudius has now been alerted to his danger. However, even in Hamlet's fury and with proof at hand, he fails, when he has an opportunity, to take vengeance on the king. He shows no hesitation in confronting his mother with her obliquity, and he leaves her wretched and ashamed. Meanwhile, he has unintentionally killed Polonius, thereby putting a strong weapon in the king's hands; and he has been visited again by the ghost, who urges him on to vengeance.

Act Three sees the conflict between Hamlet and Claudius immeasurably sharpened, for the king is now the prince's deadly enemy, and Hamlet knows it. He is under renewed pressure to kill Claudius, but it is now going to be far more difficult to do so.

ACT FOUR

[]   Scene One

Claudius hears from the queen of the slaying of Polonius. Rosencrantz and Guildenstern are summoned to locate the prince, and Claudius decides to call a meeting of his counselors.

[]   Scene Two

Rosencrantz and Guildenstern find Hamlet, who will not tell them what he has done with the body of Polonius. He taunts them and runs away, forcing them into a chase.

[]   Scene Three

Hamlet is brought before Claudius and ordered to leave for England at once. Rosencrantz and Guildenstern are to escort him. After the slaying of Polonius, the king tells Hamlet, his safety requires that he be spirited away. Hamlet has no choice but to go.

[]   Scene Four

Hamlet, Rosencrantz, and Guildenstern pass Fortinbras and his Norwegian forces on their way to Poland. In another soliloquy Hamlet compares the energetic conduct of Fortinbras and his army, who lack the personal motive for action that he has, with his own failure to avenge his father's death. Hamlet is puzzled by this failure, and determines to act boldly from now on.

[] *Scene Five*

There is a lapse of time between this scene and the last one—probably a matter of some weeks. With her father dead and her brother away, Ophelia has lost her reason. Her pitiful behavior greatly shocks the king and queen.

Laertes, hearing of Polonius' death and suspecting the king of foul play, has returned to Denmark. He bursts furiously in upon the court, sees what has happened to his sister, and is with some difficulty calmed by the king, who leads him off to talk in confidence of all that has occurred.

[] *Scene Six*

Sailors bring Horatio a letter from Hamlet, telling about an encounter with pirates at sea and saying that he has returned to Denmark. At Hamlet's urging Horatio goes to meet him.

[] *Scene Seven*

Claudius, having given Laertes his own version of recent events, says that he could not proceed against Hamlet directly for two reasons: Gertrude's maternal feelings and the prince's popularity among the people.

A messenger brings the astonishing and unwelcome news of Hamlet's return. Claudius and Laertes then plan that the king will wager on Hamlet in a friendly fencing match with Laertes that will, however, result in Hamlet's death. Laertes will use an unblunted rapier with a poisoned tip, and, to make doubly certain of the prince's demise, Claudius will prepare a poisoned drink to be given him. Their plotting is interrupted by the queen, who brings word that Ophelia has drowned.

[] *In Brief*

The play now begins to move very swiftly, in a series of short scenes. Although his plan to have Hamlet slain in England goes awry, Claudius is the principal aggressor in this act.

Hamlet returns to Denmark, partly by chance and partly as a result of his own action. Seemingly he is in a slightly different mood, not quite so subject to the bitterness and melancholy that have characterized him before. Can he finally bring himself to carry out his vengeance, and find a way to do it? Claudius lays an elaborate plot to kill Hamlet first, and in such a way that even his mother will think it was an accident.

ACT FIVE

[]   Scene One

Two rustics (Elizabethan clowns) are digging a grave. Hamlet and Horatio come upon them. Without knowing to whom he is talking, one of the gravediggers speaks of Hamlet's madness and his being sent to England. A skull tossed out of the ground is identified as that of Yorick, a jester Hamlet had known and loved as a child.

A funeral party approaches. It includes the king, the queen, and Laertes, and Hamlet learns that the corpse is Ophelia's and that the rites have been curtailed because she probably took her own life. Laertes jumps into the grave with extravagant expressions of grief, which anger Hamlet, and he reveals his presence, protesting his own love for the girl. Laertes attacks him, but attendants pull them apart. The king quietly reminds Laertes that his vengeance is imminent.

[]   Scene Two

Hamlet tells Horatio that he found, aboard ship, Claudius' instructions that he should be slain upon arrival in England, and that he forged an order that Rosencrantz and Guildenstern be put to death.

Osric, a foppish courtier, brings word that the king would wager on Hamlet against Laertes in a fencing match. Horatio is full of foreboding, but Hamlet is fatalistic and agrees to the match. It begins at once, with the king and the queen in attendance.

Hamlet apologizes to Laertes for his recent rudeness, and Laertes hypocritically returns his civilities. Hamlet scores twice as the dueling starts, and the king genially offers him the poisoned wine, but he refuses it. Although Claudius tries to stop her, Gertrude herself takes the cup and drinks to her son's fortune.

Catching Hamlet off guard, Laertes wounds him with the poisoned rapier. There is a brief scuffle, in which the weapons are exchanged. Laertes is pricked by the same deadly rapier. The queen dies and Laertes collapses. Stung with remorse, he begs Hamlet's forgiveness and accuses the king of the dueling plot. Hamlet stabs Claudius and then forces him to drink the poisoned wine. In Hamlet's death throes the nobility of his spirit is manifest: he forgives Laertes; he bids his mother farewell; and he asks Horatio to live on and tell his story.

Outside, Fortinbras is heard saluting the English ambassadors, all approaching the castle. As he dies, Hamlet indicates his preference for Fortinbras to sit on the Danish throne.

The visitors enter. An ambassador from England reports that the king's orders have been carried out—Rosencrantz and Guildenstern are dead. Fortinbras takes command, and Hamlet's body is solemnly removed to lie in state.

[] *In Brief*

Now that all is in dramatic readiness for the climactic confrontation between Hamlet and Claudius, the play can afford a brief breathing space, and we meet the gravediggers and hear about Yorick. Then we get an obligatory scene—Hamlet's learning of the death of his beloved Ophelia. Finally we are into the whirling, inevitable climax, as Hamlet achieves his long-delayed vengeance at the cost of his own and other lives.

Protagonist and Objective

Hamlet is the protagonist, and his objective is clearly and forcefully stated in I-5:

> *Ghost:* If thou didst ever thy dear father love,—
> *Hamlet:* Oh, God!
> *Ghost:* Revenge his foul and most unnatural murder.
> (*There follows a description of the murder.*)
> Adieu, adieu, adieu! remember me.
> *Hamlet:*
> O all you host of heaven! Oh earth! What else?
> And shall I couple hell? O fie! Hold, hold, my heart!
> And you, my sinews, grow not instant old,
> But bear me stiffly up. Remember thee?
> Ay, thou poor ghost, while memory holds a seat
> In this distracted globe. Remember thee?
> Yea, from the table of my memory
> I'll wipe away all trivial fond records,

All saws of books, all forms, all pressures past
That youth and observation copied there,
And thy commandment all alone shall live
Within the book and volume of my brain,
Unmixed with baser matter. Yes, by heaven!
O most pernicious woman!
O villain, villain, smiling, damned villain!
My tables, my tables! Meet it is I set it down
That one may smile, and smile, and be a villain;
At least I'm sure it may be so in Denmark. (*Writes.*)
So, uncle, there you are. Now to my word:
It is "Adieu, adieu! Remember me."
I have sworn't.

There can hardly be a question in anyone's mind, after this, as to
what this play is about. In fact, it is the very eloquence and force
of the statement of objective that make it possible for Shakespeare
to show Hamlet procrastinating and so beset by doubt and reluctance
to act. We know that sooner or later this oath must be fulfilled.

The dramatic question is "Will Hamlet be successful in avenging the murder of his father?" The answer, of course, is "yes."

Obstacles

Hamlet is a splendid illustration of the fact that, although the protagonist can have no more than one main objective if a play is to have
unity, there can be many obstacles. It should be noted, furthermore,
that these obstacles do not arise in a connected line of cause and
effect, but from many different quarters, one after another.

It is hard to think of any figure in drama beset by more difficulties and frustrations than Hamlet. There is, first of all, the active and determined enmity of Claudius and those acting under his
orders. But the more interesting battleground is in Hamlet's own
mind, for here are all kinds of emotional and psychological conflicts
that impede his purpose. His mother's hasty remarriage to her
brother-in-law, the detestable Claudius, tears him apart. He loves
Ophelia, but his feelings must be denied: the girl might betray him.
The melancholy brought on by the shock of events at court has almost
immobilized his will to act. (Modern psychiatry is familiar with this
mental condition and its consequence.) There is also, right up to
Claudius' betrayal of his guilt at the play, a question in Hamlet's
mind as to whether the ghost was truly his father's spirit. It takes a

man of great balance and courage to cope with such a host of obstacles between him and his objective.

Major Crisis and Climax, Theme

The last moment in the play in which the issue can swing either
way (that is, the major crisis, when the answer to the dramatic
question is still uncertain) is Hamlet's duel with Laertes. The major
climax is Hamlet's killing of Claudius. He succeeds in his objective.

Hamlet, in all its richness and density, has meant so many
things to so many men that it seems presumptuous to attempt to
define a theme for the play. We may surmise that it signified to the
Elizabethan public the ultimate triumph of justice and the continuity of the state under a legitimate government.

Resolution

Laertes and Hamlet die; Fortinbras arrives, and the future of the
Danish throne is indicated; the deaths of Rosencrantz and Guildenstern are reported; Horatio begins the fulfillment of Hamlet's charge
to tell his story; and Hamlet is honored.

Opening

Shakespeare might have begun the play with the murder of King
Hamlet, with Prince Hamlet's arrival back in Denmark from Witten-
berg, with the marriage of Claudius and Gertrude. But he was concerned with a man struggling to fulfill an oath of vengeance. Hence
he begins shortly before the oath is made—exactly the right spot in
the larger story.

Unity

Hamlet is a sprawling play, and certainly proves that the unities of
time and place (that we find in *Oedipus the King* and *Ghosts*, for
example) are not essential to a work of real power. The unity of place
is observed insofar as all the action occurs at Elsinore, the events in

Norway and at sea being merely reported. But the precise locale at Elsinore shifts constantly. (The simplicity of Elizabethan staging methods made changes of scene swift and effortless.)

Unity of action is carefully observed, and it is this that holds the play together so tightly. There is scarcely a line or scene that doesn't bear on Hamlet's problem. The comic dialogue of the two gravediggers might be regarded as an exception, a sop to the ground-lings who demanded some nonsense with their blood and thunder. But even here Shakespeare made effective use of the clowns. The change in Hamlet and his attitude toward death is certainly reflected in his conversation with the gravedigger. And the entire scene effec-tively slows down the action before the furious excitement of the climax.

Exposition

There is an awkward piece of exposition in I-1, when Horatio tells Marcellus about the conflict between King Hamlet and the elder Fortinbras. This is unrelieved narration. It conveys information to Marcellus that the latter could reasonably be expected to know, it has no particular effect on Marcellus, and there is no conflict between the two men that could have elicited it. Technically, Shakespeare at this point failed to employ his usual skill.

In contrast, consider the ghost's narrative when he tells how he was murdered. The material could hardly be more highly charged with emotion, both for the ghost and for Hamlet.

Exposition elsewhere in the play is conventionally handled, as in I-2, when Claudius and Gertrude implore Hamlet to end his mourning for his father, and in I-3, when Laertes and Polonius forbid Ophelia to see Hamlet again. Both these scenes exhibit a friction that helps to carry the information the audience needs to know.

Characterization

It is a truism that there is no more complex and fascinating character in all drama than Hamlet. Shakespeare achieves this depth of char-acterization in part by the contrast between Hamlet's encounters with Horatio, whom he trusts, and with those whom he mistrusts. The scenes with Horatio give us the key to Hamlet's nature and what he is really thinking. Against this we measure his actions with those with whom he must dissemble. There isn't the slightest suggestion, for example, in any of the scenes with Horatio that Hamlet is anything but sane. Neither is there any suggestion of madness in the soliloquies, which also let us explore his unguarded thoughts. It follows that his "madness" is feigned, for whenever we encounter it there is good reason for it. Knowledge of a sovereign's guilt was extremely dangerous, and pretended madness would be a logical protective device.

Hamlet is an intellectual—idealistic, imaginative, witty—and popular at court and with the common people. One factor helping us to judge his normal character, as contrasted with his behavior in the play, is what others say of him and expect of him.

As for the long delay in avenging the death of his father, there are, as already noted, two reasons for this. The more important one is psychological—the melancholy that has brought on an immobilization of the will to act. But Hamlet must also be sure that the ghost was his father's spirit, not a demon, and that it was speaking the truth. This is established for him by Claudius' reaction to the players, and from that moment on he no longer has that excuse (if excuse it is) for procrastination.

Note where Shakespeare places Hamlet's first opportunity to take vengeance—immediately after the scene with the players, when the prince is at the peak of his rage and on his way to his mother's chambers. But still he cannot bring himself to do the deed. Instead of doubts about the authenticity of the ghost, his reason for delay now is that killing Claudius at his prayers would defeat the purpose of vengeance. (It is not until the duel with Laertes that another opportunity occurs.)

Needless to say, the other characters are expertly drawn. Gertrude is a fully rounded figure, a solicitous and protective mother even after her son's dreadful indictment of her. Ophelia, dominated by her father and brother, is an immature girl, but loyal to Hamlet by her own lights; for her love is genuine and what she does, under her father's direction, is done in the hope of helping to cure the prince. Bumbling, pompous, windy Polonius is one of Shakespeare's great comic characters; and there is a splendid contrast between the hotheaded Laertes, who also lost his father, and the thoughtful, troubled Hamlet. In short, all these people are consistent and recognizable creatures trying to deal with an intensely human problem, and this gives the play a universality that makes it as valid and exciting today as it ever was.

Development

The many scenes into which the play is divided often contain two or more incidents, each with its own structure. Consider, for example, II-2:

[]   *First Incident*

Double Protagonist: The king and the queen.
Objective: To persuade Rosencrantz and Guildenstern to spy on Hamlet.
Obstacle: Their possible reluctance to betray an old school-mate. (Since they betray no reluctance whatever, there is no conflict, and the incident has little drama by itself. It is dramatic, however, in the context of the entire play.)
Climax: Rosencrantz and Guildenstern agree to the king's proposal.
Resolution: They are dispatched to find Hamlet and begin their task at once.

[]   *Second Incident*

Protagonist: Polonius.
Objective: To convince the king that the cause of Hamlet's strange behavior is madness due to unrequited love. (Here we have an occurrence that delays the action by the insertion of some exposition. The ambassadors to Norway report the success of their mission. We note this while waiting for the main thrust of the Claudius-Polonius incident.)
Obstacle: The king's skepticism.
Climax: Polonius fails to convince the king as to the cause of Hamlet's behavior.
Resolution: Claudius nevertheless agrees to spy upon a meeting between Hamlet and Ophelia.

[]   *Third Incident*

Protagonist: Polonius.
Objective: By questioning Hamlet to confirm Polonius' theory.
Obstacle: Hamlet's awareness of Polonius' purpose.
Climax: Polonius' mistaken conclusion.
Resolution: Polonius' resolve to arrange a meeting between Hamlet and Ophelia.

[]   *Fourth Incident*

Double Protagonist: Rosencrantz and Guildenstern.
Objective: To insinuate themselves into Hamlet's confidence.

Obstacle: Hamlet's awareness of their intentions.

Climax: Their inability to deny that they have been sent to spy on him.

Resolution: Hamlet reveals that he knows what they are trying to do. (Then the arrival of the players is reported.)

[] *Fifth Incident*

Protagonist: Hamlet.

Objective: To use the players for the purpose of proving the king's guilt.

Obstacle: The possible reluctance or inability of the players to co-operate. (Since the players *are* willing and able to co-operate, conflict and drama are at a minimum in this isolated incident, but as part of the larger pattern the situation is highly charged. Note the similarity to the first incident.)

Climax: The player's agreement to insert Hamlet's interpolations into the play.

Resolution: Hamlet sends the players off to prepare for the performance.

[] *Sixth Incident*

(Hamlet's "rogue and peasant slave" soliloquy. Here the drama is all in his own mind.)

Protagonist: Hamlet.

Objective: To understand the cause of his own inaction under extreme provocation.

Obstacle: The psychological complexity of the doubts and melancholy that inhibit him.

Climax: His belief that his doubts about Claudius' guilt will be resolved when the players re-enact the murder.

Resolution: His feeling that he is at last moving against his enemy.

Compare the episodic nature of II-2, above, with the tightly structured III-4:

Protagonist: Hamlet.

Objective: To wring a confession of guilt from his mother and bring her to repentance.

Obstacle: The natural feelings of both mother and son, each toward the other; Gertrude's reluctance to admit her sin.

Climax: The queen's shame and remorse.

Resolution: Hamlet leaves her emotionally exhausted.

The presence of a third person in the chamber, Polonius, draws Hamlet's wrath away from the queen for a moment, but serves to increase her terror. The ghost deters Hamlet from what would probably be an even more violent attack on his mother. Essentially, however, the basic structure of the scene is not altered by the killing of Polonius or the appearance of the ghost.

Dramtic Irony

There is a powerful use of dramatic irony during the early part of the play in Hamlet's suspicion of the king's guilt. From the time the ghost tells him of the murder until Claudius betrays himself at the play, the audience knows—and the king does not—that Hamlet suspects him. When the king realizes what we already know—that Hamlet is aware of the truth—he actively plots Hamlet's death.

Another aspect of this same irony is that, while others suspect Hamlet of madness, we know the reason for his behavior.

When Ophelia breaks with Hamlet in III-1 and returns his gifts, we know that she is acting under her father's orders. Hamlet is unaware of this, and it leads him to suspect that Ophelia, like his mother, is a perfidious woman.

Dramatic irony has seldom been used more effectively than in the scene of Claudius at the play. We know of the trap that Hamlet has laid; the king does not.

The device is used again in the final scene. We know, as Hamlet does not, that Laertes is dueling with a poisoned and unbated rapier. When the queen picks up the wine, we know that this too is poisoned.

Preparation

Very little planting is required in the play. It might be noted, however, how carefully the ultimate arrival of Fortinbras is prepared. We hear of him from Horatio in I-1, from the king in I-2, from the ambassadors to Norway in II-2; we meet Fortinbras himself briefly in IV-2. By the final scene of the play we are quite ready for his assumption of the Danish throne.

Activity

In spite of the introspective nature of the play, it fairly bursts with physical activity—the wanderings of the ghost, the hiding and eavesdropping of Claudius and Polonius, the presentation of the play, the stabbing of Polonius and near stabbing of Claudius at his prayers, the tussle at the grave, the dueling and poisoning at the end. All these activities are more than merely illustrative. They are doing their part in helping to further the story.

Dialogue

The dialogue needs no comment here, unless it be a reminder that, although it contains many words and constructions unfamiliar today, the language was perfectly comprehensible to the Elizabethan audience for whom it was written.

Plausibility

The feeling of inevitability in the play is the result not of Fate, as in the Greek tragedies, but of extraordinarily skillful character drawing. Putting a man of Hamlet's qualities into such a situation leads to an ending that is more than predictable. If Hamlet had felt less responsibility for carrying out the ghost's charge, he might have abandoned his course of action before the arrival of the players, or it might not have occurred to him to set that particular trap for the king. If he had been more impulsive, less thoughtful and subject to moods, he would probably have killed Claudius right after talking with the ghost. In either case there would have been no play. Shakespeare is nothing if not clear and plausible. (And he knew what would draw at the box office.)

MOLIÈRE
Tartuffe
1664–1669

Originally performed in a three-act version for Louis XIV at Versailles, in 1664, this satire on religious hypocrisy so offended the sensibilities of the queen mother and the Jesuits that further performances were prohibited. Molière did considerable revising and rewriting in his efforts to have the ban lifted. (This may have damaged the play. The present version, in five acts, is structurally flawed.) A 1667 production was promptly closed by the mayor of Paris, and it was not until 1669, with the king's permission, that public performances were allowed. The play then met with immediate popular success and, of all the author's works, is the most frequently performed today.

    Tartuffe is in verse. It was written for the indoor, proscenium type of theatre that France was adopting in the seventeenth century, largely from Italian designs.

Premise

Orgon, a well-to-do bourgeois, has taken into his home a sanctimonious opportunist in whom he and his mother are completely deceived. They regard him as little less than a saint, for whom no favor is too great. The rest of the family—his son and daughter by a previous marriage, his young second wife, his brother-in-law, and a bright serving maid—see through Tartuffe's pretensions, but have been unable to persuade Orgon of the hypocrite's true character.

Synopsis

The setting throughout is the salon of Orgon's house in Paris. The play is in five acts. Though no time intervals are indicated between acts, the action might be considered more or less continuous.

ACT ONE

Madame Pernelle, who has been visiting her son Orgon, is in a temper. One by one, and to their faces, she upbraids various members of the household: Elmire, her daughter-in-law, does not heed her advice and is, furthermore, extravagant; Dorine, the maid, is a talkative hussy; Damis, her grandson, an impudent fool; Mariane, her granddaughter, is two-faced; Cleante, Elmire's brother, is unprincipled. It quickly develops that the reason for all this acrimony is the family's attitude toward Monsieur Tartuffe, who has come into the house a beggar, and is now attempting to lead them all on the path to heaven. The others cannot endure him. Tartuffe is constantly criticizing them and their friends, and has so insinuated himself into Orgon's regard that he now rules the establishment. Warning them to heed Tartuffe's strictures, for their souls' salvation, Madame Pernelle storms out of the house.

Dorine tells Cleante that Orgon seems to have been bewitched, that he thinks more of Tartuffe than of his own family. Damis, the son, asks Cleante to discuss with Orgon the question of his sister's marriage to Valère. Damis is sure that Mariane is in love with Valère, but believes that Tartuffe is influencing his father against the match.

Orgon enters. He has been away for a few days, and wants to hear the household news. Dorine tries to tell him of his wife's illness during his absence, but Orgon's only interest is in Tartuffe, who has apparently gorged himself and idled luxuriously the entire time. Dorine leaves, noting sarcastically that she will inform Elmire of her husband's concern for her.

Alone with Orgon, Cleante tries to make him realize how he is being duped by Tartuffe. Orgon, however, will not listen to any criticism of his guest. Tartuffe's pious example has utterly changed his life, he says. The merest trifles are sins to Tartuffe. Heaven itself brought the man here.

Cleante thinks Orgon must be going crazy to be taken in by such an obvious fraud. There is a distinction, he says, between hypocrisy and piety, but Orgon regards such talk as irreligious. Changing the subject, Cleante asks why Orgon has postponed his daughter's wedding to Valère. Orgon avoids a direct answer, saying that in this matter he will "follow the will of heaven." Cleante foresees trouble for this romance.

[]   *In Brief*

The first act characterizes the principals, and introduces most of them. (The exceptions are Valère and, notably, Tartuffe.) The basic situation is put before us: a man that most regard as a pious fraud, by his baleful influence over the master of the house is rapidly assuming control over the lives of all, even to the point of interfering with the wedding plans of the attractive daughter. Thus we see an intense conflict brewing, and our curiosity and anticipation are whetted in spite of there being no forward movement in the act.

ACT TWO

Orgon asks his daughter her opinion of Tartuffe, as Dorine comes upon them unnoticed. What would Mariane think of Tartuffe as a husband? Mariane is appalled. Dorine, making her presence known, tells Mariane that her father must be joking. When she realizes he is serious, she asks how he can consider that bigot and pauper as a son-in-law, to which Orgon replies that he will help Tartuffe financially. Dorine then pleads with him not to force Mariane into a hateful marriage, and a fierce argument ensues between master and servant. Threatening to strike Dorine if she says any more, Orgon extols Tartuffe to his daughter. Dorine cannot refrain from making sarcastic comments, though she falls silent whenever Orgon turns to her with upraised hand. Orgon is finally so frustrated and upset by this feminine opposition that he leaves.

Dorine then urges Mariane to summon up the courage to resist her father. Mariane seems disinclined to struggle, but protests that she loves Valère passionately, and will kill herself before she will marry Tartuffe. Dorine dismisses the talk of suicide as so much drivel, and, in an attempt to arouse the girl's fighting spirit, points out with heavy sarcasm the advantages of a union with Tartuffe. Mariane, cringing under this verbal lashing, pleads with Dorine to help her.

Valère enters. He has heard a rumor that Mariane is to marry Tartuffe instead of him. Surely she can't be serious. Mariane admits that her father wishes the match. Valère, scornful and furious, tells her to go ahead and marry the man. Smarting under his sarcasm, Mariane intimates that she will do just that. Valère says there is another girl who would be glad to marry him. A lovers' quarrel quickly develops, each accusing the other of not being truly in love.

Dorine, who has stood by quietly listening to their outbursts, now intercedes and literally brings the two together, forcing them to clasp hands. Reconciled, they listen as Dorine advises them on how to thwart Orgon's scheme. Instead of defying him openly, they are to appear to acquiesce, but Mariane is to find excuses to delay the marriage. Meanwhile, the rest of the family and their friends will all be urged to help prevent it. The lovers agree.

[]   *In Brief*

The play now begins to move, though hesitantly, with Orgon informing his daughter that he wants her to marry Tartuffe. Led by Dorine, the overt opposition also begins. However, the lovers' quarrel merely marks time so far as the main story line is concerned. This would not be altered in any way if Mariane and Valère agreed to accept Dorine's advice and suggestions when they meet instead of waiting until after they have quarreled and been reconciled.

ACT THREE

Damis resents Tartuffe's interest in his sister, and wants to have the matter out with him. But Dorine tells Damis that Elmire plans to talk with Tartuffe, and since the latter seems to be attracted to his stepmother, perhaps she can exert more influence. Though Damis would like to hide and listen to the interview, he leaves reluctantly as Tartuffe enters.

Tartuffe, calling off to his servant to put away his hair shirt and his flaggelator, turns to Dorine, sees her generous expanse of bosom, and insists on covering it with a handkerchief. Dorine leaves as Elmire comes in.

Tartuffe greets Elmire effusively. As they sit down to talk, Damis slips back into the room and hides. Before Elmire can even bring up the subject on her mind, Tartuffe is paying her extravagant compliments and making unwelcome advances. Elmire asks him pointblank about his intentions toward Mariane, to which Tartuffe replies that, although Orgon has mentioned the possibility of such a match, it is not the daughter he is interested in, but Elmire herself.

He declares his passion in flowery terms, and vows that she may trust his discretion. What, Elmire asks, if she should inform her husband of this declaration? Tartuffe is sure she would never do such a thing. She will not mention it, Elmire says, providing that Tartuffe urges the union of Mariane and Valère, and gives up all thought of marrying the girl himself.

At this point Damis bursts out of hiding, in a fury. He denounces the bargain Elmire would make with Tartuffe, and says he intends to report the entire conversation to his father. Then Orgon will know what a fraud and hypocrite he is harboring. Elmire tries to dissuade him, saying that a woman merely laughs at such absurdities as Tartuffe's protestations of love; but Damis is adamant.

Orgon enters, and Damis tells him that he has overheard Tartuffe trying to make love to his wife. Elmire rebukes Damis, saying that it is enough for a woman to reject such advances; there is no need also to disturb the husband with the silly tale. She leaves.

Orgon asks Tartuffe if the story is true, and Tartuffe replies that he is a sinner, a wicked, wretched scoundrel. He goes on heaping such abuse on himself that Orgon turns on his son and upbraids him as a hard-hearted wretch, unable to recognize true piety. The exasperated Damis tries to make his father see that Tartuffe is merely playing on his gullibility, but Orgon says that to spite all those who hate this holy man he will give him Mariane's hand in marriage this very evening. Then he drives Damis from the house.

Tartuffe offers to leave this household where he has aroused so much suspicion and discord, but Orgon will not hear of it. To demonstrate his trust, Orgon says he wants Tartuffe to be seen in the constant company of his wife. Furthermore, Orgon will make Tartuffe the sole inheritor of his wealth. "Heaven's will be done," says Tartuffe.

[]   *In Brief*

With the appearance of the major and catalytic figure of Tartuffe in the third act, the play picks up considerable steam. What we see essentially, however, is merely an intensification, not a change, in the basic situation. Elmire and Damis, in their separate ways, try to open Orgon's eyes to the truth about Tartuffe. Each fails, and the only result is to intensify Orgon's blind subservience to the holy fraud.

ACT FOUR

Cleante tries to persuade Tartuffe to use his influence to reconcile Orgon and Damis, and not to accept Orgon's proffered gift of all his property. To both these suggestions Tartuffe replies with sanctimonious platitudes about following the divine will, and excuses himself.

Elmire, Mariane, and Dorine come in. Dorine asks Cleante to help in their efforts to prevent Mariane's marriage to Tartuffe. Orgon enters. Mariane begs that, if her father will not permit her to marry Valère, at least he will send her to a convent and not force her into a hateful marriage. Dorine, Cleante, and Elmire all add their entreaties, but Orgon is unmoved. Elmire insists it is true that Tartuffe tried to make love to her, but Orgon prefers to believe that she and Damis made up the story to discredit Tartuffe. Elmire says that she will prove the truth of her assertion. She asks Dorine, Cleante, and Mariane to leave, and Orgon to conceal himself under a table over which a cloth is draped. As Orgon does so, Elmire reminds him that she must pretend to an amorous response in order to trap Tartuffe. Orgon is to remain in hiding until he is convinced of Tartuffe's treachery.

Tartuffe enters. Elmire tells him that, now she is sure they are quite alone, she can reveal that she is not indifferent to his proposals. Tartuffe is at first suspicious, and Elmire continues that she opposed his marriage to Mariane because she did not want to share him. Tartuffe is delighted, but says that before he rejects marriage to Mariane Elmire must prove her sincerity by bestowing on him her ultimate favors. Elmire protests such a hasty consummation of the affair. Would not this be an offense to heaven? Tartuffe brushes aside her scruples. He can assure her that heaven will not be displeased. A secret sin is not a sin unless it is found out.

By now Elmire is coughing—a signal to Orgon to come out and put a stop to this. He stays hidden, and Elmire says she consents. But, first, will Tartuffe look around outside to make sure her husband is nowhere about? As he leaves, Tartuffe says that Orgon is so credulous he can always be led around by the nose.

Orgon emerges from under the table, convinced at last. He is furious. Elmire remarks sarcastically that nothing has happened yet; he'd better hide again to make sure. As Tartuffe returns, Orgon ducks behind Elmire's ample skirts.

Tartuffe reports that the coast is clear. Orgon jumps up, denouncing him as a traitor and a fraud, and orders him out. At this point Tartuffe turns on Orgon, reminding him that the house now belongs to him and that Orgon is in no position to order him out. He leaves.

Elmire asks the meaning of that remark, and Orgon admits that he has signed over all his property to Tartuffe, but there's something that worries him even more. There was a certain strongbox upstairs, and he must see at once if it is still there.

[] In Brief

The act begins with further efforts and entreaties to Orgon, whose belief in Tartuffe remains as strong as ever. Elmire does move him a little; though he is skeptical, she gets him to agree to hide while she attempts to demonstrate Tartuffe's perfidy. Orgon's awakening finally occurs, but Tartuffe's mischief is by no means eliminated by his exposure. By now Orgon has so deeply committed himself that he and his family, though facing a different set of problems, may be even worse off than before. We are somewhat astonished to learn, too, that there is a strongbox in the house whose possible disappearance may portend very serious trouble indeed.

ACT FIVE

The strongbox has disappeared—Tartuffe has taken it with him. Orgon explains to Cleante that the box contained papers incriminating a friend, now in exile, who had entrusted them to Orgon's care. Orgon had given Tartuffe custody of the box so that, in case of an investigation, he could truthfully deny possession of it. Now, in addition to the betrayal of a friend's trust, Orgon faces the possibility of being himself charged with treason if the contents of the box become known. In his despair Orgon rails against all pious men. Cleante insists they are not all blackguards; many are worthy, and therefore one must be reasonable and not led into extremes.

Damis enters, threatening physical violence against Tartuffe, but Cleante dissuades him from a crude and impulsive vengeance. Now all the women of the household appear: Madame Pernelle (Orgon's mother, who left the house in Act One), Mariane, Elmire, and Dorine. Madame Pernelle simply cannot believe that Tartuffe is guilty of all the misdeeds of which the others are accusing him, and even Orgon cannot convince her. As they all discuss the likelihood of Tartuffe's moving against the family with the weapons he now holds, a Monsieur Loyal appears at the door, identifying himself as a messenger from Tartuffe.

Loyal is deferential and polite, but it soon develops that he is a process server, come to evict the family from the house. Generously he offers to withhold execution of the writ till morning, but by then they must be gone. Orgon and Dorine start shouting imprecations, and Damis is ready to punch Loyal in the nose. Cleante's cooler counsel prevails. The writ is accepted and Cleante asks Loyal to leave.

Madame Pernelle is at last convinced that Tartuffe is a villain. Dorine taunts the old lady sarcastically. Elmire thinks they should tell everyone what has happened, to rally public opinion to their side.

Valère arrives hastily to inform them all that Tartuffe has denounced Orgon as a traitor to the king and offered the strongbox as evidence. Accompanied by Tartuffe, an officer is on his way there now to place Orgon under arrest. Valère urges immediate flight in his carriage, but, before they can leave, Tartuffe arrives with a police officer.

Tartuffe, intercepting Orgon as he tries to escape, orders his arrest. In the face of the family's rebukes he says that his first duty is to the king. With sanctimonious words he defends all his actions. As Cleante scathingly upbraids him, Tartuffe turns to the officer, asking him to carry out his orders.

But the officer's orders are to arrest Tartuffe. Turning to Orgon, he says that their most wise king has not been deceived by Tartuffe. He knew him for a rogue with a long criminal record. The king has declared the contract conveying Orgon's property to Tartuffe null and void. Furthermore, he pardons Orgon's offense in shielding his absent friend.

As everyone gives thanks and begins to breathe more easily, Orgon starts to attack Tartuffe. Again Cleante intercedes. Let royal justice prevail, he says, and Orgon acknowledge the king's clemency. Orgon sees the wisdom of this, and says that they must prepare for the marriage of Mariane to Valère.

[]   *In Brief*

The start of the act is given over to explaining the significance of the strongbox, and the family's dilemma is explored. Then Orgon's troubles compound rapidly—the eviction from the house, the denunciation before the king. Tartuffe is permitted a further opportunity to display his hypocritical words and behavior, and suddenly the tables are turned. The intercession of the king puts all to rights.

Protagonist and Objective

In spite of the fact that Molière named his play after its most striking and memorable character, Tartuffe is not the protagonist. Neither is Orgon. Here we have the rather uncommon instance of a group protagonist—in this case, Orgon's family: Elmire, Mariane, Damis, Cleante, plus Dorine and Valère. They all want the same thing—to rid themselves of the baleful influence of Tartuffe upon the master of the house, and hence over their own lives. They are all equally determined to accomplish this end; when not acting in concert they support one another's efforts. The play can end only when the family is entirely beyond the reach of Tartuffe's influence and machinations.

Obstacles

The prime obstacle is, of course, Orgon's credulity. It is against his blind and stupid trust of the hypocrite that the family struggles during the first four acts. Once Orgon has been disillusioned, they are faced with the absolute power that he has put in Tartuffe's hands. Against this they can only protest helplessly.

Major Crisis and Climax, Theme

The major crisis is not staged. It is Orgon's deeding his property and turning over custody of the strongbox to Tartuffe. From this point on, Orgon and the family are entirely in Tartuffe's power. Why Molière chose to omit this obviously dramatic scene, merely reporting it instead, is a mystery.

The climax is the arrest of Tartuffe, instead of Orgon, by the king's officer. But this is an example of the very ill-advised use of the *deus ex machina*. The dramatic problem has not been solved by the characters themselves, but by an agent from outside the framework of the play.

Molière maneuvered himself into this dilemma at the climax because he gave Tartuffe so much power at the crisis that the opposing forces became completely unbalanced. With the deed to the house and the strongbox in Tartuffe's hands, the family had no comparable weapons with which to fight. Hence the author's resort to an ending that calls upon a still greater power (the king's) to break the impasse. Had Tartuffe's victory not been quite so complete, had he been vulnerable at some point, perhaps Orgon and his family might have defeated him themselves. Certainly we should have had a more satisfying ending to the play.

In fairness to Molière it should be noted that the play had to be considerably revised before a public production was permitted.

It seems possible that the lengthy and flowery tribute to the king was substituted for a dramatically better ending in order to influence the authorities. As the play stands now, it seems to tell us thematically that Louis XIV in all his glorious wisdom will protect his subjects from the consequences of their own gullibility.

Resolution

This includes the paean to the king, Orgon's move to avenge himself on Tartuffe, Cleante's cooler counsel, and the indicated wedding.

Opening

Tartuffe is already living in the house when the play begins, and Orgon has been completely bewitched by his guest. The conflict is precipitated by Orgon's plan to give his daughter in marriage to Tartuffe instead of to Valère. It is this outrage that drives the family to action.

This is a valid situation for launching the dramatized portions of the story. Unfortunately Molière waited till the very end of Act One even to hint at the idea of Mariane's marrying Tartuffe, and until Act Two to put it before us frankly. Had the situation been presented near the opening of Act One, the exposition that now comprises nearly all of this act would hold greater interest.

Unity

Molière did not feel so strictly bound to observe the classical unities as his contemporaries, Corneille and Racine. *Tartuffe* does take place in one setting, however, and there are no time lapses indicated between acts. Unfortunately, unity of action is seriously violated.

We know from the many fine plays that ignore the unities of time and place that these two, though sometimes attractive, are relatively unimportant. But a play that ignores the unity of action can be conspicuously blemished, and *Tartuffe* has two such blemishes. We have already examined one of them—the use of the king's officer as a *deus ex machina*. The other is the lovers' quarrel between Mariane and Valère at the end of Act Two. This entire quarrel is structurally unrelated to the forward movement of the story, and could easily be eliminated. Though mildly amusing in itself, the play stands still so long as the scene continues.

Exposition

In spite of Goethe's enthusiastic endorsement—"Only think what an introduction is the first scene. . . . It is the greatest and best thing of the kind that exists"—that opening looks very clumsy today. For our benefit Madame Pernelle identifies in rapid succession Elmire, Dorine, Damis, Mariane, and Cleante. Then, as if it weren't difficult enough to fix the relationship of these five in our minds with only a few words to each, she goes on to discuss Orgon and Tartuffe, who have not yet appeared. Thus we are expected to remember not only the identities but the salient facts and attitudes of eight different people in the first five minutes. Immediately after this, Damis and Cleante start talking about Valère. The fact that Madame Pernelle is in such ill-humor does add a bit of spice to this nearly indigestible lump of exposition, but one wonders how Goethe, who knew how skillfully Shakespeare and the Greeks, among others, handled such problems, could have made such a statement.

Characterization

All the characters are differentiated, and behave consistently through-out. It might be argued that Orgon and Tartuffe are both overdrawn. Indeed, they seem today to be caricatures, but at the time the play was written these two may have been far more believable. (France, like England, had its puritanical fanatics then, and they could exert great pressure.)

Exaggerated or not, Tartuffe is intensely interesting. He may be a hypocrite, but it must be noted that not by a single word does he betray a hypocritical approach. He could just as well be a bigoted, avaricious sensualist, as Morris Bishop has observed. Molière left considerable room for interpretation of this comic yet sinister character.

Orgon's credulity can be a little hard to swallow, but as Molière made this a part of the play's premise (instead of showing Orgon in the process of falling under Tartuffe's influence) this is one of the given factors in the story, and we do accept it.

The others are all clearly drawn. Elmire is a charming and sensible young woman, clear-headed in a crisis; Mariane is fluttery and immature; Damis likable but impulsive and pugnacious; Cleante rational and prudent.

Development

Once past the static and expository first act, the play begins to move satisfactorily for the next couple of scenes. The first scene of Act Two has Orgon as its protagonist; his objective, to win from his daughter her acceptance of Tartuffe instead of Valère as her suitor. The obstacles are Mariane's dislike of Tartuffe, her love for Valère, and Dorine's outspoken opposition. The climax of the scene finds Orgon failing in his objective. The brief resolution is his irritated outburst against Dorine, and his walking out of the room.

The basic situation has now been altered to the extent that Orgon has openly revealed his plan for his daughter's marriage, and aroused active opposition. Thus the scene leads logically and directly into the next, in which Dorine is the protagonist. Her objective is to instill some fighting spirit into Mariane. In this she is partially successful. Had the play then proceeded straight into Mariane's and Valère's acceptance of Dorine's plan of action, we should have had an uninterrupted progression. But with the arrival of Valère the play veers off into a lovers' quarrel, and is halted until the lovers are reconciled and agree to follow Dorine's advice.

Acts Three and Four hold our interest very well, for they move logically from one situation to the next. Perhaps the play's best scene is Elmire's pretense, in Act Four, that she is willing to accept Tartuffe as a lover. She is the protagonist; her objective, to prove Tartuffe's true character to Orgon. Obstacles are Tartuffe's suspicion, at first, that she is not sincere and, of course, Orgon's own reluctance to believe ill of Tartuffe. Comedy is derived from the fact that as the situation becomes more and more compromising, and Elmire frantic to end the pretense, Orgon remains in hiding, apparently not yet convinced. The climax occurs when Orgon finally appears and Elmire wins her point. The resolution is Tartuffe's reminder that Orgon has deeded the house to him and therefore cannot order him out.

Dramatic Irony

There is irony in the fact that, while we recognize Tartuffe as a fraud and a hypocrite, Orgon does not. For the sake of the family we hope that he will wake up and save them from the consequences of his own credulity. The irony ends with his disillusionment at the end of Act Four.

The scene in which Elmire convinces him, discussed above, owes much of its effectiveness to the fact that we know, as Tartuffe does not, that Orgon is hidden under the table and is listening to every word. (Cf. the screen scene in *The School for Scandal*.) The same device is used when Damis hides during Elmire's first scene with Tartuffe in Act Three.

Preparation

There is only one component of the play for which a plant is needed, and the author unfortunately neglected to supply it. The strongbox comes as a complete surprise at the end of Act Four. Molière probably added the strongbox incident during a revision of the play, in order to motivate Tartuffe's going to the king with a charge of treason. But coming so late, without any preparation, it startles the audience unpleasantly. (We have been "cheated" in not having been given all the pertinent facts earlier.) Furthermore, the late introduction of the strongbox, with its papers that incriminate an absent friend of whom we have not even heard, necessitates a lot of rather dull exposition at the start of Act Five.

Activity

To a great degree the story is carried by its rhythmic dialogue. There are several effective bits of stage business, however. Dorine's falling silent whenever Orgon plans to strike her is amusing, and her running after each of the quarreling lovers to bring them together visualizes her frantic efforts to reconcile them. Both occur in the second act. On Tartuffe's first entrance, Act Three, he insists that Dorine cover her bosom with a handkerchief before he will talk with her. This is, of course, a sharper and funnier way to introduce us to the villain of the piece than words alone could have accomplished.

Dialogue

The fact that all the characters in a play speak in eloquent, balanced verse bearing not the slightest resemblance to speech in real life doesn't damage their credibility or obscure the differences in characterization, as Shakespeare and a host of other fine playwrights have demonstrated. In a literal sense everyone in *Tartuffe* is a poet, but they are all quite distinct from one another. Similarly, a high degree of articulateness, even in a realistic play, doesn't lessen the sharpness of the characterizations, nor our acceptance of the speakers as real people. Shaw and O'Casey, among others, knew this very well.

Plausibility

As has already been suggested, we must keep in mind that *Tartuffe* was written in an age and for a society very different from our own. Hence our difficulty in accepting Tartuffe's blatant duplicity and Orgon's credulous belief in him. Aside from these two, the attitudes and behavior of the others are entirely believable.

The fact that the play, in spite of its several faults, is still so funny, lively, and absorbing is a tribute to Molière's skill and humanity. He was one of the greatest comedy writers of all time.

RICHARD BRINSLEY SHERIDAN
The School for Scandal

1777

Following in the tradition of the Restoration comedy of manners, *The School for Scandal* was, unfortunately, the last such play until Oscar Wilde's comedies, written more than a century later. More wholesome and more amiable than the Restoration comedies, the play has been continually revived right up to the present day.

It is elaborately plotted, and its structure is unconventional, to say the least. But it is as funny as ever, and this is the principal reason for its great popularity.

The play was written for Sheridan's own theatre, the enormous Drury Lane in London, with its tiers upon tiers of galleries and its stage thrust forward between highly conspicuous boxes. The painted back cloths and flats suggested the locale of the various scenes, but, of course, there was no illusion of reality. The dialogue, too, is highly stylized—clever, loquacious, and artificial.

Premise

Sir Peter Teazle, elderly and rich, has married an extravagant and flirtatious young wife, whose chief interest is a coterie of idle, scandalmongering friends. Two brothers are seeking the hand of Sir Peter's ward, Maria. Charles Surface, a reckless, high-living, and improvident but likable young man, sincerely loves her. His hypocritical brother Joseph's interest is motivated by her fortune. The brothers have an uncle in India, Sir Oliver, whom they have not seen for many years, but from whom they expect to inherit considerable wealth.

Synopsis

The work is divided into five acts of several scenes each.

ACT ONE

[] *Scene One*

The scene is Lady Sneerwell's dressing room.

Lady Sneerwell employs a Mr. Snake to forge letters whose sole purpose is to stir up mischief and scandal. She explains that her motive in trying to cause a break between Charles Surface, an amiable scapegrace, and Sir Peter Teazle's ward, Maria, is that she herself is in love with Charles. As for Charles' brother, Joseph, Lady Sneerwell knows him to be, behind his sanctimonious façade, selfish, sly, and malicious. Joseph himself is pursuing Maria for her fortune. As his interests and Lady Sneerwell's run parallel, they are partners in trying to separate Charles and Maria. Sir Peter favors Joseph's suit, not knowing the man's true character.

Joseph Surface arrives as Snake is leaving. Joseph warns Lady Sneerwell not to put any confidence in Snake, that he would betray them both.

Maria comes to call. She is followed by various members of the scandalmongering set, who proceed at once to the task of destroying other people's reputations. Maria has no taste for malicious gossip, and soon leaves.

Joseph is asked if it is true that his uncle, Sir Oliver, is coming home from the Indies. Joseph discounts the rumor. The conversation turns to his brother Charles' extravagances. About all that is left of Charles' inheritance are the family portraits.

[] *Scene Two*

The scene shifts to Sir Peter Teazle's house.

In a soliloquy Sir Peter bemoans the fact that his young wife apparently does not return his love, and spends her time in extravagant frivolity. Master Rowley enters. He was once the servant of

Charles and Joseph's father. When Sir Peter complains that Maria favors Charles over Joseph, Rowley ventures the opinion that Charles, in spite of appearances, is the worthier man. Sir Peter is unconvinced, and says that Sir Oliver, who has been very generous with his nephews, will be disappointed in Charles.

Rowley tells Sir Peter that Oliver has already arrived from the Indies, but that he doesn't want his presence in England known to Charles and Joseph. He intends to test their dispositions.

Sir Peter asks Rowley not to tell Sir Oliver that he and his wife don't get along, for Oliver is a bachelor and would ridicule his old friend for marrying so late in life.

[]   *In Brief*

There are two complete and almost independent story lines in the play. One is Sir Peter's marital difficulties; the other is the rivalry of Charles and Joseph for Maria's hand. Both stories are set against the background of a shallow, idle, gossiping society.

The first act is almost entirely expository, depending for interest on its scintillant wit. Two of the principal characters are not even introduced to us. We must wait until the next act to meet Lady Teazle, and until III-3 to meet Charles Surface.

Meanwhile, the background against which these people move is portrayed with amusing venom. Joseph's hypocrisy and his true motives are revealed; we meet Maria and are shown her distaste for Joseph's attentions and for scandalmongering (which directs our sympathy toward her); finally Sir Peter is characterized, and, by report, his wife.

About the only forward movement in the act—and it is very slight—is the news that Sir Oliver has already arrived in England. The fact that he intends to make a test of his two nephews helps to carry our interest over into the next act.

ACT   TWO

[]   *Scene One*

The scene is still Sir Peter's house.

Sir Peter is berating Lady Teazle for her extravagance. She is defiant, and hints that he could please her greatly by making her his widow. Sir Peter also objects to the company she keeps, but when she departs for Lady Sneerwell's he follows her. In spite of her behavior he loves her.

[]   *Scene Two*

We are back at Lady Sneerwell's.

The gossips, including Joseph, are again assembled. Lady Teazle and Maria arrive, and Lady Teazle enthusiastically joins in the general blasting of reputations.

Sir Peter arrives. He is appalled by the gossip, and when a servant brings him a message calling him home he is relieved to get away.

Alone with Maria, Joseph is trying to make love to her when Lady Teazle returns to the room. She finds him kneeling to Maria, sends the girl out, and demands an explanation. Joseph pretends that he was merely urging Maria not to betray his affection for Lady Teazle to Sir Peter. Joseph urges Lady Teazle to pay a visit to his rooms.

Joseph finds himself in the curious position of having to make love to Lady Teazle to stay in her good graces, when all he really wants is her noninterference in his wooing of Maria—and her money.

[]   *Scene Three*

The setting is Sir Peter's house again.

Sir Oliver Surface, waiting for his old friend Peter, is talking with Rowley, who tells him that Sir Peter has been led to believe, by the scandalmongers, that Charles and Lady Teazle are romantically linked. It is Rowley's opinion, however, that, if Lady Teazle favors either brother, it is Joseph. Rowley is sure that Charles is a splendid fellow. Oliver says he will not be influenced by malicious tales, but will keep an open mind.

On Sir Peter's arrival the two friends greet each other warmly, and Oliver playfully commiserates Peter on his marriage to a young wife. The talk turns to Oliver's two nephews. Peter holds up Joseph as a model of virtue and rectitude, but regards Charles as lost. Oliver is skeptical of these judgments, and says that he has a plan for testing the young men.

[]   *In Brief*

The play is still moving very slowly. The first scene of the act characterizes Lady Teazle, but does little else. II-2 is a bit more eventful, as we see Joseph beginning to dig a trap for himself. And we are given further evidence of Joseph's hypocrisy. II-3 introduces and characterizes Oliver, but offers little else that is new.

Our pleasure is chiefly in the grace and brilliance of the dialogue. Our interest is carried forward by our curiosity as to what may happen in this unstable situation. Our sympathies have been strongly directed toward some characters and away from others.

ACT THREE

[] *Scene One*

The scene is still Sir Peter's house.

Oliver, Peter, and Rowley are talking. It seems that a certain Mr. Stanley, a relative of Charles and Joseph whom they have never seen, has met with financial reverses, and has appealed by letter to the two young men for help. Joseph has replied with vague promises of future aid; Charles has been as generous as his extravagance permits. It is now proposed that Sir Oliver, posing as Stanley, apply to the brothers in person.

Now Mr. Moses enters, a broker and moneylender to whom Charles is deeply in debt. He has an appointment with Charles, and expects to introduce him to a wealthy Mr. Premium, who is prepared to advance additional sums to the improvident young man. Sir Oliver changes his plans slightly. With the connivance of Moses, he will impersonate Premium at Charles' house. Later, to Joseph, he will pretend to be Stanley. Oliver, Moses, and Rowley leave.

Although Rowley has told Sir Peter that the rumors about Charles and Lady Teazle have been deliberately planted by Snake, Peter is still suspicious, and decides to ask Joseph for his opinion on the subject.

Maria enters and angers her guardian by plainly stating her dislike of Joseph and partiality for Charles. She leaves.

Lady Teazle comes to ask Sir Peter for two hundred pounds, which he is inclined to give her. But an absurd quarrel develops, culminating in Lady Teazle's statement that she will not be suspected of infidelity without cause.

[] *Scene Two*

The setting is Charles Surface's house.

Moses and Oliver, in his role as Premium, are admitted by a supercilious servant, who informs them that Charles is occupied, and they will have to wait. He then tries to borrow money from Moses himself.

[]   *Scene Three*

We are in another room in Charles' house.

Charles is entertaining a group of his cronies at dinner. Wine is flowing freely. Oliver and Moses are ushered in and are rather boisterously received. Charles' other guests soon go into an adjoining room to gamble.

Charles immediately gets down to the business of raising money. He tells "Premium" that he has no security beyond his certain feeling that he will inherit a fortune from his wealthy Uncle Oliver. He goes on to say that the climate of the Indies has weakened Sir Oliver's health, so the inheritance may come at any time.

"Premium" refuses to lend money on this dubious prospect, and asks if Charles has anything he could sell. There is nothing left but the ancestral portraits, which Charles will gladly part with, at bargain prices. Oliver is deeply shocked at such callousness.

[]   *In Brief*

Forward movement of the play has now begun. The mechanics of Oliver's test of the brothers is set up; then reference is made to Sir Peter's suspicion of his wife and Charles (which motivates Peter's later visit to Joseph's rooms).

Sir Peter's difficulties with Maria and with his wife are further illustrated, but without any real plot development.

Finally we are introduced to Charles, and Oliver's test of one of his nephews gets under way. Since we like Charles in spite of his shortcomings, we are apprehensive for him.

ACT FOUR

[]   *Scene One*

The setting is a gallery in Charles' house.

Charles proceeds to sell the pictures that line the walls, one by one at first, then in wholesale lots, and "Premium" in every case agrees to pay the price asked. Secretly, of course, he is shocked.

There is one painting, however, that Charles keeps passing over. It is a portrait of his Uncle Oliver, done before he went to India, and Charles doesn't want to part with it. "Premium" seems to take a fancy to that particular picture, keeps pressing Charles to sell it, and finally offers a huge sum for it. When Charles says "no," that he is fond of his uncle and will keep the picture as long as he has room for it, Oliver can hardly conceal his delight. He and Moses leave.

As Charles is congratulating himself, Rowley enters, and Charles peels off a hundred pounds to be conveyed to Mr. Stanley. Then he goes to join his gambling friends.

[]   Scene Two

We are still in Charles' house, in the parlor.

As Moses and Sir Oliver are about to leave, they encounter Rowley, who solemnly turns over the hundred pounds that Charles asked him to give Stanley, for Stanley will be Oliver's next impersonation.

[]   Scene Three

The setting is the library of Joseph Surface's house.

Joseph is awaiting the arrival of Lady Teazle, who has at last consented to an assignation. His real purpose in pursuing this affair is to divert her attention from his wooing of Maria, of whom she is jealous. (Joseph's reasoning—and the author's—is a little cloudy at this point. The motivations are not so clear as they should be.)

Lady Teazle arrives, and Joseph, in a display of specious and cynical reasoning, attempts to convince her that it is the consciousness of her own innocence that is at the root of her disagreements with her husband. Lady Teazle is skeptical of this argument, and Joseph is just starting off on another tack when a servant brings a warning that Sir Peter is on his way upstairs. Hastily Lady Teazle hides behind a screen.

Joseph, pretending that he has been reading, welcomes Sir Peter, who proceeds to voice his suspicion that Lady Teazle is having an affair, and that he thinks he knows the man. As Joseph wonders whether he has already been found out, Peter identifies the suspect as Charles. Joseph says that he cannot believe such an accusation, either of Lady Teazle or of Charles, but that if it is true he will henceforth deny Charles as a brother.

Peter continues that in spite of all he loves his wife, that he intends to settle an independent income on her while he lives, and leave her the bulk of his fortune on his death. Then, to Joseph's great distress, since Lady Teazle is overhearing every word, Peter goes on to encourage Joseph's courtship of Maria. At this point the servant announces that Charles Surface is below and wishes to see his brother.

Peter impulsively decides to conceal himself while Joseph questions Charles about Lady Teazle. Listening to their conversation, Peter will be able to determine whether there are any grounds for his suspicion. He starts for the screen, only to catch a glimpse of a lady's petticoat behind it. Joseph explains that it is merely a little French milliner, who was embarrassed and hid on Peter's arrival. Peter is vastly amused that the proper and virtuous Joseph is hiding a girl in his rooms. He darts into a closet.

Charles enters, and Joseph taxes him with tampering with Lady Teazle's affections. Charles denies this indignantly, and says he always understood Joseph was her favorite. On and on he goes about their flirtation, until the desperate Joseph, to stop him, says that Sir Peter is in the closet and has overheard all. Laughing, Charles drags him forth. Peter apologizes, says it was his plan to eavesdrop, that he has suspected Charles wrongly, and hopes they can now be friends.

The servant brings word that Lady Sneerwell is downstairs, and Joseph has to leave the room momentarily to get rid of her.

Charles and Peter start arguing over Joseph's character. To prove his point that Joseph is not the anchorite his brother supposes, Peter tells him of the French milliner. Incredulous, and over Peter's protests, Charles throws down the screen and reveals Lady Teazle, just as Joseph returns. Everyone seems to be stricken dumb except Charles, who, after a few sarcastic remarks, takes his leave.

Lamely Joseph attempts an innocent explanation, but Lady Teazle, to his dismay, confesses why she is here. She sees Joseph now as a despicable hypocrite, and her husband as an honorable man whom she will henceforth love and respect. She sweeps out, followed by Peter and the still protesting Joseph.

[]   *In Brief*

We are now in the heart of the play, and this superb fourth act compensates for the leisurely pace of the first half of the work.

We see Charles pass Oliver's test, and the awakening of Lady Teazle to the merits of her husband. Thus both the story lines move close to conclusion. There remains, to carry us into the final act, the testing of Joseph, the exposure to both brothers of their Uncle Oliver's imposture, and a true reconciliation between Lady Teazle and Sir Peter.

The justly famous screen scene is one of the most brilliantly conceived scenes in all comedic literature. Later we shall examine it more closely.

ACT FIVE

[] Scene One

The setting is still Joseph's library.

Joseph is very annoyed to be told that his indigent relative, "Stanley," is calling, but he receives him with a show of exaggerated politeness. Not a shilling is to be extracted from Joseph, however, even when Stanley mentions the well-known fact that Joseph has been the recipient of Sir Oliver's bounty. On the contrary, Joseph replies, his uncle has sent him no money from India, merely a few small gifts such as tea and firecrackers. Furthermore, Joseph continues, he has been obliged to lend large sums of money to his extravagant brother, and this denies him the pleasure of assisting Mr. Stanley. As Sir Oliver departs he says, in an aside, "Charles, you are my heir."

Rowley enters, to inform Joseph that his uncle has arrived from India, and will meet both brothers here at Joseph's house in fifteen minutes.

[] Scene Two

The setting is Sir Peter's house.

News of Lady Teazle's indiscretion has spread rapidly among the scandalmongers, and they are all gathering to pick up further information. Nobody has the facts straight, and rumors are flying. It was Charles, not Joseph, in whose rooms she was discovered; Sir Peter has fought a duel with Charles—no, Joseph—and has been gravely wounded by a sword cut—no, a bullet lodged in the thorax—no, the bullet continued on, smashed a bust of Shakespeare on the mantel, went through a window, and wounded a postman.

Sir Oliver Surface enters and is mistaken for the doctor in attendance on Sir Peter. But Peter comes in almost at once, and drives the gossips out of the house, hoping they all choke on their own venom.

Rowley enters. He and Oliver have both heard about the affair at Joseph's house, and Oliver is greatly entertained by his friend's discomfiture. He leaves, to keep his appointment with Joseph and Charles.

Peter observes Lady Teazle weeping in the next room, and goes to her to effect a reconciliation.

[]   Scene Three

We are back in Joseph's library.

Lady Sneerwell has come to upbraid Joseph for his blundering. Sir Peter will now be reconciled to Charles, she says, and will no longer oppose his union with Maria. So Joseph has lost Maria, and Lady Sneerwell has lost Charles. Joseph doesn't think their situation entirely hopeless, however. He is still scheming.

Sir Oliver Surface is announced, and Lady Sneerwell retires. Joseph, of course, mistakes Sir Oliver for Stanley, and is about to have him forcibly ejected when Charles comes in. Charles assumes that Oliver is the wealthy and generous Premium, and fails to understand why Joseph is so angry. There is an argument, but Charles agrees that, whether the man's name is Stanley or Premium, he can't stay here with Sir Oliver due at any moment.

The brothers are trying to force Sir Oliver out when Sir Peter, Lady Teazle, Maria, and Rowley all appear at the door. Peter demands to know what they are trying to do to their Uncle Oliver, and the truth suddenly dawns on the two young men. Joseph, ready with excuses, says that he can explain his behavior, but Oliver will hear none of it and turns to Charles, who makes no attempt to excuse or justify himself. Oliver clasps Charles' hand in forgiveness and affection.

Lady Teazle then attempts a reconciliation between Charles and Maria, but Maria believes that he has bestowed his affection elsewhere.

At this point Joseph brings in Lady Sneerwell, to accuse Charles of betraying her. But Rowley has Snake outside, and asks him in. Snake tells Lady Sneerwell that although she has paid him well, he has been offered double to speak the truth. The suspicion cast on Charles and on Lady Teazle was his own work, and entirely unfounded. Lady Teazle then contemptuously resigns from the scandalous college, and Lady Sneerwell flounces out, expressing the hope that Lady Teazle's husband will live another fifty years.

Joseph, expressing his shock and surprise that Lady Sneerwell would employ Snake in such a manner, makes his escape. Snake follows, begging them all never to let it be known that he has done an honest action.

The play ends as both couples—Peter and Lady Teazle, Charles and Maria—are happily united.

[]   *In Brief*

The last act brings us the testing of Joseph, which we have been anticipating for some time, and then a very funny but largely static scene of the busybodies' reaction to a genuinely scandalous event.

Finally the threads of this busily plotted play are drawn together and neatly tied. The brothers learn of the deception played upon them, and each gets his just deserts; Lady Sneerwell's machinations are exposed, and the kind of society she represents is denounced and forsworn; and, as the obstacles that have held the two couples apart swiftly melt away, all ends happily for the characters we like.

Protagonists and Objectives

The above heading must be in the plural, for so far as construction is concerned *The School for Scandal* is really two plays, neatly interwoven, but operating almost independently of each other. The play is not unique in this respect. Shakespeare, in *A Midsummer Night's Dream*, even managed to dovetail three significant story lines into a single work. And, of course, there are many plays, especially older ones, that have what are called subplots. But usually these are of distinctly secondary importance. The Bianca-Lucentio story in *The Taming of the Shrew* is a subplot. The two story lines in *The School for Scandal* are almost evenly balanced.

Sir Peter is the protagonist of one story line. Since his wife's behavior is humiliating and distasteful to him, his objective is to alleviate this problem in some manner. And, as Lady Teazle sincerely renounces her extravagant, flirtatious, and gossipy ways, it may be said that he is successful in attaining his objective.

Charles Surface, in spite of his delayed appearance in the play, is the protagonist of the other story. His objective is the winning of Maria, and in this he is successful. It might be supposed that his objective is to inherit Sir Oliver's fortune, but Charles does not strive toward this end. As a matter of fact, he isn't shown working very hard to win Maria's hand, either, but he does want to marry her, and the play will not be over until the question of their engagement is settled.

Obstacles

At the root of Peter's difficulty is the influence of a wanton, spend-thrift, and scandalmongering society on his impressionable young wife. In order for him to have a satisfactory marriage, this damaging influence must be negated. In this respect Lady Sneerwell and her coterie are an integral part of the play. It is also Lady Sneerwell who is responsible for the slander leveled at Charles and Lady Teazle.

The obstacles to Charles' wooing of Maria are Sir Peter's opposition, since he suspects an attachment between Charles and his wife; Maria's mistrust, on the same grounds; it may also be assumed that Charles' own extravagance and insolvency are an obstacle. At the end of the play he assures Peter that with Maria's help he intends to set about reforming.

Major Crises and Climaxes, Theme

The major crisis of Sir Peter's story is the overturning of the screen in IV-3. The climax follows almost immediately, when Lady Teazle denounces Joseph and affirms her loyalty and gratitude to her husband.

The crisis of the other story occurs very near the end of the play. Maria will not agree to marry Charles while she suspects that he is pursuing another. The climax is Snake's disclosure that the rumor is false. Maria then accepts him, and the play, all conflicts having been resolved, is over.

Thematically the work is a condemnation of the idle and flippant society of the time. It was the machinations of this society that interfered with the happiness of the four principals.

Resolutions

Although the climax of Sir Peter's story occurs in Act Four, we don't know whether Lady Teazle has really turned over a new leaf, or whether Peter will forgive her. These are matters for the resolution, and Sheridan wisely delays it until near the end of the play. It consists in our seeing that the couple is indeed happily reconciled, and in Lady Teazle's denunciation of Lady Sneerwell.

The resolution of the Charles-Maria story is the young man's statement that he intends to reform, and then his verse addressed to Maria and the audience.

Opening

Sheridan would undoubtedly have had a more swiftly moving play had he chosen to raise the curtain at a somewhat later point in the over-all story. Structurally the first act could be dispensed with almost entirely, and any essential exposition fitted into what is now the second act. As it is, the work takes an unconscionably long time to get started. (One could overlook far greater deficiencies in view of those superb scenes in Acts Four and Five. The author was twenty-six years old when he wrote the play.)

Unity

Were it not for the coherence of style, mood, and subject matter, the play's double plot line would make it sprawl disastrously. But the unity Sheridan was able to impose in his treatment of the situations was sufficient to gloss over the structural deficiencies.

Exposition

A more experienced playwright would have found ways of compressing and enlivening the masses of exposition that now encumber so many of the early scenes. The affairs of four important characters are discussed by Snake and Lady Sneerwell in the very first episode of the play, and we have not met one of them. The episode itself, furthermore, is too placid to engage our interest, even if we knew whom they were talking about. If these expository episodes are examined critically, it will be seen that the same fault is common to nearly all of them. At the start of I-2 Sir Peter has a long expository speech. It is clear enough, and we feel sorry for him; but the speech is a soliloquy—a device extremely difficult to handle convincingly.

Characterization

The characters are all sharply differentiated, but entirely by attitude, motivation, and so on, and not at all by speech patterns or mannerisms. When Joseph starts spouting sanctimonious platitudes to Lady Sneerwell, she reminds him that he is among friends. When Mrs. Candour says the town talks of nothing but Charles' extravagance, Maria replies, "I am very sorry, ma'am, the town has so little to do." By this remark the author helps to characterize Maria and direct our sympathy toward her. When Sir Peter asks if a husband is to have no influence, no authority, Lady Teazle says, "If you wanted authority over me, you should have adopted me and not married me: I am sure you were old enough." These are all very broad strokes indeed, and typical of the way everyone is characterized. But it works.

Development

Aside from the two protagonists, Charles and Sir Peter, whose objectives have already been examined, we find a diversity of objectives among the other principals. Lady Teazle wants to conform to the society that is now open to her; Maria wants Charles if he is not involved with another woman; Joseph wants Maria's fortune; Sir Oliver wants to find a suitable heir; Lady Sneerwell is attracted to Charles. It is the interaction of all these conflicting interests that build the incidents that move the play forward.

The early scenes, although the dialogue is brilliant, are clumsily constructed. The truly effective scenes have a more conventional structure. The auctioning of the pictures, for example, has Sir Oliver as its protagonist; his objective is to determine the suitability of Charles as an heir. The obstacle is the seeming contradiction in Charles' own character: his open, generous nature and yet his apparent callousness in regard to his own family. The climax is Charles' flat refusal to sell the portrait of his uncle, and the resolution is Oliver's secret delight.

Joseph is the protagonist of the screen scene, his objective being to draw Lady Teazle into an affair, since she could be jealous of his attentions to Maria. The obstacles are several: Lady Teazle's hesitancy; Sir Peter's disclosure, within Lady Teazle's hearing, that Joseph wants to marry Maria; then the arrival of Charles, whose knowledge of Joseph's attentions to Lady Teazle could turn Sir Peter against him.

Finally there is the fact that Charles and Peter are aware that there is a woman in the room, and this leads to the collapse of Joseph's plan. The climax is Lady Teazle's denunciation of Joseph, and the resolution is Peter's contemptuous exit, with Joseph still protesting.

Oliver's interview with Joseph, with Oliver masquerading as Stanley, is similar in structure to the selling of the portraits.

Dramatic Irony

Seldom has this device been used to more brilliant comic effect than in *The School for Scandal.*

When Charles starts selling the family portraits we know, as he does not, that Premium is really his Uncle Oliver, and that the impression Charles makes on him will determine whether he will be chosen as an heir. This excerpt should illustrate the tremendous effectiveness of dramatic irony.

Sir Oliver: But there is one portrait that you have always passed over.

Careless: What, that ill-looking little fellow over the settee?

Sir Oliver: Yes, sir, I mean that; though I don't think him so ill-looking a little fellow, by any means.

Charles: What, that? Oh, that's my uncle Oliver! 'Twas done before he went to India.

Careless: Your uncle Oliver! Gad, then you'll never be friends, Charles. That, now, to me, is as stern a looking rogue as I ever saw; an unforgiving eye, and a damned disinheriting countenance! An inveterate knave, depend on't. Don't you think so, little Premium?

Sir Oliver: Upon my soul, sir, I do not; I think it is as honest a looking face as any in the room, dead or alive. But I suppose uncle Oliver goes with the rest of the lumber?

Charles: No, hang it! I'll not part with poor Noll. The old fellow has been very good to me, and, egad, I'll keep his picture while I have a room to put it in.

Sir Oliver (aside): The rogue's my nephew after all!

Precisely the same construction is employed when Oliver goes to visit Joseph. Speaking in the character of Stanley:

Sir Oliver: But I imagined his [*Sir Oliver's*] bounty would enable you to become the agent of his charity.

Joseph: My dear sir, you were strangely misinformed. Sir Oliver is a worthy man, a very worthy man, but avarice, Mr. Stanley, is the vice of age. I will tell you, my good sir, in confidence, what he has done for me has been a mere nothing; though people, I know, have thought otherwise; and, for my part, I never chose to contradict the report.

Both these incidents impose on the dramatist a so-called "obligatory scene," the disclosure of Oliver's true identity to Charles and Joseph. This occurs in the final scene of the play, and the reactions of the two young men are a dramatic high point. The use of dramatic irony in these two instances cannot be said to end until this point, when the brothers know what the audience knows.

The screen scene begins with a simple use of the device, and then compounds it again and again. At the start we know that Joseph's protestations to Lady Teazle are not sincere, but are merely a blind to cover his intentions toward Maria. On Sir Peter's arrival we know, as he does not, that his wife is hiding behind the screen.

> *Sir Peter:* You can even make your screen a source of knowledge—hung, I perceive, with maps.
> *Joseph:* Oh, yes, I find great use in that screen.

A little later, after Peter has disclosed his plans for an income and inheritance for Lady Teazle, he says, "I would not have her acquainted with the latter instance of my affection yet awhile." And he continues: "We will talk over the situation of your hopes with Maria. . . . I am sensibly chagrined at the little progress you seem to make in her affections." Frantically Joseph tries to shut him up. These lines are not funny or witty in themselves, but we laugh because we know that Lady Teazle is listening to it all, and we imagine the effect on her.

On hearing that Charles is coming, Sir Peter starts to hide behind the screen. We know whose petticoat he glimpses, and we want to see his reaction when he finds out what we know.

Charles then nearly gives Joseph's game away by dwelling on the latter's attentions to Lady Teazle within Sir Peter's hearing. And after Joseph has been called from the room, this exchange takes place:

> *Sir Peter:* He had a girl with him when I called.
> *Charles:* What! Joseph? You jest.
> *Sir Peter:* Hush!—a little French milliner—and the best of the jest is—she's in the room now.
> *Charles:* The devil she is!
> *Sir Peter:* Hush! I tell you. (*Points to the screen.*)
> *Charles:* Behind the screen! S'life, let's unveil her!
> *Sir Peter:* No, no, he's coming. You shan't, indeed.
> *Charles:* Oh, egad, we'll have a peep at the little milliner!
> *Sir Peter:* Not for the world!—Joseph will never forgive me.

Charles: I'll stand by you—
Sir Peter: Odds, here he is! (*Joseph Surface enters just as Charles throws down the screen.*)
Charles: Lady Teazle, by all that's wonderful!
Sir Peter: Lady Teazle, by all that's damnable!

The use of dramatic irony in this episode ends as the screen falls. Now all the characters know as much as we do.

A critic once wrote of the screen scene, "It would no doubt have been higher art could the dramatist have deceived his audience as well as the personages of the play, and made us also parties in the surprise of the discovery." This may be history's most spectacular example of just how wrong a drama critic can be.

Besides the examples given, there are other instances of the effective use of dramatic irony in the play, such as the scandalmongers' ridiculous misinterpretation of events in V-2. But the point has already been sufficiently dwelt on.

Preparation

There is a lot of planting in the early part of the play, perhaps more than necessary. In the first scene Joseph tells Lady Sneerwell that Snake is capable of double-crossing them, as indeed he does in V-3. A bit later Joseph is asked if it is true that Sir Oliver is coming home. Then it is remarked that all Charles has left are the family portraits. In I-2 we hear that Sir Oliver has arrived, and intends to test the dispositions of his nephews. At the start of the screen scene Joseph calls attention to the screen by asking his servant to place it before the window.

The need for all these plants is open to question, but here is one that definitely helps: In V-3 Lady Sneerwell is upbraiding Joseph for the collapse of their plans. But Joseph asks if Snake hasn't undertaken to swear that Charles is bound to her by vows and honor. When she says this is true, Joseph believes that all is not yet lost, and this prepares us for his bringing Lady Sneerwell out of hiding to accuse Charles, and for Snake's double cross.

Activity

In spite of this being largely a play of conversation, the author has found several very telling pieces of business. The use of the screen and throwing it down are brilliant. So is the auctioning of the paintings, especially with Oliver's portrait in front of us, to be passed over time and again. A nice touch is the auctioneer's hammer—a rolled parchment on which is inscribed Charles' family tree. Every time the hammer comes down we can feel Oliver cringe. The brothers' attempt to eject Oliver from Joseph's rooms just as Sir Peter comes in and identifies him is also effective.

Dialogue

No group of people in real life ever conversed in such a flow of precise, literate, witty, and unhesitant speech as these characters. But Sheridan wasn't attempting "realistic" dialogue. That wasn't to be tried for another hundred years. The dialogue in *The School for Scandal* is a convention. We accept it with pleasure, just as we accept Shakespeare's iambic pentameter, the verse dialogue of Anderson, Eliot, and Fry, or the totally theatricalist approach to speech in expressionist and epic plays.

Plausibility

It seems hardly necessary to point out that everyone in the play, within the broad strokes in which he has been drawn, behaves with absolute consistency. It is true that Joseph's attempted seduction of Lady Teazle might be a bit more clearly motivated, but even here we feel that Joseph is behaving according to his own interests.

And Finally

In giving us what in effect are two parallel plays in one evening, Sheridan has managed a structural tour de force whose technique repays intensive study, both for its successes and its shortcomings. But the double story line is not recommended to the inexperienced playwright.

HENRIK IBSEN

Ghosts

1881

The late nineteenth century found *Ghosts* so shocking that the play had a hard time getting on the stage at all. Many of the early performances were subscription productions, and the work was widely and viciously attacked. It was many years before *Ghosts* was recognized not only as a highly moral work but a dramatic masterpiece as well.

Today it is almost unplayable. The Reverend Manders is so ridiculously prudish and Engstrand so transparently hypocritical that both characterizations seem preposterous and would probably, on the stage, arouse us only to laughter. And we so agree with Mrs. Alving's "advanced" point of view that we wonder at the sense of duty and decorum that ever made her put up with her husband in the first place. But these people were not caricatures when the play was written, and one of the reasons we are free of the stifling pieties pictured in the play is because a great dramatist had the courage to attack them.

All this is beside the point here, however; for, no matter how dated the play may be in content, its form has much to teach us. An unusually perceptive critic, Emmanuel Reicher, wrote of the first American production in 1899: "*Ghosts* is constructed with the scientific accuracy that a master engineer employs in building a suspension bridge. Every strand in the network of dialogue has its duty to perform in supporting the main theme. Every character, too, is as truly a part of the whole, and as necessary a part, as is each pier in the engineer's structure."

Not only in its strict observance of the unities of time, place, and action, but in its retrospective structure the play reminds us of Greek tragedy, particularly *Oedipus the King*, for it is the exposition of past deeds that relentlessly drives the action on to catastrophe. Some commentators have likened the factor of heredity in the play to Greek Fate, but, as John Gassner has pointed out, retribution in *Ghosts* could have been outwitted by a regular physical checkup. The play is by no means a tragedy comparable to *Oedipus the King*. The resemblance is a technical one, but Ibsen's method is worth the most careful study.

Premise

Mrs. Alving's son Oswald has returned home from Paris, presumably to attend the dedication of an orphanage built as a memorial to his late father. The Reverend Manders, an old friend of the family, is handling the financing for Mrs. Alving. Engstrand, a carpenter who has worked on the construction of the orphanage, plans to use the money he has made to open a "sailors' home" in the town—actually a house of prostitution. He is trying to persuade Regina, a maid in the Alving home, to leave service there and come help him run the "home." Though he publicly acknowledges Regina as his daughter, he knows that she is not. These are the facts that are evident as the play begins.

But the situation is far more complex than this. The factors hidden at the opening are gradually revealed, and the play moves forward by the disclosures of past events. Elements of the premise that are brought to light during the play include these facts: Alving was a dissolute and irresponsible man, and a syphilitic; Mrs. Alving, though in love with Manders, had been forced into marriage with Alving because of his money and social position, and spent her married life protecting her husband's reputation and keeping up an appearance of respectability; she had sent Oswald away at an early age to protect him from the pernicious influence of his father; the young man has inherited his father's disease and is on the brink of madness; Mrs. Alving's motive in establishing the orphanage is to rid herself of her "purchase price"—the amount of money Alving had at the time of their marriage; Regina is Alving's illegitimate daughter, by a servant who had been married off to Engstrand for a payment of seventy pounds.

As is obvious, there is conflict aplenty cached in this premise, ready to explode into action.

Synopsis

The scene throughout is the living room of the Alving home near a provincial Norwegian town.

The play is in three acts.

ACT ONE

Engstrand, a carpenter who has been helping to build a new orphanage, tries to persuade his daughter Regina, a serving maid of Mrs. Alving's, to come and live with him. He plans to open a house of prostitution. There are hints that he is not Regina's real father. The girl contemptuously refuses to have anything to do with him.

The Reverend Manders arrives to see Mrs. Alving, whose financial affairs in connection with the orphanage he is managing. Manders hopes that Regina will join her father, a widower, and keep house for him. She should be a good influence on Engstrand, Manders thinks. Regina declines.

Mrs. Alving joins Manders, and we learn of Oswald's arrival home in time for the dedication of the orphanage, a memorial to his father. Manders is characterized as extremely puritanical, and Mrs. Alving as far more liberal and open-minded. Manders objects to insuring the orphanage buildings on the grounds that it would show a lack of trust in Divine Providence. Then he broaches the subject of Regina's going to keep house for Engstrand, and finds Mrs. Alving adamantly opposed.

Oswald enters the room, and Manders is struck by his resemblance to his father. Speaking of his life abroad, Oswald refers to unmarried couples who nevertheless have established homes and families. This greatly shocks the minister, but not Mrs. Alving. Oswald goes on to attack conventional morality, which he has often found hypocritical.

Alone with Mrs. Alving, Manders reminds her that a year after her marriage she had come to him in desperation, wanting to leave her detested husband and join Manders, whom she loved. He had convinced her that her duty was to her husband. Manders also accuses her, in sending Oswald abroad, of having been derelict in her duty to her child.

Mrs. Alving defends her actions by telling Manders the truth about her marriage. Captain Alving had been a profligate and an alcoholic. After he had seduced a housemaid—Regina's mother—Mrs.

Alving had sent Oswald abroad to be educated. Manders is stunned by these revelations.

And now Mrs. Alving reveals her motive in building the orphanage. There are ghosts of the past that must be exorcised. She regards the Alving fortune at the time she married as her "purchase money." Once rid of it, she and her son will be free of her husband's contamination.

From the next room we hear Regina protesting to Oswald, who is trying to embrace her. It is an echo of the past, when Captain Alving made love to the girl's mother. The horrified Mrs. Alving confirms to Manders that Regina is indeed Oswald's half-sister.

[]   *In Brief*

Much of the first act is concerned with illustrating the prudery, hypocrisy, and false moral standards that Ibsen is attacking—ghosts of outmoded ideas and attitudes. By creating such a tense personal relationship between Manders and Mrs. Alving, the author is able to lead us from one startling disclosure to another as to what lies under the placid surface of the household. The building and dedication of the orphanage, far from being an act of love, is a kind of exorcism. But the ghosts are not so easily banished. As the act ends, Oswald is seen to be, in at least one respect, very like his father.

A C T   T W O

It is after dinner. Manders and Mrs. Alving agree that Regina must leave the house, but that she cannot go with Engstrand, as he is not her father. Manders was the pastor who married Engstrand and Regina's mother, and he bitterly resents Engstrand's deception in pretending that he was responsible for the bride's pregnancy, when in reality he was being paid to marry a fallen woman. Mrs. Alving points out that her case was similar—she let herself be married to a fallen man. Only the sums of money involved were different. Again Manders is shocked, and a heated discussion ensues on the ethics of her behavior, with Manders insisting that in spite of everything she acted correctly in "doing her duty." But Mrs. Alving reproaches herself for her cowardice and Manders for having denied their own love for the sake of a hollow respectability. She is haunted by the ghosts of dead ideas and beliefs, and thinks that perhaps she should have told Oswald the truth about his father, instead of letting the boy grow up venerating him.

Engstrand arrives, ostensibly to ask Manders to come to the orphanage and lead a prayer meeting among the workmen. Manders upbraids him for never informing him of the truth about Regina and his marriage. The startled Engstrand defends his actions by stating that he was only trying to help the poor wronged woman by marrying her, and that the seventy pounds had been used solely for the purpose of bringing up Regina properly. Manders is completely taken in by this hypocritical talk, and, when Engstrand tells him of his plan to establish a "sailors' home" with his current wages, the minister enthusiastically approves. Engstrand and Manders leave for the orphanage.

Oswald comes in and summons up the courage to tell his mother a dreadful truth about himself—that he is going mad. He has already had one attack. The doctor had told him that the disease was inherited, but he cannot believe this, and feels sure that he has contracted the illness (syphilis, though it is never named) himself. Mrs. Alving is distraught, since she knows the truth about the father.

Oswald then says that he loves Regina, that she is his "only hope of salvation." He wants to marry her and leave this joyless and puritanical country. In fact, on a previous visit he had half jokingly promised Regina a trip to Paris. The girl took him seriously and has been learning French. To Oswald she represents the "joy of life" that he seeks.

When Oswald invites Regina to sit with them and share a bottle of champagne, Mrs. Alving realizes that they must both be told the truth—that they are half-brother and -sister. But, before she can do so, Manders returns. He is convinced of Engstrand's moral rectitude, and says that Regina must help him in running his "sailors' home."

Oswald counters that he and Regina are going away together, perhaps as man and wife. Mrs. Alving is about to speak when they notice a glare in the sky. The orphanage is burning.

[]   *In Brief*

In this act Ibsen's attack on false moral standards reaches a peak of ferocity, Manders being the character on whom he heaps the main burden of his scorn. Mrs. Alving, who is struggling to attain an enlightened point of view, is reproached by Manders, whom she once loved, and assailed by doubts as to the wisdom of the course she has followed. A bit later Manders is made to appear an utter fool by the ease with which Engstrand hoodwinks him.

The knowledge that her husband's disease has been transmitted to her son is a further blow to Mrs. Alving, and demonstrates the folly of her compromise with puritanical concepts. The pill is made particularly bitter by the fact that Oswald, in his ignorance, not only blames himself for contracting the disease, but wants to marry a girl his mother knows to be his half-sister.

We long for Mrs. Alving to reveal the truth at last—an obligatory scene that Ibsen postpones till the third act by the fire in the orphanage, a highly symbolic occurrence. The past cannot be isolated and set aside.

ACT THREE

It is the next morning before dawn. The orphanage has burned to the ground. Engstrand, with his eye on the funds that have been set aside for the maintenance of the orphanage, convinces Manders that the minister himself is responsible for the fire, by carelessness in extinguishing a candle at the prayer meeting. (Ibsen, when asked whether Engstrand himself had set the fire, replied that he "wouldn't put it past him.") Engstrand hints that he will assume the blame for the fire, and Manders agrees that the surplus funds, which Mrs. Alving has told him to dispose of in any manner he thinks fit, will be used to help establish Engstrand's "sailors' home." Lest we miss the irony of this, it is announced that the home will be named for Captain Alving. Engstrand and Manders leave.

Mrs. Alving finally tells Oswald and Regina the truth about her husband. In spite of Oswald's protests Regina determines to leave the house at once. She indicates that she is going to ask Manders for part of the money he intends to give Engstrand, and she goes.

Alone with his mother, Oswald admits to the terrible fear of approaching insanity that shadows his life, a fear that Regina could have helped to alleviate. Mrs. Alving tries to reassure him, but he now reveals that a second attack of his disease is inevitable, and that when it comes it will mean complete and permanent imbecility. Regina, he thinks, would have cared for him and carried out his wish that he be poisoned when his mind was gone. He extracts the same promise from his horrified and reluctant mother. As the sun comes up she realizes that she already faces that dreadful responsibility. Oswald is mad.

[]   *In Brief*

In the third act Ibsen sets about destroying the last shred of respect anyone might have for Manders and the standards he espouses, as well as any remaining illusions Mrs. Alving may still hold regarding the rightness of her conduct.

Manders is gulled by Engstrand into establishing a brothel with Alving's money, Regina is revealed as a callous little opportunist, and any possible justification for Mrs. Alving's compromise with conventional morality is torn away by Oswald's descent into helpless insanity. By following Manders' advice in returning to her husband many years before, she has brought a madman into the world and ruined her own life as well.

Protagonist and Objective

It has been supposed by some critics that this is a play about Oswald, and that he is the leading character. This is a mistaken interpretation of the structure. Mrs. Alving is the protagonist. It is a play about the foolhardiness of her actions in obeying the dictates of a strait-laced and superficial moral code, and the impossibility of escaping the consequences of such misguided conduct.

Twice in the first act Mrs. Alving clearly states her objective: "The sums of money that, year after year, I have given towards this orphanage make up the amount of the property . . . which in the old days made Lieutenant Alving a catch. . . . That was my purchase money. I don't wish it to pass into Oswald's hands. My son shall have everything from me, I am determined." And a little later: "After tomorrow, I shall feel as if my dead husband had never lived in this house. There will be no one else here but my boy and his mother." In this way Mrs. Alving hopes to exorcise the ghosts of the past. She fails to achieve her objective.

Obstacles

Mrs. Alving's efforts to cut herself and her son off from the past is ultimately overwhelmed, and it is the various consequences of her husband's behavior that comprise the obstacles.

Regina is of concern because she is Alving's illegitimate daughter; Oswald's behavior with Regina, which echoes his father's with her mother, cannot be tolerated because of their close relationship; Mrs. Alving's plan to live in peace with her son is opposed by Oswald's inherited illness, and by his preference for marriage with Regina. The final destruction of Mrs. Alving's hopes comes with Oswald's madness. She must either spend the rest of her life caring for an imbecile (thus betraying her promise to him), or take the life of her son and face whatever consequences might ensue from such an act.

Major Crisis and Climax, Theme

The major crisis might be said to have occurred years before the play opens, since the last time Mrs. Alving had an opportunity to escape the consequences of her husband's profligate behavior was when she went to Manders, a year after her marriage, and begged him to rescue her from a disastrous situation. When she returned to Alving she set in motion a train of events that culminates in her defeat. (This aspect of the play is one of the reasons its construction has been compared to Greek tragedy. Mrs. Alving's decision to go back to her husband was her tragic error, and the result of this decision can be compared to Fate.)

The major climax is Mrs. Alving's realization that Oswald's madness has already come upon him. There is no further hope of evading the consequences of the past.

If we have moved beyond the specific problem raised in *Ghosts,* the fact remains that its underlying theme—the need for dropping outworn concepts and adapting to reality—remains alive. In Joseph Shipley's words, "*Ghosts* has set more minds in motion than any drama of the last hundred years."

Resolution

This is very brief. Mrs. Alving's despair reflects not only her horror of what has happened to her son, but the terrible choice she now faces—whether to fulfill her promise to kill him.

Opening

The author has chosen to begin his play less than twenty-four hours before the climax of a story that started with Mrs. Alving's marriage to a profligate husband nearly thirty years before.

The curtain rises on the eve of the dedication of the orphanage. This event has brought Oswald home, and other developments of the play follow naturally as a result of the new situation. Engstrand, with the money he has earned working on the orphanage, can now consider establishing his "sailors' home"; even the fire in the orphanage, despite Ibsen's reluctance to explain it, was probably started by Engstrand—certainly he had a motive for setting it. And it is entirely possible that the onset of Oswald's madness was hastened by the pressure of events and by his loss of Regina. The action of the play moves forward plausibly at all times, even though it may not always be convincingly inevitable.

Unity

Ghosts derives much of its power from the compression of events dictated by the observance of the three unities—time, place, and action. It requires great technical skill so to construct a play, but the result is plain to see.

Exposition

With the over-all story so greatly compressed, much of it must be carried by exposition, and to be dramatically effective this must be revealed at times when it has the maximum emotional impact on the characters hearing it. This, as has already been suggested, is the Greek method, and Ibsen is equal to the challenge of the form.

Practically all the exposition is revealed in conflict, and the disclosures never fail to elicit a reaction. Much of it is played against Manders' puritanical views. The friction between him and Mrs. Alving serves to acquaint us with the building and dedication of the orphanage, and later with the reason she has spent Alving's money in this way. Similarly, we learn that she was once in love with Manders, of her appeal to him shortly after her marriage, about Regina's parentage, and Mrs. Alving's reason for sending Oswald away. The bitterly opposed points of view between Manders and Oswald do more than characterize the two men. They tell us the kind of life that Oswald has been leading abroad—an essential factor in the story.

In the second and third acts Oswald's disclosures about the seriousness of his illness obviously are frightful blows to his mother.

Characterization

The five characters are all revealed in conflict, and are well balanced to provide the maximum stress possible in their various encounters. They are drawn with exceptional clarity, the key to each being his objective as an individual. Mrs. Alving's goal, since she is the protagonist of the entire play, we have already examined. In her attempts to explain her past actions we find the shadings of motivation that make her characterization so penetrating and believable. Oswald's objective is to escape, or at least postpone, the fate that is pursuing him. Marriage to Regina would be a part of that escape. Engstrand's objective is to start his own disreputable business, regardless of how he gets the money. Manders, a rather passive character, aims simply to uphold conventional moral standards, and Regina is moved throughout by selfishness and opportunism.

Development

As one would expect with Ibsen, the scenes are, in effect, little one-act plays jigsawed into the larger pattern. Engstrand is the protagonist of the first scene of the play. His objective is to persuade Regina to leave the Alving home and help him with his new project. The obstacle is the girl's attitude toward him; the climax, her refusal; the resolution, her turning him out of the house.

Manders' objective in the next scene is like Engstrand's in the first, the significant difference between the two scenes being that, while Engstrand is a scoundrel, Manders is a moralist. (By this device Ibsen starts attacking Manders almost the moment he appears.)

Manders is also the protagonist of the following scene, with Mrs. Alving. His objective is to help her put her affairs in order. In this he is largely successful, for he meets no significant opposition until he broaches the subject of Regina's going with Engstrand.

Oswald is the protagonist of the next scene, his objective being to defend the standards of morality in which he believes when these come under attack by Manders.

And so it goes throughout the play, scene after scene moving through the classic pattern of protagonist and objective, obstacles, climax, and resolution. The scene that follows Oswald's exit in Act One finds Manders the protagonist again, his objective being to convince Mrs. Alving of the error of her past conduct. Notice that she herself, although she is the protagonist of the entire play, has not yet become the protagonist of an individual scene. Until she defends her conduct against Manders' charges, she has been a passive character.

Dramatic Irony

As in *Oedipus the King*, dramatic irony is extensively employed, and the device serves to bolster the copious use of exposition.

By revealing early to the audience that Engstrand's "home for sailors" is really a brothel, in which he hopes to place Regina as a major attraction, Manders' enthusiasm for the project is in all three acts placed in contemptuous relief.

In Mrs. Alving's scene with Oswald in the second act we know, as the young man does not, why he was sent away, that the responsibility for his illness is not his but his father's, and that the girl he wants to marry is his half-sister. Since we rather like Oswald, we want him to learn the truth, and in this way Ibsen sets up his obligatory scene in the third act. (We don't care whether Manders ever learns the truth about Engstrand, by whom he has been thoroughly duped.)

Preparation

There are several plants in the play. Regina's use of French, in the opening scene, is one. Another, soon afterward, is the reference to the seventy pounds paid to Engstrand by "an Englishman with a yacht." Later we learn how it is that Regina knows some French, and that the seventy pounds was actually paid by Captain Alving. The idea of a fire in the orphanage is planted by a reference to some shavings' catching fire in the carpenter shop the day before. And Oswald's physical resemblance to his father, which so impresses

Manders, prepares us for the idea that Oswald is like his father in more ways than one.

Activity

There is little significant activity in the play. One effective bit, however, is Oswald's inviting Regina to sit down with him and his mother to drink champagne. The rest is mostly routine stage movement.

Dialogue

Dialogue, though a bit stiff by contemporary standards, is realistic in the sense that the author hoped it would sound like the actual speech of real people caught in such a situation. There are one or two asides—relics of an earlier dramaturgy.

Effects

About the only effects Ibsen uses in this realistic play are the rain and mist seen through the windows in Acts One and Two, the glow in the sky from the orphanage fire, and one brilliant invention—the sunrise hitting the mountain peaks as Oswald goes down into darkness.

Plausibility

Given the standards and conditions of its time, the people in *Ghosts*, as Ibsen has drawn them in his fully rounded characterizations, behave with entire consistency. The play has very nearly that feeling of inevitability that we associate with the most exalted forms of drama.

BRANDON THOMAS
Charley's Aunt
1892

The dictionary tells us that a farce is a play whose sole purpose is laughter, and that the merriment derives from situation rather than character. It might be added that a farce is rarely witty or verbally clever, and that it is unconcerned with realities and probabilities. It carries no conviction, but belief in it is not demanded. Preposterous situations are the lifeblood of farce, and we "suspend our disbelief" in order to enjoy the fun.

Probably the most successful and durable farce ever written is *Charley's Aunt*. Its initial run in London achieved a total of 1,466 performances, and for the next quarter of a century one or more companies were always on tour in England. At one time there were forty companies playing simultaneously in various parts of the world. It has been performed in every major language, turned into an immensely successful musical comedy (*Where's Charley?*), and even today is one of the most frequently produced of all plays.

It may seem a sad commentary on theatrical taste that this giddy and simple-minded exhibition can achieve such universal success when a play like *The Madwoman of Chaillot*, for example, by one of the most thoughtful, sophisticated, and genuinely witty dramatists of modern times, cannot reach more than a fraction of the other's audience. Oddly, there are certain resemblances between these two plays. Each is very funny, and each offers a bravura acting role. Neither is intended to be taken literally. Part of the explanation for their differing appeal lies in their structures. *Charley's Aunt* is built on a framework that functions like a complicated but well-oiled machine, and the other on a skeleton so rickety that it is in constant danger of breaking down altogether.

Charley's Aunt was written for the proscenium theatre.

Premise

Jack Chesney and Charles Wykeham, students at Oxford, plan to ask the two girls with whom they are in love to Jack's rooms for luncheon. Charley's aunt, whom he has never met, is the English widow of a wealthy Brazilian, and is expected to visit her nephew that day. The boys expect her to act as chaperone. Another student, Lord Fancourt Babberley, has been cast as an eccentric old lady in an amateur theatrical production.

Also antecedent to the action is the fact that Jack's father, a widower, is in financial difficulty; also that Lord Fancourt, on a trip abroad, had met a young lady, in the company of an older English-woman, with whom he had fallen desperately in love. He has since lost track of her.

Synopsis

The play is in three acts, and calls for three realistic settings.

ACT ONE

The first act takes place in Jack Chesney's rooms at Oxford.

Jack is attempting to compose a love letter to Kitty Verdun. His manservant, Brassett, distracts him, and is asked to leave the room. Jack's friend Charley Wykeham arrives. He too has been having difficulty in trying to write a letter to Amy Spettigue, declaring his love. Both young ladies are to leave for Scotland on the morrow, and the boys want their feelings known before the girls go off and forget them.

Charley, an orphan, tells Jack that his aunt, who married a recently deceased and very wealthy Brazilian, is back in England, and has written that she will be in Oxford that day to have luncheon with him. Charley has never met her. He is, incidentally, her sole heir. The boys decide that, rather than trying to declare their love for Kitty and Amy in writing, they will invite the girls to luncheon, here in Jack's rooms, to meet the aunt (who will also act as chaperone). A messenger is sent with the invitation to the girls, and luncheon is ordered. Four bottles of champagne are put out on the table.

The question arises then as to who will entertain the aunt and show her about the university while the boys make love to the girls. They decide to invite Lord Fancourt Babberley, another student, known as Babbs. Brassett is sent to fetch him. Babbs, on a recent trip to the Mediterranean on his yacht, for reasons of health, has evidently fallen in love with someone he met while traveling, and will therefore appreciate the necessity of keeping the aunt occupied.

Brassett returns with word that His Lordship cannot come as he has a luncheon party already scheduled and would like to borrow a few bottles of champagne. The boys consider this very cheeky behavior and, telling Brassett to set the table for six, leave to fetch Babbs themselves. Brassett, alone, complains of student behavior in general, and leaves the room.

Lord Fancourt Babberley appears at the window. He sees the champagne, which Brassett has not yet chilled, and puts the four bottles in a Gladstone bag he carries. Jack and Charley return, saying they have been looking for him. Babbs tries to get away, but the boys stop him and insist he stay for luncheon. Babbs isn't particularly interested in meeting Charley's aunt, or the two girls already spoken for, but the other boys plead that they are in love and need his help. Babbs confesses that he is in love too—the daughter of an English officer he met at Monte Carlo. The officer lost his fortune at the gaming tables, and later Babbs himself had played cards with him. Then the man died, and the daughter was taken in charge by an English lady on her way home to England from South America. Babbs has lost track of her.

Word comes that Kitty and Amy have accepted the invitation to lunch. Babbs, still protesting, says that he has agreed to play an old lady in an amateur theatrical, and must try on his costume before rehearsing. Unwilling to let him go back to his own rooms, the boys send Brassett to fetch the costume, saying that he can try it on here. Brassett brings it in, boxed, and Babbs, wanting to tip Brassett, tries to borrow half a crown. Neither Jack nor Charley has any money, so Jack borrows it from Brassett, hands it to Babbs, who then gives it back to Brassett. Babbs goes into the next room to try on the costume. The voices of the two girls are heard outside in the hall.

The girls are admitted, and politely take chairs. Babbs, in shirt sleeves, enters the room but withdraws quickly when he sees the girls. There is also considerable surreptitious concealment of whiskey glasses, pictures of chorus girls, and so on.

Amy tells Charley that her uncle, Mr. Spettigue (who is also Kitty's guardian), would not have let the two girls come here had he known about it, but he is in London for the day. Then Kitty, talking with Jack, complains that Mr. Spettigue always hurries Amy and herself away to some other place whenever they begin to make friends. Inquiring about the aunt, the girls learn that she hasn't yet arrived. Quickly they make an excuse to leave, promising to return later.

Charley goes to the station to meet an incoming train, hoping his aunt will be on it. Babbs comes in, still in shirt sleeves. He needs some hairpins, and Jack sends Brassett out to buy some. There is a knock at the door, Babbs returns to the adjoining room, and Jack admits his father, Sir Francis Chesney, unexpectedly arrived from London. He has brought Jack his allowance. A widower of 51, Sir Francis is handsome and vigorous, and on excellent terms with his son. But, he tells Jack, since he has come into the title, he has also had to assume the family debts. All the money he had been saving in India for Jack's education has been used up. However, he hopes to get Jack an appointment in Bengal.

Brassett returns with the hairpins, and in an aside Jack says that he must now get rid of Babbs as a luncheon partner for the aunt, and substitute his father. He then suggests to Sir Francis that he should marry again. As it happens, he goes on, Charley's aunt is expected momentarily—a charming lady, and a millionairess.

Sir Francis, obviously recalling some sacred memory, says that he will never marry again. However, Jack tells him to go back to the hotel and change, and return at one o'clock with a flower in his buttonhole. At this moment Charley rushes back in, and is introduced as the nephew of the lady they are expecting. Sir Francis leaves.

Charley has a telegram from his aunt to say that she is postponing her visit for a few days. No chaperone! What is to be done? Suddenly Babbs makes his appearance in the costume of a little old lady, complete with fichu and a ribboned bonnet. Outside, the girls knock at the door. Babbs is informed that he must impersonate the aunt; otherwise the girls won't stay. He objects strenuously, but the two boys overpower him, and when the girls are admitted he is introduced as Charley's aunt, Donna Lucia d'Alvadorez. Amy presents a bouquet, which Babbs sticks in his dress. The spray is so large that he has to separate the flowers in order to see. Amid some awkward attempts at conversation Amy takes the flowers and arranges them. Aside, Jack instructs Babbs in the role he is to play. He is a widow from Brazil, childless and very wealthy.

Babbs offers to take the girls around and show them the sights, but Jack and Charley will have none of that. Charley announces that his aunt can't stay long; she must get back to London. Babbs, getting into the swing of it and beginning to enjoy himself, crosses his legs and puts an arm around Amy's waist. Amy remarks how much Charley owes Donna Lucia, what a kind, affectionate face she has, and Babbs goes on about caring for poor, dear Charles after his parents died. Although he gets the facts and sexes quite confused, the girls accept it all at face value. By now Babbs is greatly enjoying the other boys' discomfiture, and as the girls move toward the window the boys punch him.

Brassett enters to say that Mr. Spettigue is outside. All are dismayed, for they thought he was in London. Jack, Kitty, and Amy hide. Babbs tries to get away, but Charley forcibly brings him back into the room and tells him to get rid of Spettigue. Then Charley himself hides and Spettigue enters. He is a pompous and opinionated man of middle age. He demands to see his ward and his niece, for he has been told they are here. Babbs, playing the role of an indignant old lady, upbraids him for his bad manners, and says the girls have left. As Spettigue is leaving, Babbs throws a book and knocks his hat off.

Jack, Kitty, Charley, and Amy all re-enter. The girls, running to Babbs, hug and kiss him to express their thanks for his getting rid of Spettigue. This, of course, greatly annoys the other two young men.

Now Sir Francis Chesney, Jack's father, returns, in frock coat, silk hat, gloves, and carnation. Jack introduces the girls, and Charley his aunt, Donna Lucia, from Brazil, "where the nuts come from." Prodded by Jack, Babbs reluctantly begins to play the part for the benefit of Sir Francis, but the latter turns away and quietly tells his son that he can't bring himself to woo Donna Lucia, in spite of her money.

Luncheon is ready, and Brassett looks about for the missing champagne. Babbs jumps up, saying he brought some along in a bag. Jack realizes that Babbs had intended to make off with it, but can say nothing. Suddenly Mr. Spettigue bursts back in and orders the girls away, telling that "old fool of a woman" not to interfere. He quickly changes his tune when he learns that the old woman is Donna Lucia d'Alvadorez, the celebrated millionairess. He apologizes, and is asked to stay to lunch. Babbs, now thoroughly enjoying himself, begins to flirt outrageously with both Sir Francis and Mr. Spettigue, and, in the men's tussle to hold a chair for him, he sits on the floor.

[]   *In Brief*

This very artificial, if workable, plot requires considerable setting up. We learn that Jack is in love with Kitty, and Charley with Amy; that since the girls are going away there is pressure on the boys to declare their love; and that Charley's aunt, whom he has never met, is due to arrive that day. With the aunt serving as both excuse and chaperone, the boys can invite the girls to lunch. To occupy the aunt's attention they enlist the help of Babbs, who happens to be rehearsing for an amateur theatrical and who happens to be in love too, with a girl he has lost track of. All this, of course, is part of the premise. That it plays as well as it does is due to the author's skill in handling essentially undramatic material with the aid of amusing incidents and colorful detail.

The girls arrive, and we hear about Mr. Spettigue, presumably in London today. The girls' hasty departure on learning that the aunt hasn't arrived dramatizes the boys' need for a chaperone.

Now Jack's father arrives, and we learn of his financial embarrassment. This establishes a motivation for Jack's telling him to court the aunt, as well as contributing to the dramatic irony when he later courts the real Donna Lucia, thinking she is someone else. So much exposition is seldom carried at the beginning of a play without boring the audience.

Suddenly, however, and very rapidly, things begin to happen. The aunt sends word that she will not come today. The girls return, and Babbs is pressed into service as Donna Lucia. Spettigue arrives, and is temporarily driven off by Babbs in the role of the aunt. Sir Francis comes back, ready to court Donna Lucia, but changes his mind when he sees her. Then Spettigue returns. On learning the old lady's supposed identity he becomes a serious suitor.

The act ends with Jack and Charley in a comic predicament, but one in which the stake is not really serious. If their deception were to be exposed the girls would leave, perhaps being forbidden any further contact with the boys. This is about all, so far as the story is concerned, that carries us into the next act.

ACT TWO

The setting is a courtyard outside Jack's rooms, with garden furniture.

Brassett is talking to himself as the act opens. He muses that Sir Francis seems to be the aunt's "favorite," though old Spettigue is still in the running. Jack enters and tells Brassett that tea will be served out here. Then he has a monologue, which informs us that he has asked Kitty to meet him here. Charley enters. He too has an appointment here—with Amy. Kitty arrives, and Jack tries to get Charley to leave. But Amy enters also, and each couple hopes the other will go somewhere else. Finally Charley and Amy go off to inspect the garden.

Alone at last with Kitty, Jack starts to make love (in a very stiff and proper Victorian manner, naturally). But Sir Francis interrupts them; realizing that he wants to talk to his son, Kitty also goes into the garden. Sir Francis has decided that in spite of the old lady's bizarre appearance and manners he will, for Jack's sake, ask her to marry him. This will solve the financial problem and enable Jack to continue his education. Jack does not enlighten his father, but wonders, aside, what kind of mess he and Charley have gotten themselves into. Sir Francis leaves.

Charley rushes in to ask Jack's help—Babbs has gone off with Amy, and they can't be found. Jack tells him that, what is far worse, his father intends to propose to "Donna Lucia." The boys know they will be disgraced if their deceptions are found out. They leave to hunt for Babbs.

Sir Francis returns. He tells himself (and us) that he has arranged to meet Donna Lucia here at this hour. Spettigue arrives also, obviously to declare his intentions. Each tries to get rid of the other, and expresses his exasperation in a series of asides. Finally Spettigue goes to the garden to look for Donna Lucia. Sir Francis is about to follow when Jack enters; knowing that Babbs is not in the garden, he sends his father out there. (He wants to warn Babbs before his father has a chance to propose.)

Charley enters. He hasn't been able to find Babbs. But soon Babbs and Amy stroll in, arm in arm. Charley wants to punch Babbs, right then, but Jack restrains him, and sends him and Amy off to see the chapel.

Angrily Jack tells Babbs that his job is to entertain the two older men and leave him and Charley free to court the girls. He then says that Sir Francis intends to propose marriage, and that Babbs is to remain calm and refuse. Jack leaves as Sir Francis returns. At first

Babbs flirts coyly; then he tries unsuccessfully to bolt. Sir Francis begins comparing the old lady to a wild flower. Jack appears, unseen by his father, and the two boys exchange pantomimed insults. Jack disappears again. Sir Francis continues courting, which Babbs makes as difficult and awkward for him as possible. (Both reveal their thoughts in a series of asides.) Finally Sir Francis comes to the point and proposes marriage. Babbs replies that he belongs to another, but will be a sister to him. Expressing his relief in another aside, although for Jack's sake he regrets the refusal, Sir Francis leaves.

Jack, who has been eavesdropping, comes in and berates Babbs for making a fool of his father. Babbs says he couldn't very well refuse Sir Francis until the man had proposed. Spettigue returns, sees Babbs, who runs off with Spettigue in pursuit. Jack leaves to find Kitty and the stage is empty for a moment.

Two ladies now appear, looking for Jack Chesney's rooms. They are the real Donna Lucia, a handsome and capable Englishwoman of middle age, and Ela Delahay, a beautiful girl of about twenty. Donna Lucia admits that she wanted to observe her nephew without his knowing her identity; hence the telegram canceling her visit, and her arrival now. They speak sentimentally of the beautiful Oxford buildings; then it develops that Ela dreams romantically of a young man she met on a yacht in the Mediterranean. His name was Lord Fancourt Babberley. Further conversation reveals that Donna Lucia has so successfully invested some money that Ela's father left her that Ela is now independent for life. Donna Lucia asks how it happened that Mr. Delahay had a large sum of money in his possession just before he died, after going bankrupt at the gaming tables, and Ela says he won it at cards, from Lord Fancourt Babberley. Donna Lucia smiles, and hints that Lord Fancourt may have lost the money deliberately. Then she reminisces—when she was Ela's age she too had fallen in love, but the man had suddenly been ordered off with his regiment. His name was Frank Chesney. And these rooms, oddly enough, are those of a student named Chesney. Donna Lucia is struck by the coincidence.

Now Sir Francis Chesney himself appears, and introduces himself. He does not recognize his old sweetheart at first, and she fishes in her bag for a card, but can find, we learn in an aside, only that of someone else, a Mrs. Beverley-Smythe. Though he still doesn't recognize her, something about the woman brings back memories of that early romance—even what she wore the last time they saw each other. Sir Francis says that, although these are his son's rooms, they have been loaned to another student, Charles Wykeham, who is entertaining two young ladies and his aunt, a Donna Lucia d'Alvadorez, from Brazil. On being told that the aunt has already arrived, the real Donna Lucia indicates that her own name now is Mrs. Beverley-Smythe; she hands him the card.

Ela has been watching all this with curiosity, and Donna Lucia introduces the girl as her niece. Sir Francis suggests that they all go into the garden, to find the boys and "Donna Lucia." As he follows the ladies off he muses that, if only Mrs. Beverley-Smythe had been Donna Lucia, things would turn out very differently.

Babbs runs across the stage with Spettigue in pursuit; then Brassett enters, to set the table for tea. He hopes the old gent didn't catch sight of His Lordship's trousers.

Jack and Kitty enter. Jack tells Brassett to go inside now, and set the table later. Then, shyly, he tries to express his feelings. Kitty, in asides indicating that she too is in love, nevertheless pretends she doesn't know what the embarrassed young man is talking about. They finally declare their love openly and embrace. She will marry him even though he has no money and will have to work.

Kitty says that she must have the consent of her guardian, Mr. Spettigue, and that it had better be in writing, so that he can't retract. She thinks Donna Lucia would be a valuable ally; telling Jack to find the old lady, she herself goes off in search of Amy.

Charley comes in, and Jack tells him he has proposed to Kitty, and that she thinks "Donna Lucia" can help her to get Spettigue's written consent. Babbs runs in again, hides, and the pursuing Spettigue dashes on past.

Charley, in a mildly hysterical outburst, wants to confess and end the masquerade right now, but Jack calms him down. Then the boys start blaming Babbs for their predicament: Babbs is not co-operating; instead of behaving like a lady and entertaining the two older men, he runs after the girls himself. Resenting this unfair criticism, Babbs quietly steps out of the dress, but is chased into hiding by the two boys as Spettigue appears. They get rid of Spettigue and drag Babbs into the open again. He is now in rebellion, but the boys manage to get him back into the dress.

The girls enter. They want to talk with "Donna Lucia" alone, and the two boys move off a bit, but stay within sight and hearing. To their distress, Babbs puts an arm around each of the girls as they ask for help. Both girls are in love, and they need Spettigue's consent to marry. Will "Donna Lucia" use her influence? Babbs agrees to try, and the girls run off to find Spettigue.

Babbs asks Brassett for a brandy and soda, but withdraws the request as Spettigue comes on. Before anything can be said, the real Donna Lucia appears, and Spettigue is obliged to introduce "Mrs. Buttercup-Smith" and "Donna Lucia d'Alvadorez." Babbs shakes hands, remarking that he is Charley's aunt, from Brazil, "where the nuts come from." "Mrs. Beverley-Smythe" smiles and replies that she knew Donna Lucia's late husband intimately. At this Babbs turns to flee, but is met by Jack and Charley, who lead him back to the tea table, which Brassett has set and where Babbs is to pour. The girls have returned, and all sit down.

Babbs, greatly flustered, says all the wrong things to Mrs. Beverley-Smythe, pours tea into Spettigue's silk hat, and pours it back into the pot when he discovers his mistake. Sir Francis now joins the group and sits with the real Donna Lucia. Spettigue, in an aside, says that he must create an opportunity to talk with "Donna Lucia" alone; he then invites them all to dinner at his home.

The real Donna Lucia says that she is accompanied by her niece, Miss Delahay, and Ela comes in at that moment. Babbs sees her, and in great agitation tells Spettigue that he can't come to dinner. At first Ela recognizes his voice; then she sees who is speaking and betrays her disappointment. Babbs throws his skirt over his head and faints in Spettigue's arms, as Jack kneels and tries to hide the young man's trousers.

[]   *In Brief*

We are on very thin ice now, so far as motivations are concerned, for if anyone stopped for a moment and behaved sensibly the play would end right then. But with the breakneck tempo characteristic of farce, the complications pile up as Sir Francis and Spettigue start courting the false Donna Lucia. Probably Spettigue, if he learned how he had been hoodwinked, would forbid the girls ever to see the boys again. But actually the boys have never been guilty of anything more than a college prank. However, since they believe in dire consequences to themselves if they are found out, we do too.

The arrival of the real Donna Lucia and Ela Delahay necessitates another long scene of exposition to set up the ensuing developments, but the scene holds our interest because the presence of these two women intensifies the predicament of the three young men. This is especially true for Babbs, for Ela is his lost sweetheart, and he doesn't want to be caught impersonating the girl's friend and protector.

The extravagant coincidences disclosed when Donna Lucia

and Ela arrive will have been noticed. Although they would never be acceptable in comedy and drama, we don't seem to mind them in farce. Were the play less funny and less fast, we would probably reject them anyway.

ACT THREE

The setting is Spettigue's drawing room.

Brassett has been pressed into service as Spettigue's butler, he tells himself in an aside; further, dinner is finished, and His Lordship has kept up the masquerade wonderfully. And, if worst comes to worst, Brassett has brought His Lordship's dress clothes along. (Exposition was certainly a simple matter in 1892). Babbs enters, still in costume, and sends Brassett for a cab. He's going home.

Jack and Charley enter. They aren't going to let Babbs run out on them now. But Babbs retorts that Ela Delahay wasn't around when he agreed to impersonate the aunt. He tells the boys that Ela is the girl with whom he fell in love at Monte Carlo, and this "Mrs. Butterscotch-Smythe" is the woman who took her away. All Babbs wants now is to appear as Lord Fancourt Babberley and tell Ela the same things the other two boys are telling their girls. It makes Babbs very uncomfortable to have Kitty and Amy kissing him in front of Ela.

Before Babbs can get away, Donna Lucia and Ela enter the room. "Mrs. Beverley-Smythe" has noticed that "Donna Lucia" seems to be indisposed, and inquires politely how she is feeling. At the same time Ela offers smelling salts, which makes Babbs sneeze. Amy and Kitty enter, telling the boys to return to Mr. Spettigue, that they will look after "Donna Lucia." Jack and Charley leave the room.

Brassett enters and serves coffee. Quietly Ela and the real Donna Lucia speculate on the identity of the impostor. Apparently neither one suspects that she is a man. From the next room comes the sound of male laughter, and "Mrs. Beverley-Smythe" starts to tell an anecdote about Dom Pedro, Donna Lucia's late husband. Babbs regards this as a dangerous turn in the conversation. ("Mrs. Beverley-Smythe" had earlier said that she was well acquainted with Donna Lucia's husband.) Babbs tries to change the subject, but is only urged to tell the story himself. He pretends to have forgotten, and "Mrs. Beverley-Smythe" mischievously relates a mild adventure of Dom Pedro's. Music is suggested, and Babbs plays the piano.

The men are heard approaching, and Kitty quietly urges Babbs to get from Spettigue the letter consenting to her marriage. She will arrange for them to be left alone together. Spettigue enters, with Sir Francis, Jack, and Charley. Spettigue applauds Babbs' playing. Cigars are passed, and Babbs, who sits staring at Ela, nearly gives himself away. Sir Francis tells Jack quietly that he approves of Kitty.

Spettigue, tête-à-tête with Babbs at the piano, says they must talk things over alone before he writes the letter. Amy and Charley go into the garden. Kitty tells Jack she will be happy with him even if they have no money. They go into the garden, followed by Sir Francis and "Mrs. Beverley-Smythe," of whose identity as Donna Lucia he is still unaware. Clearly he adores her. Babbs is alone with Spettigue.

The two play a sort of flirtatious hide-and-seek around the piano; then Babbs starts insisting that Spettigue write the letter. He wants only to pursue the courtship, but finally, since he thinks it is the only way the old lady will ever consent to marry him, goes off to compose the letter. Relieved to be rid of him, Babbs lights a cigar, as "Mrs. Beverley-Smythe" and Ela enter and catch him at it. He tries to conceal the cigar and swallow the smoke, to his acute discomfort. Ela goes off to get a wrap for her friend.

Donna Lucia starts teasing the impostor by talking about Dom Pedro. Then Babbs, on being informed that many Brazilian ladies smoke, produces the cigar he has been trying to hide and puffs contentedly. Ela returns with the wrap, Babbs gets rid of the cigar, and Donna Lucia goes into the garden to join Sir Francis.

Ela, who still thinks Babbs is an old lady posing as Donna Lucia, confides that years ago "Mrs. Beverley-Smythe" and Sir Francis were sweethearts, but both were shy and failed to declare their love before being separated. Another fine man was shy too—a young man who deliberately lost a large sum of money to her father at cards. But she has the money now, and if ever she meets the young man again she intends to give it all back. And how she longs to see him again! She leaves.

Spettigue enters with the letter consenting to Kitty's marriage, and, on Babbs' promise that "she" and Spettigue are now betrothed, gives it to him. Babbs goes out with the letter. As Sir Francis and "Mrs. Beverley-Smythe" enter, Spettigue tells them the happy news, and leaves.

In the garden Sir Francis has proposed to Donna Lucia, whom he still supposes to be a penniless widow. They are both very happy. Ela returns, followed by Spettigue, Kitty and Amy, Jack and Charley. Brassett enters with a tray. With rhetorical fanfare Spettigue announces that under the spell of a good fairy he has consented to the engagement of his niece Amy to Charles, and his ward Kitty to Jack. Finally the good fairy herself has consented to become Mrs. Spettigue. Brassett drops the tray.

Charley can take no more. He loves Amy too much to espouse her under false pretenses. "Donna Lucia" is not his aunt. There is general consternation, and Jack comes forward to help to explain and take the blame. Brassett leaves with an aside to say that he must go tell His Lordship that the game is over.

Jack and Charley continue their explanation without saying just who "Donna Lucia" really is. Spettigue is furious. He denounces the frump who has deceived him and demands that she be turned out of the house.

Lord Fancourt Babberley appears, in evening clothes, and when Spettigue angrily asks who he is, replies that he is Charley's aunt from Brazil, "where the nuts come from." Ela suddenly realizes that she has confessed her love to him, and in great embarrassment moves off with Donna Lucia. Babbs, Jack, and Charley all apologize to Spettigue for the deception, but he is still angry and demands the letter that was obtained from him under false pretenses. "Mrs. Beverley-Smythe" takes the letter from Babbs, saying it is addressed to Donna Lucia, and that she is Donna Lucia. The letter is hers. Spettigue leaves the room, raging.

In the general surprise Donna Lucia and Sir Francis disclose that they are to be married. Babbs proposes to Ela and promises to resign to Sir Francis Chesney all claims to "Charley's aunt."

[]   *In Brief*

There is a rather tired old play formula that reads: Act One—chase your hero up a tree; Act Two—throw stones at him; Act Three—bring him down again. *Charley's Aunt* almost perfectly illustrates the formula.

Once Babbs has succeeded, in Act Three, in getting the letter from Spettigue, Jack and Charley are reasonably sure of being able to marry their girls; hence there is no pressing reason to continue the masquerade. Charley wants to end it because it is dishonest; Babbs, so that he can declare his love for Ela. (Babbs-Ela is a secondary story line.) End it they do, and since there has never been any real danger to the boys as a consequence of their prank, the dramatic situation dissolves in mere rumblings and empty threats from Spettigue. (The Donna Lucia-Sir Francis story is also secondary.) And the four couples are quickly brought together as the obstacles vanish.

Protagonists and Objective

The play has a double protagonist. Jack and Charley want the same thing—to become engaged to their respective girls. They pursue this objective by the same means and are caught in the same predicament.

Babbs, of course, is the starring role, but this does not mean that he is the protagonist. After Ela's arrival he has his own romantic problem, but structurally the play is still built on the desire of the other two boys to win Kitty and Amy. Not until this is accomplished (by Babbs' securing the letter) is the way clear for Babbs to propose to Ela.

Obstacles

The first obstacle facing Jack and Charley in the winning of the two girls is simply the difficulty they have in composing letters that will adequately declare their feelings. This is solved by inviting the girls to lunch. A second and major obstacle arises when the girls won't stay without a chaperone. And when the expected chaperone fails to arrive, Babbs is pressed into service. The dramatic situation develops from the fact that Babbs is an unreliable and unsatisfactory substitute: he is not only none too convincing, but he does not seem to take his duties seriously; he himself is attracted to the girls; he is pursued by the two fortune-hunting older men; and he is reluctant to carry on the masquerade in Ela's presence. Finally we are aware that his deception can be exposed at any moment by the real Donna Lucia.

Once the girls indicate their acceptance of the two boys, in Act Two, a new obstacle appears: Spettigue's permission must be obtained before the girls can marry. To overcome this, Babbs' aid is again enlisted.

But once Spettigue delivers the letter there is no reason to continue the masquerade, although he does try to withdraw his permission when he learns of the hoax, and this leads to the climax.

Major Crisis and Climax, Theme

In securing the letter, which is necessary to the accomplishment of the objective, Babbs is acting as a surrogate for Jack and Charley.

Hence we have a rather unusual situation, technically, in which both major crisis and climax are staged without the active participation of the real protagonists.

The crisis occurs in Act Three when Babbs insists to Spettigue that the letter must be written before he will consider Spettigue's proposal of marriage. (If Spettigue refuses to furnish it, the boys' whole scheme collapses.) The climax hinges on the question of whether the letter is still valid after it is revealed that it was obtained under false pretenses. Donna Lucia's claiming the letter as hers settles this question (more or less, but satisfactorily for the present purpose).

The theme, as banal as much of the play itself, is simply "Love will find a way."

Resolution

This merely ties up the two remaining romances—Donna Lucia-Sir Francis and Babbs-Ela—and gives Babbs a play on words with which to bring down the curtain.

Opening

The play begins as Jack and Charley decide to declare their love for the two girls. The fact that the girls are about to leave for Scotland puts pressure on them to act at once. Coincidentally, Donna Lucia is expected to visit Charley that same day. The right moment to raise the curtain has been chosen, neither too early nor too late in the over-all story.

Unity

The play takes place in one day, and in three locations in and near the university, giving it a sense of unity in these respects. The far more important unity of action is observed insofar as the two subsidiary love affairs bear upon those of the two protagonists.

Exposition

As a glance back over the outline of the first act will show, a lot of exposition is required to get this play under way. Audiences at the turn of the century were apparently far more tolerant of informative but static conversation than we are. Today we accept the exposition in *Charley's Aunt* as part of the play's quaintness and naïve charm. Each act opens with a single character on stage, talking to himself; people tell each other facts that one would suppose both to be acquainted with; and they are continually breaking into asides that reveal their thoughts, all others within earshot turning conveniently deaf for the moment.

These methods of dealing with exposition would seem extremely clumsy in a modern play, and are certainly not to be recommended unless the play is so stylized and theatricalized, as in the epic form, that there is no attempt whatever to create the illusion of reality.

Characterization

The characterizations are crude but serviceable. There is little distinction between Jack and Charley, and Babbs is the same uncomplicated type, fun-loving but equally susceptible to feminine charm. The girls are two-dimensional and interchangeable. Sir Francis and Donna Lucia are high-minded "mature" adults, and Spettigue a curmudgeon whose fancies swing according to the requirements of the plot. Any of these characterizations, in a more serious play, would be totally inadequate.

Development

Most of the scenes progress by the introduction of new obstacles, new complications. Thus in Act One Charley gets a telegram that his aunt is postponing her visit. Babbs, against his will, is pressed into service; the girls enter and he is introduced as the aunt; Babbs finds that he enjoys the role, to the boys' annoyance; then Spettigue unexpectedly arrives.

Jack and Charley serve as the dual protagonist of this scene, their objective being to produce a chaperone so the girls will stay. The obstacle is Babbs' initial reluctance to play the role. The boys achieve their objective (the climax of the scene is the girls' acceptance of Babbs as the aunt), and the resolution is Babbs' changed attitude. He enjoys the part. Spettigue is the new complication that begins the next scene. Similar examination of other scenes would show them following much the same pattern.

All the women in the play are rather passive, seldom initiating any action, their reciprocated affection being the objective of the various men. Jack and Charley, of course, have this objective all the way through; Babbs, Sir Francis, and Spettigue only after the play is well advanced. They occupy secondary places in the structure.

Dramatic Irony

It must be obvious that *Charley's Aunt* is built on dramatic irony for almost its entire length. Four people know what the audience knows—that Charley's aunt is a man: Jack, Charley, Brassett, and Babbs himself. Two know only that he is an impostor: Donna Lucia and Ela. Four are unaware of the deception: Kitty and Amy, Sir Francis and Spettigue. The major use of the device begins when Babbs is introduced to the two girls, and ends when he appears in male clothing in the last act.

There are many other instances in the play when dramatic irony is employed, though less extensively. One important use, however, lies in our knowing the true identity of Donna Lucia and Ela—that the former is the real aunt and the latter the girl Babbs fell in love with. The scene in which Ela confides to Babbs that she loves the young man who let her father win at cards owes its effectiveness to our knowing that Ela is talking to the young man himself. Sir Francis' courtship of Donna Lucia when he thinks she is Mrs. Beverley-Smythe is similarly handled.

Dramatic irony is used less significantly in other parts of the play. For example, we know that the missing champagne is in Babbs' Gladstone bag, and that it is Jack's own champagne Babbs offers for the luncheon. In the cigar scene we know, as Babbs does not, that Donna Lucia is aware that he is trying to conceal a lighted cigar.

Preparation

Considerable preparation is carried in the long expository scenes in Acts One and Two. Babbs tells of his experiences at Monte Carlo; we are informed that Spettigue would not permit the girls to come here if he knew about it; Sir Francis tells Jack of his financial problem; Donna Lucia reminisces about her youthful romance. All these plants, among many others, help to lay the groundwork for later scenes.

Activity

The script of *Charley's Aunt* is crammed with explicit descriptions of comic business. In all probability many of these were developed by various actors and directors working on the play over the years, and by now have become traditional. A few examples will suffice: the girls bring "Donna Lucia" a spray of flowers that Babbs sticks in his dress and then can't see through; Babbs frequently forgets his role and crosses his legs as a man does, takes an unfair advantage by embracing the girls, steps out of the dress in response to criticism by the other boys, throws his skirt over his head when he recognizes Ela.

Dialogue

With the exception of the many asides, in which the characters speak their thoughts aloud, the dialogue is realistic in that it simulates conventional upper-class speech of the period.

Plausibility

We accept all these cardboard figures because they are unfolding a very funny story. Anyone in real life behaving as these people do would be regarded as a mental case. All of which suggests that plausibility of characterization is not essential to farce if the fun is genuine. The people must act consistently, however, in the light of their objectives and such characterization as they have been given.

OSCAR WILDE

The Importance
of Being Earnest

1895

Sometimes rather disparagingly pigeonholed as a farce, *The Importance of Being Earnest* has, nevertheless, beneath its glittering surface
enough satirical bite and social comment to evade this easy classifica-
tion. Many of the characteristics of the comedy of manners and the
comedy of ideas are evident. Even the punning title is a satirical
thrust, by the rebellious movement of which Wilde was a part, at the
Victorian ethos.

The plot, by the standards of normal human behavior, is improbable nonsense. The long arm of coincidence is practically jerked
from its socket, and the conduct of the characters is preposterous.
But the audience "suspends its disbelief," as with a fairy tale or
fantasy, and demands only that the story conform to its own absurd
logic, which it does.

Structurally the work is built in the usual way, like most other
great and successful plays, of whatever kind. There are three acts in
the acting version usually performed today, each taking place in a
different setting. The play was written for a proscenium theatre and
was staged realistically. It lends itself, however, to highly stylized
interpretations and production forms, such as arena staging.

Premise

Jack Worthing, a young man who lives a virtuous and high-minded
life in the country, maintains the fiction of a scapegrace younger

brother in London, whose role he assumes when in town. He wants to marry a particular girl of impeccable social position. (This is a perfectly good premise, with the potential of conflict, but the play does not develop in the way one would expect. The obvious course of action would be for the girl to learn of her suitor's profligacy. In this play she does not, in spite of the fact that she knows him only by the name of the fictitious brother.)

Antecedent to the action is the fact that Jack is a foundling, discovered in a handbag left at a railway station. He is actually the elder brother of his friend Algernon.

Synopsis

ACT ONE

The setting is Algernon's flat, London.

Jack Worthing, an attractive man in his late twenties, who lives in the country, calls on his friend Algernon in London. Jack has come to the city to propose marriage to Algy's cousin Gwendolyn. But Algy knows Jack as "Ernest" Worthing, and demands to know why the latter's cigarette case is inscribed "From little Cecily, with fondest love to her dear Uncle Jack." Jack reluctantly explains that Cecily, eighteen and very pretty, is his ward, the granddaughter of the late Thomas Cardew, Jack's foster father. As for "Ernest," that is a fictitious brother invented by Jack as an excuse for visits to the city. Jack has assumed the name himself in London; for, should any of his escapades reach the ears of the pure and innocent Cecily, they could then be attributed to the scapegrace brother. Jack will kill off Ernest, however, if Gwendolyn accepts him.

Gwendolyn and her mother, Lady Bracknell, a formidable dowager, arrive for tea. Alone for a few minutes, Jack proposes and is immediately accepted by Gwendolyn, who asserts that the moment her cousin Algernon first mentioned that he had a friend named Ernest she knew that she was destined to love him passionately. But, she asserts under questioning, she could never love anyone named Jack.

Upon being told of the proposal, Lady Bracknell sends Gwendolyn from the room and examines Jack as to his eligibility. All seems to be going well until Jack admits that he doesn't know his parentage. Mr. Cardew found him, as a baby, in a handbag at Victoria Station. Will the aristocratic Lady Bracknell permit her daughter to marry into a cloakroom and form an alliance with a parcel? Hardly. She sweeps out indignantly.

Gwendolyn returns surreptitiously to declare her eternal devotion to "Ernest," and asks him for his address in the country. As Jack gives it to her, Algy, who has been much intrigued by Jack's description of Cecily, copies it down on his cuff.

[]   *In Brief*

If we disregard the artificiality of the plot and consider only its technical aspects, it is seen to be conventional in form, with a steadily progressing story, each scene altering to some degree the situation that preceded it. Jack wants to marry Gwendolyn, but she loves him because she thinks his name is Ernest. Furthermore, her mother forbids the match because Jack is a foundling. Gwendolyn's cousin, Algy, who has the incriminating and therefore dangerous knowledge that "Ernest" is a fiction, may further complicate matters by pursuing Jack's ward, Cecily.

ACT TWO

The setting now is the garden of Jack's house in the country. It is the following afternoon.

We are introduced to Cecily and her governess, Miss Prism. Cecily wishes that her Uncle Jack's unfortunate brother, Ernest, would sometime pay a visit. She believes that she and Miss Prism might exert a good influence over him. There is a reference to a three-volume novel written by Miss Prism many years ago, the manuscript of which was unfortunately lost. Dr. Chasable, rector of the local church, enters, and he and Miss Prism go off for a short stroll.

The butler then announces the arrival of "Mr. Ernest Worthing," and Algernon enters. Cecily, assuming that he has come to see his elder brother, tells him that her Uncle Jack is in London, and is not expected until Monday. Unfortunately, "Ernest" replies, he must be back in London by then. He is enchanted with the girl. They go into the house.

As Miss Prism and Dr. Chasable return, Jack Worthing unexpectedly arrives. He is dressed in deep mourning, for he says he has received word from Paris that his brother, Ernest, has contracted a sudden chill there and died. After the condolences he arranges with Dr. Chasable to be rechristened later in the afternoon, changing his name to Ernest.

Cecily comes into the garden and greets her Uncle Jack with the news that his brother, Ernest, is here in the house. Jack is baffled, and it is assumed by Miss Prism and Dr. Chasable that the report of Ernest's death in Paris was erroneous. When Jack sees Algy he is furious, but there is nothing he can say until the two of them are alone. Then he orders Algy to return to London by the next train, and goes in to change from his mourning clothes.

Algy then makes love to Cecily, and proposes marriage. She confirms that it has been her dream to fall in love with someone by the name of Ernest. She could never give anyone named Algy, for example, her undivided attention. Algernon leaves for the rectory, obviously to make arrangements to have himself rechristened.

Gwendolyn arrives then, and is ushered into the garden, where she meets Cecily, of whom she has never heard. Since Gwendolyn knows Jack only as "Ernest" Worthing, confusion and suspicion between the two girls mount rapidly as each insists that she is engaged to marry Ernest. Their animosity is mounting when Jack and Algy enter, greet their respective fiancées, and explain that neither one of them is named Ernest. The girls, resenting the deception, return to the house. Alone, the two men quarrel. Algy refuses to return to London. Each is determined to be rechristened.

[]   *In Brief*

The second act continues the artificial pattern of the first. Jack's attempt to dispose of his fictitious brother and assume the name Ernest himself is thwarted by Algernon's masquerading as that iniquitous young man. Gwendolyn, when she learns of the deception, is piqued and unforgiving, as is Cecily. Algy will not co-operate—he intends to stay on and, like Jack, be rechristened.

ACT THREE

The setting is the drawing room of Jack's country house. Immediately following.

Upon being told that each of the young men pretended to the name Ernest in order to have an opportunity of meeting the lady of his choice, and that each of them intends to be rechristened in order to conform to feminine taste, Gwendolyn and Cecily forgive them. There remains the problem of securing Lady Bracknell's approval, however, and the dowager arrives at this moment, having traced her daughter's movements. She intends to take Gwendolyn back to London at once.

When her nephew informs her that he is engaged to Cecily, she views the matter with lofty unconcern until she learns of the enormous fortune that Cecily will one day inherit. She urges that the marriage take place as soon as possible. But Jack intervenes; as Cecily's guardian he will not give his consent until Lady Bracknell permits Gwendolyn to marry him. Lady Bracknell is adamant on this point, and, with the issue deadlocked, she prepares to leave.

Dr. Chasable enters to say that all is in readiness for the dual christening, and mentions Miss Prism. On hearing this name Lady Bracknell starts in astonishment, and imperiously demands that the governess be summoned.

Miss Prism quails in Lady Bracknell's presence, and admits that many years ago she had absent-mindedly placed a novel she had written in a perambulator and a baby in her care in a handbag, which she then checked at the cloakroom of the Victoria Station. Jack disappears for a moment and returns with a battered handbag that Miss Prism identifies as hers. Jack assumes that Miss Prism must be his mother, to that maiden lady's horror. Lady Bracknell establishes that he is actually the lost son of her deceased sister, and that he is therefore Algernon's elder brother. Jack's real name, it is disclosed, is Ernest.

[]   *In Brief*

The third act moves from its opening situation—the girls' forgiveness and acceptance of the two young men—through Lady Bracknell's consent to the Algy-Cecily marriage, her refusal to permit Gwendolyn to marry Jack, and Jack's refusal to permit Cecily to marry while Lady Bracknell opposes him. But, once Jack's identity is established, the only basis for Lady Bracknell's opposition is removed, and both young couples are free to marry. Miss Prism and Dr. Chasable make a third happy pair.

It might be noted that the question of Cecily's preference for a suitor named Ernest is ignored at the end, nor is any notice paid to the improbability of the governess being employed in the house of the very man whom she had lost when he was a baby.

Wilde, of course, realized the frail and artificial nature of his story line. It is, in fact, a plot that perfectly matches the grace and insolent elegance of his dialogue, this being, in John Gassner's words, "uncontaminated with any real feeling." Indeed, the plot may well be a deliberate burlesque of a type of popular melodrama of the day.

Protagonist and Objective

Jack is the protagonist; his objective, to become engaged to Gwendolyn. He says, early in the first act: "I am in love with Gwendolyn. I have come up to town expressly to propose to her." It is his pursuit of Gwendolyn that motivates his actions throughout the play. He succeeds in his objective.

It seems, at times, almost as though there were a double protagonist—Algernon as well as Jack. For Algy pursues Cecily with equal fervor, and the two suits run parallel much of the time. But Algernon's courtship begins later than Jack's, is less beset with difficulty, and its outcome is entirely dependent on the success of Jack's suit. And it is the solution to Jack's difficulties for which the audience waits.

Algernon is, therefore, a subsidiary figure. His chief function in the plot is to complicate, in Act Two, Jack's effort to kill off his fictitious brother Ernest. The motivation for this, presumably, is that Jack wants to be rid of "Ernest" so that he may assume the name himself, as it is favored by Gwendolyn. The structure of the play is none too sturdy in this area.

Obstacles

Though trivial by the standards of normal behavior, the factors that hinder Jack's courtship of Gwendolyn are valid in the context of the unreal world presented by the author. There are two such obstacles: Gwendolyn's preference for the name Ernest and Lady Bracknell's opposition to the match.

The first obstacle is apparently overcome early in Act Three when Gwendolyn seems to forgive Jack his deception on learning that he assumed the name Ernest in order to create opportunities for coming to London to see her—an explanation, by the way, not entirely accurate. She is further mollified on learning that Jack is to be rechristened Ernest. (Cecily forgives Algernon at the same time and for similar reasons.)

The second obstacle is surmounted by the disclosure of Jack's parentage, which makes him acceptable to Lady Bracknell as a husband for her daughter.

Major Crisis and Climax, Theme

The crisis—a totally artificial one—depends on a fortunate coincidence, and not any effort on the part of the characters. It is the disclosure that Miss Prism, who just happens to work there, once misplaced a baby left in her charge. Could that baby have been Jack?

The climax is Lady Bracknell's telling Jack that he must be the son of her sister, and consequently Algernon's elder brother. Since Jack's lack of family connections has been the basis of Lady Bracknell's opposition, it is assumed that she will now consent.

However, Gwendolyn's preference for the name "Ernest" is revived as an obstacle at this point—one that will have to be overcome quickly, for it is not strong enough to carry the play more than a few moments, once Lady Bracknell retires from the field. On being told that he was named after his father, Jack consults a directory and learns that his father's name was Ernest. With this disclosure the last shred of conflict evaporates and the play is substantially over.

Even so gossamer-like a play as this can have a theme, and a devastating one. Surely it is a comment on the social distinctions of the British aristocracy, their shallowness and triviality. Perhaps, odd as it may seem, the play is a distant cousin of Osborne's *Look Back in Anger*. (Better humored, though!)

Resolution

There is almost nothing that can be regarded as a resolution, unless it is Jack's final line, "I've now realized for the first time the vital Importance of Being Earnest," a triple pun that embraces the title of the play, the factual denouement of the plot, and a satirical comment on contemporary mores.

Opening

The author begins his play soon after Jack's decision to come to London in order to propose to Gwendolyn, and before the actual proposal. Opposition and complications can arise quickly thereafter.

Unity

It is unity of style, more than anything else, that gives this work its feeling of coherence. As originally written, the play had four acts and contained scenes and dialogue omitted in the version we know today. Some of this material satirized movements and arguments in the Church of England, long since resolved and forgotten by the general public. Unity of action suggests that perhaps that material should never have gone into the play in the first place.

Exposition

Exposition, of which this highly synthetic story requires a good deal, is handled initially by having Jack explain his actions to Algy. The fact that Jack is reluctant to do so, that Algy has Jack's cigarette case with its possibly incriminating inscription, and the fact of Algy's relationship to Gwendolyn introduce a note of conflict and irritation into the exposition that enlivens it and makes it playable.

Characterization

All the characters belong to the same hothouse milieu and all subscribe to the same standards; so there is little difference among them, and conflict has to arise out of situation, whim, and caprice, not out of character traits.

But it is only in an imaginary world that a plot like this will work. Were any of the characters to behave like reasonable human beings, the whole house of cards would collapse. (It should be observed that in performance, however, the actors must impress the audience as being totally committed to their own objectives, dismayed by their own predicaments. Once they betray the fact that they know they are funny, they no longer are.)

Development

Many of the individual scenes are built in the conventional pattern. Even the opening scene of exposition between Algernon and Jack follows the form: protagonist, Algy; his objective, to probe the mysteries of Jack's behavior; obstacle, Jack's reluctance to explain; climax, Algy succeeds in prying out of Jack the admission that Ernest is not his own name, but that of a fictitious brother; resolution, Algernon, revealing that he has a similar fictitious friend serving the same purpose, agrees to leave Jack alone with Gwendolyn. (It may be noted that, although Algy is the protagonist of this scene, Jack is revealed in the same scene as the protagonist of the entire play.)

Later in the act Jack is the protagonist of an individual scene, as well as of the play, when Lady Bracknell quizzes him as to his eligibility. His objective is to obtain Lady Bracknell's approval of his engagement; obstacle, the disclosure that he is a foundling; climax, Lady Bracknell's refusal to consider the match; resolution, Jack's anger and dejection.

Gwendolyn's scene with Cecily, on her entrance in Act Two, is another example. Protagonist, Gwendolyn; her objective, to find out what Cecily is doing in the home of her fiancé; obstacle, the misunderstanding that arises from the fact that both Jack and Algy are known to the girls as Ernest; climax, the entrance of the young men and their explanations; resolution, the girls' statement that under the circumstances they are not engaged to anyone and their exit into the house.

Dramatic Irony

Dramatic irony is employed frequently during the play, always as a comedic device. In Act One Algernon uses the excuse of his sick friend to get out of dining with Lady Bracknell, when we know that the sick friend is fictitious.

In Act Two Algernon pretends to Cecily to be Jack's brother Ernest. We, of course, know who he really is.

On Jack's entrance, dressed in mourning, dramatic irony is doubled and the comedy enhanced by our knowledge that not only is Jack's grief spurious but that Algy is in the house masquerading as Ernest. The audience anticipates Jack's discomfiture when he learns the truth. This particular use of dramatic irony ends when he does so.

Other instances of the device occur later in the act when Cecily tells Algernon that it has been her dream to love someone named Ernest (we enjoy Algernon's discomfiture); when Cecily muses that Gwendolyn must be one of the many good elderly women associated with Uncle Jack in his philanthropic work in London (we eagerly anticipate Cecily's reaction when she sees Gwendolyn and learns what we already know about her); and the scene between the two girls when each claims to be engaged to Ernest. (Our knowledge that there are two men, neither named Ernest, is what makes the scene so effective.)

Preparation

Although the exchange of the baby for the three-volume novel propounded in the last act is totally preposterous, it is interesting to see how carefully Wilde planted the existence of the novel earlier in the play. It occurs in the beginning of Act Two, when Miss Prism tells Cecily: "The manuscript was unfortunately abandoned. I use the word in the sense of lost or mislaid." There is a kind of mad logic at work when it later develops that the manuscript turned up in the perambulator. The scene would not be so funny had we not already known of the novel's existence.

Another instance of careful planting that makes the humor effective occurs in these lines of Dr. Chasable's: "Were I fortunate enough to be Miss Prism's pupil, I would hang upon her lips. (*Miss Prism glares.*) I spoke metaphorically. My metaphor was drawn from the bees." Moments later the author plants the joke again: "But I must not disturb Egeria and her pupil any longer." "Egeria? My name is Laetitia, Doctor." "A classical allusion merely, drawn from the Pagan authors." Quite a bit later Wilde is ready to reap what he has sown. Miss Prism, in response to Dr. Chasable's observation that a married man is often not even attractive to his wife, replies: "That depends on the intellectual sympathies of the woman. Maturity can always be depended on. Ripeness can be trusted. Young women are green. (*Dr. Chasable starts.*) I spoke horticulturally. My metaphor was drawn from the fruits."

Activity

Food is used several times as a comedic activity. In Act One the cucumber sandwiches that have been especially prepared for Lady Bracknell are all eaten before she arrives; when Gwendolyn asks for bread and butter, and tea without sugar, Cecily serves her cake and drops four lumps of sugar in her cup; the quarrel between Jack and Algy at the end of Act Two is made to seem even more ridiculous by the two young men's voraciously eating muffins.

Lady Bracknell's solemnly taking notes as she quizzes Jack, and Algernon's tearing up the unopened bills his manservant brings him, both help characterization early in the play. And in Act Two Jack's arrival at his country home in full mourning clothes is a very funny visual effect.

Dialogue

Wilde's dialogue is a triumph of poised insincerity and aplomb. The wit is based largely on paradox, the turning upside down of more widely accepted standards of behavior. The lines glitter with a high literary polish, but there is almost no difference in characterization, since all the people belong to the same artificial world and think the same thoughts. Many of the witticisms are practically interchangeable.

ANTON CHEKOV

The Cherry Orchard

1904

This is the great Russian dramatist's last and perhaps greatest play. It was first produced by the Moscow Art Theatre shortly before his death.

Chekov is unique. Though others have tried, no one has ever written plays quite like his, before or since. *The Cherry Orchard* has very little plot or forward movement. It is a work of intense mood, realistic in form, but with important symbolist elements. Never pressing a particular social program or point of view, the play nevertheless illuminates the passing of one social order and the growth of another with humor, poetry, and heartbreak.

It is impossible for a synopsis to do justice to the work, or to give its full flavor and impact. The play's great value lies in its wonderful interplay of dialogue and swift changes of mood, all so seemingly casual but so revealing of character.

The play was written for the proscenium theatre.

Premise

Madame Ranevsky (Lyubov), after some rather extravagant and profligate years in Paris, returns, nearly penniless, to her ancestral home in Russia, to find that the heavily mortgaged estate is to be sold to meet indebtedness. She is ill equipped by training or temperament to grasp the seriousness of the situation, much less to deal with it. Her brother and her daughter are equally innocent of practical matters, and her adopted daughter helpless, beyond petty economies, to do anything about it.

Synopsis

The play is in four acts, and covers a period of several months during the summer of a year at the turn of the century.

ACT ONE

The setting is a room in the Ranevsky house. The time is a May morning, before sunrise.

Lopahin, a wealthy merchant whose father was a peasant and grandfather a serf, is awaiting the arrival of Madame Ranevsky, due home after five years in France. With Dunyasha, a rather silly housemaid, he talks of the past. Then Epihodov, a clerk on the estate and a very clumsy fellow, appears with a nosegay, also to welcome Madame Ranevsky and her retinue. A sound of carriages is heard, and they leave to meet the travelers. Firs, an ancient butler, also crosses the room to join in the welcome.

Madame Ranevsky ("Lyubov" from here on) appears, followed by her lovely seventeen-year-old daughter Anya and Charlotta, an eccentric woman of middle age, Anya's governess. Two other members of the household who have gone to meet the train also enter. They are Gaev, Lyubov's brother, and Varya, her adopted daughter, aged 24. Pishtchik, a hearty neighboring landowner, is also part of the welcoming committee, as are now, of course, Lopahin and Dunyasha.

It is a sentimental homecoming, with Lyubov somewhat tearfully reunited with her adopted daughter, her brother, and the servants. As the group scatters with luggage, Dunyasha tells Anya that Epihodov has proposed to her.

There is then an affectionate reunion between Anya and Varya, and we learn that Anya and Charlotta had made the trip to Paris in order to accompany Lyubov home, that Lyubov had had to sell her villa at Menton in order to pay her debts, and that although she has almost no money left she is as extravagant as ever. Anya learns that the estate will be sold at auction in August, since the arrears on the mortgage have not been paid.

Lopahin appears momentarily, and Varya tells Anya that although everyone assumes that she and Lopahin are in love, he on his part has never spoken of it, much less proposed marriage. Varya doesn't think anything will ever come of it. She wishes that Anya could marry some rich man.

Yasha, Lyubov's valet, a shallow and affected young man who has also been with her in Paris, crosses with luggage, and stops to embrace the flirtatious Dunyasha.

Anya, who is very tired from the journey, wants to retire, but she tells Varya that their mother ought to be prepared for the fact that Petya Trofimov is in the house. Trofimov was the tutor of Lyubov's son, who was drowned in a nearby river at the age of seven. It was the sorrow brought about by the deaths of both her husband and her son that led Lyubov to go to live in Paris some years before.

Coffee is to be served, and Lyubov, Gaev, Lopahin, and Pishtchik gather for it. Anya says good night and leaves. Lyubov, fatigued and deeply moved by her homecoming, is in no mood to discuss her financial problem, but Lopahin insists on talking business. He grew up on this estate, a peasant boy, and he has the deepest affection for the family. Now he has a solution to their difficulty, and it is an eminently practical one—cut down the cherry orchard, subdivide the property, and lease the lots as building sites for summer villas.

To Lyubov and Gaev the idea of destroying the cherry orchard is unthinkable, and they dismiss Lopahin's proposal as hardly worth discussion. As the guests prepare to leave, Charlotta crosses the room, and rebuffs Lopahin's clumsy attempt at courtesy. After Lopahin goes out, Gaev refers to Varya's presumed engagement to him. Then Pishtchik tries to borrow some money from Lyubov.

Varya opens a window, and they all look out at the blossoming cherry orchard. Lyubov recalls her youth and happier times.

Trofimov, the tutor, now about thirty years old and a student, comes in to pay his respects. Lyubov is moved to tears, and embraces him.

All are tired and ready for sleep. Pishtchik again asks for a loan, and Lyubov tells her brother to give him the money, which, since he has no money, he does not. Lyubov, Pishtchik, Trofimov, and the old butler go out.

Varya tells Yasha, the valet, that his mother has come from the village to see him. Irritated, Yasha leaves. Gaev and Varya are alone. Gaev wishes there might be a legacy from someone, or that Anya might marry into wealth, or that a rich aunt might come to the rescue.

Anya, who hasn't been able to sleep, enters the room, and Gaev rambles on—perhaps he can raise a loan at the bank, or Lopahin will lend them the money. In any case, he swears, he will never allow the estate to be auctioned. Anya, reassured, embraces him.

Firs, the old butler, whose meddlesome admonitions are tolerated because of his age and long service, comes in to tell Gaev to go to bed, and the two men leave. Varya speaks of household matters, but Anya is asleep. Varya leads her out as the visionary student, Trofimov, appears, looks outside, and murmurs of the sunshine and the spring.

[] *In Brief*

The first act introduces us to Chekov's large cast of characters at a moment charged with emotion, to some degree, for each of them, for Lyubov's return from self-imposed exile means that the real head of the family is again among them. (Her brother Gaev is far too ineffectual to be so considered.) Everyone is briefly but sharply characterized, and the dilemma facing the family is explicitly set forth. We hear from Lopahin of a possible solution to their difficulties, and are shown their reluctance to make the necessary adjustments to a changing social situation. Thus, though there is little forward movement in the conventional sense, the entire situation is put before us, and the question is posed whether Lyubov can face reality, or whether she will do nothing and simply let disaster overtake them all.

A C T   T W O

Some time has passed. The setting is a garden on the estate, about sunset on a summer evening.

Epihodov is playing a guitar, while three of the other servants— Charlotta, Yasha, and Dunyasha—sit listening, plunged in thought. There is some flirtatious byplay between Yasha and Dunyasha, as well as a few satirical thrusts at metaphysical speculation and futile intellectualism. All except Yasha leave when they hear Lyubov, Gaev, and Lopahin approaching.

Lopahin is urging, as vehemently as he can, that the land must be divided into building lots, but his argument gets scant attention from Lyubov or her brother. She drops her purse. Yasha picks up the scattered coins for her, then leaves. Lopahin says he has never met such unbusinesslike people—they can't seem to understand that the estate will be sold unless something is done to meet the arrears. Lyubov dismisses the idea of villas and summer visitors as vulgar, and Gaev agrees.

Offended, Lopahin starts to go, but Lyubov persuades him to stay. It is more cheerful with him present, and perhaps they will think of some solution to their problem.

Lyubov reminisces about her marriage to an extravagant man and about his death. She loved another, and as "punishment" her son was drowned. She then fled Russia, bought a villa on the Riviera, where she cared for her lover through a long illness. Then, in Paris, he betrayed and robbed her. In despair, and almost without funds, she has come home. But her lover sends her telegrams, pleading for her to forgive and come back to him.

A local orchestra is heard playing in the distance. Lopahin speaks of his father, a peasant who beat him. Lyubov tells him he should marry Varya. Lopahin agrees that she is a good girl. Gaev has been offered a position in a bank, but his sister tells him to "stay as he is."

Firs brings an overcoat for Gaev, and recalls the emancipation of the serfs, so many years before. He regards this as a national calamity, and would not himself consent to be set free. Gaev remarks that he is going to town on the morrow to try to arrange a loan.

The two girls, Anya and Varya, enter with Trofimov, and there is a rather acrimonious exchange between the idealistic student and Lopahin, the self-made businessman, in which each expresses his own point of view about contemporary Russia. Epihodov crosses, playing his guitar, and the attention of the family is quickly diverted.

Suddenly there is a sound, from far off, as of a breaking harp string. All are startled. It is a disturbing occurrence, without explanation. A tramp appears and asks the way to the station. He begs for money, and frightens Varya. Impulsively Lyubov searches her bag and, finding no silver, gives him a gold piece. He leaves. Varya is near tears. She hasn't enough to feed the servants properly, and Lyubov has squandered gold. Lyubov says that Lopahin will lend them more, that he and Varya are to be married. Varya is embarrassed, and Lopahin passes off the remark with a clumsy attempt at humor. Once more he reminds Lyubov that the cherry orchard is soon to be sold. All leave the garden except Anya and Trofimov.

Trofimov envisions the Russia that is to come. To him the cherry orchard represents the nation's fearful past, with its slavery and backwardness. But by work and suffering Russians can expiate that past, and go forward with hope and joy. Anya is not only impressed by his eloquence; she is clearly falling in love with him too. Trofimov, however, is too enraptured by his visions to think of love. Varya calls, but they don't answer. Instead they go down to the river.

[] *In Brief*

The second act deepens and develops our understanding of the principal characters without altering the basic situation. We see that the cherry orchard means different things to different people, but Lyubov is no nearer consenting to its destruction, in spite of Lopahin's repeated warnings.

ACT THREE

It is August, the day the estate is to be sold, and Lyubov is giving a ball. The scene is a drawing room.

Gaev and Lopahin are not present; they are in town attending the auction. But all the others, plus a number of local guests, are dancing and celebrating. They drift in and out of the room.

Trofimov teases Varya by calling her Madame Lopahin. She resents this, and incidentally remarks that they have no money to pay the musicians. Lyubov wonders whether the estate has been sold, and why her brother hasn't returned. She muses that this was not the time to give a party. Charlotta entertains the crowd with card tricks and an exhibition of ventriloquism.

Varya, trying to cheer her mother, says she is sure her wealthy aunt has authorized Gaev to buy the estate, but Lyubov knows this isn't true. She urges Varya to marry Lopahin, but the girl says that, while she likes him, he has not proposed. He is much too busy making money to think of marriage.

Lyubov and Trofimov have a few moments alone. She is very worried about the estate—whether it has been sold. Trofimov tells her to face the truth—that it doesn't matter; the cherry orchard is part of a past that is gone. Lyubov weeps as she remembers her drowned son. Another telegram from Paris has informed her that her lover is ill. She knows he is a millstone about her neck, but she loves him and cannot live without him. Trofimov is shocked, and a quarrel develops, Lyubov saying that he knows nothing of love. He runs out, trips and falls, but Lyubov calls her apologies, and soon they are waltzing together.

Firs remembers balls in earlier days, attended by the aristocracy. There is a rumor that the estate has been sold, but no one knows to whom. Lyubov wonders what will happen to old Firs. Yasha, the valet, begs Lyubov to take him back to Paris when she goes, and Pishtchik asks her for a loan.

Epihodov rebukes Dunyasha for her coldness. Varya enters, and tells Epihodov to be off. A quarrel ensues, with Varya chasing him out of the room with a stick. As she swings it, she inadvertently strikes Lopahin, just coming in. He has had too much to drink.

Everyone rushes in to hear whether there has been a sale, but Lopahin avoids a direct answer. Soon Gaev appears, asks Firs to help him change, and goes out again. Lopahin then reveals that he himself has bought the cherry orchard. Lyubov is crushed, beyond speech. Varya takes the house keys from her belt, throws them on the floor, and walks out.

Lopahin exults, and tells how he outbid everyone else. Now he is the owner of the estate where his father and grandfather were slaves. Stumbling drunkenly over the furniture, he goes into the next room, calling on the musicians to play. Anya tries to comfort her weeping mother.

[] *In Brief*

Character development continues in Act Three with added force and clarity, since this is the day of the sale, and the gaiety of the party is in sharp contrast to the underlying sadness of the family's plight. With Lopahin's disclosure that he is the one who has bought the estate, we have a sudden dramatic development of great power, because of the long and careful preparation that has preceded it. The announcement is the first—one might almost say the only—significant plot development of the entire play.

A C T   F O U R

It is now October. The setting is the same room as in Act One, but it has been stripped of most of its furnishings, and trunks and traveling bags are piled up near the door. There is a great deal of passing back and forth, moving of luggage, and general confusion.

To her brother's dismay Lyubov has given her purse to the peasants who have come to say good-bye. Lopahin has brought champagne, but no one wants to drink except Yasha. Trofimov intends to go to Moscow to pursue his studies, but at the moment cannot find his galoshes. He proudly refuses a proffered loan from Lopahin.

Let Lopahin work and make money; he has no need of it in his search for truth and happiness. We hear the stroke of an ax cutting down a cherry tree.

As Lopahin and Trofimov are bidding each other good-bye, Anya comes in to ask that the cherry orchard not be cut down until Lyubov has left. Lopahin goes outside to give the orders.

Anya inquires whether Firs has been taken to the hospital, and Yasha says he gave orders to have it done. Varya, who has found their note to the doctor, wonders why that wasn't taken along too. Dunyasha bids Yasha a tearful farewell, to which he is quite indifferent. And his mother, to his annoyance, has come to bid him good-bye.

Lyubov, Gaev, Anya, and Charlotta enter the room, ready for the journey. Yasha starts carrying out the luggage. Lyubov is returning to Paris, at least temporarily; Gaev has been offered a position in a local bank; Anya will live nearby and continue her education at a local high school. Charlotta doesn't know what she will do, but as Lopahin returns he tells her not to worry, that he will find her a position.

Pishtchik rushes in, ebullient and excited. He has just leased some mineral rights on his land. To their amazement he pays Lyubov and Lopahin each part of what he owes them, then hurries away.

Lyubov says she is concerned about two things. One is leaving Firs ill. Anya assures her that Firs has already been taken to the hospital. The other concern is Varya's future. Dismissing the other people in the room, Lyubov quietly urges Lopahin to ask for Varya's hand. The girl loves him, she says. Lopahin agrees to propose right now. Calling Varya, Lyubov leaves the two of them together.

Self-consciously Varya busies herself at the luggage. Lopahin asks what she intends to do, and she tells him of a position as housekeeper that she has secured with a family living some seventy miles away. Though she gives him every opportunity, Lopahin cannot bring himself to speak of marriage, taking refuge instead in small talk. Both are acutely uncomfortable, and when Lopahin's name is suddenly called from outside he runs from the room. Varya begins to sob.

Lyubov returns, takes in the situation without comment. It is time to start. Suddenly everyone appears and begins carrying out luggage and saying farewell. Lyubov and Gaev are left alone for a moment after the others have gone ahead. It is the last time they will ever see this house or the orchard. Emotionally they turn away. We hear the doors being locked, as they go, and the carriages driving away.

There is silence, broken only by the sound of an ax cutting down a tree. Firs appears. Slowly he crosses to a sofa and sits. Gaev has gone off in his thin overcoat, he muses; life has slipped by as though he hadn't lived. He lies down. Again we hear from a distance a sound like a harp string breaking, then the axes, chopping down the trees.

[] In Brief

Chekov has no surprises for us in Act Four, no twists of plot or any development that couldn't be long foreseen. But we have come to know these people so well that we follow their rather prosaic fates with deep concern and no feeling of anticlimax. And the larger pattern of the play is completed: one social order has outlived its time; it passes and another takes its place.

Protagonist and Objective

It has been suggested that *The Cherry Orchard* has a group protagonist—the entire family. But only one person is capable of making the decision to lease the land, as Lopahin urges, and that is Lyubov. Indeed, he invariably addresses his arguments to her. Gaev is too weak and too preoccupied for such an action, and the two girls could not in any case act independently of their mother. Lyubov is the protagonist; her objective, somehow to escape the pressure that will force her to give up the estate. The fact that she does not (in fact, cannot) do anything to save herself doesn't alter her position as the focus of the play. It simply means that the energy which usually drives a play forward has been greatly reduced. Chekov has compensated for this lack of force by employing his unsurpassed skill at characterization to engage our sympathies.

Obstacle

There is but one obstacle, and that is within Lyubov herself. She is incapable of dealing realistically with the financial situation in which the family finds itself. Were she to follow Lopahin's advice, the chances are that the family could make a far more comfortable adjustment to the social changes that are pressing on them.

Major Crisis and Climax, Theme

The final opportunity to lease the land, so far as we are shown in the play, occurs in Act Two, in the near quarrel that develops between Lyubov and Lopahin. This is the only dramatized crisis. Presumably there are other times when she could have made such a decision before the date of the auction.

The climax is Lopahin's announcement, in Act Three, that he has bought the estate.

Thematically the play tells us that an outworn social order has no defenses against the relentless pressure of a new one.

Resolution

Most of Act Four (with the exception of the scene between Varya and Lopahin) may be considered a resolution of the main story line. Here we learn what happens to the various people as a result of the family's losing the estate. This is an exceptionally long and detailed resolution, only possible dramatically because of our intense absorption in the characters.

Opening

The thematic pattern of *The Cherry Orchard* is indicated by the family's loss of the estate. Chekov has thrown this into bold relief by beginning the play with Lyubov's arrival (just as he ends it with her departure). Doubtless the span of dramatic action could have been compressed by starting the play closer to the climax, and perhaps with some gain in tension. But to what purpose? Tension is not required here, nor even desirable, and the author's intention is better served by showing us that the threat hanging over Lyubov and her family cannot move her to action even over an extended period of time.

Unity

As noted, the play is framed by Lyubov's arrival and departure, and this gives it a sense of unity as well as emphasis on the theme. There are many subsidiary characters (Pishtchik and Epihodov, for instance) whose presence is of little importance dramatically. But Chekov is painting the picture of a social order, and this certainly justifies their inclusion in the play. Tightness of structure serves a play ill if it prevents the author from filling out his complete picture. It is a tool and a discipline to be used when appropriate, and the playwright must be the judge of the degree to which he will adhere to its demands. It serves *Ghosts* and *The Little Foxes* very well indeed. It would destroy *The Cherry Orchard*.

Exposition

Much of the play's exposition is quite unconventionally handled, with little trace of the conflicts that are usually employed as carriers of such information. For example, there is no conflict whatever between Anya and Varya in their scene together in Act One. However, what they are telling each other (and the audience) is so fraught with emotion that we are entirely absorbed. This is one of Chekov's methods of handling exposition. Another is a speech of reminiscence and self-examination, such as Lopahin's to Dunyasha at the beginning of the play. It is almost a soliloquy. Again and again people in Chekov look inward and talk about themselves. It is as though the character was trying to explain himself, not to others, but to himself. Charlotta's long speech at the opening of Act Two is another example. It is tangential to the course of the play.

Such introspective musings could be disastrous in the hands of an unskilled playwright. Though it looks easy, it is probably the most difficult form of exposition there is.

Characterization

The many flights of introspection encountered in the play certainly help to advance the richness and variety of its characterizations. But it is not entirely what they say about themselves that lets us know these people so intimately. They also react characteristically to one another, and to the situation that confronts them. Consider Gaev's baseless and futile optimism at the end of Act One, when he tells his niece: "We shall pay off the arrears, I'm convinced of it. (*Puts a caramel in his mouth*) I swear on my honour, I swear by anything you like, the estate shan't be sold. (*Excitedly*) By my own happiness

I swear it! Here's my hand on it, call me the basest, vilest of men, if I let it come to an auction! Upon my soul, I swear it!" Note the caramel, too! What kind of man chews candy when making such a statement?

Here is Lyubov's reply to one of Lopahin's many exhortations: "Villas and summer visitors—forgive my saying so—it's so vulgar." The play abounds in such telling strokes.

One would have to understand the original Russian to know to what degree Chekov has also characterized by means of speech patterns, grammar, et cetera.

Development

Gaev and Anya have objectives similar to Lyubov's; Gaev's may be even weaker than his sister's, for it is clear from the beginning that he will do nothing to stave off disaster. Lyubov might—at least, Lopahin thinks so. (Technically one must designate this wish to postpone or avoid action, undynamic though it is, as the objective, for it is Lyubov's failure to act that brings on the climax.)

Lopahin's objective is to help the family, according to his own lights. He is motivated by friendship and gratitude. Trofimov wants to "build the future." His absorption in his visionary dreams is the obstacle to Anya's awakening love.

Varya wants to marry Lopahin, and the intensely moving scene in the last act, when he cannot bring himself to propose to her, is one of the few conventionally structured scenes in the play.

For the most part these people move about within the larger framework of the play, drifting along on currents they but faintly comprehend, and with which they certainly cannot cope. It must be stressed, however, that the structural pattern is almost unique with Chekov.

Dramatic Irony

In one sense the first two acts are ironic, for we believe Lopahin's warnings, and Lyubov does not, preferring to think that somehow things will turn out all right. In other words, we see the cliff toward which the blind are walking; they have been told it is there, but they pay no heed. This subtle use of dramatic irony accounts in large part for the structural vitality of the first half of the play. In a more conventional sense there is no further use of the device.

We could have known, in Act Four, that Firs had not been taken to the hospital, but this would have made us unduly concerned about him at a time when our attention is properly centered on the major figures. Furthermore, it would have destroyed the shock of seeing Firs come into the room after the house has been locked. The author made the right choice. Dramatic irony isn't always better than surprise.

Preparation

We are told early that Trofimov is in the house, and that he was the tutor of Lyubov's drowned son. Knowing this makes their first meeting very dramatic, for there has already been speculation about Lyubov's reaction to seeing him again.

Varya, at the end of Act One, tells of a report that she is feeding the servants nothing but pease pudding. By Act Two this is what she is actually doing.

Varya's feeling for Lopahin is planted again and again. By the time of their final scene together we have been carefully conditioned for Varya's disappointment and all its heartbreak.

Twice in Act Four we are told that orders have been given to take the ailing Firs to the hospital. When we see him at the end of the play we think back to the careless way the family dealt with this matter.

Activity

For all the floods of speech in *The Cherry Orchard*, Chekov has found plenty of significant and dramatically effective activity for his people.

Lyubov drops her purse and scatters the contents. She gives a gold coin to a beggar. The telegrams she receives and tears up remind us of her lover and the kind of life to which she has grown accustomed. Characteristically, without even money to pay the musicians, she holds a ball on the very day of the auction. The dancing, music, and gaiety of the ball beautifully counterpoint the underlying situation.

Lopahin is drunk at his moment of triumph, and Varya, in her disappointment and disgust, throws the house keys at his feet. Earlier, pursuing Epihodov with a stick, Varya had unintentionally hit Lopahin.

Epihodov plays the guitar and is forever stumbling over the furniture. We know something about the man from these two facts alone. Charlotta's parlor tricks are used as a foil for her loneliness and rather desperate situation. Trofimov, the dreamer, can't find his galoshes. Firs is forever fussing over Gaev, and the irresponsible Yasha is the only one to drink Lopahin's champagne.

Dialogue

Chekov's people often seem to be talking half to themselves, with the person addressed only half hearing, perhaps replying indirectly or with a comment that isn't really a direct reply at all. Realistic dialogue handled in this way can be tremendously effective in a thoughtful, introspective kind of play like *The Cherry Orchard*. Most plays require far more force and directness from their characters.

Effects

The breaking string that is heard in the second act and again at the end of the play is a highly theatrical effect, but the only one the author employs that is outside the realistic form in which he is working. Even here, he offers a possible explanation for the mysterious sound: it might have been a bird, or a mine bucket falling. The effect on stage is eerie, and the symbolism inescapable.

There is also the sound effect of an ax, far off, cutting down the trees.

Plausibility

It need scarcely be pointed out that all that happens in *The Cherry Orchard* is logical and believable. Seldom are such fully realized people achieved in dramatic writing. Their motives, their inmost thoughts are all opened to us, and their actions are totally credible.

GEORGE BERNARD SHAW
Pygmalion
1913

One of Shaw's most popular and engaging comedies, frequently revived, *Pygmalion* was also made into a successful motion picture; it further provided the characters, story line, and much of the dialogue of the triumphant musical comedy *My Fair Lady.*

Building on the ancient tale of the sculptor Pygmalion, who created a figure that came to life and with whom he fell in love, Shaw shaped the myth into a modern and immensely appealing Cinderella story that is, at the same time, a hilarious satire on British class distinctions.

The play is realistic in form and treatment, although the dialogue is characteristically Shavian—meaning that the lines are far more amusing, eloquent, and penetrating than one is accustomed to hear in real life. (Hearing such lines competently delivered can be one of the greatest pleasures of theatre-going.)

Premise

A London professor of phonetics, Henry Higgins, makes notes on the speech of an ignorant and totally uncultivated flower girl. She overhears him tell a friend that her poor speech will keep her in the gutter to the end of her days; that after three months of training he could pass her off as a duchess. Eliza, the flower girl, comes to Higgins' home and asks to be taught to speak properly.

An antecedent fact that will have a bearing on the developing situation is the mother-fixation that, in John Gassner's words, "deprives Higgins of the conventional qualification of sexual passion."

Synopsis

The play is in five acts, and requires three settings.

ACT ONE

The scene is the portico of a church near the Covent Garden vegetable market.

A number of people coming from the theatre have taken shelter here from a rainstorm. Mrs. Eynsford Hill and her daughter Clara are waiting for Freddy, Clara's twenty-year-old brother, to fetch a cab. Freddy returns, saying there are no cabs to be found. As he starts off again he collides with a flower girl, a dirty, wretched little creature who upbraids him for his carelessness. Her speech proclaims her a member of the lowest social class. Mrs. Eynsford Hill pays the girl for the flowers her son knocked into the mud.

An elderly gentleman, Colonel Pickering, enters. The flower girl, Eliza, urges her wares upon him, and he gives her a bit of small change. A bystander warns her to give the gentleman a flower for it, for there is another man standing nearby who is writing down every word she says. Thinking he must be a police informer, Eliza is greatly alarmed, and protests her innocence of any wrongdoing. The note-taker shows her his notes, which she can't read. But he can—and imitates her accent precisely. People gather round, and he tells two or three speakers where they live or where they were born. He then identifies the colonel's schools and his residence in India. Mrs. Eynsford Hill and Clara go off to catch a bus, the rain having stopped.

The colonel, curious, strikes up a conversation with the note-taker, who says he is a phonetician and that there is a living in it. People on the upgrade socially pay to have their speech habits changed, he says. Eliza, meanwhile, is muttering and whining, and is told to be quiet. The phonetician remarks that the girl's speech will keep her in the gutter, that given three months he could pass her off as a duchess, that he could even get her a place as a lady's maid or a shop assistant.

The colonel says that he is a student of Indian dialects, and the phonetician introduces himself as Henry Higgins, inventor of a phonetic alphabet. The men know of each other, and form an immediate friendship. Higgins mentions his address (which Eliza overhears). The girl again importunes, and Higgins, annoyed, starts to walk off with Pickering. The church bell rings, like a rebuke for his want of charity. Amused and contemptuous now, Higgins throws a handful of coins into her basket. The men leave.

Freddy returns, having found a cab, but finds that his mother and sister have gone. Eliza has been counting the change, and grandly announces that she will take the cab.

Many years after *Pygmalion* was written Shaw added a few brief scenes that may have been intended for inclusion in the film version of the play. Although they are not practical for stage production, they have been printed in recently published texts.

At the end of Act One we are shown Eliza and the taxi driver arguing over the fare. Finally, with great good nature, he tells her to keep the shilling and drives off.

Then we see Eliza in her shabby room, counting her riches (the money Higgins tossed her way) and climbing into bed.

[] *In Brief*

Act One is more like a prologue than an act. Although its sharply drawn characterizations are very entertaining, it does little more than introduce the principals and indicate the potential of the situation. There is no significant forward movement. All we know is that a spectacularly knowledgeable and arrogant phonetician has boasted that he could pass a flower girl off as a duchess and that the girl has overheard the remark. We are curious to know whether she will do anything about it.

ACT TWO

The setting is Higgins' laboratory, in his home.

Higgins has been explaining his work to Pickering, who has moved in with him, when Mrs. Pearce, the housekeeper, announces that a young woman wants to see him. It is Eliza, and she has come to take speech instruction. Higgins, amazed at her presumption, is very rude. Pickering, on the other hand, has courtly manners, and the girl responds to his courtesy. She would like to be a lady in a flower shop, but knows that no one will hire her unless she talks like one. She offers to pay a shilling per lesson, and it strikes Higgins that, considered as a percentage of the girl's income, it is a magnanimous offer.

Pickering reminds Higgins of his boast—flower girl into lady— and Higgins accepts the challenge. He orders Mrs. Pearce to bathe the girl, burn her clothes, and order new ones. Pickering and Mrs. Pearce protest this highhanded procedure, even though Eliza has already admitted that she has no mother and that her father long ago kicked her out. Higgins rides roughshod over all objections. Bewildered and offended, Eliza tries to go, but Higgins lures her with chocolates and promises of luxuries. When asked what is to happen to the girl at the end of six months, Higgins says that they will simply throw her back in the gutter again. With many misgivings Mrs. Pearce leads Eliza off to be made a little more presentable.

We now have the second of Shaw's interpolations. Eliza is taken to the spare bedroom, whose grandeur frightens her. She is then initiated into the mysteries of the bathroom, where Mrs. Pearce, much against the girl's will, gets her into the tub and starts scrubbing.

In normal staging the action continues without interruption in the laboratory. Pickering wants to assure himself that Higgins will not take advantage of Eliza, but there can be little doubt that her honor is quite safe. Higgins admits that he finds women jealous, exacting, suspicious; they upset him. He is a confirmed bachelor.

Mrs. Pearce enters, bringing the girl's hat, which Eliza insisted on saving. She pleads with Higgins not to swear in front of Eliza, and particularly not to use a word (which the English consider vulgar) that begins with *b* (bloody). He must also set an example of tidiness. Mrs. Pearce goes on to criticize Higgins' personal habits at some length. After she goes, he expresses amazement that Mrs. Pearce can have formed so erroneous an impression of him.

Mrs. Pearce returns. There is a dustman (refuse collector) asking to see Mr. Higgins. It is Alfred Doolittle, Eliza's father, who had learned her whereabouts from a boy who accompanied her there in a taxi; she had sent him back for some personal effects. Higgins correctly surmises that Doolittle wants money, and he deals with the situation by ordering the man to take his daughter away at once. Doolittle isn't prepared for this tactic. He has brought Eliza's luggage, but she had told the boy she didn't want any clothes, and what is a father to make of that? But if Doolittle brought the rest of Eliza's things, Higgins points out, he must have expected her to

stay. He says that Doolittle and Eliza have concocted a plot to ex-
tort money from him, and goes to the phone to call the police. Doolittle backs down, and Higgins rings for Mrs. Pearce, telling her to
turn Eliza over to her father.

But Doolittle wants to strike a deal, and Mrs. Pearce goes out
again. Doolittle asks Higgins for five pounds in trade for the girl.
When Pickering remarks that Higgins' intentions are entirely honorable, Doolittle replies that if they weren't he'd ask fifty.

Higgins and Pickering protest the man's lack of morals. Doolittle explains that he is one of the undeserving poor, who must constantly struggle against the prejudices of middle-class morality.
Though his needs are as great or greater than those of the most deserving pauper, he is invariably refused any kind of charitable assistance. But he enjoys his status, and intends to go on being undeserving. Higgins is so taken with Doolittle's views and personality
that he offers him ten pounds. But Doolittle doesn't want that much.
More than five pounds would make him feel prudent, and he wants to
remain carefree. There is a reference to the woman with whom Doolittle is now living, and Pickering wants to know why he doesn't marry
her. Doolittle says that he'd like to, but the woman refuses. Married,
she would have no hold over him. As it is, he has to be agreeable
and buy her clothes and presents to induce her to stay.

As Doolittle starts to leave, Eliza and Mrs. Pearce enter the
room. Eliza, washed and combed, is wearing a Japanese kimono,
and at first her father doesn't recognize her. Eliza sees her hat, sits
grandly, and begins to talk about the wonders of the bathroom. Only
the mirror failed to meet with her approval. She considers it im-
modest. Doolittle tells Higgins to apply the strap if she doesn't behave. Eliza knows that he has come here only for money to get drunk
on, and they rail at each other. After he goes, she says they have
seen the last of him.

It is obvious that Eliza enjoys Colonel Pickering's little courtesies, and being called Miss Doolittle. She'd like to go back and put
the other flower girls in their place. Mrs. Pearce says that her new
clothes have come, and Eliza rushes out with shrill cries of joy.
Higgins and Pickering begin to realize the magnitude of the task
ahead.

Shaw here, in the current printed text, gives us a scene in
which Higgins is actually teaching the girl. His overbearing manner
reduces her to tears, but Pickering comforts and encourages her.

[] *In Brief*

Higgins now commits himself to the task of remaking a human being. The complication he is too blind or irresponsible to envision is foreshadowed in Mrs. Pearce's query about what is to become of the girl afterward. As will be seen, this is one of the most important elements in the play. On this consideration the last two acts are built almost entirely.

The long scenes with Doolittle, both in this act and later, are structurally unimportant, but they are carried by the brilliance of the dialogue and characterization, and by the wonderful role for an actor that Shaw has provided.

ACT THREE

The setting is the drawing room of Higgins' mother.

It is Mrs. Higgins' At Home day. A cultivated lady of commanding presence, she is awaiting her callers. Higgins bursts into the room, to his mother's annoyance. He would like to ask a favor. There is a young woman—and Mrs. Higgins, interrupting, hopes that at last her son has fallen in love, and with somebody under forty-five. But Higgins doesn't care for young women; they are all idiots. He could become seriously interested only in an older woman—someone like his mother. This subject is not pursued.

Will Mrs. Higgins receive this afternoon a common young woman that he has been teaching to speak properly? He tells of the wager and of Eliza's progress. Already her accent is that of a lady, he says, but what she says still reflects her background. However, Higgins is sure that Miss Doolittle will not disgrace herself, as she has been ordered to confine her conversation to just two topics—the weather and people's health.

Mrs. and Miss Eynsford Hill come to call. Higgins greets them perfunctorily. Pickering arrives, then Freddy, and Higgins does little to conceal his boredom with the Eynsford Hill family. Clara remarks that she has no small talk, and wishes people would say what they really think. Higgins shudders at the idea.

Eliza arrives—poised, beautiful, and exquisitely gowned. She is introduced, and Freddy and his mother feel sure they have met somewhere before. Freddy is instantly infatuated. Eliza's speech is flawlessly correct, but overarticulated. Higgins, making no effort at polite conversation, stumbles over furniture, curses, and behaves in general like a bull in a china shop.

Mrs. Higgins, making conversation, asks whether it will rain, and Eliza, to everyone's amazement, offers her opinion in the words of an extended weather report, such as those that appear in the papers. Freddy is enchanted. His mother hopes it will not turn cold—so much influenza about. At this point Eliza launches into a detailed account of illnesses among her relatives, and her conviction that her aunt was murdered for her new straw hat. As the others sit open-mouthed at this recital, Higgins interposes that this is the new small talk. Eliza continues with a lively defense of liquor as an aid to the contented life.

Higgins signals Eliza that it is time to leave, and she rises. Freddy asks if he may walk across the park with her. But Eliza is not walking, not bloody likely. She goes down to her cab, leaving the others gasping. There is a brief discussion of the decline of manners. Clara finds the new small talk delightful, and, as the Eynsford Hills prepare to go, she says Victorian prudery is bloody nonsense. Freddy and Clara go on ahead, and in a confidential moment with Mrs. Higgins we learn from Mrs. Eynsford Hill that the family is in quite straitened circumstances. She goes.

Pickering and Higgins now ask if Eliza isn't presentable, and Mrs. Higgins quickly disillusions them. The girl is a triumph of the phonetician's and the dressmaker's art, but, of course, she gives herself away by what she says. And it hardly seems likely that Eliza will grow in refinement so long as she is in Higgins' care. Higgins is puzzled and offended, but his mother silences him, and starts to question Pickering about the situation under which Eliza is living and learning. The two men paint an enthusiastic picture of their fascinating experiment. They are both working very hard to transform Eliza, and she, for her part, helps Mrs. Pearce and keeps track of Higgins' appointments.

Mrs. Higgins asks what is to happen to Eliza afterward, once she has been given the manners and habits of a lady, without the means of living as a lady must. Higgins is inclined to dismiss this as so much quibbling. They will find some light employment for her somewhere, he says. The men leave. Mrs. Higgins is totally exasperated.

An interpolated scene here shows Higgins, Pickering, and Eliza arriving at an embassy reception. Everyone's eyes are on Eliza, gowned and jeweled to perfection.

A bearded young man named Nepommuck, a Hungarian linguist and former student of Higgins', is present to interpret for foreign guests. He claims the same skill as Higgins in his ability to determine people's origins by their accents. Soon he is reporting to his hostess that Eliza is a fraud. In spite of her name she cannot be English. Only foreigners have been taught to speak so well. She is Hungarian, undoubtedly of royal blood. When he spoke to her in that language she pretended not to understand him. Higgins ventures the opinion that she is English, an ordinary London girl taught to speak by an expert.

Eliza, tired and feeling the strain, wants to leave. She believes she has failed the test, but Pickering tells her she has won the wager ten times over. They go.

[]   *In Brief*

Act Three presents Eliza in transition, with Higgins making progress but encountering the not fully foreseen obstacle of the girl's lack of educational background. The comedy implicit in the contrast between what she says and the way she says it is exploited hilariously. And the complication of what is to be done with her afterward is explicitly set forth.

The interpolated scene at the embassy presents the actual achievement of passing Eliza off as an aristocrat, and if the play were solely concerned with Higgins' winning of his bet, this would be the major climax. But, as the author has been careful to make us understand, Higgins has involved himself in a responsibility to Eliza after the bet has been won. It is this factor that carries us into the next act.

ACT   FOUR

The scene is Higgins' laboratory again. Midnight.

Higgins, Pickering, and Eliza, in all her finery, arrive home after the embassy reception. The men are tired, Eliza brooding and silent. Higgins wonders where his slippers are. Eliza brings them, but he is quite unaware of this little service. The slippers could as well have appeared by magic.

Pickering congratulates Higgins on having won his bet. Higgins thanks God his ordeal is over. This has been a tiresome, boring day. In fact, the whole idea of the wager was silly. He should have chucked it long ago. However, tonight he can go to bed without dreading the morrow. Still, Pickering observes, it has been a real triumph for Higgins. He goes.

Higgins tells Eliza to put out the lights, and, without a word of appreciation for her part in his accomplishment, he leaves the room. Eliza is clearly ready to explode, and when he returns momentarily to get his slippers, she throws them at him.

What's wrong? Higgins wants to know. Eliza ferociously tries to claw him. He's won his bet, but she doesn't matter. She wishes he'd left her in the gutter. What is to become of her now? Higgins makes her admit that she has not been mistreated here. Now she is free and can do what she likes. Eliza asks what she is fit for, where she is to go. Higgins tells her to stop worrying. She can probably marry somebody—not all men are confirmed bachelors like himself and the colonel. In fact, Eliza can be quite attractive when she hasn't been crying and making herself ugly. He imagines that his mother can find some chap to marry her.

Eliza replies scathingly that the flower girls sold only flowers. They were above selling themselves. Higgins, unruffled, says that perhaps Pickering could set her up in a florist's shop.

Eliza's manner turns suddenly formal. She wants to know whether her clothes belong to her or to Colonel Pickering. The astonished Higgins wants to know why she asks. Eliza replies that she doesn't want to be accused, when she goes, of stealing anything. Higgins tells her to take the whole damn houseful of clothes—all except the jewels. They have been rented. Eliza hands over the jewels; she doesn't want any of them to turn up missing. She also gives Higgins a ring that he had bought for her in Brighton. She doesn't want it any more. Higgins, smarting badly under the girl's attack, dashes the ring into the fireplace. He towers over her threateningly. "Don't you hit me!" she cries. This is too much. He slams out, damning everything and everybody, including himself for ever having spent his talents on a heartless guttersnipe.

Eliza picks up the ring, flings it down again, and goes out raging.

An interpolated sequence now takes us to Eliza's bedroom, where she changes to street clothes, then leaves the house. Outside, on the street, she runs into Freddy, who has been gazing up at her window. He admits that he spends his nights here. He kisses her. A constable asks them to move on.

Some distance away they stop again to embrace and make love. Finally they take a taxi. They will drive around all night, and in the morning Eliza will go to Mrs. Higgins for advice.

[]　*In Brief*

Once the wager has been won, the question of what is to become of Eliza comes to the fore. As the girl realizes the seriousness of the problem and Higgins, characteristically, does not, the teacher-pupil relationship quickly dissolves in a fury of recrimination. Eliza, with her new awareness, knows where Higgins is weak and how to avenge herself for the weeks of overbearing behavior to which she has been subjected. She definitely has the upper hand at the end of the act— she has made him lose his temper. But the question of her future is still unsettled. There has been a hint that Higgins himself might be in love with Eliza. The violence of his reaction to her attack suggests that he is not totally immune to her charms. Will there be a reconciliation?

The new sequence with Freddy suggests a way out of Eliza's dilemma, and points to a romantic ending if Higgins does not marry her. We are concerned to know whether it will be Freddy or Higgins.

ACT FIVE

The scene is Mrs. Higgins' drawing room. Next morning.

A maid informs Mrs. Higgins that her son and Colonel Pickering are downstairs, phoning the police. Mrs. Higgins asks her to go upstairs and tell Miss Doolittle not to come down until she is sent for.

Higgins bursts into the room, informing his mother that Eliza has disappeared. Mrs. Higgins takes the news calmly, and says that the girl has a right to leave if she wants to. Pickering enters, reporting that the police, instead of being co-operative, appear to suspect him and Higgins of some improper conduct.

The maid announces that a Mr. Doolittle is asking to see Professor Higgins, having been sent on here from the other house. The maid describes him as a gentleman, not a dustman, and Higgins thinks it must be some other relative of Eliza's to whom she has gone for help. But it is Eliza's father who enters. He is formally and fashionably dressed, complete to silk hat and boutonniere. He immediately launches into recriminations: Higgins has delivered him into the hands of middle-class morality. It seems that Higgins, in correspondence with an American millionaire, the founder of a league for moral reform, had mentioned that one Alfred Doolittle was the most original moralist in England. The millionaire, in his will, has bequeathed Doolittle a considerable income, on condition that he deliver a series of lectures to Moral Reform Societies.

It isn't the lecturing that Doolittle minds; it's being made into a gentleman. As a dustman he was happy and free. Now everybody is trying to borrow money from him; lawyers and doctors squeeze him for fees; suddenly he has fifty penniless relatives and responsibilities. Now he has to live for others instead of himself. He will doubtless even have to come to Higgins to learn to speak properly. And he expects to find Eliza back on his doorstep as soon as she learns that he has money.

Mrs. Higgins tells him he needn't accept the bequest, but Doolittle admits he hasn't the nerve to refuse it. Unfortunately, the prospect of an income has shoved him into the middle class, with its concern for the future. Happiness for Doolittle is gone forever.

Now that Doolittle can provide for her, Mrs. Higgins says, the problem of Eliza's future is solved. Higgins protests. He paid five pounds for the girl, he says, and he won't have her going back to her father now. At this point Mrs. Higgins reveals that Eliza is upstairs, and has told her all about the brutal way she has been treated. Higgins and Pickering are shocked at being thus maligned, but Mrs. Higgins goes on. She knows how they behaved after Eliza's triumph at the embassy reception—not a word of appreciation, just how bored they were, how glad their trials had ended. Mrs. Higgins says she wouldn't have thrown the slippers—she'd have thrown the fire irons. Eliza will never go back to them, she reports; but the girl is willing to let bygones be bygones. Reluctantly Higgins promises to behave himself if Eliza comes down, and Mrs. Higgins asks Doolittle to step outside on the balcony for a moment, which he does.

Eliza enters, completely at ease, and flabbergasts the men by her cool and formally correct manner. Furiously Higgins demands that she stop that game and come home at once. Eliza pays no attention to him, but hopes that Colonel Pickering won't drop her, now that the experiment is over. It was from him that she learned manners. If she'd had only the example of Professor Higgins, she'd never have known how to control her temper or behave properly. Of course, Higgins taught her to speak, but that is his profession. It was like learning to dance. Her real education began that first day, when Colonel Pickering called her Miss Doolittle. And there were his many little courtesies. The real difference between a lady and a flower girl isn't in the way she behaves, but how she's treated. She will always be a flower girl to Higgins, because that's how he always treated her and how he always will. She would like Colonel Pickering to call her Eliza now, and Higgins to address her as Miss Doolittle. To Pickering's dismay, she says she will not go back to them, at which Higgins roars that without him she will be back in the gutter in three weeks. But Eliza won't relapse. She can't go back. She's even forgotten the language of the gutter.

At this moment she catches sight of her immaculately groomed father coming into the room, and proves that she hasn't forgotten gutter sounds after all. Doolittle admits that he has come into some money, but the reason he is all dressed up is that he's getting married today. Eliza is shocked—marry that common woman! Pickering wants to know why the woman changed her mind about marriage, and Doolittle replies that respectability has intimidated her and broken her spirit. Eliza agrees to come to the wedding, and leaves the room to get her hat. Doolittle admits it's the first time for him. He wasn't married to Eliza's mother—but asks them not to tell Eliza. Pickering says he'll come to the wedding too, and so does Mrs. Higgins, who leaves to change as Eliza returns. Eliza will go with her in the carriage; Colonel Pickering had better go ahead with the bridegroom.

Pickering hopes that Eliza will forgive Higgins and come back. Doolittle observes that, if the two men hadn't been so clever as to chaperone each other, Eliza could probably have captured one of them. He goes, followed by Pickering. Higgins and Eliza are alone together.

Eliza tries to leave the room, but he stops her. She says he only wants her back to fetch and carry for him. He replies that he hasn't said he wanted her back at all. It is clear that he does, however—on his own terms. He insists that he treats everyone alike. He hasn't singled her out for special rudeness. But he also confesses, rather humbly, that he has grown accustomed to her voice and appearance and that they do not displease him. Well, he has her voice on the gramophone, Eliza replies, and her face in photographs. He can turn to those when he misses her. They don't have feelings.

But these aren't Eliza, and he wants the real girl. She has become a part of his life. She should come back for the sake of good fellowship, for the fun of it. And get thrown out tomorrow, Eliza asks. She is free to walk out herself, Higgins points out. She could go back to her father, or sell flowers. Or perhaps she'd like to marry Pickering. She wouldn't. Nor would she marry Higgins. Not that she hasn't had chances—Freddy wants to marry her.

Higgins has nothing but contempt for Freddy. Does Eliza want him to be as infatuated with her as that young fool? What Eliza wants from Higgins is kindness, friendship—nothing more. Higgins calls Eliza a fool too. If she's to be a lady she must stop expecting men to either worship her or beat her. He tells her to go marry some rich and sentimental oaf who will kiss her and kick her. That's all she can appreciate.

Ruefully Eliza says that she intends to accept Freddy's proposal, as soon as she can afford to support them both. At least Freddy loves her. Higgins explodes. What will she do? How will she earn enough to support them? By teaching phonetics, Eliza replies coolly. She knows just how to do it. Higgins himself had told her she had a finer ear for it than his own.

Higgins can hardly contain his fury now, and starts to hit her. She always knew he'd strike her someday, Eliza says. Suddenly she realizes she is free of his dominance, and Higgins that this creature of his fashioning has become a woman of spirit and independence. He likes her this way.

Mrs. Higgins returns, dressed to go to the wedding. Higgins isn't going. Eliza says she will not see him again, and bids him a very formal good-bye. Higgins ignores this and gives her some household instructions. But she has already taken care of the matters he mentions. Whatever will he do without her, Eliza asks, as she sweeps out.

The possibility of Eliza's marrying her son crosses Mrs. Higgins' mind. He, laughing uproariously, tells her that Eliza is going to marry Freddy.

[]   *In Brief*

Higgins, though he may not be aware of it himself, has apparently fallen in love with his creation, as Pygmalion did with Galatea. But he is proud and overbearing; she, proud and resentful. A successful marriage would require adjustments that neither seems likely to make. In their long last act scene together Eliza grows in awareness and stature, and Higgins betrays occasional signs of a new humility. Finally Eliza realizes that she need no longer be subservient, that she is independent of him, and Higgins is forced to admire this creature that has turned into a woman. Now perhaps they could be fitting mates, but their pride and old wounds will probably prevent it. (In his afterpiece Shaw specifically says that Eliza married Freddy, and that with money advanced by Pickering they opened a flower shop.)

As with Doolittle's earlier appearance, his second one is a

vastly amusing set piece, attached to the play but not an integral part of it. Structurally the main story would not be altered if Doolittle were cut out entirely.

Protagonist and Objective

Higgins is the protagonist. From a structural standpoint his objective is an extremely interesting one, for it demonstrates that in proceeding with an apparently simple objective the protagonist can involve himself in a course of action that must be pursued after the original objective has been achieved.

We are reminded again and again that the limited objective—to pass a flower girl off as a lady—is going to open larger questions. What is to be done with the girl afterward? She can't go back to being a flower girl. What will be her source of income? Higgins has a responsibility to her now. We see how attractive and appealing she is. Will Higgins fall in love with her? Will Pickering? Will Freddy? Would a marriage work with any one of them? As we watch the development of a woman of sensitivity and feeling, we realize that Higgins has molded a creature far different from the one he took out of the gutter. In other words, Higgins has started with one objective, and one clear but simple problem (simple for Higgins, anyway); suddenly he finds himself with major complications on his hands. The play cannot end until Eliza is no longer a problem for him.

Obstacles

As the objective is a complex one, so also are the obstacles. The simple goal of passing a flower girl off as a lady is made difficult by Eliza's uncouth speech and her lack of education. But, once that goal has been reached, these obstacles are no longer operative. Larger problems intrude. Higgins' reluctance to see them, much less to deal with them, sets up an external conflict with Eliza and with his mother, and an internal conflict within himself. He is drawn to Eliza, and yet is a confirmed bachelor. There is his rudeness, which deflects the affection Eliza feels for him. And there is the knotty problem of her future, for which Higgins must be held responsible. Eliza can no longer go back to her life as a flower girl, nor has she the means or position to live as a lady.

Crises and Climaxes, Theme

The crisis of the "flower girl into lady" strand of the play occurs during Shaw's interpolated scene at the embassy reception, when the Hungarian interpreter determines to learn who Eliza really is. This leads directly into a climax—her acceptance as an aristocrat. But neither this crisis nor this climax is the major one in the play.

The major crisis may be found at the beginning of Act Four, when it becomes clear that Higgins doesn't realize his responsibility for what he has done, and we realize Eliza's deep resentment of his attitude. This crisis will precipitate the major climax in the last act when Eliza, a real lady at last, declares her independence, and the tie that has bound them together is broken. Higgins has succeeded both in the limited objective—to pass Eliza off as a lady—and in the evolving one—to solve the problem of her future. He has inadvertently created a woman capable of living independently of him.

The main theme, evident at both climaxes just mentioned, is a satirical one suggesting the superficiality of class distinctions: the difference between a lady and a girl from the slums is primarily a matter of education, speech, and appearance. (This was doubtless a more iconoclastic view in the England of 1913 than it is today.) But Shaw, always generous with the riches of his mind, leaves us as well the observation that the difference between a lady and a flower girl may be less in her behavior than in how she is treated. He also suggests that the social graces require an income to support them. While set forth at various times during the play, all these ideas are implicit in the major climax.

Resolution

This is very brief. Mrs. Higgins wonders about the possibility of marriage between her son and Eliza, but Higgins, in his laughter, shows his relief in being rid of the girl, who has said she's going to marry Freddy.

Opening

Structurally Act One is unnecessary, for the story doesn't really get under way until Eliza comes to ask Higgins to teach her. But, even if the play were built to start with what is now Act Two, it would still be desirable to show us Eliza's background and to demonstrate Higgins' skill in phonetics. As Act One covers all this material very entertainingly, as well as establishing the relationship between Higgins and Pickering and introducing us to the Eynsford Hills, Shaw's decision to begin the play where he does seems entirely justified. It may be questioned, however, whether a less skillful dramatist could keep us absorbed in an entire act of what is essentially exposition.

Unity

None of the classic unities is observed—time, place, or action. (Doolittle's two long scenes are not an integral part of the play.)

Exposition

Act one repays careful study. It consists of a whole series of minor conflicts. Freddy can't find a cab. His mother and sister are unreasonable and impatient, and we become acquainted with the Eynsford Hill family in just a few broad strokes. Freddy bumps into Eliza, knocking her flowers into the mud, and Eliza, in all her squalor and vulgarity, is brought into focus.

Then we have Eliza's alarm when she learns that someone is writing down her words, and the hostility of the bystanders to the notetaker. Even Pickering is hostile before he knows who Higgins is. There is further conflict with Eliza as the two men leave. And finally, for a bit of rueful comedy, Freddy returns with a cab, only to find that his mother and sister have gone, and Eliza takes the cab. Nothing of real importance has happened (little to carry us into Act Two), and yet we know the major characters of the play, their backgrounds, and their relationship to one another.

Characterization

Shaw, as usual, has drawn his people with broad, sure strokes. He stops, however, this side of caricature. Each one is distinctly individualized. The humor arises from character and situation. There are no witticisms, such as we find in Wilde, or gags, as in Neil Simon's plays. If most of Shaw's people seem a bit larger than life, it is doubtless because they hold their convictions so passionately and express them so eloquently.

Higgins, wholly dedicated to his work, is rude and inconsiderate to a degree that makes it easy to believe his confirmed bachelorhood. (What woman would ever put up with him?) If Shaw had made Higgins as considerate as Pickering, he would have anticipated the problem of Eliza's future, and there would have been no conflict to carry the play through Acts Four and Five. As previously noted, it is also briefly hinted that a mother fixation contributes to Higgins' intolerance of young women.

Eliza, before her transformation, is eager, naïve, defensive, and quick-tempered. Her later behavior still reflects these traits, but they are modified by her training. She is still independent enough to defy Higgins and rise to the challenge of determining her own future.

Doolittle is one of Shaw's masterpieces of comic characterization. Accepted values are turned upside down in the dustman's philosophy, but he expounds it with such frankness, conviction, and sweet reason that audiences are captivated.

There is a slight inconsistency in the characterization of Pickering. After the men return from the embassy reception, Pickering is almost as indifferent to Eliza as Higgins is. On the strength of his earlier courtesy and consideration, one would think he'd know that the girl expected some attention now, and that he'd give it to her.

Development

Most of the scenes are constructed in the conventional manner, and, with the exception of the Doolittle episodes, which are thrust into the play quite arbitrarily, they lead naturally from one to the next. The first scene in Act Two has Eliza as its protagonist; her objective, to become a pupil of Higgins; obstacle, Higgins' disdain; climax, his decision to teach her; resolution, her acceptance as a pupil under conditions she had not foreseen.

This situation leads logically into the next scene, in which Higgins becomes the protagonist; his objective, to persuade the girl to stay; obstacles, the reluctance of Mrs. Pearce and Pickering to go along with the plan, and the girl's own fears; climax, Eliza's decision to stay; resolution, her defiance.

Doolittle is the protagonist of his scenes. In Act Two his objective is to get five pounds out of Higgins by pretending to be concerned for his daughter. The obstacle is Higgins' instant recognition of Doolittle's hypocrisy and true motive. In pursuit of his goal Doolittle defends his request for money and expounds his odd social and philosophical views. This brings Higgins around, and Doolittle gets his five pounds. The resolution is Doolittle's encounter with the scrubbed Eliza, and his advice to Higgins on how to handle her.

It might be noted that, while Eliza is the central figure in her scene in Act Three at Mrs. Higgins' home, she is not the protagonist. Higgins is. His objective is to test her speech and behavior among cultivated people. The obstacle is her lack of background as revealed in the subject matter of her conversation. Higgins overcomes this hurdle by suggesting that it is the new "small talk"; he achieves his objective with the Eynsford Hills, but not with his mother.

Dramatic Irony

The brilliantly comic scene in Act Three, in which Higgins tests Eliza's speech in his mother's drawing room, employs the device of dramatic irony. We know Eliza's background; the Eynsford Hills do not, though Freddy and his mother think they have met somewhere before. (We know where.) After Eliza has left, Mrs. Higgins takes it for granted that her son has no manners, and Higgins is puzzled. We know that his mother's assumption is correct.

In the interpolated scene at the reception, the Hungarian's conclusions about Eliza are played against our knowledge of who the girl really is.

In Act Four we can well understand why Eliza is resentful of her treatment by Higgins and Pickering, and why she throws the slippers—behavior that the men are too self-centered to comprehend.

We know, in Act Five, long before Higgins and Pickering do, that Eliza has come to Mrs. Higgins and is in the house then.

Preparation

The use of the adjective "bloody" is prepared by having Mrs. Pearce warn Higgins against using a vulgar expression in Eliza's presence that begins with *b*.

Doolittle's rejection of Higgins' offer of ten pounds instead of the five he asked for, on the grounds that such a large amount would make him prudent, foreshadows his distress later on inheriting a large income. In fact, Doolittle's entire second appearance is built as a contrast to the first. He has been living happily with a mistress; with an assured income he must marry the woman.

Eliza has been told to confine her conversation at Mrs. Higgins' home to the weather and people's health. Incredibly, that's what she does talk about, with such hilarious effect.

In the same scene Clara remarks that she has no small talk, thus establishing the term for Higgins to use when he says that Eliza's conversation is the new small talk.

Both Mrs. Higgins and Mrs. Pearce early bring up the problem of Eliza's future; as we have seen, this consideration is to modify the play's objective to such a degree that the last two acts are built upon it.

Activity

The play is full of inventive and splendidly telling activity. Freddy's knocking Eliza's flowers into the mud sets up the contrast of his attitudes toward the girl before and after her transformation. Higgins' identification of various bystanders by their accent alone, in the same scene, dramatizes his skill far better than any mere discussion of phonetics. His tempting Eliza with chocolates, in Act Two, and eating half of one himself to allay her suspicions, is fine illustrative activity.

Eliza's business with the slippers, in Act Four—first placing them out for Higgins, who doesn't notice the little favor, then throwing them at him—is even more significant than the business with the chocolates. A few minutes later Eliza hands Higgins the jewels she has been wearing, including the ring he gave her. Infuriated, he throws the ring in the fireplace. After he has left the room, she recovers the ring, then throws it away again. Her thoughts are effectively conveyed without words.

Dialogue

Shaw's people, educated or not, all know what they want, and are never at a loss for words with which to express themselves. They are, of course, not only the creations but the reflections of an exceptionally lively mind, brimming with intelligent fun. Hence the dialogue of all the characters is exuberant and acutely responsive. This universal articulateness tends to make Shaw's characters sound somewhat alike, but one is compensated by the pleasure of hearing passionately held and often unconventional views stated with such eloquence and humor.

Plausibility

Pygmalion's premise stretches credibility somewhat. But if we can accept the wager and even the remote possibility that Higgins' teaching can turn Eliza into a lady in a few months, then what follows is logical. (Though it hardly seems likely that even the most eccentric American millionaire would bequeath a large income to an English dustman he had never met or heard, on condition that he deliver a series of lectures to the millionaire's pet charity!)

But the play's rewards are so great that the audience willingly suspends its disbelief and accepts it all. It seems unlikely that a lesser dramatist than Shaw could get away with the play's improbabilities.

Note: The reader may at this point wish to turn ahead and examine *My Fair Lady,* while *Pygmalion* is still fresh in his mind.

SEAN O'CASEY

Juno and the Paycock

1924

O'Casey's early plays, of which this and *The Plough and the Stars* are the best known, are realistic in form. Later he abandoned realism, and became one of the most daring experimenters in the modern theatre.

Juno and the Paycock mingles broad humor with searing tragedy, and achieves a kind of poetry from the uncultivated speech of the Dublin slums. It is, incidentally, an actors' holiday for those capable of performing it.

The play was written for the proscenium theatre.

Premise

An indomitable woman is managing to maintain a home for her family, in spite of poverty, the shiftlessness of her husband, the mental and physical incapacity of her son, and the ignorance and lack of judgment characteristic of them all.

Synopsis

The entire action takes place in the living room of a two-room tenement flat. There are three acts, with an interruption in Act Three to indicate a lapse of time.

ACT ONE

Johnny and Mary, the grown son and daughter of the Boyle family, are on stage at rise as their mother, Juno, enters from shopping. Mary has been reading a newspaper account of the finding of the body of their neighbor, young Robbie Tancred, traitorously murdered in the course of the movement for political independence. Johnny cannot listen; he tells his sister to stop reading, and goes into the other room.

From Juno's conversation with Mary we gather that the situation for this poverty-stricken family is serious, with little prospect of improvement. Juno works to bring in a little money, but her husband, Jack, a strutting, idle braggart (hence his sobriquet, "the paycock"), prefers to spend his time in a nearby pub with his crony, Joxer. Mary is on strike in support of a discharged fellow worker. Johnny was shot in the hip during the 1916 Easter rebellion, and later lost an arm in street fighting. He is unable to work and is the prey of nameless fears.

Jerry Devine, a young labor leader and friend of the family, brings word of a possible job for Jack. Juno sends him to the pub, but feels sure that Jack will find some way of avoiding the job when he hears of it. Moments later the voices of Jack and Joxer are heard on the stairs, and Juno goes into the next room.

Jack and Joxer enter, looking about cautiously for Juno. Jack invites his pal to sit down for a cup of tea, remarking that the only comfort he enjoys is when Juno is away. She, having overheard it all, comes out of the bedroom, and sarcastically invites Joxer to make himself at home. Hastily, with Joxer's connivance, Jack improvises word of a job for which he intends to apply right after lunch. Joxer leaves.

Juno has not been deceived; she asks whether Jack met Jerry Devine outside. He didn't, but Jack is immediately suspicious. He says he'll go look for Jerry, but Juno isn't taken in by this maneuver either. She tells Jack to sit down and eat his breakfast—Jerry will be back. She produces some sausages; but Jack, offended, refuses to eat, and she puts the sausages away.

Jerry returns and tells Jack of the job opportunity. Jack is suddenly afflicted with pains in his legs. Juno views this ailment with crushing sarcasm, tells Jack to go change into his work trousers and apply for the job. Then she goes off to work.

Mary enters the living room. Jerry, who is in love with her, reproaches her for neglecting him in favor of another suitor. Mary tells him that it is true and that she no longer cares for him. Jack comes back in, and there are some angry words as he tries to fulfill the role of the concerned father. Mary and Jerry leave.

Jack sits down, vowing not to touch his breakfast. But hunger soon overcomes his wounded pride, and he sings a popular song as he fries the sausages and boils the tea. Joxer returns, now that Juno has gone.

There is a thundering knock at the street door. Johnny comes out of the next room in great alarm, and Jack peers out the window. It is a man in a trench coat. Fearfully Johnny goes back to his room, and the caller goes away.

Jack invites Joxer to share his breakfast. Joxer picks up a book of Mary's—three Ibsen plays. Jack expresses his contempt for such nonsense. Both men sit down; Jack pours two cups of tea, puts the grease and gravy on Joxer's plate, and keeps the sausages for himself. Jack tells Joxer of Jerry's visit, then complains of the pains in his legs. Gradually he builds a case for not going after the job at all. Soon he is talking of his experiences (imaginary) as a sea captain.

There are steps outside the door. It may be Juno returning. Jack tries to hide the breakfast things, and Joxer nearly jumps out the window in his haste to get away. But it is only a coal vender. Jack roars at him to get out, then declares that he won't let Juno bully him any longer. But now her voice is heard outside, and both men fly about as before. Joxer actually goes through the window to an adjoining rooftop. Jack hides the dishes as Juno enters. He denies that Joxer was here. Juno tells him to go change back into better trousers, and put on a collar and tie. A visitor is on his way here, with Mary, and he brings good news. As Jack goes to change, she discovers the remains of the two breakfasts.

Mary enters with Charlie Bentham, a young law student. Juno fusses about hospitably, calls Johnny in and introduces him, and urges Jack, in the next room, to hurry. Jack appears, uncomfortable in his best clothes; suspicious that Bentham is there to offer him a job, he starts describing the pains in his legs. But Bentham is there to read the will of a deceased relative who has left his cousin two thousand pounds.

Overjoyed, Jack tells Juno that from now on he is a new man. He's done with Joxer—and at this moment Joxer comes in through the window. Furiously ridiculing his pal's pretensions as a sea captain, he crosses the room and leaves. As the act ends Jack is clasping his wife's hand and singing a sentimental ballad.

[] *In Brief*

Very little happens in the first act to move the story forward until the arrival of Bentham. Our interest is chiefly held by the sharply drawn characterizations and by the comedy. (Jack and Joxer's breakfast scene is, in performance, hilarious.) But before the act ends there does occur a change in the basic situation, from the apparent hopelessness of the family's position to the sudden promise of affluence that would mean the solution of many of its difficulties.

ACT TWO

Two days later the flat has been decorated with paper streamers and artificial flowers, and refurnished with furniture bought on credit. Jack, half asleep on the sofa, jumps up and pretends to be very busy with various documents as Joxer arrives. Mrs. Madigan, a neighbor, has pawned some of her belongings to help tide the Boyle family over and has entrusted the money to Joxer, who has brought it here. Jack magnanimously tells Joxer to keep five bob for himself, and does his best to give the impression that he is now a man of weighty affairs and responsibilities. There is a suggestion that Mary will become engaged to Charlie Bentham. Jack insists that Bentham, who is studying law, will get no financial help from him. Joxer leaves.

Johnny comes into the room, and Juno and Mary arrive, bringing a gramophone bought on credit. As Juno arranges the table for tea, we learn that Johnny spends some of his nights at the home of an aunt or an uncle. He obviously lives in a state of fear.

Charlie Bentham arrives, and they all sit down to tea. Jack comments on trends in the stock market, and soon he and Bentham launch into a discussion of theosophy, about which Jack knows even less than he does about finance. The conversation shifts momentarily to ghosts, and suddenly there is an outburst from the fearful and overwrought Johnny, who thinks he sees the ghost of Robbie Tancred, the young neighbor and revolutionary patriot who was slain in ambush. Juno calms her son.

Joxer and Mrs. Madigan arrive, and in celebration of the family's good fortune a real party is soon under way, with music and singing and much laughter. Mary and Charlie are apparently in love, and Mrs. Madigan urges the match.

The mood changes suddenly as Mrs. Tancred comes down the hallway on the way to her son Robbie's funeral. In a deeply moving speech (to be repeated later by Juno when she loses her own son)

Mrs. Tancred appeals to Christ and the Virgin to "take away this murdherin' hate, an' give us Thine own eternal love!"

After Mrs. Tancred goes there is considerable talk about the young men who have lost their lives in the movement for Irish independence, and Johnny becomes upset. Mary and Bentham excuse themselves and go for a walk. An attempt is made to recapture the gaiety of the party. Jack recites a verse he has written, and they start playing the gramophone.

The door is opened by Nugent, the tailor, to remind them that the Tancred funeral procession is passing below. All except Johnny go down to the street.

A young man enters, ordering Johnny to appear at a battalion staff meeting. It is suspected that he knows something about who betrayed Tancred. Johnny protests that he won't go, says he has done enough for Ireland. From the street we hear the crowd chanting a "Hail Mary."

[]   *In Brief*

Forward movement in the act is slight, with little plot development. As in the first act it is often the humor of sharply drawn characterization, such as Bentham trying to explain his theosophist beliefs to Jack, that carries our interest.

Such change as exists is largely one of mood, as the euphoria of the early scenes is dissipated by our suspicion that Johnny is an informer, and by our apprehension for the family if the inheritance should fail to materialize. It is clear that they would be in far worse trouble than before.

ACT THREE

Two months later a mood of dejection hangs over the flat. Mary, who seems ill, tells her mother that Charlie Bentham has gone to England, leaving no address. Although she still loves him, she has had no word from him for a month. Mary thinks that maybe "we weren't good enough for him."

Juno is taking Mary to see a doctor. On the way out she urges Jack to go to the law office and try to get an advance on the inheritance. He protests that he can't keep going there morning, noon, and night. The money has not arrived.

Joxer comes into the flat with Nugent, the tailor. They don't see Jack, who is in the next room. Nugent says he has been to the lawyers' office to try to collect on a suit of clothes he had made for Jack, and has learned that due to a technicality in the will it is defective, and there will be no inheritance. When they discover that Jack is in the flat, Nugent goes into the bedroom and demands payment of seven pounds for the suit. Jack orders an overcoat, saying that will be thirteen pounds he owes the tailor. Nugent grabs the suit and flees. Joxer, meanwhile, pockets a bottle of stout that Juno had left for her husband.

Jack emerges, and Joxer pretends to know nothing of the tailor's having been here, or of the missing stout. Mrs. Madigan then comes in to demand payment of the money she advanced on her pawned articles, and when Jack can't pay her she makes off with the gramophone. Joxer also goes, jeering.

Johnny enters, followed by Juno, who has left Mary at her sister's. Juno tells the two men that Mary is pregnant, by Bentham. Jack and Johnny, who regard the situation as a disgrace to themselves, think Mary should be driven from the house. Juno tells them that if Mary goes she will go too. But Juno believes the situation not to be hopeless. When they get the money—and then Jack tells her that there will be no inheritance. He has known it for some time. Juno is stunned; Johnny, full of self-pity, turns on his father with furious invective. Jack calls Joxer down from upstairs, and together they leave for the pub.

Moving men arrive to take away the unpaid-for furniture, and proceed to strip the apartment. Mary comes in; Juno briefly explains this new crisis, and leaves to find Jack—perhaps he can stop the moving men.

Jerry, the young labor leader, arrives. He tells Mary that he still loves her, that he knows Charlie has left her but that he is willing to forget and hopes that she will marry him. Mary suspects that Jerry doesn't know the whole truth. When she reveals it he is horrified, though he tries to be sympathetic. But he is no longer willing to marry her. He goes. Mary, unable to bear Johnny's recriminations and the sight of the furniture being taken away, runs out.

Two armed men enter and drag Johnny off, screaming for mercy. He is to be executed for betraying Robbie Tancred. The curtain falls.

An hour later Juno and Mary are sitting in the nearly empty flat. They know that Johnny has been abducted, and Juno is in despair. Mrs. Madigan comes to say that the police have found a body they believe to be Johnny's, and Juno is needed to identify it. Mary bursts out that "there isn't a God, there isn't a God." Juno tells Mary they will let Jack "furrage for himself" from now on, that they will go to her sister's until Mary's confinement, and that then they will work together for the sake of the baby. Then, recalling the words of Mrs. Tancred when she lost her son, Juno goes off to her sad duty.

Moments later the door of the empty flat is opened, and Jack and Joxer, roaring drunk, come in. They talk some patriotic nonsense, and Jack, as the curtain falls, utters a malapropism that has become famous—"th' whole worl's in a terrible state o' chassis!"

[]   *In Brief*

As can be seen even in this outline, the plot elements of the last act, so carefully prepared in the first two, rush headlong to conclusion as one disaster after another overtakes the family. It should be noted too that the tempo and seriousness of the calamities increase as the act progresses. The effect of the play upon an audience, when well performed, is very powerful. This may be due in part to the slow early tempo and the gradual rush of events toward the end. In any case, O'Casey appears to have found the perfect structure for telling the story. One would not know where it could be strengthened.

Protagonist and Objective

Although there is no specific statement of objective, it is evident early in the first act that Juno, the wife and mother, is the protagonist. The family situation, as indicated in their relationships to one another, makes it clear that it is she who holds them together and that all her strength and spirit would be marshaled to protect them from disaster. She is an intensely sympathetic protagonist, whose hopes and fears can be shared by the audience.

Specific clues to Juno's objective are indicated in these lines from Act One: "Amn't I nicely handicapped with the whole o' yous! I don't know what any o' yous ud do without your ma." "I killin' meself workin', an' he sthruttin' about from mornin' till night like a paycock." "It ud be easier to dhrive you out o' the house than to dhrive you into a job. Here, sit down and take your breakfast—it may be the last you'll get, for I don't know where the next is goin' to come from." In Act Three she says to her son: "If you don't whisht, Johnny, you'll drive me mad. Who has kep' the home together for the past few years—only me? An' who'll have to bear the biggest part o' this throuble but me?" But we are well aware by now that what she says is true. It has been evident from the start. She fails, at the end, to achieve her objective.

Obstacles

Forces tending to break up the family are the shiftlessness of Juno's husband, Jack Boyle, who would far rather be drinking with his pal Joxer than working to help to support the family; the physical and mental disability of her son, Johnny, who is unable to work; and the waywardness of her daughter, Mary. The circumstances of both son and daughter worsen disastrously as the play develops. Johnny, whose constant state of terror betrays a secret guilt, is at first suspected of betraying a revolutionary comrade, and is finally kidnaped and executed for the deed. Mary, out on strike to protest the discharge of a fellow worker, throws over a decent and acceptable suitor who loves her for the young law student who brings the news of the inheritance. She is made pregnant and later abandoned by him. Few families could survive these repeated and terrible shocks.

In a larger sense all the obstacles derive from the basic ignorance characteristic of everyone in the play. Jack Boyle is too benighted to sense his responsibilities as a father, or to appreciate the problems faced by individual members of his family (witness his scorn of Mary's reading matter, followed by his total lack of sympathy and understanding when he learns that she is pregnant), too ignorant to hold any but the most menial kind of job. Juno doesn't know better than to permit the family to go deeply into debt before the inheritance is actually in hand. (Indeed, none of them senses the danger in this course.) Mary doesn't understand the significance of the labor movement in which she is involved, any more than Johnny understands the social upheaval in which he has participated or his responsibilities to his revolutionary comrades.

Crises and Major Climax, Theme

This is a story of cumulative misfortunes that overwhelm a family. Hence it isn't possible to designate as a major crisis a single spot in the play where the action can swing one way or the other. We are faced with a series of crises or turning points: the pattern of Jack's shiftlessness was set, of course, many years before the start of the play; Johnny's betrayal of Tancred also takes place before the play opens; Mary's acceptance of Bentham as a lover is not disclosed until Act Three; and the general ignorance and lack of judgment common to all the Boyles is a condition of their lives.

The climax, however, takes place on stage, as Juno fails to accomplish her objective. It is rather lengthy, for it is not one but a series of disasters that overtake and destroy the family. The climax reaches its peak when Juno, knowing that her son has been killed and realizing that she cannot ask the pregnant Mary to go through the ordeal of helping her to identify the body, repeats the words spoken earlier by Mrs. Tancred, the mother of the boy Johnny had betrayed: "What was the pain I suffered, Johnny, bringin' you into the world to carry you to your cradle, to the pains I'll suffer carryin' you out o' the world to bring you to your grave! Mother o' God, Mother o' God, have pity on us all! Blessed Virgin, where were you when me darlin' son was riddled with bullets, when me darlin' son was riddled with bullets? Sacred Heart o' Jesus, take away our hearts o' stone, and give us hearts o' flesh! Take away this murdherin' hate, an' give us Thine own eternal love!" With this speech she leaves the flat forever. The family unit has been shattered.

O'Casey was a man of strong social and political views, and the play illustrates the waste and degradation that are the result of poverty and ignorance. The author never preaches. Like Shaw, among others, he aimed to provide, first of all, an absorbing experience in the theatre, but the meaning of what he wrote is inescapable.

Resolution

Jack Boyle and Joxer return drunk to the empty flat, totally insensitive to the tragedy around them. Jack is uncaring and unaware of the hopeless future. Unlike Juno, who has grown in strength and understanding, he has not changed in any way. One can read into this, perhaps, O'Casey's comments on certain types of his countrymen.

Opening

The over-all pattern of the play is: poverty and shiftlessness, the promise of riches, disintegration when the riches fail to materialize. Obviously the point to begin the play is just before the news of the inheritance. Thus the poverty can be shown, and the family's joy on learning of the inheritance. This provides a contrast with their later disillusionment.

Since the author wants us to become only gradually aware of Johnny's betrayal of Robbie Tancred, he has properly made the actual betrayal an antecedent action.

Most important, the play begins at a time when the situation for the family as a unit, and for every member individually, is precarious and subject to drastic change, for better or worse.

Unity

The play, though held together by its theme, is not so tightly structured as it might have been. (In view of its force and stature few would regard this as a flaw.) There are digressions in which the author's aim seems to be pure hilarity, and the party scene almost turns into a vaudeville show.

The story of the retribution taken on Johnny for his betrayal of Tancred runs coincidentally in time with the main story of the vanishing inheritance, but neither plot line substantially affects the other. They simply run parallel. Mary's story, on the other hand, has been rather loosely woven into the inheritance story by having Bentham, who drew up the will, the man who becomes her lover. Juno is involved in the fortunes of all.

Exposition

Exposition, whenever needed, is handled with great skill, being so thoroughly embedded in conflict and character portrayal that we are not aware that the author is feeding us information. Consider, for example, the scene that opens the first act. Mary is reading aloud a newspaper account of the finding of Robbie Tancred's body. This so upsets Johnny that he has to leave the room. Juno prepares breakfast for the absent Jack, and, when Mary questions why her father can't get his own breakfast, we learn that Juno is afraid her husband will bring his cadging pal, Joxer, home with him. In a rather sharp exchange between mother and daughter we learn of Jack's unemployment, the family's poverty and indebtedness, and the fact that Mary is out on strike. Within two minutes of the opening of the play we know a great deal about this family, our sympathy has been guided toward Juno, and our curiosity aroused about them all. Yet nothing has "happened." It was all exposition, superbly done.

Characterization

Seldom do we encounter, on the stage, such fully rounded characters as Jack and Juno. They have no purely utilitarian speeches, as in so many plays, whose sole function is to move the plot along. Everything these two say or do reveals some facet of their personalities. In the theosophy scene with Bentham, for example, Jack never lets down his guard, and his obvious ignorance of the subject in contrast to his pretended familiarity makes for delightful comedy. Juno, who has no pretensions whatever, is frankly puzzled and mistrustful. In adversity we find equally characteristic responses. To protect Mary from her father, Juno leaves the girl at her sister's until after she has broken the news of the pregnancy. She knows quite well how Jack will react. And Jack, instead of showing any sympathy or understanding for his wife, let alone his daughter, chooses this moment to break the news of the loss of the inheritance—surely the act of a very callous man.

Johnny, Mary, and the others are not so fully drawn, but they are, after all, secondary to the principals. Joxer is a marvelously comic invention. He and Fluther Good, of *The Plough and the Stars,* are worth careful study by anyone interested in character comedy.

Development

Just as O'Casey's humor and invention permit a rather loosely organized structure, so they enable him to dispense with the more conventional pattern in building his individual scenes. (Though it must be quickly noted that all the scenes fit into the larger framework of the play.)

The scene in Act Three, when Jerry comes back and asks Mary to marry him, does follow a conventional structure: protagonist, Jerry; objective, to obtain Mary's consent to their engagement; obstacle, Mary's pregnancy; climax, Jerry's refusal when he learns of the pregnancy; resolution, Mary's sadness as she ruefully recites the verses Jerry had included in a lecture on "Humanity's Strife with Nature."

Dramatic Irony

The device is employed occasionally during the play, most notably in Act Three:

> *Joxer (to Nugent, the tailor)*: An' you really think there's no money comin' to him afther all?
> *Nugent*: Not as much as a red rex, man; I've been a bit anxious this long time over me money, an' I went up to the solicitor's to find out all I could—ah, man, they were goin' to throw me down the stairs. They toul' me that the oul' cock himself had the stairs worn away comin' up afther it, an' they black in the face tellin' him he'd get nothin'. Some way or another that the will is writ he won't be entitled to get as much as a make!

From this moment on the audience knows there is no inheritance, but Juno, Mary, and Johnny do not know. The device ends sometime later when Juno and Johnny hear the truth in this exchange:

> *Mrs. Boyle*: But, Jack, when we get the money . . .
> *Boyle*: Money—what money?
> *Mrs. Boyle*: Why, oul' Ellison's money, of course.
> *Boyle*: There's no money comin' from oul' Ellison, or anyone else. Since you've heard of wan throuble, you might as well hear of another. There's no money comin' to us at all—the will's a wash-out!
> *Mrs. Boyle*: What are you sayin', man—no money?
> *Johnny*: How could it be a wash-out?
> *Boyle*: The boyo that's afther doin' it to Mary done it to me as well. The thick made out the will wrong; he said in the will, only first and second cousin, an' now anyone that thinks he's a first cousin or second cousin to oul' Ellison can claim the money as well as me, an' they're springin' up in hundreds, an' comin' from America and Australia, thinkin' to get their whack out of it, while all the time the lawyers is gobblin' it up, till there's not so much as ud buy a stockin' for your lovely daughter's baby!
> *Mrs. Boyle*: I don't believe it, I don't believe it, I don't believe it!

Briefer uses of dramatic irony occur on the first entrance of Jack and Joxer, who do not know, as does the audience, that Juno is in the flat. And in Act Three, when Joxer pretends ignorance of the tailor's making off with Jack's suit, the audience knows that Joxer was present, and that Joxer, furthermore, is responsible for the theft of a bottle of stout, for which Jack is blaming the tailor.

Preparation

There is plenty of preparation for Johnny's abduction at the end of the first scene of Act Three—most notably the knocking at the street door by the man in the trench coat, and Johnny's imagining he sees the ghost of Robbie Tancred.

A very effective bit of preparation is Mrs. Tancred's brief appearance on her way to her son's funeral. Juno, near the end of the play, uses the same words when she is called to identify Johnny's body.

Activity

Two very funny pieces of stage business occur in Act One: the division of the breakfast, with Jack getting the sausages and Joxer the grease; then their trying to hide the breakfast so that Juno won't see it.

Later in the play we find the tailor taking Jack's suit back, Mrs. Madigan carrying off the gramophone, and finally the moving men taking out the furniture. We see as well as hear what happens when the money isn't forthcoming.

Dialogue

O'Casey has few peers in the writing of trenchant dialogue. Every line characterizes the speaker as well as fulfilling its other intended functions—exposition, conflict, or whatever. The speeches are full of emotion and humor as well, poetic in their rhythm and imagery, and superbly aural. These lines are intended to be spoken and heard, rather than read. It may be questioned whether so much phonetic spelling was necessary to capture the Dublin accent on the printed page. But it is the effect in the theatre that counts, and here the dialogue cannot be faulted.

Effects

The play calls on no theatrical resources beyond those of ordinary realistic treatment. This is not true of O'Casey's later plays.

Plausibility

Characterization has been so rich, consistent, and complete throughout the play that one never questions the probability, even the inevitability, of the events. They seem to spring from the deepest roots of character, formed, or perhaps malformed, by poverty and ignorance. Given the people O'Casey has drawn, one can hardly imagine a different course of events than those presented. It is the author's consummate skill in making his story seem to flow from the characters (rather than having the characters controlled by events) that gives the work its impact in the theatre.

EUGENE O'NEILL

Desire Under the Elms

1924

Few modern plays of any country have achieved the tragic stature of this one, and the work has lost none of its distinction since it burst upon an American public then accustomed mainly to machine-made comedies and romantic claptrap. The struggle it depicts is timeless, the emotion generated is overpowering, the events it sets in motion lead to an inevitable end. These are the hallmarks of genuine tragedy.

Some are inclined to place *The Iceman Cometh* or *Long Day's Journey into Night* as greater plays. But whatever claims may be made for these two works, it can hardly be denied that both are inordinately long, and give an impression of overwriting and repetitiveness. *Desire Under the Elms,* on the other hand, is all muscle and grace and symmetry. It is certainly one of the finest plays ever written by an American.

The play was intended for the proscenium theatre.

Premise

Ephraim Cabot, a hard-bitten farmer of 76, marries a young, attractive, and passionate woman. He has two older sons by his first marriage, men in their late thirties, and another son, Eben, about 25, by a second marriage. All three sons hate their father for his grasping ways, and realize that he intends to cheat them of their inheritance, the farm. Abbie, the new wife, has married not for love but solely to have security and a home of her own.

Synopsis

The single setting shows a New England farmhouse, yard, and porch, shaded by elms. With the removal of the siding, four rooms can be revealed, separately or in any combination: the kitchen, parlor, and two upstairs bedrooms. The action moves from one location to another without awkward changes of scene, and frequently takes place in more than one location simultaneously. The time is 1850.

The play is in three parts (or acts) of four scenes each.

PART ONE

[] *Scene One*

We see the exterior of the house. It is sunset of a day in summer.

Eben comes out on the porch and rings the dinner bell. He is a good-looking young man, with a trapped, resentful manner. He goes inside as his two older half-brothers, Simeon and Peter, come from the fields. Peter says there is gold in California, fortunes to be picked up off the ground, instead of stones. They are tempted to make the long trek west, but that would mean giving up their right to the farm, on which they have labored for so many years. Eben, in the window, stands listening.

Their father has been gone for two months. He drove off without saying where he was going or why. Maybe he is dead. Eben breaks in and says he prays that his father is dead. The other two shoulder their way in to supper.

[] *Scene Two*

Twilight falls, and the kitchen is now visible.

The three brothers sit down to eat. Simeon and Peter are somewhat shocked that Eben prays for their father to die. Eben retorts that they want to see him dead too; anyway, he disowns his father. Every drop of his blood comes from his mother. The older men concede that their stepmother had been good to them. Eben maintains that their father killed her through overwork, just as he is driving the three of them.

Eben taunts the others about going to California. It's too far to walk and they haven't the money to get there any other way. In any case, they'd never give up their chance of inheriting the farm.

Eben insists that the farm belonged to his mother, and is rightfully his. And why, Eben wants to know, didn't the older boys help protect his mother from old Cabot's slave-driving? After her death, when he was fifteen, Eben took over her work—the cooking and the household chores. Now he can appreciate what she has done for them all. He feels that her spirit is still in the house, close to him. One day he will tell his father what he thinks of the way his mother was treated.

Simeon and Peter discuss their father's mysterious departure—the way he ordered the boys back to their plowing as he drove off in the buggy, singing hymns and shouting that he'd live to be 100. They should have stopped him. Eben remarks scornfully that their father is stronger than both of them put together. Then he puts on his coat and says he's going to the village. Simeon and Peter assume that he intends to pay a visit to the local prostitute, and jeer that they have both been with Min too, and their father before them. Violently Eben storms out of the house. The brothers remark how like his father he is. Then they head for bed, dreaming of California.

Eben stands outside, looking at the stars. In the warm night his mood changes, and he strides off to enjoy Min's favors.

[]   *Scene Three*

Just before dawn Eben makes his way back to the house and up to the bedroom where Simeon and Peter are sleeping. He wakens them and, laughing bitterly, passes on a bit of news he has heard in the village: their father has married again—a pretty woman much younger than himself. All three men are angry and dismayed, for now the new wife will inherit the farm.

Simeon and Peter think that now there is little reason for them to stay here. They should go to California. Eben, pulling a document from his pocket, says he'll give them three hundred dollars apiece if they will sign it. With the money they can buy passage on a boat to California. The agreement provides that they assign their claim to the farm to Eben. And where did Eben get six hundred dollars? It's money old Cabot hid many years ago, and Eben knows where. His mother told him before she died. Simeon and Peter want to think over the proposition.

Defiantly Eben says that he spent the night with Min. Maybe Min was his father's once, but now she is his. Simeon jeers that perhaps he'll want to make the new stepmother his own too, but Eben expresses nothing but hatred and contempt for the woman who has come to take his mother's place and steal the farm—his mother's farm—from him. He goes down to prepare breakfast.

Simeon and Peter decide to wait till they see if the report of the new wife is true before making a decision. Meanwhile, they'll do no more work on the farm. Simeon hopes she's a devil who will make life hell for old Cabot.

[] *Scene Four*

It is dawn. The kitchen and the exterior of the house are visible.

The three men are finishing breakfast. Eben believes that his father and the bride are due to arrive at any moment. Mechanically the older men start out to begin the chores, then remember their decision not to do any more work and sit down again. Startled, Eben asks if this means they're going to sign the agreement. They say they are thinking of it. Meanwhile, Eben is the sole farm hand. He'd better go milk the cows. Exultantly Eben says the farm once more belongs to his mother and him, and he leaves. Outside, he gazes around at the property possessively, then goes off toward the barn.

In the kitchen Simeon and Peter light their pipes, put their feet up on the table, and reach for a jug of whiskey. They drink to the gold in California. But idleness soon makes them uncomfortable, and they go outside. Thirty years of their lives are buried in this land. California promises freedom from slavery. Soon they are wondering how Eben is getting along with the milking. The cows don't know Eben. They start toward the barn as Eben hurries toward them. He has seen his father's buggy approaching on the road. There was a woman on the seat beside the old man.

Angrily Simeon and Peter run upstairs to fetch their belongings. Eben goes to the kitchen, pulls up a floorboard, and brings out a small bag of gold pieces. When the brothers come down he counts out six hundred dollars. They take the money and sign the agreement, say good-bye, and go outside. Eben remains in the kitchen.

Looking off toward the barn, Simeon and Peter see their father unhitching the horse. The two brothers are unnaturally merry, and decide to wait long enough to see what the bride is like. They pull the gate off its hinges, for spite and good luck.

Cabot and Abbie appear. He is 75, gaunt and powerful; she is about 35, buxom, vital, and sensual. Cabot says they are home, and Abbie repeats the word. She can hardly believe it's really hers. Cabot asks his two elder sons why they are not working, and Simeon replies ironically that they're waiting to welcome him and his bride home. Cabot introduces them to their new mother. The men regard her contemptuously. Abbie starts inside—she wants to see her new house. Peter calls that she'd better not call it her house in front of Eben. Cabot tells her that Eben is a fool, to pay him no heed. As Abbie goes in he orders the brothers back to work. Exultantly they laugh and dance, and tell him they're going to California. Cabot thinks they've gone mad. The brothers pick up stones and send them crashing through the parlor window. In a fury Cabot chases them off the property, and we hear their voices singing about California as they retreat down the road.

Abbie leans out of one of the upper windows and asks if this is her bedroom. Cabot replies that it's their bedroom, and a look of aversion crosses her face. She shuts the window. It suddenly occurs to Cabot that the brothers may have poisoned the stock, and he runs off toward the barn.

Abbie comes into the kitchen and introduces herself to Eben. She says she doesn't intend to play mother to him. She hopes they'll be friends. Perhaps she can make things easier for him with his father. Eben tells her to go to the devil. She replies calmly that she understands his resentment—a stranger coming in and taking his mother's place. Abbie lost her own mother, too, as a girl. She's worked hard for other people, to earn a living. Once she married, but her baby and husband both died and she was forced to work again as a servant. Then she met Eben's father. Eben retorts that Cabot then bought her, like a harlot. Her price was the farm, his mother's farm, his farm now. What if she did marry to get a home, Abbie asks. Why else would she marry an old man? Eben says he'll tell his father she said that; Abbie replies that she'll say he lies, and his father will drive him off the place. This is her home now, her kitchen, her bedroom. Once more she asks that they be friends. In a fury Eben brushes her aside and rushes out the door. Abbie looks after him with a smile and remarks to herself that he is nice. She starts washing the dishes.

Eben, in the yard, comes on his father, who has meanwhile returned from the barn. Cabot stands watching the road down which the two older brothers are marching. He shouts a curse after them. Eben mocks him, and Cabot turns on him viciously. Why isn't he at work? Eben says he can't work the place all by himself. Together they start toward the barn as the strains of the California song are heard from the distance.

[]   *In Brief*

The first act is largely given over to exposition, preparation, and characterization, carried by the minor conflict between the two elder brothers and the younger one, and the play is slow in getting under way. But there is such a sense of foreboding in the first three scenes that our attention is held in spite of their static nature. With the arrival of Cabot and Abbie in I-4 the important conflicts begin and the play is set upon its course to disaster.

PART TWO

[]   *Scene One*

We see the exterior of the house, on a Sunday afternoon two months later.

Abbie sits in a rocker on the porch. Eben looks out of an upstairs window; she senses his presence. Eben comes outside, neatly dressed and groomed; their eyes meet, then he starts toward the road. Abbie laughs, taunting him. He turns on her, but she tells him not to try to deny that he is attracted to her. Eben is defiant: she is a schemer, bent on getting possession of all that is his. But he intends to fight her.

Seductively Abbie asks if he isn't on his way to see Min. Why does he want to waste time on her? Eben retorts that at least Min is not a hypocrite. Furiously Abbie orders him off the place, or she'll have old Cabot drive him off with a horsewhip. Saying that he hates the sight of her, Eben strides off.

Cabot comes from the barn, asks what they were quarreling about. Abbie doesn't tell him, but jeers that Cabot is getting soft. He admits feeling his age, but she has no sympathy for him. He remarks that the house is lonesome and cold, while the barn is warm and friendly. He seems to regret that Eben is his only heir. When Abbie reminds him that he has a lawful wife, the old man grows amorous and quotes from the *Song of Solomon*. Abbie pulls away, asks if he intends to leave the farm to Eben. Cabot replies that he'd like to burn down the farm when he dies; the cows and Abbie he'd turn loose.

Abbie is furious. So Eben, who hates him, will get the farm while she is turned out on the road. Vindictively she tells the old man that Eben tried to make love to her, and when she repulsed him went off to see Min. That's what the quarrel was about.

Cabot, raging, says he'll shoot Eben, and Abbie is frightened. Now she tries to make light of the matter. Eben was only joking, and she lost her temper at the thought of his inheriting the farm. She pleads with the old man not to drive Eben away—he is needed to help on the place.

Cabot doubts that Eben is capable of running the farm by himself, and, as for Abbie, she's just a woman. If only he had a son, then the farm would still be his, even after death. Abbie looks at him craftily, and with loathing. But she says that maybe the Lord will give them a son. Cabot is startled; Abbie says she prays for it to happen. It's not impossible, even at his age. Overwhelmed, Cabot says there is nothing he wouldn't do for her if she'd bear him a son— will the farm to her—anything. He falls to his knees and begins to pray. Abbie regards him with a scornful smile.

[]   *Scene Two*

We see into the two bedrooms. It is early evening. Eben is in one room, half dressed, and Abbie and Cabot in the other, in night clothes.

Cabot is in a strangely excited mood. He and the farm need a son. Abbie tells him to go to sleep. In the next room Eben stretches his arms toward the dividing wall. Abbie seems to sense this, and watches the wall fixedly.

Cabot talks at some length about his life. He came here fifty years ago, and people thought he'd never be able to turn such rocky soil into a farm. Discouraged after a couple of years, he joined a party going to the western plains, but God told him to return home, and he came back and piled the stones up into walls around his fields. He was always lonesome, even after marrying his first wife. After she died he married Eben's mother, whose folks were contesting his deed to the land. Her death left him more lonely than ever. The boys all coveted the farm and hated him. Then he found Abbie. Suddenly he realizes that Abbie hasn't been listening. To placate him she promises that she will bear him a son. How can she promise, he wants to know. Profoundly troubled and uneasy, he says he's going down to the barn to sleep, where it's warm and restful. We see him outside, before he plods off, raising his arms to heaven in a baffled appeal for help.

Abbie and Eben almost seem to be able to see each other through the wall. Finally she comes into his room, throws her arms about him, and covers his face with kisses. He responds at first, then throws her off, saying he hates her. He pretended it was Min when he kissed her, he says. They hurl threats and insults at each other, Eben maintaining that she is only trying to use him to gain possession of the farm. Abbie laughs confidently. There's only one room in the house not hers yet—the parlor. She invites him to come courting her down there. Eben, torn between hatred and longing, slowly dresses. Plaintively he calls to his mother for guidance.

[] *Scene Three*

The setting is the parlor, a short time later.

Abbie sits waiting, and Eben enters and sits beside her. Both seem fearful. Abbie feels there is another presence in the room; he replies that it is his mother. He talks of her—of her gentleness and kindness. Abbie says she'll take his mother's place. She will be kind; she'll sing to him, protect him from the man they both hate. She kisses him, chastely at first, then lustfully, and soon he is responding the same way. When she plainly indicates that they must become lovers, he jumps up and calls to his mother. What is she telling him? Prodded by Abbie, he comes to the conclusion that this would be his mother's vengeance on Cabot. She wants him to love Abbie. He falls on his knees beside her and they kiss fiercely.

[] *Scene Four*

We see the exterior of the house, just before dawn.

Eben comes outside, dressed in work clothes. Abbie raises the parlor window, calls him, and they kiss. Both are exhilarated, confident. Abbie says she's going to leave the parlor shutters open, let in the air and sunshine. The room is hers now. Quickly she corrects herself—the room is theirs. Their loving has made it so. Eben reflects that his mother can rest quietly now. Abbie turns to go upstairs; she will tell Cabot she isn't feeling well today.

Eben meets his father coming from the barn. Laughing and joking crudely, he tells the old man they are quits now, and offers his hand. Cabot is puzzled, and Eben asks if he didn't feel his mother's spirit passing back to her grave. Then he tells his father to go to work. Yes, Eben is bossing him—he's the prize rooster here now. He marches off toward the barn. Cabot calls him a fool—soft-headed, like his mother.

[]   *In Brief*

The second act consists entirely of forward-driving action. Eben moves from an overt rejection of Abbie to full acceptance of her as his beloved; Abbie, from greed and self-interest to actual love for her stepson. Cabot moves unwittingly closer to the dreadful tragedy he himself has set in motion.

There isn't a superfluous moment in the act, nor is there a scene that isn't entirely gripping.

PART THREE

[]   *Scene One*

The setting shows the kitchen and the two bedrooms. It is the following spring, nighttime.

Eben sits alone in his room, torn by conflicting emotions. In the kitchen a dance is in progress, celebrating the birth of a boy. Many neighbors are present, and they seem to share a secret joke. Cabot, who has had too much to drink, is serving whiskey to the men. Abbie sits, preoccupied, as though waiting for someone. She asks where Eben is, and why he isn't here to enjoy the dancing. These inquiries are greeted with titters and leering guffaws. It is obvious that all the guests believe Eben, not Cabot, to be the father. The insinuations grow very coarse and open, but Abbie seems oblivious to them.

Cabot becomes annoyed at the undercurrent of laughter. Unaware of the reason for it, he urges them all to celebrate properly the arrival of his son and heir. There are other snide remarks, but he doesn't catch their drift. A square dance follows, during which Abbie remains apathetic. Cabot suddenly pushes the dancers out of the way and, with great swagger and energy, kicks up his heels in a grotesque, capering dance, shouting all the while that he's a better man than anyone else in the room. Finally even the fiddler is exhausted, and has to stop playing.

Upstairs, Eben creeps into the next room, and bends over the cradle. Abbie seems to sense his movement. She excuses herself, saying she wants to go up to the baby. Cabot offers to help her up the stairs, but she shrinks from his touch. Feeling dizzy, he goes out to the porch, and the gossip about Abbie and Eben becomes overt.

Abbie goes to Eben, kisses him, and they admire the baby.

But Eben deeply resents the celebration, pretending that what's his is his father's. Abbie tries to comfort him, saying that something is bound to happen to change the situation. They embrace.

Outside, Cabot has a presentiment of evil. There is something about the place he doesn't comprehend, something that makes him very uneasy. Wearily he goes off toward the barn. Inside, the dancing starts with renewed vigor.

[]   *Scene Two*

We see only the exterior of the house. It is half an hour later. From the kitchen come the sounds of the dance.

Eben is looking up at the sky as Cabot returns from the barn. Why isn't Eben inside dancing the old man wants to know. There are eligible girls in there. Perhaps Eben could marry one with a farm of her own. Furious, Eben retorts that he doesn't intend to come by a farm the way his father did. Anyway, he has a farm— this one. Cabot, in a rage, tells his son that he'll never inherit a stick or stone of it; he intends to leave it to Abbie and his new son. Abbie wants the farm for herself and the boy, and she's wise to Eben's tricks. She has already told him how Eben tried to gain her sympathy by making love to her.

This really shakes Eben, and he calls his father a liar. But Cabot presses his advantage. Had not Abbie interceded, pointing out that Eben was needed to work on the place, Cabot would have blown his son's brains out. Furthermore, Abbie told him she wanted Eben cut off so the farm would be hers on Cabot's death. And with her giving him a son that's just the way it's working out.

It doesn't occur to Eben that Abbie's feeling toward him might have changed since she said this. Almost blind with grief and fury, he starts in with the intention of killing Abbie, but his father stops him and a violent struggle ensues. Abbie runs out of the house and forces Cabot to let go of his son's throat. As Eben lies gasping and choking on the grass she tries to help him, but he throws her off. Laughing triumphantly, Cabot goes into the house, and soon he can be heard whooping at the dance.

Eben tells Abbie that he hates her, and calls her a tricking whore. Baffled, Abbie insists that she loves him, but Eben says she has been lying to him all along. Didn't she make Cabot promise to disinherit Eben and give the farm to her if only she'd bear him a son? Abbie can't deny it, but begs Eben to realize that it was said in pique and jealousy, long before they became lovers. This is not her attitude any more.

Abbie begs forgiveness, but Eben, raging hysterically, says that he intends to tell the truth about the baby and that he's going to California to prospect for gold. When he's rich he'll come back and fight them for the farm they've stolen, and he'll kick the three of them out on the road.

Brokenly Abbie reminds him that the baby is his child too. Eben replies that he wishes the child had never been born. Abbie asks if he believed, before the baby came, that she loved him. Eben admits it, but says he was a fool to think so. Is it true he's going west on account of the baby? Eben doesn't answer this directly, but swears he intends to leave in the morning. Abbie replies that if this is what the baby has done to her, killing the only joy she's ever known, then she too hates the child.

Bitterly Eben retorts that the reason she loves the baby is because he will steal the farm for her. What Eben can't bear is the thought of her getting him to father the child in order to cheat him of his inheritance. Abbie says the baby won't steal the farm—she'd kill him first. She'll prove that she loves Eben. He tries to break away from her now, but she clings to him and asks whether he would love her again if she could prove she wasn't scheming to steal the farm. Eben admits he would, but asks how she could prove such a thing. He doesn't believe her protestations for a moment. He goes into the house, as Abbie cries she'll prove that she loves him—better than anything else in the world.

[]   *Scene Three*

The setting shows the kitchen and Cabot's bedroom. It is just before dawn of the following morning.

Eben is sitting in the kitchen, his carpetbag packed. Upstairs Cabot lies asleep. Abbie is bending over the cradle. She sobs, then pulls herself together, backs away in horror, and goes down to the kitchen. She embraces Eben and kisses him wildly, but he remains impassive.

Abbie urges him to respond. She needs his love now, after what she has done. Dully he says that he's going away, and without telling Cabot who the baby's father is. Cabot is just mean enough to take his vengeance on the child, and the baby is not to blame for what his mother is. Abbie protests that there's no sense in Eben's leaving now, after what she has done. She says she has killed him, and Eben assumes she means Cabot. It serves him right, Eben remarks savagely. But it is the baby whom Abbie has killed. She smothered him with a pillow. Eben, horrified, calls on his mother's spirit. Why didn't she stop Abbie? Eben is sick with rage and grief as Abbie tries to explain—Eben has said that he hated her for having the child, that he wished the baby had never been born, for it was he that had come between them.

Eben cries out that he'd kill himself before he'd hurt the baby. Abbie pleads for his understanding, but he threatens to kill her. She must have done it because the child looked like him, and she couldn't bear that. Wildly he rushes to the door. He's going to notify the sheriff; then he'll go to California and out of her sight forever. Abbie struggles after him, crying that she loves him. She doesn't care what he does, if only he'll love her again. She collapses.

[]   Scene Four

The setting continues to show the kitchen and Cabot's bedroom. It is an hour later, and full daylight.

Abbie is in the kitchen, her head in her arms. Cabot wakens, sees that he has overslept, goes to the cradle and remarks how soundly the baby is sleeping, then goes downstairs. Abbie hasn't prepared breakfast, and Cabot assumes she isn't feeling well. He tells her the baby will be needing her soon. Bluntly Abbie says that she killed him. Cabot rushes up to the bedroom, touches the baby, and stumbles back to the kitchen. Grabbing Abbie violently, he demands an explanation.

Abbie pushes him away, shouting that she hates him, that she would never bear him a son, that she loved Eben, and that the baby is his. It's Cabot she should have murdered. So this is the unnatural thing that Cabot had sensed in the house. If the baby was Eben's, he's glad it's dead. He'll go notify the sheriff. Abbie tells him Eben has already done so. Abbie ought to have loved him, Cabot observes. The child ought to have been his. Then he'd never have sent for the sheriff, no matter what she'd done. Well, the chores are waiting.

Outside, Cabot meets the returning Eben. After learning that the sheriff has indeed been notified, Cabot knocks him down and tells him to get off the farm, or the sheriff will have another murder on his hands. Cabot goes off to the barn.

Eben comes into the kitchen, throws himself on his knees beside Abbie, and sobs brokenly. He begs her forgiveness. Though he has told the sheriff, he loves her still—he knows that now. Abbie responds with anguished joy. Eben says there may be time for them both to get away before the sheriff comes. But Abbie says she'll stay and take her punishment. Eben replies that he will share it with her. It was he who put the idea in her head, wished the baby dead. The guilt is his too. Abbie doesn't want him to suffer, but Eben insists that they face the consequences together. They cling to each other.

Cabot walks into the kitchen. Telling the lovers they should both be hanged from the same tree, he says that he has turned the cows and other stock loose. He intends to burn down the farm and follow his other sons to California. Luckily he has the money to take him there. Pulling up the floorboard he reaches for the bundle of gold pieces. He turns to look at Eben, who tells him, tonelessly, what he did with the money. Cabot sees the hand of God in this. It's His way of telling him to stay on the farm.

The sheriff and his men arrive, and Cabot admits them. Eben tells them to take him too—he helped her do it. This brings a moment of grudging admiration from Cabot, who then goes off to round up the stock.

Before they leave, Abbie and Eben declare their love for each other and kiss. Then they go outside, and pause briefly to admire the beauty of the morning. The sheriff remarks that it's a fine farm. He wishes it were his.

[]   *In Brief*

With the beginning of III-1 the play rushes headlong to its inevitable end, each event leading inexorably to the next. Cabot's presumed triumph over his son and Eben's resentment of this false situation leads the old man to depict Abbie as she was at one time, though not at present. But the story is plausible, and it drives Eben to denounce Abbie and drives her, in response, to offer the "proof" that her love is genuine. Eben, torn between his grief and horror and his terrible passion, can only sacrifice himself along with Abbie; while Cabot, his money gone, is left without even the means of putting these dreadful events behind him and building a new life.

All this is accomplished with breathless speed as the tragic events pile up one on another in the final scenes of the play.

Protagonist and Objective

Abbie is the protagonist; her objective can perhaps best be defined as her own fulfillment as a woman. What seems to her to be her most pressing need, as the play opens, is security, represented by the ownership of the farm. Actually, as she and we discover, it is emotional security she requires—the affection and protection of the man she loves.

Obstacles

Eben's hostility is the first obstacle Abbie must deal with, for he considers that she intends to steal the farm from him. However, since it is Cabot who will dispose of the farm, Eben seems to pose no real threat. When it appears, however, that Cabot may leave the farm to Eben after all (II-1), Abbie determines to fight: she will bear Cabot a son. Now she faces the fact of Cabot's age, and Eben's still active resentment should she have a child by her husband.

With the seduction Abbie falls in love with Eben, and now the obstacle that emerges is the social pressure that prevents an acknowledgment of the truth. This is followed by Eben's renewed hostility when he believes she has had the child only in order to defraud him. Now Abbie must find a way to convince him of the genuineness of her love. Finally she must face Eben's horror and revulsion at her deed.

Major Crisis and Climax, Theme

The crisis is the murder of the child; the climax is Eben's rejection of this "proof" of Abbie's love. A genuine tragedy in the Aristotelian sense, the play cleanses by pity and terror. Greed, physical passion, and an inhibiting environment have worked in combination to destroy three lives.

Resolution

This includes Eben's decision to notify the sheriff; his return to Abbie, declaring both his love and his own guilt; Cabot's frustration when he finds the money gone; and finally the ironic comment of the sheriff about the farm.

Opening

Although the initial scenes are skillfully handled, we may question whether O'Neill didn't begin his play a bit early for maximum impact. A tighter construction would have raised the curtain at I-3, incorporating the exposition of the first two scenes in a revised I-3 and I-4.

Unity

Simeon and Peter are not really necessary to the main problem of the play, and, having served their expository function, they disappear at the end of the first act. Beyond this point the play drives on relentlessly, with no extraneous or superfluous scenes whatever. Structurally, Simeon and Peter could be eliminated without altering Parts Two and Three, except for the fact that it was to the older brothers that Eben gave the six hundred dollars, thus forcing Cabot to stay on the farm after the tragedy.

Exposition

As already noted, there is a lot of exposition in the early scenes. Most of it is carried by the hostility between Eben and the older brothers. Eben believes the farm to be rightfully his by inheritance from his mother; Simeon and Peter scorn this claim. At the same time the older brothers are attracted by the promise of riches in California, which, except as a way of getting rid of these rival claimants to the farm, interests Eben not at all. (O'Neill didn't create any differences between Simeon and Peter. The two men, for dramatic purposes, are essentially one character.)

Eben's detestation of his father is more intense than that of his brothers, and this creates further friction. These factors combine with the mystery of Cabot's absence to hold our interest until the news of their father's marriage starts the forward movement of the plot.

Characterization

Eben, Cabot, and Abbie are characterized not only by their actions and what others say of them, but by what they say, at some length, about themselves. Eben reveals the bitterness of his life and his feelings about his father and his dead mother in I-2. In II-2 we learn a great deal about Cabot as he tries to tell Abbie of his devotion to the farm and about his two previous marriages. Abbie is the most complex of the three, for it is she who undergoes the most profound changes during the course of the play. We observe one facet of her character in her first meeting with Eben (I-4), another and far less attractive aspect, indicating her greed .and her resentment of Eben, in II-1; and in succeeding scenes we see what began as a scheme to inherit the farm slowly overwhelmed by her blind, consuming passion.

All three major characters are motivated at first by their need for security that the farm represents—Cabot cherishes and tries to guard it even beyond his own death; Eben longs for it beyond anything else in the world; Abbie contracts a distasteful marriage in order to secure it.

Simeon and Peter are more crudely drawn, but, as they operate on the periphery of the main story, this is not a serious defect.

Development

The play's many scenes are constructed for maximum movement and change, and each leads inevitably into the next. Consider II-1: structurally this consists of two episodes—the first between Abbie and Eben, the second between Abbie and Cabot. Abbie is the protagonist of each. In the first her objective is to attract Eben physically. The obstacle is Eben's resentment of her. At the climax she fails to elicit the desired response, and the resolution is her anger.

The second episode of II-1 finds Abbie struggling in a situation of conflicting pressures—her detestation of Cabot, Eben's attraction for her, and the overwhelming need to gain possession of the farm. Her objective is to find a way out of this trap. The climax is her decision to have a child. The resolution is Cabot's joyful reaction. The basic situation in the play has now changed, and this leads directly into the next unit of dramatic action, II-2 and II-3, which may be considered as one episode.

Abbie is also the protagonist here, her objective being to

seduce Eben in order to become pregnant. There are two obstacles—Cabot's presence in the house and Eben's continued hostility. But we are aware that Eben is undergoing an inner struggle, for he is strongly attracted to his stepmother. The suspense engendered by this situation holds us through Cabot's long speech about his own history; when Cabot realizes that Abbie hasn't been listening to him he goes to the barn, and one obstacle to Abbie's objective is removed. Abbie then approaches Eben directly, and her physical appeal for him slowly overcomes his scruples and his reluctance. Although the locale shifts to the parlor, dramatically the scene continues unbroken. Eben has rationalized his surrender and is responding to Abbie as she intends. She has attained her objective.

The basic situation, altered once again, leads directly into II-4, in which we see that Abbie seems to have fallen genuinely in love with her stepson, while Eben finds an exhilarating independence and release from his father's domination. Similar careful building of scenes that flow naturally from one to the next may be found throughout the play.

Dramatic Irony

The device is employed frequently. There is a very brief use in I-4 when Simeon and Peter jeer at their father and his bride, for we know, as Cabot doesn't, that they are going to California.

The basic situation—that Abbie and Eben are lovers—is, of course, known to the audience, and thus constitutes a major irony until Cabot also learns the truth in III-4. We know why the neighbors at the dance are laughing at Cabot, and why the old man senses an evil presence in the house.

In III-2 Cabot quotes Abbie's earlier statements about Eben's making love to her, and that she wants him disinherited so that she will inherit the farm herself. We know, as Eben in his blind rage doesn't realize, that Abbie's feelings toward him have changed, that she truly loves him.

We also know that Abbie has killed the baby before either Eben or Cabot find out. And we are aware that Cabot isn't going to find the six hundred dollars in gold pieces under the floorboards.

Preparation

An interesting plant, used symbolically, is Eben's relationship with Min, whom his father also used to visit. The older brothers even speculate (I-3) that Eben may inherit his father's wife as well.

Activity

Playing Cabot's ignorance of the baby's paternity against the background of a country dance is a brilliant theatrical stroke. Nothing O'Neill might have devised could have thrown Cabot's isolation and humiliation into bolder relief than this snickering crowd of neighbors, come to celebrate an event of which they have guessed the scandalous truth. The gaiety and music offer an opportunity to demonstrate Cabot's high spirits and to emphasize, by contrast, Abbie's and Eben's unease and apprehension.

Another significant bit of business is the older brothers' pulling the gate off its hinges (I-4); later in the scene they throw stones through the parlor window. And, of course, there is a great deal of physical contact in the play, both amorous and contentious. All this helps to make vivid the underlying emotions, so powerful that they keep bursting through the dialogue into physical activity.

Dialogue

O'Neill's speeches are direct, colorful, and vigorous throughout the play. He did, however, attempt to indicate the regional and period accent by phonetic spelling. This makes for irksome reading, and is of doubtful assistance to the actors, who depend on aural observation and training, not the printed page, in the reproduction of regional speech.

Effects

Except for the removal of the walls in order to reveal the various rooms in the house, the effects are all in the realistic tradition. The combinations of interior and exterior lighting, however, made possible by the unusual setting, can be highly atmospheric.

Plausibility

As in all great plays, the characters' motives and actions are understandable and believable. Even Abbie's smothering of her baby becomes plausible in view of the intensity of her emotions. The author has been at great pains, in the second half of III-2 (just before the actual killing), to convince us that Abbie is desperate enough to be capable of this horrifying act.

HOWARD LINDSAY
and RUSSEL CROUSE
Life with Father

1939

This comedy achieved a record run of nearly eight years on Broadway. Its popularity can be accounted for, in part, by its mood of gentle warmth, innocence, and nostalgia, which held a special appeal during a particularly ominous period of our century. The play broke no new ground; it is entirely conventional in form and content. But Clarence Day's many short sketches about his lovable bear of a father, which appeared originally in *The New Yorker,* have been woven together and given dramatic form with such consummate technical skill that the play is well worth study. It is realistic in treatment, and like all Broadway shows was, of course, written for the proscenium theatre.

Premise

Father Day presides over his comfortable New York home, in the late 1880's, as a benevolent despot. Although they love and respect him, his frequent outbursts of temper usually cause his somewhat scatter-brained wife and four growing boys to run for cover. Father Day's parents neglected to have him baptized, which bothers him not at all. His devout wife learns of this lapse.

Synopsis

The setting throughout is the "morning room" of the Days' house on Madison Avenue. There are three acts of two scenes each, with II-2 being interrupted to indicate a passage of time.

ACT ONE

[] *Scene One*

Vinnie, wife and mother in the Day household, is breaking in a new maid as the family comes down to breakfast. We meet the four boys: Clarence, Jr., 17; John, 15; Whitney, 13; Harlan, 6—all redheaded like their parents. They all stand somewhat in awe of Father Day, who is due downstairs momentarily. House guests are expected today, and Father, who hasn't yet been told, isn't going to like it. We hear Father storming around upstairs, looking for a favorite necktie, as Whitney practices reciting his catechism.

Father enters, sits down to breakfast, and starts opening the mail. Vinnie tells him that Clarence needs a new suit, which Father says the boy will get when he goes to Yale in the fall. Meanwhile, one of Father's suits can be altered to fit him. Vinnie tells Whitney that he must study his catechism before going out to play ball. Father thinks that Whitney could study his catechism any old day. Vinnie is shocked. Unlike her husband, she sets great store by the forms and rituals of the church.

Father's outspoken comments on the new maid terrify the poor girl. Vinnie plans a musicale to benefit a missionary fund, and Father protests. While he is meticulously exact in money matters, it is apparent that Vinnie is incapable of understanding money at all, and he knows that the money for the missionaries will ultimately come out of his pocket. He tells her that he must put his foot down about the musicale, just as he has had to put his foot down about visiting relatives. Moments later he opens a letter assigning him exclusive rights to sell a popcorn popper in Staten Island. The letter is addressed to his eldest son, but Father hadn't noticed the "Junior" after his name. He apologizes.

Clarence has been invited to have tea with a girl his own age. He objects. He doesn't care for the company of girls.

Father tries to persuade Vinnie to keep household accounts. She counters by saying that if they had charge accounts at the stores she wouldn't need to keep track of the figures herself. Father reluctantly agrees to open accounts at two stores.

Vinnie tells him that the rector is coming to call this afternoon. Father plans to avoid this encounter by coming home late from the office. As the others finish their breakfast and go about their business for the day, Father, alone, settles down to read his paper. Suddenly he launches into a tirade against Tammany politicians, as though they were in the room. The family, passing by in the hall, is used to this sort of thing, and ignores it. But the new maid thinks he is addressing her. Finally Father goes off to work, and the maid falls down the stairs with a tray of dishes.

Clarence protests to his brother John that he has no use for girls. We learn that the expected visitors are Cousin Cora, a relative from the country, and her friend Mary Skinner. They arrive. Mary is sixteen, coquettish and beautiful. Clarence is smitten.

[] *Scene Two*

Late that afternoon the rector and Vinnie hear Whitney recite his catechism. Then the rector, who had hoped to see Mr. Day, asks Vinnie if her husband had ever been injured in a fall. He has never seen Mr. Day kneel at prayers in church.

Father arrives home unexpectedly—he had forgotten that the minister was to call. As a new maid serves tea, the rector informs Father that he will be expected to subscribe five thousand dollars toward the building of a new church. Father is appalled at the rector's ignorance of financial matters, and indignantly points out that his family pew has dropped two thousand dollars in value since he bought it.

Cora and Mary return from a shopping trip and the rector leaves. Not knowing that the girls are staying at the house, Father welcomes them cordially, even invites them to stay for dinner. The truth dawns on him, however, as the girls start upstairs, and Clarence and Vinnie hastily shut the doors into the hall so the expected outburst will not be heard by the guests. Vinnie refuses to send the girls to a hotel, and Father has to acquiesce to their presence. He stomps out.

Mary is as dazzled by Clarence as he by her. They are somewhat disturbed by the fact that while Clarence is an Episcopalian, Mary is a Methodist. Father returns, and then Vinnie, and Father admits that although he attends the Episcopal Church his free-thinking parents never had him baptized. Vinnie is horrified, and says that he must be baptized without delay. Otherwise, how can he enter heaven? Father says this is all folderol, and he isn't going to have any minister splashing water on him at his age. Vinnie wonders if, in the sight of God, they are even married. And then her stricken glance falls on her children.

[] *In Brief*

There are so many plot elements to be set up in this loosely constructed play that the first act hardly moves forward at all. That it plays as well as it does is due to both the broad, sure strokes of characterization and to the skillful use of suspense and dramatic irony from moment to moment.

The main plot line hangs on Father's efforts to avoid the indignity of submitting to baptism, and Vinnie's determination to get him into heaven. But the authors were wise to delay the statement of these opposing points of view until the end of the act, for it would mean little until we know Father and Vinnie quite well. When the clash does come, we know that this isn't going to be any petty disagreement over an ecclesiastical formality, but a real battle between two determined opponents.

ACT TWO

[] *Scene One*

It is Sunday morning and the family is returning from church, where evidently Father has made a noisy and embarrassing scene in front of the whole congregation. Baptism was the subject of the sermon, and Father is sure it was directed toward him. He decides that this is the time to straighten out the household accounts, and goes to get the current bills.

This is the day that Cora and Mary are to leave New York to visit other relatives, and Clarence is despondent. Furthermore, he must have a new suit, one of his own. He tells his mother that the reason *he* didn't kneel in church was because in Father's altered suit he can't do anything that Father wouldn't do. At a party, for instance, during a game of musical chairs, when a girl sat on his lap he had to jump up. She was sitting on Father's trousers.

Alone with Mary, Clarence urges her to write to him, but Mary thinks it improper for a girl to write first. There is a near quarrel, which Mary tries to patch up by sitting on Clarence's lap.

Clarence tells her to get up, and now she is really angry. She leaves the room as Father enters.

Father then has a man-to-boy talk about women, the substance of which is that women are always getting stirred up and men have to be firm. When Mary enters a moment later to retrieve a handkerchief, Clarence tries to be firm. She simply ignores him.

Father calls Vinnie in for an explanation of certain expenditures. The house must be run on a businesslike basis. But he runs headlong into Vinnie's total illogic on money matters, and ultimately her most effective weapon—tears. He winds up giving her money. Vinnie is sure, however, that Father's checks aren't legal if he hasn't been baptized. She leaves, and Father, as he follows, tells Clarence that there will be no new suit.

Clarence tries to borrow money from John for a suit. John has found a "Boy Wanted" ad in the paper, and promises that when he applies he will try to get a job for Clarence too.

A cab arrives to take the girls to the station. Cabs charge by the hour, and if there's one thing Father can't stand it's to keep a cab waiting. Mary is very frosty with Clarence, but when she asks if he is going to write first he tells her that men have to be firm. The girls are shepherded out, and Clarence immediately sits down, pen in hand, and begins writing "Dear Mary."

[]   *Scene Two*

Two days later another new maid is serving breakfast. Vinnie has not come down. She isn't feeling well. John has already gone out to see about the job. Clarence is anxiously awaiting the mail, and when a special delivery arrives it is handed to Father, who opens it. Some woman claims to have sat on his lap, and this is followed by a lot of mush! As Clarence squirms, Father crumples the letter and throws it away. Practical jokers!

Vinnie, having heard his indignant protests about jokers, comes hurrying downstairs to see what is wrong. Father tries to make her eat breakfast, which she doesn't want, and then tries to persuade her that her indisposition is all imaginary, that what she needs is cheering up. Vinnie finally tells him to get out and go to his office. Baffled and hurt, he leaves. Vinnie goes back to bed, asking that a cup of tea be brought up to her.

Clarence rescues the letter his father tossed away and reads it happily. Then John comes in, bringing two heavy packages containing bottles of a patent medicine. It is obvious, though not to the boys, that it is a quack nostrum, and they decide that before going out to sell it to the neighbors they'd better be able to say they use it at home. As Vinnie's tea is brought in, they pour a generous dose into the cup.

The curtain is lowered to denote the passage of three hours.

The doctor is upstairs with Vinnie. Whitney has been sent downtown to fetch Father, who arrives in a cab and goes straight up, and straight down again, not having been allowed in the room. The doctor comes down, saying that Mrs. Day appears to have been poisoned. He hurries out, saying he'll be back shortly. Father is very worried. He agrees to hear Whitney's catechism, but quickly loses interest when there is a reference to baptism.

The minister has been summoned, and now appears. He begins to talk of Vinnie as though she were already dead, and Father is furious. The doctor returns, bringing another physician with him, and they go upstairs.

Father tells the rector there is something he can do to help speed Mrs. Day's recovery, for there is a situation that has been worrying her deeply. As soon as the doctors let the minister see her, will he please explain to Vinnie that baptizing Father would just be a lot of damn nonsense?

The doctors come down and ask to be shown to a room for private consultation. The rector says that all they can do now is pray, and he starts in, asking mercy for a miserable sinner. This is too much for Father, who takes over the prayer himself. Vinnie is not a miserable sinner, but a damn fine woman, and her suffering has got to stop, damn it!

The uproar draws Vinnie down the stairs, and Father, torn between joy and fear, blindly promises to be baptized if only she will get well. As Vinnie faints in his arms he suddenly realizes what he has said, and bellows in dismay.

[]   *In Brief*

While keeping the main story line of Father's effort to escape baptism well in the forefront, subsidiary strands are woven in and out, and the whole play begins to move forward.

The subplot of Clarence's infatuation with Mary includes, in this act, the handicap of Father's clothes, then Mary's leaving, Father's reading her letter, and Clarence's decision to sell medicine in order to earn enough to buy a suit.

Father's effort to make Vinnie keep accounts is funny in itself, but it is also preparation for an episode in the next act.

Vinnie's illness serves to show that Father, for all his bullying, loves his wife dearly. It also furthers the plot by motivating Father's involuntary promise to be baptized.

ACT THREE

[]   Scene One

A month later, in midafternoon, Vinnie is instructing the cook to prepare an especially good breakfast for the morrow—things that Mr. Day likes. Cora and Mary are stopping by again on their way back to their home town. Clarence comes in from McCreery's with a box containing a china pug dog that Vinnie had ordered.

John arrives home, having been down to collect his and Clarence's commissions for selling the patent medicine. But the boys have been paid off in more medicine, not cash. Clarence is in despair. He has ordered a suit from McCreery's. It costs fifteen dollars and is already being altered. When Father comes in, Clarence pleads in vain for a suit of his own. What if he should want to kneel in front of a girl? Father can't imagine such a contingency.

Vinnie enters with the happy news that a young minister out in the suburbs has agreed to baptize Father quietly and privately. Father protests that his promise to be baptized was made when he thought Vinnie was dying. She's well now, and that makes a difference. As the argument mounts, his eye falls on the pug dog, and he roars that he will never be baptized while that hideous thing is in the house. He stomps out.

Vinnie interprets this as an agreement, and she tells Clarence to take the pug dog back to McCreery's. As it happens, the price of the dog and the suit are identical, and credit on one would pay for the other. Vinnie thinks this a splendid idea, for then the suit wouldn't cost Father anything.

Father enters in time to see Clarence leaving the house with the pug dog, and there is an affectionate scene with Vinnie. Father is in a good mood again, but then, as he says, "in this house you never know what's going to hit you tomorrow."

[]   Scene Two

Another new maid is serving breakfast next morning when Clarence's suit is delivered. Vinnie tries to explain to Father that the suit cost him nothing, since it was exchanged for the pug dog. Father sees

Cora and Mary approaching the house, and Clarence rushes upstairs to put on his suit.

Vinnie and the girls sit down to talk as Father opens the mail. There is a letter from a neighbor saying that their dog died from a dose of John's medicine and demanding ten dollars for a new dog. Father insists that the purchasers of all 128 bottles be reimbursed out of John's allowance.

On learning that the girls aren't staying in New York at all on this trip, Father suddenly becomes cordial. But then a cab draws up outside, and Vinnie announces that it is here to take them to the baptism. Father demands that the cab be dismissed. Vinnie accuses him of going back on his word, the sacred promise he gave her the day she almost died. John maintains she would have died if he and Clarence hadn't given her some of their medicine. Father is furious—at the boys and at Vinnie's arrangements for the baptism.

Suddenly he notices the cab again, and, on learning that this one costs two dollars an hour instead of one, he explodes, and tells Vinnie to get her hat on. In a stream of profanity he leaves to be baptized. Clarence, who has come downstairs in his new suit, kneels at Mary's feet.

[] *In Brief*

Again, this act never loses sight of the main dramatic problem—the question of who will win the struggle over Father's baptism, he or Vinnie. The subsidiary stories are brought to a close coincidentally: Father and Vinnie learn that it was the boys' medicine that made her so ill, and, partly as a result of Vinnie's noncomprehension of money matters, Clarence finally gets his suit—and his girl.

Protagonist and Objective

Let us say that Father is the protagonist. His objective is stated repeatedly, the first time near the end of I-2, when he thunders that he will *not* be baptized, he *will* be a Christian, but that he will be a Christian in his own way. Since he does, in the end, submit to baptism, we may say that he fails to achieve his objective.

With equal logic Mother might be regarded as the protagonist and Father as the (comic) antagonist. If we examine the play this way, then Mother's objective is to get Father baptized, and she succeeds. Structurally the result is the same, so in this case the matter seems to be one of semantics, and of no real importance. For purposes of this analysis, Father is the protagonist.

Obstacles

Vinnie's determination to have Father baptized so that he can get into heaven is the only obstacle in the main story line. However, this is a play with subsidiary stories running along coincidentally, and these have their own protagonists, objectives, and obstacles.

Major Crisis and Climax, Theme

The crisis of the main story line occurs in III-2, when Vinnie challenges Father to make good his promise to be baptized, and he states that he would never have promised if he hadn't thought she was dying. This is the last moment in which the issue could swing either way. But it is immediately followed by Father's finding out that the cab is costing not one dollar an hour but two, and this is the straw that breaks his opposition and provides the climax.

Even so lightweight and sentimental a work as this has a theme; it informs us that a wife's love and persistence, when it's for a man's own good, can overcome a stubborn man's obstinacy.

Resolution

This is very brief, and includes Vinnie's forgiving John for putting the nostrum in her tea (an obligatory tag to the medicine story) and Clarence's kneeling to Mary, which resolves the teen-age romance.

Opening

The time chosen to begin the play is just ahead of the two coincidental events that set the two principal story lines in motion. The first is Mary's arrival, which leads to Clarence's infatuation and his problem of getting a new suit; the second is Vinnie's discovery that Father has never been baptized, and this leads to her campaign and Father's defensive position.

Unity

Being a work based on incidents drawn from a number of short sketches, structural unity is not inherent in the material, but had to be supplied by the adapters. Lindsay and Crouse achieved it, first, by focusing strongly on one of their story lines, the baptism, returning again and again to this conflict once it had begun, and, second, by creating a unifying mood made up of family affection, benevolent tyranny, and nostalgia. The result, in spite of the many threads that weave in and out of the dramatization, is a work that seems all of a piece.

Characterization and Exposition

Characterization is of prime importance if this thin story line is to work. In fact, it can't even begin to work until Father and Vinnie have been carefully delineated.

The authors are far too skillful, however, to do but one thing at a time. They also have some exposition to cover, and a lot of planting to do before they can proceed with the play's forward movement; so they combine characterization, exposition, and planting all in one.

In gentle conflict, I-1 explores the contrasting attitudes of Father and Vinnie toward the church: Vinnie insists that Whitney learn his catechism, Father attaches little importance to it; Vinnie wants to benefit the missionary fund, Father doesn't (this episode also contrasts their approach to money matters); Father wants to avoid meeting the rector when he comes to tea. By the time we have heard Father discuss the family pew as a financial investment, in I-2, we are ready for the setting up of the main conflict. Whatever exposition is required in the first act flows effortlessly from these various situations.

Preparation

Simultaneous with the characterizations are the various plants. In the first scene we learn that Clarence wants a new suit, and intends to go to Yale; that Cora and Mary are expected; that Clarence is interested in selling from door to door as a means of earning money (the corn popper); and that Father opens mail addressed to Clarence Day without bothering to notice the "Jr."; that Clarence maintains a profound disinterest in girls; that Vinnie plans to open a charge account; that the rector is expected to call; and, once more, Clarence's attitude toward girls, just before Mary arrives. All these plants will bloom later.

The planting continues in Acts Two and Three. In II-1 Clarence tells his mother that when a girl sat on his lap he had to jump up because she was sitting on Father's trousers; Vinnie's total incomprehension of simple accounting procedures prepares for the pug dog and new suit episode in Act Three; John reports that he has found a "Boy Wanted" ad; when the girls start for the station we learn that Father can't stand wasting money by keeping a cab waiting; and in II-2 Vinnie rushes downstairs when she hears Father roaring angrily. This last sets up Vinnie's coming down, in spite of her illness, at the end of the act.

In III-1 anticipation about the next day's events is whetted by Vinnie's instructions to the cook regarding breakfast. This prepares for the girls' arrival and Vinnie's coincidental plans for the baptism. Clarence's saying that he can't kneel to a girl while he's wearing Father's trousers prepares for the final moment of the play when, in his own suit, he does kneel.

Development

Mary's arrival and Clarence's immediate infatuation comprise the only forward movement in I-1, and the drawing of the battle lines on the question of baptism the only progression in I-2. The rest of the act is given over to the characterization, exposition, and planting already noted.

Many of the individual episodes hold attention because of characterization, dramatic irony, their function in the larger pattern of the play, or a combination of these elements. Other episodes utilize a more conventional structure. Consider these two examples, both in II-2:

Clarence is the protagonist of the episode with Mary in which they discuss who is going to write first. His objective is to establish a closer relationship with Mary. The obstacle is the inhibiting effect of Father's trousers on Clarence's behavior. The climax occurs when Mary tries to sit on his lap. The resolution is her anger.

Father is the protagonist of the episode with Vinnie in which he tries to bring order into the household accounts, and that is his objective. The obstacle is Vinnie's irrationality about money. The climax comes when Vinnie weeps and Father agrees to sign the checks. There is a delay before we come to the resolution, as Vinnie again insists that Father be baptized. The resolution is Vinnie's shaming Father into giving her a dollar and a half.

Dramatic Irony

The device is used extensively, right up to the final scene. In I-1 we learn that guests are expected; the news is being kept from Father. Later, when Father berates Tammany, the maid thinks he is addressing her. We know he is merely self-dramatizing. In I-2 we are aware, as the rector is not, that Father deliberately tries to avoid him. When the girls arrive home from shopping, Father thinks they are just paying a call, and even invites them to dinner. At the act curtain the humor of Vinnie's wondering whether her children are legitimate is based on our knowledge that Father's not having been baptized has nothing to do with it.

In II-1 we know that Clarence cannot behave naturally with Mary while he is wearing Father's trousers. Mary doesn't know this. In II-2 we know that the special delivery letter Father has opened is Clarence's letter. Later, as Clarence reads the label on the bottle, we realize that the medicine that the boys intend to sell is a quack remedy. And when they put some into their mother's tea we know what may be expected. Not even the boys realize the reason for Vinnie's sudden turn for the worse.

In III-1 we learn that Cora and Mary are returning. Again, Father doesn't know. And Father doesn't know, either, that Clarence has already ordered a suit and can't pay for it. When Vinnie reasons that the suit will cost Father nothing because she is returning the pug dog, we can imagine what Father will have to say about that. At the end of III-1, when Father remarks that "you never know what's going to hit you tomorrow," we can well imagine what is going to hit him. Dramatic irony is not required in the final scene, for by now the various plot elements (the suit, the medicine, Clarence and Mary, the baptism) are being drawn together, and the play is moving rapidly toward the climax.

Activity

There are a number of expert uses of physical activity. One of the best, and perhaps the funniest, is the family's rush to shut the doors into the hall whenever Father loses his temper. The terror of the maid is conveyed by the way she handles the breakfast dishes. Mary's sitting on Clarence's lap and later his kneeling to her carry a burden of meaning far beyond the simple actions themselves.

Dialogue

Dialogue is straightforward "realistic" speech of the period, but while of its kind it is very well done it has no special distinction. It carries the play forward, and that is all that is required of it.

Plausibility

These people are all slightly caricatured, and the authors faced a real danger that they might broaden out into cartoons. In that case, though we might have laughed at them, we would no longer have believed in them as people. This pitfall was avoided by depicting the genuine emotion and affection that underlay the bluster and storms characteristic of the household.

HERMAN J. MANKIEWICZ
and ORSON WELLES

Citizen Kane

1941

Film, with its exact control of just what an audience will see and hear, and far more flexible than the stage, is generally considered a director's medium rather than a writer's. But films have to be written too, and the same basic principles govern audience attention that prevail when the actor is present in person.

Citizen Kane, one of the most famous and influential of all American films, is not a profound work, by any means, but it has a vitality and an exuberant theatricalism that have seldom been equalled, and have made it a landmark in motion picture history.

This analysis and the numbering of the scenes are based on the shooting script, the authors' screenplay with which the film went into production. This differs slightly from the cutting continuity, an exact record of what finally appeared on the screen. (The two versions may be compared in *The Citizen Kane Book*, published by Little, Brown and Company.)

Premise

Charles Foster Kane, owner of a chain of newspapers and a man of enormous wealth and power, has recently died. A brief motion picture review of his life is in preparation by a rival publishing house, but the producer feels that, while the film covers the known facts of Kane's life satisfactorily, it fails to provide the key to his somewhat enigmatic character.

Synopsis

[] *Scenes 1–14*

The opening shot is a lighted window in the distance. The camera pans down to a large iron gate with the initial *K* above it. Beyond is an enormous fairy-tale sort of castle on a hill. Then a series of shots take us through the neglected gardens, zoo, swimming pool, and finally into the bedroom beyond the lighted window. The picture dissolves to a snowstorm, with a farmhouse and snowman, and we hear Kane mutter the word "rosebud." As the camera pulls back, we find that the snow scene is a toy, contained in a glass globe in Kane's hand. Kane is dying. The globe slips from his hand to the floor. A nurse pulls the sheet over his head.

[] *Scene 15*

A newsreel biography of Kane fills the screen. Called *News on the March*, it deliberately imitates and satirizes the pompous manner of the old *March of Time*. The narrator, with appropriate pictures, announces that Charles Foster Kane, builder of the vast Florida estate Xanadu, has died. Headlines flashed before us indicate what a controversial figure Kane was—regarded by some as a pacifist and idealist, by others as a warmonger or a traitor. The narrator goes on to outline Kane's career as a publisher of a host of newspapers and magazines. The foundation of his fortune, we are told, was a gold mine in Colorado. The presumably worthless deed to the mine was left to his mother in payment of a board bill.

We next see a congressional investigating committee questioning an important and influential financier, Walter P. Thatcher, who says that he was, many years before, appointed trustee for the fortune and guardian of the child. An investigator asks if it is true that the boy attacked him, on their first meeting, with a sled. Ignoring the question, Thatcher reads a prepared statement in which he denounces Kane as a communist.

A newsreel clip shows a speaker at an outdoor rally calling Kane a fascist. Another clip shows Kane making a speech in which he claims that he is only one thing—an American. Next follows a newsreel shot of Kane returning from Europe, predicting that there will be no war.

We then see pictures of a wedding party on the White House

lawn. Kane's first wife, Emily, is identified as the President's niece. After their divorce Kane married a singer, Susan Alexander, and we see Kane attacking photographers after the couple's civil wedding ceremony. There follows a drawing of an opera house in Chicago, built by Kane for his second wife; then pictures of the building of Xanadu, its parks, its zoo, its phenomenal collection of art objects from all over the world.

Newspaper headlines indicate that Kane urged our participation in the Spanish-American War, opposed our entry into the First World War, supported the campaign of one president, and attacked another so viciously that he was blamed for the latter's assassination and was hanged in effigy.

We next see Kane in the midst of an apparently successful campaign for governor; then a headline, appearing just before the election, saying that he had been caught in a love nest with a singer.

The film-within-a-film continues with an account of the gradual shrinking of Kane's empire, as many of his newspapers are forced out of business by the depression. It ends with shots of Kane, an invalid, at Xanadu. Finally we see the moving electric sign in Times Square announcing his death.

[]   *Scene 16*

The setting is a small projection room, in which the preceding newsreel has been run for its producer and his staff. They agree that something seems to be missing—the facts are there, but there is no new light on this extraordinary and controversial man. The producer recalls Kane's last word, "rosebud," and assigns one of his men, Thompson, to interview people who knew Kane intimately for an explanation of this cryptic utterance. Perhaps "rosebud," when they know what it means, will provide the key to Kane's drive and personality.

[]   *Scenes 17–18*

We are in a cheap night club in Atlantic City, run by Susan Alexander Kane. The headwaiter brings Thompson to a table where Susan sits, drunk, her head on her arms. A thunderstorm rages outside, and there are no customers in the club. She looks up, orders another drink, and Thompson sits down. She refuses to talk to him, however, and orders him out of the club. Thompson goes to a phone booth, calls his boss in New York, reports his lack of success with Susan, but says he's going to the Thatcher Library in Philadelphia in the morning to read Thatcher's diary; then he will return to New York to interview Bernstein, Kane's general manager. Thompson then asks the head-waiter whether Susan, in talking about Kane, ever mentioned "rose-bud." He replies that when this utterance was reported in the papers he had asked Susan what it meant, but she didn't know.

[] *In Brief*

Scenes 1–18, in a highly ingenious but logical form, introduce us to Kane, give us some startling but superficial facts about him, and pique our curiosity as to the meaning of his puzzling last word, which Thompson is assigned to explain. Susan's refusal to talk with Thompson suggests how difficult his task is going to be. (The fact that Kane's career so closely parallels that of William Randolph Hearst adds more than a fillip of interest to the story, but from a structural standpoint this is immaterial.)

[] *Scenes 19–31*

Thompson is ushered into the marble fastness of the Thatcher Library, and permitted to examine the section of Thatcher's unpublished memoirs that deal with Kane. Alone in a vast hall, except for an armed guard, he begins to read. Thatcher is recounting his first meeting with Kane, then a small boy. We first see a snowstorm and a house, similar to the toy scene in the glass globe. Inside Mrs. Kane's boarding house are Charles' father and mother, and Thatcher, aged 26. Against her husband's strenuous opposition, Mrs. Kane signs papers making Thatcher's bank trustee of the fortune the mine will produce, and Thatcher himself the boy's guardian until his twenty-fifth birthday.

The three then go outside, and Mrs. Kane tells the child that he is going off on a trip with Mr. Thatcher, to New York, where he will live and be educated, for when he grows up he will be one of the richest men in the world. Learning that his mother isn't coming too, Charles grows suspicious and resentful, and when Thatcher tries to make friends with him, he rushes at him with his sled, then kicks him. The boy then runs to his mother's arms for comfort.

It is many years later; Kane is now a young man. Thatcher, as an adviser and no longer his legal guardian, is objecting to Kane's recently acquired newspaper, the *Inquirer*, stirring up hostility to

Spain by means of fraudulent news stories. Bernstein, Kane's general manager, enters with a cable from an *Inquirer* reporter in Cuba. It says that he can provide poems about the scenery, but that there is no war. Kane dictates a reply: the reporter may provide the poems; Kane will provide the war.

Thatcher then protests the *Inquirer's* campaign against a company in which Kane himself is a large stockholder. Kane replies that he is really two people—a man of wealth and property, but also a publisher; and as a publisher he considers it his duty to protect the underprivileged from grasping and unscrupulous financial interests. If he doesn't, perhaps someone *without* money and property will rise to defend them. Thatcher finally reminds Kane that the *Inquirer* is losing a million dollars a year. At that rate, Kane replies, he'll have to shut the paper down in sixty years.

Thompson, in the library, closes the manuscript of Thatcher's memoirs, and as he is ushered out caustically inquires of the formidable librarian if she happens to be Rosebud.

[]   *In Brief*

Thompson begins to put together a more complete picture of Kane from Thatcher's testimony—the first of five such segments. The first scene, with Kane as a small boy, will be important later, but its significance is not revealed at this time. We are also shown Kane in action early in his career—his ruthlessness and contradictory views. The final sarcastic reference to "rosebud" reminds the audience that the investigator has not found what he is looking for.

[]   *Scenes 32–50*

Thompson is interviewing Bernstein, who has always been Kane's general manager, and is now chairman of the board. Bernstein can offer no explanation of "rosebud." Thompson mentions that he is going back to Atlantic City, hoping that Susan Alexander will be willing to talk. Bernstein suggests that he ought to interview Jed Leland, who was Kane's closest friend; he begins to reminisce about Kane's arrival at the *Inquirer* offices, the day he took possession of the paper.

Kane and Jed arrive in a cab at the shabby old building. They are followed by Bernstein in a wagon loaded with furniture, including a bed. In the city room Carter, the editor, and his staff rise to greet the new publisher. Kane introduces Jed, who will be the paper's new drama critic. At the door Bernstein appears with the furniture, and Kane tells Carter that he intends to live here, that the office will be open twenty-four hours a day, not twelve.

Sometime later Kane is pointing out to Carter that the *Chronicle,* a rival paper, has played up a suspected murder and made a big story out of it. Why hasn't the *Inquirer* done the same? Carter objects that the *Inquirer* is not a scandal sheet. At this Kane gives some very explicit instructions on the handling of the story. The *Inquirer* is going to be written, edited, and illustrated so that it will sell.

In the pressroom, still later, Bernstein makes some derogatory remarks about the paper in the presence of both Kane and Carter. Carter is offended and offers his resignation, which is promptly accepted. Then Kane turns to the foreman of the composing room and tells him they will remake the front page. When the foreman objects that they go to press in five minutes, Kane upsets the forms, scattering the type onto the floor, and directs the foreman to reset the pages according to his instructions.

The front page having been made over four times, Kane, Bernstein, and Leland are very tired. However, Kane decides to remake the page once more, this time to include a "Declaration of Principles." This states that he will tell all the news honestly, and that he will champion the people's rights. Leland asks the foreman to bring the declaration back to him after it has been set up in type. It may be a historic document.

Kane, Bernstein, and Leland stand in front of the *Chronicle* building. The *Chronicle*'s circulation is roughly twenty times that of the *Inquirer.* Bernstein remarks that, with the *Chronicle*'s fine staff, its circulation is no mystery. Some years later, in the city room, sits the *Chronicle*'s former staff, now all working for the *Inquirer,* whose circulation has jumped spectacularly. A party is in progress. Kane announces that he is taking a vacation in Europe, and it is suggested that he will pursue his hobby of buying art objects, of which he already has a large collection. Then a line of dancing girls appears. As the entertainment proceeds Bernstein and Leland speculate as to whether Kane will change the *Chronicle* veterans into his kind of newspapermen, or whether they will change him. Leland declines Kane's offer to send him to Cuba to cover an as yet nonexistent war. Leland strongly objects to Kane's policy of promoting trouble between Spain and the United States. Later Kane tells Leland he may write a column of personal opinion without editorial interference.

Kane is in Europe, and his office is crammed with crates of

paintings and statuary he has shipped back. Bernstein suggests to Leland that art objects aren't the only things Kane is collecting abroad.

On his arrival home Kane hands a short bit of copy to the *Inquirer*'s society editor. Avoiding the welcoming ceremony that the staff has prepared, he goes down to his carriage, where the niece of the President awaits him. They are engaged to be married. Then we see the wedding party on the White House lawn, as in the newsreel.

This ends Bernstein's testimony to Thompson. Bernstein remarks that Kane's first wife was no "rosebud," and again advises Thompson to interview Jed Leland.

[]   *In Brief*

As in the first segment of testimony, a portrait of Kane begins to emerge from these bits and pieces of his business career, which, it should be noted, do not follow chronologically except within the segments. We are introduced to Leland as a young man and to Emily, Kane's first wife. Leland, having had a closer personal relationship to Kane than Bernstein, may be expected to shed some light on the man from quite a different angle.

[]   *Scenes 51–79*

Leland is in a wheel chair on a hospital roof during his talk with Thompson. Leland reflects that Kane never believed in anything or anyone but himself; that his papers never told the truth; that, though he wasn't brutal himself, he sometimes behaved brutally. Leland doesn't know the significance of "rosebud." But he remembers Emily. She and Kane seldom saw each other except at breakfast.

There follows a montage of very brief scenes showing Emily and Kane at the breakfast table over a nine-year period. At first Kane is attentive and loving. As the years pass he grows more preoccupied with business. He is also attacking the President, Emily's uncle, and hints that he may occupy the office himself someday. The final scene shows Kane reading the *Inquirer* and Emily the *Chronicle*, and neither saying a word.

We are again at the hospital. Leland remarks that all Kane ever wanted was love from others, but he had no love to give, except to himself and perhaps his mother. Then he begins the story of Kane and Susan Alexander, who became his second wife.

Susan, suffering a toothache, is coming out of a drugstore as

Kane is splashed with mud by a passing cab. She laughs at him but invites him to her nearby flat to clean himself up. Susan is a totally uncultivated girl who has no idea who Kane is even after he tells her his name. He confides that he had intended, this evening, to make a sentimental journey to the warehouse where his dead mother's things are stored. Susan tells of her own mother's ambition for her to be a singer. Kane urges her to sing something for him, and she does so, in a small, quavering voice.

Inquirer headlines announce that Boss Rogers picks both the Republican and Democratic candidates for governor; a cartoon shows Rogers in prison stripes, and urges that he be jailed.

Kane, running as an independent and promising to prosecute Rogers, addresses a cheering crowd in Madison Square Garden. It would appear that he stands a very good chance of being elected. Emily and his son listen from a box. After the rally Emily has their chauffeur take the boy home, and insists that Kane accompany her to an address in a note that she has received. It is Susan's address. They go there in a cab, without speaking.

They are met by Susan and Boss Rogers. Susan protests hysterically that Rogers forced her to write the note. Kane starts to bluster and threaten Rogers; Emily demands an explanation of the message, which hints at dire consequences for herself and their son. Susan insists that Kane is merely paying for her singing lessons. Rogers cuts in to say that he is fighting for his political life; unless Kane withdraws from the race, his relationship with Susan Alexander will be publicized. Susan is panic-stricken; Emily says coldly that Kane has no choice but to withdraw; Kane himself, raging, refuses to submit to blackmail. He can't believe that the people of the state would turn against him now—they love him. Emily and Rogers leave, with Kane shouting defiance after them. He still intends to send Rogers to prison.

A headline in the *Chronicle* says that Kane has been caught in a "love nest." The *Inquirer*, in announcing his defeat, claims an election fraud.

Leland, slightly drunk, comes to Kane's office. Kane senses his contempt; both men know that he has betrayed the principles to which he had pledged himself when he took over the paper. Leland tells him he has always behaved as though the people belonged to him; he thinks he loves the people so much they ought to love him in return, but that actually he loves only himself. Leland asks to be transferred to the Chicago paper, as drama critic there. Reluctantly Kane agrees.

Kane, besieged by reporters as he and Susan emerge from their wedding, announces that the new Mrs. Kane is going to be an opera star.

The *Chicago Inquirer* carries a picture of a new opera house in that city, which is to be inaugurated by Susan Alexander. On the stage we see a terrified Susan just before the curtain rises, then hear her pitiful effort to sing a difficult role. The camera travels up to the flies where two stagehands are listening. They glance at each other sourly, and one of them holds his nose.

We are in the city room of the *Chicago Inquirer*. Bernstein has also come to Chicago for Susan's debut and the opening of the opera house. The news, music, and social coverage of the event is all ready for tomorrow's paper, but Leland's review, from the dramatic angle, is still not finished. Kane enters, in evening clothes, learns from Bernstein that the drama review isn't ready, and walks into Leland's office. There is an empty bottle on the desk. Leland has passed out, his head on the typewriter. Bernstein follows Kane into the office and reads the notice aloud, as far as it goes. It is severely critical. Kane takes the sheet and asks Bernstein for a typewriter. He will finish the notice himself.

Leland wakens some minutes later and sees Kane in the city room typing. Bernstein tells him that Kane is finishing the notice as Leland started it—unfavorably. Leland approaches Kane and asks if they are on speaking terms. Indeed they are. Leland is fired.

At the hospital Leland tells Thompson that Kane finished his bad notice to prove his own honesty. But Kane, Leland muses, was a disappointed man, and must have been very lonely in his last years.

[] *In Brief*

Kane's personality, with all its contradictions, becomes clearer with Leland's contribution. Again, many years of Kane's career are covered, even though the period in time is the same as in the preceding segments. It is the device of examining that career from several different points of view that imposes order on the material and keeps it from dissolving into chaos. As in the preceding segments, we are introduced to the narrator of the next segment—in this case, Susan—so that she is no stranger by the time we hear her contribution. As for "rosebud," the search must continue.

[]   *Scenes 80–108*

Thompson returns to Susan's night club in Atlantic City, and this time she is willing to talk. She maintains that she never wanted a career in music—that was Kane's idea. And she describes her singing lessons.

Matisti, a high-priced voice teacher, competent and conscientious, is at the piano; Susan is singing and Kane listening. Matisti stops in exasperation. He can do nothing with this voice, and he tells Kane so. Kane overrides his objections, insists that the lessons continue.

We are in the opera house again, at the opening performance. Susan is on stage, singing an aria. Matisti, in the prompter's box, is apprehensive. Kane, Bernstein, and other members of the staff are in the audience, their eyes all riveted on Susan. At the end of the performance the applause is scattered and feeble, except for Kane and his party, who applaud vigorously. Susan takes a bow, but it is obvious that the occasion has been a disaster.

In a Chicago hotel room Susan sits on the floor surrounded by newspapers. The notices of her debut are terrible. Humiliated and rebellious, she tells Kane that she will not continue singing, but he says she will—he isn't going to be made to look ridiculous. Susan retorts that he isn't the one being made to look ridiculous. During this scene an envelope is delivered—from Leland. It contains the original copy of Kane's Declaration of Principles. Susan remarks that sending a man a check for twenty-five thousand dollars when you fire him is a peculiar thing to do. Kane slowly tears up the declaration and tells Susan that she will continue her singing career. Then we see a newspaper picture of Susan, and hear her singing, as the names of the papers carrying the picture—the *New York Inquirer,* the *St. Louis Inquirer,* the *Los Angeles Inquirer,* and so on—dissolve from one to another.

Susan lies unconscious in her New York bedroom as Kane and a servant break down the locked door. She has taken an overdose of sleeping pills. Later a doctor tells Kane that she will be all right, and both men maintain the pretense that she confused two bottles of medication. When Susan recovers consciousness she says that she simply could not face another hostile audience, and Kane at last capitulates. He will not force her to sing again.

In a huge hall at half-built Xanadu Susan is doing a jigsaw puzzle. She is surly and rebellious; she misses the life of a big city. Kane is indifferent to her pleas that they move back to New York.

As the years pass there are more jigsaw puzzles to be solved, but Susan's disposition does not improve. A picnic in the Everglades is planned.

A Kane picnic expedition somewhat resembles the march of a triumphant Roman army. Susan and Kane sit in the lead car of a long procession, taciturn and glum. That night, in a luxuriously furnished and carpeted tent, Susan starts complaining. Apparently Kane has limited the amount of liquor the guests may consume. Knowing that she can be heard by others in the nearby tents, Kane tries to quiet her, but only makes her more furious. He never gives her anything she really wants, she says. He does things only to please himself. He has spent his life trying to bribe people. He doesn't love her, but he wants her to love him. Finally Kane slaps her face.

Back at Xanadu Raymond, Kane's butler, tells him that Mrs. Kane would like to see him. Susan is packed and dressed for travel. She makes it clear that she is leaving him, and doesn't care about appearances. Kane is reduced to pleading with her piteously not to go; when she realizes that he is thinking not of her but of himself her determination hardens and she walks out.

We return to Thompson's interview with Susan at the night club. He remarks that he and a photographer are going down to Xanadu to take pictures of the castle and its contents for a magazine his firm publishes. Susan suggests that he talk with Raymond, the butler. She admits that she felt sorry for Kane.

[]   *In Brief*

With Susan's account we move still closer to an understanding of this compelling and dangerous man, for this is the most personal of the four statements made so far. Raymond will supply the fifth and last.

[]   *Scenes 109–118*

At Xanadu Thompson is interviewing Raymond, who asks to be paid for what he knows about "rosebud." Thompson agrees to a thousand dollars. Raymond says that Kane was a strange man, especially in his last years.

We then see the butler, in his reminiscence, releasing for the papers a very tactful and bland announcement of Kane's separation from his wife. He is interrupted by a servant bringing word that there is some kind of disturbance in Mrs. Kane's room. Raymond rushes to the scene and finds Kane in a silent and terrible fury smashing every bit of furniture and bric-a-brac in the room. His eye lights upon the glass globe with the snow scene inside.

With the globe in his hands Kane moves into the corridor, where a group of servants, attracted by the noise, fall back deferentially. Kane tells Raymond to lock the door of his wife's room and keep it locked. Staring at the globe with its miniature snowstorm, he walks down the hall, a very old man, and is heard to murmur, "Rosebud."

Thompson is dissatisfied. Raymond's story is hardly worth a thousand dollars, and "rosebud" is as deep a mystery as ever. Raymond confirms the fact that Kane said the word just before he died, when the globe slipped from his hands and broke. Thompson says that he and the photographer will be leaving Xanadu as soon as all the pictures have been taken.

We are now looking down the length of the great hall. The enormous room is jammed with crates into which the statuary, paintings, tapestries, and other works of art are being packed. It is obviously a collection not only of enormous size but of great value. Among the objects being sorted are the furnishings from the elder Kanes' boardinghouse in Colorado—a desk, a stove, a sled.

Thompson tells another reporter that he's been building a picture of Kane, piece by piece, like a jigsaw puzzle, and he mentions some of the contradictions: his honesty and dishonesty; how he lost the respect of his closest friend; how both his wives, whom he sincerely loved, finally left him. Thompson says that if he could have learned what "rosebud" meant it might have explained everything—or nothing. In any case, "rosebud" is the missing piece in the jigsaw.

Later that night the debris from the packing job is being fed into a furnace. Raymond directs a workman to throw in a nearby pile of junk—the furnishings from the Colorado house. The camera moves in close to the fire, and on the sled, just before the flames devour it completely, we can read the word "Rosebud."

The film ends with a long shot of Xanadu, smoke pouring from one of its chimneys. The camera pans down to the gate and a "No Trespassing" sign.

[]   *In Brief*

Raymond contributes little beyond the account of Kane's uncontrollable rage when Susan leaves him. To what degree his tantrum was due to the loss of a creature he really loved and how much to humiliation and frustration we must judge for ourselves. Thompson fails to learn the meaning of "rosebud," but we are shown how the word entered Kane's consciousness and what associations it would have for him. We must form our own conclusions about this too.

Protagonists and Objectives

Since the story of Kane's life is contained within an outer framework, we have, in film, the equivalent of a play-within-a-play, and the inner story and the framework each has its own structure.

Kane is the protagonist of the inner story. His objective is to conduct his life on his own imperious and unbending terms.

In the framing story Thompson is the protagonist. His objective is to learn more than is generally known about Kane, especially the meaning of the word "rosebud." When he has learned all he can, but failed to discover the meaning of "rosebud," the film is over.

Obstacles

Kane inspires his own opposition. Jed turns against him because of his opportunism and lack of integrity, Emily leaves him because of his indifference and ultimate unfaithfulness, Susan because of utter boredom and incompatibility. Nor will the public, which does not love him, follow where he wants to lead. They reject him at the polls, and in spite of extravagant promotion and publicity they refuse to accept Susan in opera.

In the framing story the first opposition that Thompson meets is Susan's hostility and unwillingness to talk. The principal obstacle he encounters later is simply the fact that no one is able to give a wholly satisfactory explanation of Kane's personality and behavior. Each person interviewed casts some light on the subject, but not enough for Thompson's purpose. As for "rosebud," which may be the key to unlock the entire riddle, that secret died with Kane. No one can explain it, for it was only in his own head that it ever meant anything.

Major Crises, Climaxes, and Themes

The major crisis of Kane's story is his pleading with Susan (Scene 107) not to leave him, and the momentary weakening of her resolve. The climax is her decision to go.

In the framing story the crisis is Raymond's telling Thompson that he knows about "rosebud" and Thompson's agreeing to pay for the information. The climax is the failure of Raymond's story to shed any light on the meaning of the word. Thompson has nowhere else to look for an explanation.

The theme implicit in much of Kane's story, and made explicit in the climactic scene of Susan's departure, is that love and respect cannot be purchased, but must be earned by unselfishness, consideration, and reciprocal love.

The theme to be found in the framework is plainly that a complex personality like Kane's, lacking a key that would explain it, may always have to remain enigmatic.

Resolutions

In Kane's story the resolution is his rage and frustration as he breaks up Susan's bedroom and has the room permanently locked (Scene 113). There follows a teasing reference to the objective of the framework—the glass globe with its snowstorm and the word "rosebud." This is also an obvious clue to the fact that there is a connection between "rosebud" and Kane's present state of mind.

The entire resolution of the framing story is built toward the moment when the audience, in an omniscient view, is given the clue denied Thompson. We see the vast array of objects Kane has accumulated; we hear Thompson recapitulate Kane's contradictory traits; then we are shown the word "rosebud" on the sled; and, as a final ironic comment, see the smoke coming from the chimney—the destruction of the only piece of evidence—and the "No Trespassing" sign, which tells us that Kane's secret is wholly lost.

Opening

The film establishes, first of all, that a man of immense wealth has died with the word "rosebud" on his lips. Then we are shown an admittedly superficial summary of the man's life. Because this account does not explain him satisfactorily, the producer assigns a reporter to dig deeper into Kane's background. In this way the framework's protagonist and his objective are established.

The inner story begins with the reading of Thatcher's diary. The opening chosen is Kane as a small boy, and his traumatic experience when Thatcher takes him away from his mother and his home.

Unity

The original script of *Citizen Kane* was more than twice as long as the shooting script, with which the picture went into production. In the process of cutting the original down to a practical length, the nonessentials were clearly eliminated. It would be hard to find now a superfluous scene or incident, for everything contributes to the development and understanding of the two interlocking stories.

Exposition

In one sense practically all of Kane's story is expository, for Thatcher's diary and the people Thompson interviews are all reporting what they remember of Kane. But in no case does the film remain for any length of time at the actual interview, which would be dull indeed. The recalled incidents are immediately dramatized as individual scenes of conflict, and thus lose the character of exposition.

Characterization

We have been led to believe, throughout the film, that there is a psychological explanation for Kane's personality and behavior, and that the word "rosebud" is the key that could unlock the puzzle. When we see the word on the sled our minds go back to Kane's childhood, when he used the sled to attack the man who was taking him away from his mother. Any interpretation we put on this is certainly apt to be very superficial psychiatry, but, for whatever it is worth, the revelation suggests that taking the child forcibly from his mother left a permanent psychological scar, giving him an intense drive for power over others, and damaging his capacity for love.

Other principals in the film are, of course, far more simply drawn, but they are clear and effective. Thatcher is depicted as a haughty but conscientious man, doing what he believes to be his duty toward his young charge and loathing every minute of it. The shrewd and charming Jed has an integrity that will not permit him to remain friends with Kane when he feels the latter is dishonest. (Kane's bad review of Susan's opening is probably an attempt on his part to match Jed's honesty.) Emily remains cool and dignified at the dreadful meeting with Rogers and Susan (Scene 68). Susan herself is a small masterpiece—an attractive but common girl floundering in an artistic and social milieu she is incapable even of understanding. As for Thompson, he is a device reflecting our own curiosity. (All the shots of Thompson, until the end, are of the back of his head.) We know next to nothing about him, and care less. Fortunately there is another protagonist who interests us.

Development

As the framing story is a relatively uncomplicated search for information, the progression of scenes simply follows Thompson as he moves from one witness to another. He doesn't even have any difficulty in finding them. The first time he tries to interview Susan he finds her drunk and hostile. (The authors, although they wanted to stress her importance early in the film, also wished to save her interview for the climax of the Kane story.)

This inner story, since segments of it are presented successively from five different sources, has many overlapping chronological sequences, but none within the segments themselves. The individual segments are built somewhat like short plays.

Thatcher is the protagonist of Scenes 19–31; his objective, to instruct and guide Kane into patterns of behavior he considers proper for a young man of enormous wealth. The obstacles are Kane's hostility, willfulness, and determination to go his own way. The climax is Thatcher's vain attempt to persuade Kane to behave responsibly with the deficit-ridden *Inquirer;* the resolution, his frustration and exasperation.

Kane is the protagonist of Bernstein's segment (Scenes 32–50); his objective, to publish the kind of newspaper he wants to establish. This segment also includes, as expository details, the beginning of Kane's passion for collecting and his engagement to Emily.

Jed is the protagonist of his segment (Scenes 51–79). He would like to remain with Kane, because of their long friendship and because of his job, but both men are ultimately driven apart by Kane's improbity.

Susan's segment is really two short plays, Kane being the protagonist of each. In the first his objective is to establish Susan as an opera star; the obstacle, of course, is her incompetence. The crisis is her suicide attempt; the climax is Kane's capitulation. Scene 98 begins the second short play. Kane's objective here is to establish a proper relationship with Susan consistent with his own life style. The obstacle is Susan's inadaptability and lack of breeding. The climax of this episode, her departure, is also the climax of the entire inner story.

Thompson is the protagonist of the brief segment with Raymond.

Dramatic Irony

The entire film is full of dramatic irony, for the newsreel of Kane's life near the beginning of the picture tells us that his editorial policies made his publications phenomenally successful, that both his marriages ended in divorce, and that a scandal defeated him in his campaign for governor.

Hence we know a good deal more than the principals as the various developments occur. However, since the entire orientation of the film is directed toward a character analysis of Kane, the authors do not employ the ironies for the purpose of tension, but to help us arrive at an understanding of the man.

Preparation

As the newsreel has already given us a summary of Kane's life, very little planting is required. The exception is the word "rosebud," which is planted again and again, and the use of this device is far more effective than an explicit statement by someone who knew him that Kane's personality was the result of a childhood trauma.

Activity

The versatility and easy maneuverability of the camera inclines the films to tell their stories in terms of physical action. The test of the value of such action is whether it is meaningful. We may be sure that the authors of *Citizen Kane*, especially with Welles serving as his own director, have made every activity count dramatically.

Some of the more significant pieces of business include: the boy using the sled with which to attack Thatcher; Bernstein bringing the bed to the *Inquirer* office at the very moment Kane meets his staff; Kane's upsetting the forms and scattering the type when the foreman argues with him; his tearing up his Declaration of Principles when Leland returns it; his furious destruction of Susan's room after she leaves him. There are many other visually effective moments due to imaginative and significant business.

Dialogue

Contemporary reviews of the film speak of the dialogue as "mature," and it was—remarkably so for its time. Today we are more accustomed to dialogue of this kind in pictures. It is "realistic" speech, somewhat heightened and directly to the point, and it uses words and phrases skillfully tailored to the person uttering them, as a comparison of Susan's lines with Emily's, for example, will quickly show.

Effects

Films are far more resourceful than the stage in the matter of expressive pictorial and aural effects, and *Citizen Kane* abounds in them. Among the most striking visual effects are the long shots of the castle and its grounds at night; the silhouetted forms of the newsreel staff against beams of light in the projection room; the camera's movement into the Atlantic City night club through a skylight; the spectacular shot of the performance in the opera house, with the camera rising up through the flies until it comes to rest on the two listening stagehands. (The camera work of Gregg Toland in this film is a landmark in cinematography.)

The film's sound track is also used with great skill and imagination. The echoing quality of the scenes in the Thatcher Library and in the great hall at Xanadu are major contributions to the atmosphere of these scenes. And it is often sound rather than sight that gives us the feeling of crowds and excitement when Kane is speaking or being interviewed.

Plausibility

This is the study of one man, a highly controversial figure. To what degree the events that befall him seem ultimately logical and inevitable depends, it would appear, on our willingness to accept the "rosebud" theory.

JEAN GIRAUDOUX

The Madwoman of Chaillot

1943

A stinging condemnation of predatory capitalism is embedded in this poetic and comic fantasy, one of Giraudoux's last and best-known plays. Its rueful humor, the delightful improvisations of its crack-brained protagonist and her cronies, have earned the play long runs in Paris and New York. But the truth is that it is a curiously unsatisfying work in spite of its moment-to-moment felicities, for the story is weak and the play is poorly constructed. Attempts to turn it into a motion picture and a musical comedy (*Dear World*) were not successful.

The play was written for the proscenium theatre, and is composed of highly theatrical elements—bizarre costuming and local color, heightened speech and frolicsome verbal play, extravagant characterizations—all offered, for the most part, in the realistic form.

Premise

A financier, ruthless and socially irresponsible, heads a syndicate searching for some way to increase its already considerable wealth. The financier is approached by a prospector who tells him that oil may be found under the city of Paris. Near the café where they meet lives a mad countess, eccentric but pure in heart. In her view the world is divided between exploiters and men of good will.

Synopsis

The play is in two acts, and requires two settings.

ACT ONE

The first act takes place on a café terrace, in a fine quarter of Paris. The time is late morning, in the spring.

At one of the tables sits the Prospector, carefully sipping a glass of water. The President and the Baron enter, and a waiter ushers them to a table. The President is clearly a highly successful entrepreneur; the Baron, an impoverished nobleman. All the latter has left is his name, but the President tells him that is just what they need on their Board of Directors.

As the life of the street passes by, the President discloses something of his past. In collaboration with various shady characters—counterfeiters, narcotics peddlers, and the like—he has risen from a poverty-stricken childhood to the directorship of many companies, and is now head of a new international combine. Its stock is booming on the exchange, but so far the company has no name, nor does the President have any idea what business it will engage in. A Ragpicker finds a hundred-franc note near the President's table, and the latter claims it. All hundred-franc notes belong to him.

Suddenly the President spies the Prospector, sipping his glass of water, and knows by the Prospector's face that this is the man he needs. The Prospector will recognize him as a kindred spirit also, the President declares, and will soon come to their table.

A Deaf-Mute, whose gestures can be interpreted only by Irma, the waitress at the café, observes, according to her, that it is a beautiful morning, but a better one before the arrival of the President. A Peddler offers shoelaces to the Baron, but the President urges him not to buy from such a person.

Now the President's Broker arrives and, as a street mountebank prepares to juggle his colored clubs, describes the activity of the company's stock in this morning's market. As the stock climbs the Juggler's clubs are thrown higher and higher. Then a rumor is launched to make the stock fall; the Juggler's clubs come down too. Insiders, who have sold high, wait till the stock has fallen very low, then buy it all back again. The Broker then describes how the enormous funds gathered in this manner are manipulated through a series of intricate and totally incomprehensible financial transactions that double and triple the sum again (and up go the Juggler's clubs).

A Little Man, who has been listening, rushes forward and presses his life's savings into the Broker's hands, then runs off joyfully. A Professor, passing by, joins a Street Singer in a song, to the President's disgust.

The Prospector rises and moves slowly to the President's table. The two men understand each other so completely that a minimum of conversation is required. The President needs a name for his new corporation; the Prospector needs fifty thousand francs. He offers the name "International Substrate of Paris, Inc.," for which the Broker pays him with the Little Man's money. The Prospector explains that there are deposits of oil under Paris—in fact, the largest deposit is directly under the spot where they are sitting. He has traced it by tasting the water in various parts of the city.

As the men start planning how to get the oil out of the ground, an eccentric old lady appears, dressed extravagantly in the style of 1885. She has come for table scraps to feed stray cats and dogs that she has befriended. The President requests Irma, the waitress, to ask the old lady to move on. Irma, identifying her as the Madwoman of Chaillot, refuses. The Madwoman asks the Doorman whether her feather boa has been found. Addressing her as Countess, he says that it hasn't, but produces for her inspection three scarves that have been left in the café. She chooses one, flinging it about her shoulders and upsetting the President's glass of water in his lap, and sits at a nearby table.

The President, furious, deplores a social system that permits anarchic individualism, as exemplified by the Madwoman and other characters on the street, to disturb the tranquillity of this district, the citadel of management. Ideally there would be only two classes of people—the entrepreneurs and, on the other hand, standardized workers with interchangeable parts. The Baron tries to calm him down; the Prospector points to a building opposite, the office of the City Architect, who has refused him a permit to drill for oil anywhere within the city limits of Paris.

A little old man, a retired Doctor now specializing in the removal of bunions and corns, solicits the patronage of the President, then takes a seat and exchanges pleasantries with the waiter and the Countess. The President wants to go elsewhere to talk, but the Prospector says that a bomb is about to explode in the office of the City Architect, and that the man appointed to replace him will be more reasonable about granting a drilling permit.

But no bomb goes off, and suddenly a Policeman carries in an unconscious young man. The Prospector recognizes him as Pierre, his agent, whom he had engaged to drop the bomb down the coal chute of the Architect's office. An argument ensues between the dim-witted Policeman, a novice at his job, and the Prospector as to what to do with the young man. The Policeman had slugged him to prevent his jumping off a bridge into the Seine. It would now appear that the only way the Policeman can abide by the rule book and avoid trouble for himself is to take the man back and throw him off the bridge, then jump in after him and rescue him from drowning. But, as the Doctor points out, the Policeman, who can't swim, would undoubtedly drown himself if he followed such a course of action. As this argument is pursued, the President, the Broker, and the Baron steal away. The Broker appears momentarily to advise the Policeman that people are calling for help in a nearby street. The Policeman runs off, followed by the little Doctor. Of the plotters, only the Prospector remains at the café.

Irma and the waiter cross to Pierre and determine that he still lives. Irma is smitten by the handsome young man's appearance. The Prospector, who also would like to reach Pierre, gives up and follows after the President and his friends. Irma primps and Pierre opens his eyes. For him too it is love at first sight. As Irma is called back inside the café, the Countess takes her place at his side. She holds his hand firmly and calls a police Sergeant. Fearing that she will turn him in, Pierre struggles weakly to rise. The Countess says she will not let him go. More than thirty years before she let a young man, Adolphe Bertaut, go, and she never saw him again. When the Sergeant arrives it is only to be told that Pierre agrees with him that the iris the Countess wears on her bosom is becoming to her. Impatiently the Sergeant turns away—there is a man drowning in the Seine. Informed that Pierre is the drowning man, the Sergeant starts writing a report. The Countess tells him it is his duty, with attempted suicides, to speak out in praise of life. The young man's name is Roderick, she continues. Every man's name is changed each hour on the hour. Women find this a simpler system than changing the men.

Prodded by the Countess, the Sergeant tries to convince the young man that life is worth living, but his enthusiasms seem to be limited to cards and beer. As Pierre struggles to rise, the Countess tells him she knows why he tried to kill himself. It is because the Prospector, who years ago stole her feather boa, has now ordered Pierre to kill her. But she's not so easy to get rid of, as she has no wish to die. Addressing the young man as Roderick, and speaking at some length, she describes how she wakens in the morning, how she dresses, puts on her make-up and her jewels, the pleasure she gets from reading the morning paper (it is always the same one—an issue of March 22, 1903, now unfortunately in tatters), how she feeds her cats, pets her dogs, waters her plants, how she then goes outside and, by cutting across their paths from the left, thwarts the evildoers of the district—those who hate people and plants and animals. Gathering around to listen are other neighborhood characters, who nod approvingly. Pierre, who has listened, fascinated, to all this, begins to take an interest in life.

The Prospector returns and tells Pierre to come with him. But the Countess holds the young man firmly. The Prospector tries to take him away from her, and she squirts a soda water siphon in his face, then hits him over the head with the bottle. The Prospector calls for help and more people of the district run in. The police Sergeant, on arrival, sees no reason for telling the Countess she must release Pierre, and when the Deaf-Mute indicates that Pierre's life is in danger if he accompanies the Prospector, the Sergeant orders the latter to move on.

Pierre reveals that the Prospector has been blackmailing him; that he couldn't bring himself to plant a bomb in the City Architect's office and therefore attempted suicide. The Prospector and his associates, he says, are convinced that a lake of oil lies under Paris. They need this oil in order to make war, and are prepared to destroy the city to get it. The Countess is incredulous, but the Ragpicker convinces her that there is a new and different breed of people on earth. They are pimps—the middlemen, the nonproducers who demand their cut of every transaction without ever producing or contributing anything. Gradually they are taking over the world. Pierre confirms the Ragpicker's words. Indignantly the Countess says that they must get rid of these men. But that will not be simple, the others believe. Their enemies are strong, clever, powerful, and rich.

Nothing daunted, the Countess starts making plans. She sends word to three friends—Constance, Gabrielle, and Josephine (all mad)— to meet at her cellar lodging at two o'clock. Then she asks Irma to bring her a bit of kerosene and mud in a little bottle. To the Deaf-Mute, through Irma, she dictates a letter, addressed to the President, informing him that an outcropping of oil has been found in the cellar of a building at 21 Rue de Chaillot, now occupied by a lady of unstable mentality. The accompanying bottle contains a sample of the outcropping. The President may examine the premises himself at

three o'clock that afternoon. The Countess then asks Pierre to sign
the Prospector's name to the letter, and the Doorman to deliver it.
The President will come, she is sure, and bring all his villainous associates with him.

The Countess must now return home. Since her feather boa
hasn't been found, the Doorman gives her an ermine collar that someone left in the café. Pierre will accompany her and take care of some
household chores at her cellar. The ermine collar turns out to be
rabbit, and Pierre's name changes from Roderick to Valentine as the
clock strikes one. They leave.

Irma, clearing the table, muses that she has never told any
man she loved him; but, looking after Pierre, she whispers, "I love
you."

[]   *In Brief*

There is such a wealth of color, wit, and invention in the first act of
The Madwoman of Chaillot that one may think at first there is considerable forward movement. In fact, the act consists almost entirely
of exposition and characterization, and the play is nearly half over
before an important conflict develops. This is a very long wait, and
other factors that are offered to hold our interest must be arresting
indeed to compensate for the lack of dramatic progression.

Stripped of the bizarre extravaganza and improvisations that
embellish it, the framework of the act may be quickly summarized.
The predators are introduced and characterized at considerable
length, and we learn of their plan to drill for oil even at the risk of
destroying Paris. Except that they have been refused a drilling permit,
there is no suggestion of opposition until much later.

The Countess makes her flamboyant entrance; her eccentricity
and her indifference to the President are established. Then Pierre is
brought in—a young man to whom both Irma and the Countess are
attracted. As the Prospector identifies Pierre as an employee, and we
know that his life is in danger, the lines of conflict between the predators and the pure in heart begin to emerge—but up to this point
only so far as Pierre is concerned. This conflict is secondary to the
principal one that will lead us to the play's climax.

As the Countess and her friends win the skirmish over Pierre,
the outlines of the entrepreneurs' plot are disclosed to the Countess,
who then promises to take action against them and starts arranging
her countermeasures. But by now the act is almost over, and this is

half the play. All that remains before the first act curtain is Irma's declaration that she is in love with Pierre, a factor in the secondary story of which we are already aware.

ACT TWO

The scene is an ancient, vaulted cellar in which the Countess lives. It is cluttered with the accumulation of centuries, and there is some furniture of the 1890's. A stairway leads to the street.

Irma, the waitress, comes in to announce that a Sewer Man is calling on the Countess. He and the Countess are old friends. There is some discussion about life in the sewers, whose romantic aspects have been greatly exaggerated; then the Countess asks him to reveal to her the secret of the moving stone. The Sewer Man presses a brick in the masonry, and a huge block of stone swings open to disclose a staircase winding down into the bowels of the earth. The steps lead nowhere, except to death. The Sewer Man presses another brick, and the stone swings back into place. He leaves as Irma returns to announce the arrival of Madame Constance and Mademoiselle Gabrielle.

These two ladies are as outlandishly garbed as the Countess, and are, if anything, slightly madder. Constance is accompanied by an imaginary dog, Dickie, to whom she talks continually. Gabrielle is deaf, except on Wednesdays, when she hears perfectly well. One more lady is expected—Josephine; but she, we are told, is waiting in front of the palace for President Wilson to come out.

The Countess explains that she has called them together to decide the future of the human race, but this matter is momentarily sidetracked as Dickie wants to sit in the Countess' lap, and she doesn't want him there. Sweetly Gabrielle offers to take Dickie in her own lap, but this merely provokes Constance into reminding the Countess that Gabrielle brings along to tea people who exist only in her imagination. Constance begins to cry. The Countess, to make peace, says that she will hold Dickie in her lap. Irritably Constance replies that she didn't bring Dickie today.

The Countess gets down to business: there exists a group of men who are planning to tear down the city. The other ladies are skeptical, and the discussion turns to men in general, men as a sex. This is delicate ground, for Gabrielle is a virgin. Men, who used to be so considerate and polite, are turning into beasts. Constance and Gabrielle are inclined to think better of men than the Countess, but the latter warns them against male deceptions. Men worship the

Golden Calf these days. Humanity is doomed. What do the ladies suggest? Constance would write to the Prime Minister; Gabrielle would like to go home and consult her voices, but the Countess says there isn't time. She has conceived a plan for bringing the evildoers here this afternoon. Does she have the moral right to exterminate them? The others aren't sure. Besides, how could it be done? The Countess isn't ready to disclose that.

Constance is suspicious that some of Gabrielle's invisible friends are present, and refuses to commit herself before witnesses on a matter of life and death. The Countess insists that, of all the millions of beings prowling about in space, some must be here in the room. Her house is always full of invisible guests, and she welcomes them. As a matter of fact, the reason the Countess entertains Madame Constance is only because the latter is always accompanied by her charming, though invisible, sister, a far pleasanter person than Constance herself. Indignantly Constance gets up to leave, as Irma announces the arrival of Madame Josephine.

Once again Josephine has waited for President Wilson to come out of the palace, but he didn't appear. When the Countess points out that, since he died in 1924, she'll have a long wait, Josephine replies that she has plenty of time. The Countess puts her question: if she had all the world's criminals here in this room, would it be right to get rid of them? Josephine, whose sister's husband was a lawyer, speaks with great authority. She approves their extinction, but says they must first be tried. A trial, however, would make them suspicious and would spoil the Countess' plan. Then they must be tried *in absentia*. The Countess asks Irma to summon the Ragpicker to act as their defense attorney.

The Ragpicker asks Josephine, who is now presiding, if he may be allowed to speak directly as defendant. It will be more convincing that way. His request is granted. A motley assortment of vagabonds is invited in to watch the trial.

The Ragpicker swears to tell the truth; Josephine reminds him that as an attorney his duty is to lie, conceal, distort, and slander. He gets no farther than "May it please the Court" when the defense is declared closed and the Countess begins the cross-examination. The accused insists that he doesn't worship money—money worships him. He attracts it. Every transaction, every move he makes brings in more money, and he can't get rid of it, no matter what his extravagances. The Countess asks him what he will do with the oil under Paris, if it is found to exist. He proposes to make war, to conquer the world. The verdict is "guilty," and the Countess is told she has the right to carry out the sentence, to exterminate all the evil men. Court is adjourned. The guests all leave, singing and dancing, Constance with her invisible dog Dickie, who has run in and found his mistress.

The Countess lies down for her nap. Irma will keep watch and waken her should the President and his cronies arrive. Irma tiptoes out, and presently Pierre comes down the steps, carrying a feather boa. He kneels beside the Countess and takes her hand. She believes him to be Adolphe Bertaut, her lover of many years before, and Pierre compassionately joins in the deception. He begs her forgiveness for deserting her, tells her that he loves her still, and always has. He asks her pity. The Countess bids him farewell, and he pretends to leave. When she opens her eyes Pierre has taken the place of the lover. She sees the boa, and Pierre tells her he found it in the wardrobe, when he took down a mirror she had asked him to remove. But a sewing box that had been stolen from her as a child is still missing.

Irma runs in excitedly to report that a procession of taxis and limousines is arriving. Pierre leaves, and Irma gives the Countess another bottle of kerosene and water. The Countess reminds her that she will pretend to be quite deaf, so that she can overhear remarks not intended for her ears. Then she presses the brick that swings back the great stone over the stairway.

The President enters from the street above, followed by many other presidents, all looking alike and all smoking cigars. Irma tells them they will have to shout if the Countess is to hear them. A contract is presented for the Countess to sign. In it, we learn from the conversation of the presidents, she waives all rights to any oil that may be found. She signs the contract, then is presented with a gold brick, which the presidents intend to reclaim on their way out. As the various presidents start down the stairway the Countess stops them. She asks if anyone has brought back her little sewing box, missing since her childhood. No one has, and they disappear down the deep stairway.

Now the Prospector arrives, followed by other prospectors, all alike. They sniff their way to the bottle of kerosene and water, sample it, present the Countess with what they say is an agreement for dividing the profits but is actually an application to enter a lunatic asylum, and go down the stairway.

The prospectors are followed by a group of press agents, one of whom steals the gold brick as he goes down the stairway. Then three women enter, beautiful but soulless creatures whose greed leads them down also. Finally an unidentified man rushes through and disappears just as the Countess is closing the stone door.

Irma comes back to find the room empty, except for the Countess, who tells the girl that the others have vanished because wickedness evaporates. The room is suffused with a radiant light, leaving only the closed trap in shadow. Now Pierre returns, and all the vagabonds. They report great changes in the world outside. The air is clear, new grass is sprouting, strangers are greeting one another warmly. Unearthly music is heard, and voices thanking the Countess on behalf of the animals, people, flowers.

A group of three Adolphe Bertauts appears, professing their love for the Countess and proposing marriage, but she tells them it is too late and they vanish. It is not too late for Pierre and Irma, however, and the Countess urges them to grasp love now, not to wait until his hair is white and there is another madwoman in Paris. The Countess then goes out to feed her cats, remarking that it would be a dreadful bore for them if humanity had to be saved every afternoon.

[] *In Brief*

Like *Alice in Wonderland*, which it resembles in more ways than one, the play continues episodically rather than organically. Many delightful bits of poetry and fantasy are found in the second act, particularly the conference of the four madwomen, with its flights of moon-struck logic. But the events do not grow out of each other as a result of pressure and counterpressure—they simply occur. Our interest is dependent on the charm and imagination of the author, parading before us one brilliant improvisation after another. The "story" is minimal.

The first episode in Act Two deals with the Sewer Man, who discloses the secret of the moving stone and the stairway to nowhere. This is exposition, static and totally devoid of forward movement. Then we have the meeting of the madwomen, a very funny scene dependent on bizarre characterization, and the trial. Although the outcome of the trial is scarcely in doubt, it does proceed to the point where the Countess obtains the sanction she desires to destroy the evildoers.

This aspect of the play is then dropped as Pierre becomes the surrogate Adolphe Bertaut. Next the President and all his followers arrive and, led purely by greed and with no show of resistance, march unwittingly to extinction. The play closes with reports of a better and happier world, and the union of Pierre and Irma.

One feels that it has all been too easy. The Countess may be mad, but her enemies are fools. The opposing forces are unevenly matched.

Protagonist and Objective

The Countess is the protagonist. Her objective is stated near the end of the first act when, after hearing from the Ragpicker and her other friends that evil people are plotting and coming into power, she says that the world must be saved.

Obstacles

If the President and his cohorts realized for one moment that the Countess was a dangerous enemy, they would, of course, move against her. As it is, they see in her only an eccentric old woman, harmless but useful to them; hence they put up no struggle. This fact seems to be the core of the play's trouble; it produces a blandness in the story line for which hardly any degree of sophisticated wit and brilliance of invention can compensate.

Major Crisis and Climax, Theme

Since there is no active opposition to the Countess in her scheme to rid the world of evildoers, both crisis and climax are extremely weak, almost unidentifiable as such. However, we may regard the arrival of the President and his associates at the Countess' cellar as the crisis. (Will they be trapped underground? There is little doubt that they will, and therefore no suspense.) The Countess' closing of the stone door is the climax. (She succeeds in ridding the world of evil.)

As to theme, it would appear at first glance that Giraudoux is telling us that men of good will have only to act imaginatively to cure the world's ills. Is this it, however? We have been given the solution of a madwoman. Perhaps the madwoman's scheme has been offered ironically, in a profoundly pessimistic view of society. Or is her madness a metaphor of sanity? Is our "sane" world the truly mad one? There is no simple answer. Each of us must decide for himself what the play means. The author's point of view, in this case, is delightfully ambiguous.

Resolution

This includes the report that the world has been cleansed, the acknowledgment of their love by Irma and Pierre (the denouement of the secondary story line, in a more conventional structure, would have occurred before the major climax), and finally the Countess' observation about saving humanity.

Opening

As we have seen, the statement of objective does not occur until the play is nearly half over. Hence the author appears to have raised the curtain too soon, and indeed the long scene of plotting by the conspirators comes dangerously close to tedium before it ends. If the Countess had been introduced earlier, if she were aware of what the President and his associates were planning, and if we knew of her determination to thwart them, then opening the play with the arrival of the President and the Baron at the café would seem more justifiable.

Unity

The unities of time and place are closely enough observed, along with a unity of mood, to give the impression that the play is all of a piece, but the unity of action is given scant obeisance. Not only is the Pierre-Irma romance unconnected with the main problem (it almost seems dragged in to give the play some love interest) but the forward movement is continually being interrupted by further, if less conspicuous, irrelevancies. They hold our interest not because of their bearing on the story (thus heightening our emotional involvement) but because they bear the stamp of one of the wittiest and most sophisticated writers of modern times. He can just about manage it. Most of us, were we so to disregard the basic principles of structure, would find our plays unreadable and unplayable.

Exposition

Beyond the peculiar nature of the conversation and the *outré* characterizations, there is little support for the long scene of exposition that opens the play. We are not emotionally involved with the people as yet, nor is there any conflict to help in holding our attention. The President, Baron, Prospector, and Broker are all pursuing the same ends. The Ragpicker, Deaf-Mute, Peddler, and other denizens of the neighborhood are good local color but little more until Pierre is brought in. His arrival acts as a catalyst, and we begin to "take sides." A great deal of unrelieved exposition has poured forth in the meanwhile.

Once an emotional relationship has been established between the Countess and Pierre, exposition flows more easily. The Countess tells him how she spends her day (this long bravura passage is both characterization and exposition); and Pierre tells how he has been blackmailed. But then the Ragpicker describes to the Countess how the entrepreneurs are plotting to take over the world—something we already know. Although this disclosure does move the Countess into her statement of objective, the structure sags again during the Ragpicker's speech.

The second act opens with another long expository scene. As the stairway and the swinging stone are established for us by the Sewer Man, whom we now meet for the first and only time, interest must depend entirely on the bizarre nature of the people and the subject matter. None of the usual methods of carrying exposition is employed.

Characterization

The Madwoman of Chaillot lives and breathes by its characterizations, and extravagance is the key to everything that contributes to the individuality of its principals—motivation, dialogue, deportment, costume, gesture—all are drawn in the broadest and most theatrical strokes.

The exploiters push their chicanery to the farthest possible limits, caring not even whether they maintain the appearance of legitimate enterprise. The Countess is concerned with saving more than Chaillot, or even Paris. She intends to save humanity, the entire world. Pierre and Irma are wildly impulsive and romantic, impossibly beautiful. The young Policeman is impossibly thickheaded. And so on.

John Gassner has pointed out that the Countess exists simultaneously on planes of reality and theatricality. He could have observed the same thing about them all.

Development

There are but few characters in the play, aside from the protagonist, with strong individual objectives. The President, of course, wants to get the oil, but his cohorts merely echo his own greed. (For structural purposes they are all one character.) The Countess' three mad cronies, delightful as they are, exhibit no desire to change their own circumstances or anything around them. Pierre and Irma want each other, but nothing stands in the way of their romance. Hence the interlocking conflicts that comprise the usual building blocks of a sturdy play are conspicuous mostly by their absence.

The situation, the inventiveness, the peculiarity of the events and the people all contribute to holding our interest in this highly unconventional play, but there are few scenes that do so because of any inherent drama. Even the conference of the four madwomen lacks any kind of suspense; and, when the Ragpicker is permitted to serve as surrogate for the President at the trial, the conflict that would normally develop, were the latter actually defending his actions, loses all force.

Preparation

There are several references to the feather boa the Countess had lost many years before, which is apparently associated in her mind with Adolphe Bertaut. When Pierre brings the boa into the room near the end of the play, the way has been gracefully prepared for the romantic scene in which he pretends to be the lost lover.

Pierre's first entrance is prepared by the expectation that a bomb will explode at noon in the office of the City Architect. The young man couldn't bring himself to plant the bomb.

The purpose of the Sewer Man is to acquaint us with the moving stone and the hidden stairway. While the Sewer Man provides another amusing characterization, there is no movement or conflict in the scene, and it certainly seems risky to devote so much time exclusively to this kind of preparation.

Activity

The Countess' contempt for the entrepreneurs is vividly conveyed when she lets her scarf upset the President's water glass, and later in the business with the soda water siphon. Another effective bit is the Little Man's pressing his life's savings on the Broker, who then turns it over as payment to the Prospector.

The Juggler and the Deaf-Mute contribute two truly spectacular inventions in performance. It should be noted, however, that the Juggler is simply illustrating (however delightfully) what is already clear in speech, and that the Deaf-Mute's gestures are a substitute for speech, and have to be interpreted for us in speech.

Dialogue

Like the characterizations (and dialogue is, of course, an important ingredient of characterization), the play's dialogue is real and theatrical at the same time. The "realistic" prose speeches abound in inventive imagery and playful improvisations. Giraudoux was one of the wittiest of modern playwrights, and his dialogue compensates for many of the play's shortcomings.

Effects

The situations, though highly theatrical and imaginative, are presented realistically until the entrepreneurs are safely behind the stone door. Then the stage directions call for a change of lighting, suggesting an unworldly radiance, and music and voices are heard that cannot be logically accounted for.

Tennessee Williams similarly introduced subjective elements near the end of A Streetcar Named Desire. Whether such a change from one form to another can be successfully accomplished seems to depend on the play itself. Certainly it would be wildly inappropriate in Ghosts or Juno and the Paycock, for example.

Plausibility

One must accept the people and the events of *The Madwoman of Chaillot* on faith, as a child does a fairy tale. Certainly there is little that is plausible in the play, even on its own terms. As for the entrapment of the entrepreneurs being the inevitable result of the Countess' efforts, quite the reverse would seem to be the logical outcome. But, as with all fantasy, one dismisses mundane logic in order to let other factors take over. The practice, though it may afford some momentary delights, has not produced many masterpieces.

BERTOLT BRECHT

The Caucasian Chalk Circle

1944

Suggested by the Chinese play *The Chalk Circle* (ca. 1300 A.D.) and strongly influenced by the conventions of the Chinese theatre, this modern parable is one of Brecht's most admired and successful works. As with most plays intended for "epic" presentation, no attempt is made to convey the illusion of actuality. Quite the contrary. The play continually calls attention to its own theatricality by introducing such devices as direct address to the audience, signs describing the action, and interpolated songs. The Berliner Ensemble, Brecht's own theatre, has even used masks in its production of the work.

The author's purpose, here as elsewhere, was not only to entertain but to instruct and make a social comment. But Brecht's humor and his lyrical gifts keep surfacing in spite of the play's solemn intent, and what results is a spendidly entertaining work along with its message.

Although Brecht probably had the proscenium theatre in mind when he wrote the play, it is adaptable to nearly any kind of stage.

Premise

A tyrant is deposed during a revolution. His wife, in her concern over what dresses to take as she prepares to flee the country, neglects to take her baby. Grusha, a goodhearted young serving maid, is left with the child in her arms.

Synopsis

A stylized setting is called for, the different locales being indicated by the simplest means—projections, banners or signs, significant properties, and so on. A realistic treatment would not only be inappropriate, but contrary to Brecht's method and theories.

The full text consists of a prologue and two parts (or acts), the first part being divided into three scenes, the second into two.

PROLOGUE

Frequently omitted in production, and even in the early printed English translation, the prologue is set in Georgia, U.S.S.R., in 1945, presumably in an area recently recovered from the Nazi invaders. In it, two groups of peasants debate their right to cultivate a certain piece of land. Before the invasion it had been worked by one collective farm, but it now appears that another collective can put the land to more productive use. A number of questions are thus raised, a major one being: who has the better claim to the land, those with an established right of possession or those who can accomplish more for it and with it? This relates directly to the theme of the play that follows.

A professional entertainer, called the Singer, appears in the prologue to perform for the assembled peasants, and the play itself is, presumably, the story that he tells. The Singer will remain on stage throughout the play, commenting on the action and serving as a sort of master of ceremonies. There is no other connection or overlapping of characters between the prologue and the play.

PART ONE

[]   Scene One: The Noble Child

The Singer, or Story Teller, sits on the floor surrounded by a group of listeners, the Chorus. He tells us that in olden times a wealthy tyrant governed this province. The Governor himself, with his Wife and son Michael, a babe in arms, appear in procession on their way to church. Beggars and petitioners crowd about them, and are driven back by soldiers. A relative, the Fat Prince, comes forward to greet the family, and we learn that the governor's army has met with reverses in a current war. The Governor's Wife is concerned for little

Michael, and two doctors in the party argue about his care. As the procession enters the church the Governor is detained by the Adjutant and a messenger from the capital. The Governor isn't interested in hearing any news just then, however, and goes inside, followed by the Adjutant. The messenger leaves in disgust.

The Singer now introduces Simon, a young palace guard, and Grusha, a kitchen maid. They know each other, and there is a flirtatious exchange. It is clear, though, that Grusha is a very proper young woman. She runs off, and Simon steps into the church doorway to listen to the service.

The Singer hints at a revolution that is brewing in the country. The Fat Prince appears, signals to some confederates, and we hear the shouting of orders in the distance. Now the governor's procession comes out of the church and crosses to the palace. The Adjutant lingers behind and tells the messenger, who has reappeared, that the Governor doesn't wish to hear depressing news before dinner. Suddenly the Adjutant is confronted by the rebellious palace guards.

The Singer comments editorially on the nature and weakness of tyranny as the Governor is brought from the palace in chains and led off to be executed. Panic follows, as the palace servants rush outside and run for their lives. Simon searches through the crowd for Grusha, and tells her that he has been ordered to accompany the Governor's Wife on her flight from the country. Grusha thinks he is foolish to obey, but Simon intends to follow orders. Hastily he proposes marriage, and Grusha accepts. He assures her that he will return as soon as the war is over, and Grusha, breaking into song, pledges to be faithful. She runs off.

The Adjutant appears and orders Simon to harness the horses. Simon leaves as servants appear with trunks of clothing. They are followed by the Governor's Wife and Maro, a woman carrying Michael. The Adjutant says there won't be room in the carriage for the trunks, that the Governor's Wife can take only what she needs. She orders the trunks opened, and tries to decide among the many gowns. Grusha enters, and is told to fetch hot-water bottles from the palace. The Adjutant urges haste, for there is fighting in the city. The Governor's Wife tells Maro to put Michael down and bring from the palace a pair of shoes that match a dress she favors. The Adjutant, frantic by now, says they must leave at once, on horseback. But the Governor's Wife is still rummaging through her gowns when the sky turns red and the firing comes very close. Maro and Grusha have returned from the palace, and the Governor's Wife tells Maro to bring the baby. Then she and the whole party flee on foot. But Maro is carrying the shoes, and as she flies off after the others the baby is left with Grusha.

More servants emerge from the palace, and we learn that the tyrant has already been slain. They warn Grusha it is dangerous to be seen with the baby; she must pack her things and flee with the others. Grusha puts the baby down, wraps a blanket around him, and re-enters the palace.

The Fat Prince enters with some drunken soldiers. They have the governor's head, which they hang over the gateway. The Prince wishes he had Michael too, but he doesn't notice the child, and they leave. Grusha returns, screams as she sees the severed head, and goes to the baby. The Singer then describes what follows, with Grusha suiting her actions to the words. She seems to hear the baby calling for help, telling her that those who ignore a fellow human being in need will never know love. Grusha sits, watching the child. Night comes, and eventually the dawn. Finally, unable to resist the appeal of the helpless infant, she picks him up and steals away.

[]   *Scene Two: The Flight Into the Northern Mountains*

The Singer and the Chorus tell us, in song, that Grusha walked along the highway toward the Northern Mountains, singing, with Michael in a sack slung over her shoulder. Grusha sings "The Song of the Four Generals," a ditty about four incompetent generals and one capable soldier.

She arrives at a peasant's cottage and knocks at the door. An old man appears and Grusha asks for a little milk. The peasant asks an exorbitant price for it, and Grusha puts the baby at her own breast. But her breast is dry, and she finally buys the peasant's milk. Then she resumes her journey.

The Singer and Chorus inform us that soldiers loyal to the Fat Prince are pursuing her, in an effort to capture the child. Two Ironshirts appear, singing and discussing the war, military duties, and a soldier's life.

The Singer continues that Grusha went on till she came to a farmhouse, and the girl reappears as the Ironshirts are left behind. In a monologue to the child Grusha tells him that she's going to leave him here on the doorstep. She is sure he will be well cared for at this farm. She herself must get back to the city to rejoin her sweetheart when he returns from the war. She puts the baby down and hides behind a tree. The farmer's wife comes outside, and over the protests of her husband takes him inside the house. The Singer and the Chorus reflect Grusha's conflicting emotions—her relief at being rid of the responsibility, her sadness at the parting.

Grusha walks away from the farmhouse and runs into the two Ironshirts, a Corporal and a Private. They question her but don't suspect at first that she is the woman who took Michael away. The soldiers make advances, and Grusha, frightened, runs back into the farmhouse. She tells the farmer's wife to hide the baby quickly, that the Ironshirts are searching for it. The woman is frightened, but reluctantly agrees to say the baby is hers. The Ironshirts come into the house. The Corporal, wanting to be alone with Grusha, orders the Private to take the wife outside. However, he then discovers the child, in its fine linen. As he bends over the crib Grusha picks up a log and brings it down on his head. He collapses. Quickly Grusha snatches up the baby and rushes off again.

The Singer and Chorus pick up the narrative. After twenty-two days' journey Grusha decided to adopt the child as her own. Grusha sings to the baby of her affection for him, and how their fates are now joined. Then, the Singer tells us, Grusha and the child arrived at a deep chasm, spanned by a rope bridge, some of whose strands are broken. There are several travelers who also want to get across, but they are afraid the bridge will collapse under their weight. Grusha must take the chance, however, for the Ironshirts are following her, and her brother's farm, on the opposite side, promises safety. Grusha sings "The Song of the Rotten Bridge" to the baby, and crosses safely to the other side.

The Ironshirts appear, the Corporal with a bandaged head. Grusha, laughing, holds up the infant for them to see. They cannot pursue her farther. Snow begins to fall, and Grusha sings "The Song of the Child," a kind of lullaby.

[]   *Scene Three: In the Northern Mountains*

The Singer relates that Grusha journeyed for seven days down the mountain slopes with the baby until, ill and exhausted, she reached the house of her brother and sister-in-law. The brother, assuming that the baby is Grusha's son, and illegitimate, pretends to his straitlaced wife that Grusha is on her way to meet her husband, a soldier. The wife, suspicious of the story, further believes Grusha to be coming down with some contagious disease. Grusha collapses in her brother's arms, and the Singer tells us that she and the child stayed at his house through the winter.

We next see Grusha sitting at a loom, weaving. She sings "The Song of the Center," about a girl who pleads with her soldier lover not to fight in the front lines or the rear, which are more hazardous than the center. The brother tells her that when spring comes she must leave, unless a husband can be found, for his wife is very religious. The brother continues that a neighboring peasant woman has a dying son, and a marriage could be arranged with him that would soon leave Grusha a widow. Naturally the mother expects a substantial dowry.

Grusha is tempted. A marriage certificate would help to protect Michael if she were to be questioned by the authorities. The brother leaves to get his wife's milk money to make up the dowry, and Grusha ruefully tells the baby that he is causing a lot of trouble.

The next scene is the peasant's hut, where the dying man lies under a mosquito net. His mother objects strenuously when she sees that Grusha has a child, and has to be persuaded with another large addition to the dowry before she will permit the marriage. Neighbors enter to witness the ceremony, which is conducted by a tipsy monk. The bridegroom is unconscious, and his mother answers for him. Grusha's brother holds the baby, which he tries to hide. The ceremony ended, the brother pays the dowry to the mother and leaves. Grusha is then introduced to the neighbors, who begin to gossip about her and the baby as they sit around consuming the combined wedding and funeral feast. The mother is dissatisfied with the monk she hired.

Suddenly the dying man comes to life and sits up, then falls back again unnoticed. Three musicians enter to play for dancing, and a drunken peasant sings a ribald verse. The guests then begin to talk about the war: it is over, and the soldiers are coming home. Grusha hears this with mixed feelings, and she prays. The mother-in-law is passing cakes when the dying man again comes to life, and this time he speaks and climbs out of bed. The frightened guests run out of the house.

The Singer reflects on the confusion in Grusha's mind. She has a child and a husband now, and her lover is on his way back to her.

The peasant, recovered, is bathing in a wooden tub. His mother pours water over him. Grusha cowers in a corner, with Michael. Her husband orders her to scrub his back, and berates his mother for saddling him with a stupid and sluttish wife. At the same time he upbraids Grusha for not submitting to him.

The Singer continues: as time passed the child learned to walk and talk. And Grusha, yearning for Simon, imagines that she sees his face in the stream where she washes the clothes. Michael and the other children, playing, recreate the execution of the Governor and the flight of his Wife. They run off.

Suddenly Simon appears on the opposite side of the stream.

He has risen in the ranks, is now prosperous, and wants to marry. But Grusha cannot accept his proposal. Weeping, she begs him to cross the stream so she can explain.

The Singer tells of the soldier's experiences in the war, how Simon survived while men all around him fell. Then Simon notices Michael's cap in the grass and assumes the child to be Grusha's. She says there is a child, but he is not her own. Simon doesn't believe her. The Singer recapitulates the story of Grusha's taking the baby to protect it. Simon tells Grusha to return the keepsake he gave her. Grusha cries that she is not the child's mother.

Suddenly voices call out that soldiers have come to take Michael away, and two Ironshirts appear with the boy between them. They say they have orders to take him back to the city, as it is suspected that he is the son of the Governor. Grusha runs after them, pleading.

The Singer tells us that when they arrived in the city Grusha faced a trial. The judge was a man named Azdak.

[] *In Brief*

Structurally, the Prologue may be disregarded. Nearly all of Brecht's plays are intended to instruct and propagandize. The theme of *The Caucasian Chalk Circle* seems entirely clear, but perhaps he felt that for unsophisticated audiences the ancient fable's lesson should be made specifically applicable to today's problems.

Part One, so far as the story line is concerned, proceeds in quite a conventional manner. An intensely sympathetic young woman places herself, through the goodness of her own heart, in a situation in which she is opposed and pursued by morally indefensible authority, and the more she clings to what her instincts tell her is right, the more her troubles multiply. No simple movie western could more clearly differentiate the good guys from the bad, or more unashamedly engage our emotions, in spite of all the "alienating" effects the author has introduced—the Singer-narrator, the songs, the stylization.

PART TWO

[] *Scene One: The Story of the Judge*

We now drop the story of Grusha for a considerable time, and take up that of Azdak. The Singer, in another song, tells us we are to learn how Azdak came to be a judge. On the day the Grand Duke was overthrown and the Governor lost his head, the village scrivener, Azdak, brought a fugitive beggar to his cottage.

The scene is the hut. Azdak, in rags and a bit drunk, questions a taciturn old man and gives him food. It develops that the old man is not what he seems, but is an aristocrat fleeing the revolution. He tries to bribe Azdak to hide him from his pursuers, but Azdak orders him out of the hut. Just then a police officer comes to arrest Azdak for poaching, and the aristocrat hides. Azdak talks himself out of the arrest, and the officer leaves. Azdak has not betrayed the presence of the aristocrat. Azdak takes a kind of rough pity on the old man as he comes out of hiding, and gives him more food.

The Singer then tells us that Azdak learned, to his amazement, that his guest was none other than the Grand Duke himself, fleeing to avoid the fate that had overtaken the Governor. Azdak was so horrified at having helped this archenemy of the people that he called back the police officer and had himself arrested and brought to trial.

The next scene is a courtroom. From a beam hangs the body of the judge. Three Ironshirts sit drinking as Azdak enters, in chains, and dragging the arresting officer along. Azdak denounces himself, saying that he let the Grand Duke escape. The Ironshirts aren't very interested, and when Azdak demands to be taken before the judge they point to the hanging corpse. Azdak protests that forty years ago, when all the officials in the Persian revolution were slaughtered, peasants took their places. He and the policeman then sing "The Song of Injustice in Persia," which tells of an imperialistic war and its effect on the common people at home.

The Ironshirts report that the common people are in rebellion against the new regime here, but have been put down. Why has Azdak come here and denounced himself? Is he some kind of troublemaker? Deciding that he is not to be taken seriously, they unchain him.

The Fat Prince appears, bringing his nephew, whom he proposes as the new judge. He leaves it to the Ironshirts to decide, and quietly tells his nephew that when the Grand Duke is caught they will no longer have to defer to such rabble as these soldiers. Laughingly the Ironshirts propose that Azdak be the judge, but Azdak suggests that the candidates be tested. He himself will play the defendant, while the nephew assumes the role of the judge.

A mock trial ensues, with Azdak playing the part of the Grand Duke, advised by five hundred lawyers. He denies starting the war, and accuses the Fat Prince and his associates of having been war profiteers. The nephew passes sentence on Azdak—death by hanging.

The mock trial over, the Fat Prince orders the Ironshirts to

ratify the selection of his nephew as judge. The soldiers pull the robe
off the corpse, but put it on Azdak, who sits in the judge's seat.

The Singer and Chorus tell us that Azdak remained a judge
during the civil strife of the next two years.

We now see how Azdak carried out his duties. In the case of
a doctor accused of malpractice he fines the patient, and a black-
mailer is ordered to split his loot with the public prosecutor. The
Singer and Chorus comment that for those who could not afford to
bribe the courts there was only one way to secure justice—to appear
before Azdak.

We next see Azdak as a traveling judge, holding court in the
open air. A stableman is accused of rape. Azdak finds the girl guilty
because of her plump figure and seductive behavior. The Singer and
Chorus extol Azdak as the poor man's magistrate.

Azdak next holds court in a tavern. An old woman is accused
of various thefts by three farmers. Azdak puts her in the judge's chair
and likens her to the nation itself, which has been exploited by the
rich. The farmers are fined. The Singer and Chorus tell us that for
two years Azdak befriended the downtrodden, who didn't have to
bribe him to obtain justice. The Singer continues that at last the
Grand Duke and the Governor's Wife returned to power, and Azdak
felt himself to be in great danger of reprisal.

We are again in the courtroom. As the Fat Prince's head is
carried by on a lance, Azdak talks with the officer of his court, telling
him of the changes to be expected. Together they sing "The Song
of Chaos," an account of the reversals of position brought about during a revolution, with a plea to the military to restore order.

Azdak searches the statute book to see what punishment may
be in store for him. The Governor's Widow enters, and an attendant
informs Azdak that she is looking for her infant son, believed to have
been stolen by a young woman who took the baby into the mountains and is now passing him off as her own. Obsequiously Azdak
assures the Governor's Widow that the boy will be found and the
young woman beheaded.

[]   Scene Two: The Chalk Circle

The scene is a courtroom. The Singer tells us that we are to hear how
the child's true mother was found by the test of the chalk circle.
Michael is led across by Ironshirts; then Grusha is brought in. Her
friend, the governor's cook, says that she's lucky to have Azdak as
a judge. Simon enters, and the cook tells Grusha he knows the baby

isn't hers, but that he can't understand why she married. Simon comes forward and says he is willing to swear at the trial that he is the father of the child. Grusha thanks him. An Ironshirt, recognizing her voice, whirls around. His face is scarred. It is the Corporal she hit over the head. Though he would like vengeance, he can't accuse Grusha without implicating himself as a potential abductor of the child.

The Governor's Widow enters, followed by her Adjutant and two lawyers. The latter advise her to curb her disdainful remarks about the common people so long as Azdak is the judge. Several Ironshirts run in, accompanied by the three farmers Azdak had fined. Azdak himself and his court officer are in chains. The Ironshirts strike and kick them, and prepare to hang them. The Governor's Widow is delighted at this development.

Suddenly a Corporal runs in, with a rider from the Grand Duke. Azdak had saved the Duke's life, and is now appointed permanently to the judgeship. The Corporal and rider leave. Azdak, who has fainted, is unchained, revived, and dressed in the judge's gown. The Ironshirts, fawning, leave, and the court officer fetches the statute book for Azdak to sit on. The trial begins.

One of the lawyers, after handing Azdak a bribe, begins a long dissertation on mother love and the ties of blood. Azdak, who has interrupted to ask what the lawyer's fee is, says he listens differently when he knows the attorney is high-priced. Grusha, without claiming that she is the natural mother, says the child is hers. It was she who cared for him and protected him.

The Governor's Widow begins an elaborate show of grief and longing for her abducted child. The second lawyer, in her support, interrupts indignantly, but betrays the fact that without custody of the heir she cannot claim her late husband's estate. The first lawyer tries frantically to shut him up, and then to present the matter in a favorable light. Slowly the story of Grusha's flight to the mountains with the baby is put before Azdak, but with Simon insisting that he is the father. Azdak doesn't know whether to believe this, and that the child is illegitimate, or whether he is actually the Governor's Son, as the Widow insists. Azdak and Simon start insulting each other with folk proverbs; then Grusha and Azdak get into furious argument.

The case is adjourned for a few minutes, and an old couple come in to ask for a divorce. After forty years of marriage they don't like each other. Azdak reserves judgment, and calls Grusha back. She has only to say that Michael isn't hers and the boy will be wealthy. Doesn't she want this for him? The Singer tells us that Grusha believes that with riches he would grow up powerful and cruel; she refuses to give him up, and the Widow tries to attack her.

Azdak orders a circle to be drawn on the floor and the child placed in it. Whichever woman can pull him out will be declared the mother. Despite the objections of the Widow's attorney, the women come to the circle. Each takes a hand, but Grusha lets go and the Widow pulls the boy outside the ring. It is assumed that she has won her case. Grusha begs the judge for custody of the child for a short time longer. The test is repeated, and again Grusha cannot bring herself to risk hurting the boy. Azdak then declares that the child belongs to Grusha, and that the governor's estate shall be converted into a playground for children. The Widow faints and is carried outside.

Azdak removes his robe, and suggests a dance. But he has forgotten to sign the divorce decree for the old couple. He writes, and the court officer, picking up the paper, says he has made a mistake—he has given Grusha a divorce instead. Azdak pretends it was an error, too late to correct now. Grusha and Simon will marry and leave the city with Michael. All dance.

The Singer says the people of the country remember Azdak as presiding in a golden age of justice. Then he points the moral: what there is on this earth shall go to those who are good for it.

[]   *In Brief*

Brecht clearly fell in love with his creation, the rogue Azdak, and he devotes an entirely disproportionate segment of the play to establishing Azdak's history and character. Structurally the play would hardly be altered if II-1 were eliminated entirely. Azdak is such an engaging fellow and his exploits are so amusing, however, that we don't mind this long diversion from the main story. Audiences would undoubtedly grow restive if the material were less interesting.

II-2 follows a conventional structure, of calculated naïveté, that brings the play to a satisfying conclusion, at least on its own terms.

Protagonist and Objective

Grusha is the protagonist; her objective, to protect the child she has grown to love.

Obstacles

The pressures on Grusha are both external and internal. There is, first, the great inconvenience and danger to herself in keeping the child. She is in conflict with the authorities, with her relatives, with the peasant she marries, and ultimately with the Governor's Widow. Her internal struggle is evident from the moment she finds the abandoned infant, and the rift with Simon, her hunger, poverty, and physical peril must all be weighed against her love for the child, which ultimately prevails.

Major Crisis and Climax, Theme

The crisis is the test of the chalk circle, when the decision can swing either way. The climax is Azdak's decision in favor of Grusha, thus stabilizing the situation. The theme, implicit in the climax, is made explicit by the Singer in the play's final moments.

Resolution

This is very brief. It consists of Azdak's giving Grusha a divorce, Simon and Grusha's plan to marry and leave the city with the child, the dance, and the Singer's summary. No words are wasted in covering these topics, for Brecht knew that, once he had passed the climax, the play was really over.

Opening

While the main story line begins when Grusha is left alone with the baby, near the end of I-1, considerable preparation is required to show who the child is and to establish the character of the Governor's Wife. We are also shown the revolution and the reasons for it, and introduced to Grusha's sweetheart, Simon.

The need for putting all this material before the audience before getting under way with the main story pushes the opening farther back in time than is customary in most plays. However, there is so much activity and excitement up to the moment Grusha is left with the child that the lack of focus is hardly noticeable.

Unity

As has already been noted, the concentration throughout II-1 on Azdak, a subsidiary character, seriously damages the play's structural unity. There is, however, a unity of style and point of view that imposes its own sense of wholeness on the work. The unities of time and place are disregarded; but, again, the unconventional manner of staging minimizes the play's episodic nature.

Exposition

Practically all of the play's exposition is carried as straight narrative by the Singer, and, within the convention established by the author, this is satisfactory so long as there isn't too much of it. The music helps.

Characterization

Though Brecht professed to shun emotional involvement for the audience, he appears to have done absolutely everything to enlist our sympathetic response to Grusha. The girl is bright and attractive, in love with the good man and faithful to him, and so good-hearted that she puts her life in mortal peril for two years for the sake of a helpless child. Whether the author intended it or not, we are bound to like such a creature. (On another occasion Brecht seemed astonished and annoyed that audiences were prepared to admire a character he had named Mother Courage.)

Motivations for all the secondary characters, except for Azdak, are quite clear. The Governor, his Wife and the Fat Prince are moved by self-interest. Grusha's relatives, the peasant she marries, and his mother are also looking out for themselves. Simon is in love. Azdak is a little more complicated, and this is what makes him so interesting. He is a careless, happy-go-lucky rogue, but with decent instincts and a contempt for authority that lead him to dispense a kind of rough justice much fairer than the common people could hitherto expect.

Development

Part One follows a chronological sequence of events in very brief scenes, the narrative intervals being bridged by the Singer. Most of the scenes are conventionally built. Grusha's marriage to the peasant, for example, has Grusha as the protagonist; her objective is to become a respectable widow. Obstacles include the greed of the peasant's mother, her objection to Grusha's supposedly having a bastard child, and the fact that the peasant's illness isn't mortal. The climax is Grusha's realization that her dying husband isn't going to die after all, the bitterness of her situation being underscored by her learning, right after the ceremony, that the war is over and the soldiers are coming home. After a brief interlude in which the Singer reflects Grusha's state of mind, the scene's resolution follows—Grusha is legally tied to a brutish man.

     II-1, although it goes back in time to the day of the revolution, proceeds in the same manner structurally. By II-2 both Grusha's story and Azdak's are concurrent.

Dramatic Irony

We know, of course, that Michael is the Governor's Son, and various people who would be concerned by that fact may suspect, though they certainly don't know, that the baby with Grusha is the same child. However, little tension is developed as a result, and Brecht clearly didn't employ dramatic irony here for that purpose.

     He does use the device for both pathos and comedy, though very briefly, when the bridegroom sits up in bed before anyone else in the room is aware that he is alive.

Preparation

Very few plants are required. Two incidents in II-1 prepare for developments in II-2: the farmers that Azdak fined come back to denounce him after the counterrevolution; similarly, Azdak's rescue of the Grand Duke, which is staged for us, motivates the Duke's appointment of Azdak to a permanent judgeship. The old couple who come into court seeking a divorce provide for a more graceful and comic handling of Grusha's divorce at the very end.

Activity

The play is packed with effective stage business, and the full text can profitably be studied for scores of wonderfully inventive things the author has found for his actors to do that help to characterize and carry the story forward.

A few may be pointed out: the governor's guards drive back his subjects when he appears in procession; his Wife rummages through her luggage trying to decide which gowns to take with her on her flight (and how forcefully that imaginative piece of business characterizes the woman!); the governor's severed head is hung up in full view, and later, after the counterrevolution, the severed head of the Fat Prince is carried by; Grusha sits with the abandoned child, unable to tear herself away; she tries to feed the baby from her own dry breast; she carries the child across a dangerous bridge that others dare not step on.

Hamlet tells us that "The funeral baked meats / Did coldly furnish forth the marriage tables," but Brecht gives us the actual meal, hilariously celebrating the two events simultaneously.

The body of the judge hangs from a beam over the bench; later the robe is pulled off the corpse and put on Azdak; Azdak's opinion of the law is suggested by his using the law books mainly to sit on; and, of course, the test of the chalk circle is itself a striking visualization of the issue in the trial.

Dialogue

It is generally felt that Brecht's dialogue in English translation does not have the pungency of the German original. Be that as it may, the totally unrealistic pattern of the plays makes acceptable what seems to us the rather stiff and mannered speech of his characters. In the realistic form we simply would not believe in people who talked that way.

Effects

Epic Theatre has always employed theatricalism with a profusion of effects, often unconventional and startling. As has been already noted, they are much in evidence here—unfamiliar locale and costumes, stylized settings and projections, direct narration, signs and symbols, plus music, singing, and dancing.

Plausibility

Within the very broad strokes in which they have been drawn, the characters behave consistently. (Though we may wonder whether Azdak was quite the type to have himself arrested and brought to trial for having inadvertently helped an aristocrat.) Again it must be noted that only the highly theatricalized form in which the story has been cast makes the action credible. We accept it as we would a fairy tale or fantasy.

JEAN-PAUL SARTRE

No Exit

1944

Written and produced in Paris during the closing days of the German occupation, *No Exit* reflects the existentialist philosophy of its author. Though not successful in the commercial theatre, the play has achieved wide recognition as a work of artistic and philosophical importance. It is in one long act, and is something of a tour de force in construction. It can be performed equally well on a proscenium thrust or stage.

Premise

One man and two women, strangers to one another, all recently deceased and all guilty of thoroughly reprehensible acts during their lifetimes, are condemned to spend eternity in one another's company.

Synopsis

The setting is a windowless, ugly drawing room in hell. The furnishings consist of three ill-matched sofas.

Garcin, a middle-aged man, is ushered into the room by a somewhat supercilious bellboy. Garcin asks about the instruments of torture, and is told that such an idea is merely an earthly superstition. There is no light switch in the room, no mirror, and the only ornament is a hideous and immovable piece of sculpture. There is an electric bell, but the bellboy says that it doesn't always work. He leaves.

Garcin, alone, tries the bell, but it is silent. He attempts to open the door, but it is locked. He beats on it. Nothing happens.

The door opens and Inez, a woman in her thirties, is admitted. She assumes at first that Garcin is the torturer. He introduces himself—a Brazilian journalist and man of letters. He suggests that, since they are to be locked up together, they make an effort to be quiet and polite. Inez does not appear especially co-operative.

Now a beautiful young woman, Estelle, is admitted. Inez is immediately drawn to her. Each of the three tells how he died: Estelle of pneumonia, Inez by suicide, and Garcin by twelve bullets through the chest. Garcin appears to be in some distress of mind, and buries his head in his hands. The trio reminisces briefly, but it is apparent they are going to get on one another's nerves.

They wonder why they have been lodged together. Estelle and Garcin think it must have been mere chance. Inez is sure that it wasn't chance, that their punishment has been carefully planned, and the three of them deliberately chosen to share this room. Estelle speculates that she may have been sent to hell by mistake. Protesting that she is innocent of any wrongdoing, she says that she married a wealthy man much older than she in order to provide for an ailing brother. Then she met the man she was "fated to love." He asked her to run away with him. She refused, but caught pneumonia and died. Garcin protests that he too is blameless. He ran a pacifist newspaper. When war broke out he stuck by his principles and was executed.

But Inez faces the truth. They are all three criminals, and each is to act as the torturer of the other two. Garcin says the solution to their plight is simple. Each will remain silent and pay no attention to the others. They agree on this procedure.

Inez, however, begins to sing, and soon Estelle is asking Garcin for a mirror. Eagerly Inez reaches into her bag, but finds her hand mirror gone. She helps Estelle to apply lipstick, and becomes somewhat amorous. Estelle is both fascinated and repelled by Inez. Secretly she is trying to attract Garcin, who attempts to ignore the two women. When he can no longer do so, he says he isn't interested in Estelle. He asks merely to be left to his own thoughts.

There is silence for a few moments; then Inez bursts out that it is impossible for them to ignore one another. She says that Estelle's behavior is entirely conditioned by Garcin's presence, and that he has already stolen Estelle from her.

Garcin gives up trying to impose silence. He demands that they all stop pretending, and tell the truth about themselves. He leads off. He is here because of his cruel treatment of his wife. Drunk, he would bring other women into the house, and his wife, loving him, was spared nothing.

Inez is next. She tells how she seduced her cousin's wife, how the cousin was killed in an accident, then how the wife turned on the gas one night, killing herself and Inez as she slept.

Estelle is far more reluctant to tell her story, and, when pressed, tries to break out of the room. Gradually the truth is forced from her. She had an unwanted baby by a lover, and drowned the child. The lover killed himself.

Perhaps now that everything is in the open, Garcin observes, they can help one another. On second thought, he and Inez see that this triangle is made for torture. Not one of them can respond naturally to another while the third one is present. Inez tells him, however, that if he will leave her and Estelle in peace she will not harm him.

Suddenly, in deep distress, Estelle appeals to Garcin for help. She envisions another lover, on earth, in the arms of a rival, and hears the other woman telling her lover about the drowning of the baby. Estelle appeals to Garcin to take her in his arms. He tells her to go to Inez for comfort. Inez attempts to talk to her as her lovers did, but Estelle spits in her face. Inez tells Garcin that he will pay for that.

Estelle then makes advances to Garcin. Physically he begins to respond, and this enrages Inez. She tells them to make love, but reminds them that she is there, watching every move. Garcin is distracted by a vision of his associates discussing him. He reveals that he wasn't shot for sticking to pacifist principles, but for trying to flee the country. Estelle tries to reassure him that he acted rightly, but Inez knows it was cowardice that made him run away. Estelle doesn't think his motives matter, so long as he kisses well. Garcin admits the truth of Inez's accusation, for he faced death badly too. He sees that his friends all think of him as a coward, that this is the legend he has left, with no possibility of changing it.

Garcin appeals to Estelle to have faith that he didn't run away, that he wasn't a coward, and she agrees—but all too easily. Laughing, Inez points out that Estelle doesn't give a damn either way. All she wants is a man.

Desperately Garcin tries to get out. Estelle repels him even more than Inez. But the door won't open and the bell doesn't ring.

Furiously he bangs on the door and throws himself against it. Estelle begs him, if he should get out, to take her with him. He rebuffs her scornfully. Inez says that if he gets out she and Estelle will have the place to themselves, but Estelle replies that if Garcin escapes she will leave too.

Suddenly, after a violent outburst from Garcin, begging for any kind of torture but this, the door opens. Neither Garcin nor Estelle, however, has the boldness to go through it. Estelle tries to force Inez out, but cannot. Garcin shuts the door and says he is staying because of Inez, for she knows the meaning of wickedness, shame, and fear. She knows from experience what it means when he admits to cowardice. Ultimately it is Inez he must convince; he couldn't leave her here gloating over his defeat. Estelle doesn't matter; Inez is the one to help to restore his faith in himself.

Inez says his earthly dreams and intentions are of no consequence, that he "died too soon" is no excuse for his behavior on earth, for when one dies one's life is complete, ready for judgment. Now Garcin was a coward because she wills it; he is at her mercy.

Garcin realizes that Inez is at his mercy as well. He kisses Estelle, arousing the other woman's furious jealousy. She watches and taunts Garcin until he finally walks away from Estelle. At last he realizes what it means to be damned. "Hell is—other people."

Estelle pleads for love, but Garcin thrusts her away. Then she tries to stab Inez with a paper-knife, but Inez only laughs. She is dead already. And they are all three there—forever.

Protagonist and Objective

Garcin is the protagonist; his objective, to escape the self-torment that gnaws at him because of cowardice in life. Only the faith of some other person can save him. He fails to achieve his goal.

Obstacles

Estelle's professed faith in Garcin is self-motivated lip service, and means nothing. Inez cannot and will not, because of her jealousy, give him the assurance he needs.

Crisis and Climax, Theme

This is a play, like *Oedipus the King*, *Ghosts*, and *Death of a Salesman*, of inexorable Fate pursuing its victim. And as in those plays the crisis occurs before the rise of the curtain, for the protagonist's last opportunity to escape retribution happens long before that part of the over-all story that the dramatist chooses to present.

The climax, just before the end, is Garcin's realization that he is trapped with two other people from whom there is no escape, that they are his torturers, the manipulators of his mind. At this point he gives up fighting the inevitable.

Thematically the play implies that each of us builds his own world, and his own heaven or hell.

Resolution

Estelle tries to stab Inez, but Inez knows that there is no release for any of them. All three begin to realize what "forever" means.

Opening

Sartre has obviously chosen the only satisfactory point at which to begin the play—the arrival of the three people in hell. Nothing would be gained by showing us their lives on earth; starting later, after they had become acquainted, would be to deprive the play of their dawning comprehension of their fate.

Unity

All three classic unities—time, place, and action—are observed. The play's structure is very tight. There isn't a superfluous element anywhere.

Exposition

As in the three plays of "inexorable Fate" already mentioned, exposition of past events is unfolded late and slowly, and with maximum dramatic effectiveness. Not only is it exceedingly painful for each of the three characters to reveal the truth about himself; but, once the truth is exposed, the relationships are altered in subtle ways. One is never conscious of these recitals of earthly guilt as exposition, for it is the truth about these people that we seek. This is the very essence of the play.

Characterization

Garcin's courtesy reflects a certain breeding. Inez is blunt and outspoken, a totally different kind of person. Estelle is emotional and transparently insincere. These are the foundations on which the disclosures of their pasts are built. Although all are guilty of abhorrent acts in life, the contrast in their characters is very pronounced.

Development

No Exit is essentially one long scene, with a single protagonist following one objective all the way through. Estelle and Inez are secondary, but each is given a strong objective, and obstacles similar to Garcin's. Each of the women is driven by a desire to escape her inner torment by contact with another being. Each is frustrated: Estelle by Garcin's preoccupation and inability to make love with Inez present, Inez by Estelle's indifference and hostility.

It might be supposed that what we have in this play is three protagonists, equally balanced, all moving toward similar goals—an impressive structural feat indeed. But examination shows that it is Garcin's story we are following, and that his full realization of his fate is the play's climax. Estelle's realization occurs during the resolution. Inez has known their fate almost since her arrival.

Preparation

Very little preparation is needed. The bellboy plants the fact that the bell doesn't always work. It is better, when Garcin pushes the button, that we know that this is in all probability a vain act. It is also noted, early in the play, before Estelle's need for a mirror, that there is none in the room. Garcin refers, also quite early, to his execution, implying that it was because he stuck to his principles. We learn the real reason later.

Activity

As a play of ideas expressed largely in conversation, there isn't a great deal of physical activity; but such activity as there is is very telling. There are the colors of the costumes clashing against those of the sofas, the ugly sculpture that is too heavy to lift, the worthlessness of the paper-knife as a weapon. And, above all, the door that swings open after Garcin has pounded on it for so long. This visualizes the means of escape they all think they want, but that none can bring himself to act upon.

Dialogue

The realistic, matter-of-fact tone of the dialogue is exactly right for the play. The horror of the situation in which these three ordinary people find themselves would be much diluted were their speech given to flights of poetry, rhetoric, or symbolism.

TENNESSEE WILLIAMS
A Streetcar Named Desire
1947

Produced while the author was still in his early thirties, this play is theatrically one of his most effective, and has enjoyed enormous commercial success.

Action and dialogue are realistic and convincing. But Williams has also added highly theatricalist elements, such as mood music, sound effects, and a colorful and imaginative nonillusionistic setting that combine with the realism to produce a work poetic in feeling, formidable in power.

Premise

Blanche Du Bois, a sensitive young high school teacher of some refinement, has grown up on a plantation that has been lost because of financial reverses. Without funds, she arrives in New Orleans to live with her younger sister Stella, now contentedly married to coarse, lusty, and totally plebian Stanley Kowalski. They live in a squalid flat in a disreputable section of the city. The flat is not big enough to insure any measure of privacy, and it is plain, in any case, that Blanche's presence is a disruptive influence on the marriage.

Facts antecedent to the play but disclosed as it proceeds include the following: Blanche, some years before, had married a young poet who turned out to be homosexual and committed suicide; in a search for compensating affection she had seduced a high school student and been discharged. She has since been engaged in prostitution, but has finally been obliged to leave her small home town.

Synopsis

The setting throughout is a combination interior and exterior. It includes a cross section of the Kowalski flat, with a door leading to a bathroom. Visible at stage right is a street corner. Outside stairs lead to a flat above the Kowalskis'.

The play is divided into eleven scenes, with intermissions suggested after Scenes Four and Six.

[] *Scene One*

Blanche arrives at the flat, and, not finding her sister Stella at home, is admitted by Eunice, a young housewife who lives upstairs. Blanche is dismayed that her sister and brother-in-law live in a slum. We learn that Blanche has been a school teacher and had lived on a Mississippi plantation. Eunice goes off to tell Stella that Blanche is there. Blanche, alone, finds a bottle of whiskey and fortifies herself.

Stella runs in and there is an affectionate reunion of the sisters. Blanche reveals her distaste for the shabby flat, and, pretending that she hasn't already had a drink, has another. Stella appears to be quite satisfied with her surroundings. It is apparent that Blanche is in a nervous and overwrought condition, and that she needs reassurance about her own attractiveness, among other things. She tells Stella that the superintendent of schools has suggested that she take a leave of absence. Stella tries to warn her sister that Stanley, whom she clearly loves, and his friends are not the kind of people to whom Blanche will respond.

Blanche reveals that their mortgaged plantation, Belle Reve, has been lost. She is resentful that the burden of trying to keep it fell on her, while Stella, "in bed with her Polack husband," gave her no help.

Stella, crying, goes into the bathroom, and Stanley arrives. Blanche introduces herself. Stanley is polite, and asks if she's going to stay there. He shouts a vulgarity to his wife in the bathroom, and asks Blanche if she wasn't married once. Blanche admits that she was and that the boy died. Suddenly she feels ill.

[]   *Scene Two*

Stella tells Stanley that she is taking Blanche out to dinner and a show, because of Stanley's poker party scheduled for this evening. She then informs him that Belle Reve has been lost, and asks him to be nice to Blanche and flatter her a bit. She also asks him not to mention her pregnancy until Blanche is "in a quieter condition."

Stanley is very suspicious that Stella has been swindled out of her (and by extension, his) share of the plantation. He wants an accounting. Angrily he pulls clothes, furs, and costume jewelry out of Blanche's trunk. Where did she get the money to pay for all this stuff? Not from a teacher's pay! Failing to calm him down, Stella goes outside as Blanche emerges from the bathroom.

Playfully flirtatious, Blanche fishes for compliments and asks Stanley to button up her dress in back. He demands to see papers on the sale of Belle Reve. Blanche denies any wrongdoing, but Stanley begins pawing through her trunk. He finds a packet of letters, which Blanche furiously snatches away from him. They are poems written to her by her dead husband. She then gives Stanley all the papers pertaining to Belle Reve. The plantation was apparently lost when mortgage payments couldn't be met. Stanley says he will have a lawyer go over the documents, that he must look after his wife's interests, now that she is going to have a baby.

Blanche goes outside and tells Stella that she and Stanley have thrashed things out. The sisters start off for their evening as two of the poker players arrive.

[]   *Scene Three*

It is after two in the morning, and the poker game is still in full swing. One of the men, Mitch, thinks he should go home. He lives with his mother, who is ill.

Blanche and Stella return home and pass through the kitchen, where the game is, to the bedroom. Mitch is coming out of the bathroom, and Stella introduces him. Blanche senses that he is more of a gentleman than the others. Mitch returns to the game, and the two women start preparing for bed. As Stella goes into the bathroom Blanche turns on the radio. Stanley, half drunk, comes into the bedroom and turns it off, then goes back to the game. Mitch decides to go to the bathroom again. Blanche tells him it is occupied. He offers her a cigarette. The case, given him by a girl he was once in love with, now dead, is inscribed with a quotation from Elizabeth Barrett Browning.

Mitch and Blanche are soon deep in sympathetic conversation. She pretends that she is a little younger than Stella, and that she has come here for a while to help her sister, who is run-down. Blanche has bought a paper lamp shade, and asks Mitch to put it over a light bulb. She tries to impress him with her refinement and her superiority to her present surroundings. As Stella comes out of the bathroom Blanche turns on the radio, and she and Mitch dance for a moment. Stanley, infuriated, comes into the bedroom and throws the radio out the window. Stella asks the poker players to leave, and Stanley charges after her. He hits her, and the other men pull him away and quiet him down.

Blanche leads Stella to the flat upstairs to spend the night. Stanley is too drunk to realize what he has done, and the men lead him into the shower, then pick up their winnings and go.

Dripping wet, Stanley emerges from the bathroom. He knows Stella is upstairs, goes outside, and bawls for her lustily. Eunice appears and says that Stella won't come down. But after a few moments she does, and Stanley bears her off to the bedroom.

Blanche comes down, looking for Stella, and runs into Mitch, who has not gone home. He tells her not to worry about Stella and Stanley; they are crazy about each other. He offers Blanche a cigarette. They sit on the steps, and Blanche thanks him for being so kind to her.

[]   *Scene Four*

Early the following morning Blanche comes in to find Stanley gone and Stella lying contentedly in bed. Blanche expects Stella to leave her husband, and is puzzled and shocked that Stella intends to do no such thing. Stella maintains that last night's fracas wasn't nearly so serious as Blanche thinks.

But Blanche is not persuaded, and recalls a college beau, Shep Huntleigh, of Dallas, now well-to-do. Impulsively she tries to compose a telegram to Shep appealing for money, so that she and Stella can escape. Stella wants no part of this, and tries to give Blanche five dollars. Blanche insists that Stella must leave her husband, but Stella is not leaving. Her marriage works.

Stanley enters the kitchen, and, unseen by the two women, hears Blanche launch into a diatribe against him. He is common, has an animal's habits, is a thoroughgoing brute. Pretending to have just arrived and heard nothing, Stanley calls Stella, who enters the kitchen and in full view of her sister throws her arms around Stanley and kisses him. Stanley grins at Blanche.

There is now an intermission.

[] *In Brief*

From the moment we first see Blanche we sense that she has entered an environment in which she cannot survive. The author has set up a marvelous contrast between her refinement, her pretensions, her helplessness, and the earthy vitality of the slum.

Perhaps Blanche could be saved by sympathy and understanding, and while either Mitch or Stella could respond to her need, Stella's ties to her extravagantly virile husband are stronger than her ties to her sister. And sympathy and understanding are the last qualities Blanche can look for in her brother-in-law, who quite correctly sees in her a threat to his marriage.

Trapped in this situation, Blanche tries to extricate herself by persuading Stella to flee with her. But Stella chooses her husband, now Blanche's implacable enemy. Unless Blanche finds some means of escape she will be destroyed.

[] *Scene Five*

It is late afternoon. Blanche is writing a letter to Shep Huntleigh, and reads some of it to Stella. Asserting that life is a continual round of cocktails and luncheon parties here at her sister's, she tells him that she may decide to visit Dallas. Upstairs Eunice and her husband are fighting. She runs down the steps with him after her. They head for a bar. Stanley enters, and Stella comments that going for a drink is better than calling the police.

Blanche is making polite but barbed conversation with Stanley when he suddenly asks her if she knows someone by the name of Shaw, who claims to have met Blanche in her home town at a disreputable hotel. Blanche, visibly shaken, denies it. Stanley goes outside as Eunice and her husband return, arms around each other.

Blanche tries to find out how much Stella knows about her recent life. She admits there was a good deal of talk about her during her last two years at home. She is so nervous she spills a drink. She tells Stella she is going out with Mitch tonight. Perhaps Mitch will be the one to take her away from this intolerable situation. Stella assures her sister that it can and will happen.

Stanley appears outside, calls Stella, and they go off to a bar with Eunice and her husband. Blanche is alone as a young man appears to collect for the newspaper. Blanche is immediately coquettish, and finally plants a kiss on the embarrassed young man's lips. He escapes as Mitch arrives with a bunch of roses. Blanche welcomes him affectedly.

[] *Scene Six*

Blanche and Mitch return from their date about two o'clock. They have not had a particularly good time, for which Blanche takes the blame. She invites Mitch in, as Stanley and Stella haven't come home yet. *"Voulez-vous couchez avec moi ce soir?"* she asks, knowing that he understands no French. She fixes drinks, and they go into the bedroom. There is a tentative fumbling embrace, which she discourages, saying she has old-fashioned ideals.

Blanche tries to learn what, if anything, Stanley has told Mitch about her. She complains of Stanley's coarseness and says that he hates her, that she must get away from there. Mitch says he told his mother about Blanche, and the old lady wanted to know Blanche's age. He admits that he will be lonely when his mother dies.

Blanche tells him of her marriage to the young poet, that she discovered his homosexuality, and that he had shot himself. Mitch is deeply moved by the story. He embraces Blanche, and suggests that each of them needs the other. She responds with grateful sobs.

This is the second intermission.

[] *In Brief*

Frantically looking for a way out, Blanche considers an appeal to Shep Huntleigh, which even she realizes is useless. Meanwhile, Stanley has begun his counterattack. He has already learned something of her disreputable past, and under this added pressure Blanche is near panic.

However, Mitch, in his loneliness, is susceptible to Blanche's warmth and understanding, and it would appear, at the end of Scene Six, that Mitch may offer the means of her salvation. The unknown factor that makes her still vulnerable is Stanley's reaction to such a union, for Mitch is his wartime pal.

[] *Scene Seven*

Some months later Stella is planning a little party in celebration of Blanche's birthday. Stanley tells Stella that he has at last found out the truth about Blanche. After Belle Reve was lost she moved into a hotel and became notoriously promiscuous. Stella doesn't believe this, but Stanley says the information has been thoroughly checked by his traveling friend. He continues that she lost her high school teaching job when it was discovered that she was having an affair with a student. After this she had to leave town.

Blanche emerges momentarily from the bathroom, and senses that Stella is upset. Stella defends her sister to Stanley, calling the stories exaggerated. She tells Stanley that she has asked Mitch to the birthday party. Stanley replies that he has already told Mitch about Blanche's past, and Mitch will not be coming. Stella is utterly dismayed. With no job and no prospect of marriage, what will her sister do? Stanley continues that he is presenting Blanche with a return ticket home.

As Blanche comes out of her bath she realizes that something has happened, something has gone very wrong.

[] *Scene Eight*

A short time later Blanche, Stella, and Stanley are finishing the birthday supper. Even though she has been "stood up" by her beau, Blanche pretends to a gaiety she doesn't feel. When Stella criticizes Stanley's manners he throws his dishes on the floor and stalks outside. Blanche asks Stella what has happened. Why didn't Mitch come to the party? Vainly she tries to reach Mitch by phone.

Stella goes outside and rebukes Stanley for his behavior. Stanley assures her that things are going to be all right, the way they used to be, after Blanche goes. They return to the kitchen.

Stanley, confronting a very tense Blanche, gives her his birthday present, a bus ticket home. Blanche tries to laugh it off, but can't, and runs into the bathroom. Stella is furious, and demands to know why Stanley has behaved so cruelly. Stanley protests that he has taken all the insults from Blanche that he can swallow, and repeats that once she is out of here he and Stella will be happy again.

Suddenly Stella's labor pains begin, and she asks to be taken to the hospital.

[]   *Scene Nine*

Later that evening, after Stanley has taken his wife to the hospital and Blanche is alone, drinking, Mitch appears. He has had a few drinks himself. She rebukes him gently for "forgetting" her party.

Mitch is belligerent and surly, and observes that he has never seen her except under soft lights. She has made sure he hasn't. He tears the paper shade off the lamp and stares at her under the harsh light. He could forgive her for being older than she pretended, but not for her other lies, he says. Stanley has told him all about her, and he has confirmed the truth of the stories.

Bitterly Blanche admits the truth, but defends her actions as the consequence of her young husband's death, the need to care for her dying mother, and the eventual loss of the plantation.

When Mitch proposes to have "what he has been missing all summer," she asks him to marry her. He refuses: she is not good enough to bring into the home of his mother. Hysterically Blanche drives him out of the flat.

[]   *Scene Ten*

A few hours later Blanche is packing. She has dressed in her finery, but when she examines her face in a mirror she smashes the glass.

Stanley comes home, reporting that the baby isn't expected before morning. Blanche claims that she has had a wire from Shep Huntleigh, inviting her to a cruise on his yacht. Stanley pulls off his shirt and opens a bottle of beer. Blanche elaborates on her relationship with Huntleigh, who simply wants the companionship of a lady of intelligence and breeding. She goes on to say that Mitch had the nerve to come and repeat the slanders that Stanley had spread about her, that later he tried to apologize, but that she had sent him packing.

Stanley puts a stop to these fancies. There is no telegram, and he knows where Mitch is now. Stanley has been wise to Blanche from the start. He goes into the bathroom to change into pajamas.

Frantically Blanche tries to phone Huntleigh in Dallas, or to reach him by wire. Shadows, reflections, and weird cries surround her, and we become aware of the prostitution, drunkenness, and thievery taking place outside.

Stanley comes out of the bathroom and approaches her. She is very frightened and smashes a bottle, threatening him with the broken top. He makes her drop it, then picks her up and carries her to the bed.

[] *Scene Eleven*

It is some weeks later. Another poker game is in progress. Mitch is one of the players. In the bedroom Stella tells Eunice she has informed Blanche that someone is calling to take her to the country for a rest, and that Blanche has got this all mixed up in her mind with Shep Huntleigh. Blanche appears at the bathroom door long enough to give Stella some instructions about her wardrobe.

Stella tells Eunice that she couldn't do anything else but have Blanche committed. If Stella had believed Blanche's story about Stanley she wouldn't be able to go on living with him.

Blanche comes out of the bathroom, senses that something threatens her, and demands an explanation. She is obviously unbalanced, and the other two women try to distract her while they are waiting.

A doctor and matron appear outside. Blanche is persuaded to cross through the kitchen. Mitch does not look at her. When she sees the doctor she protests that he isn't Shep Huntleigh, and returns to the flat. Strange lights and sounds surround her, and the voices echo. Stanley comes in to help the matron. Stella, outside, cries out in remorse as Eunice tries to comfort her. Mitch starts toward the bedroom, but Stanley stops him, and Mitch collapses, sobbing. As Blanche fights back, the matron forces her to her knees.

The doctor comes into the bedroom, removes his hat, and speaks to Blanche gently and politely. He indicates to the matron that a strait jacket won't be necessary. He leads Blanche out through the kitchen, past the poker players and past the weeping Stella.

Stanley comes outside and comforts his wife. The three players in the kitchen resume the poker game.

[] *In Brief*

Over the summer Blanche has been cultivating Mitch, now her only hope of escape. But we learn of the weapon Stanley now holds, and that he has already used it. Stella, caught in the middle of the struggle, is powerless.

It is Mitch who reveals to Blanche that he knows the truth about her—a far more effective and affecting treatment of the incident than if Stanley had told her, for she and Stanley are already enemies. With Mitch, Blanche has farther to fall.

With no defenses left, and Stella refusing to believe that Stanley attacked her, Blanche's reason gives way. She is saved from complete humiliation by a sympathetic doctor, who treats her as a lady.

Protagonist and Objective

Blanche is clearly the protagonist. It is her story, not Stanley's, that we are following. And her need for shelter, sympathy, and peace is so obvious that a specific statement of objective isn't necessary. But Blanche asks more of life than life can deliver. She demands gentility and is met with crudeness. She dreams of romance but finds only sex. She is close to being an alcoholic. This is a woman on the ragged edge, near desperation, who is trying to save herself. And her resources—spiritual, emotional, financial—are gone or rapidly vanishing.

Obstacles

While Blanche's own weakness contributes to her downfall, Stanley is the principal obstacle that she faces. Were it not for him she might possibly find a tolerable place in society, even marry such a man as Mitch and live happily. But her airs and pretensions to refinement, even her presence in the little flat, lead Stanley to regard her as a threat to his marriage and his way of life. And so her need for protection is assaulted by crude forces of vulgarity and brutality.

In another sense it is Blanche's world of financial and social security, now reduced to decadence and pretense, that is ultimately destroyed by a world that has managed, with a set of earthy values, to survive.

Major Crisis and Climax, Theme

The crisis is not shown. It occurs just before Scene Seven, when Stanley tells Mitch that Blanche has been a harlot. From this point on, Blanche is doomed, for Mitch was her last hope.

The climax is the rape, Stanley's ultimate triumph over Blanche.

The play is rich in thematic material. Probably one is most apt to read into it the inability of a weak and decadent culture to adapt to a totally different environment, the ultimate triumph of a healthy life force over a cultural and sexual impotence.

Resolution

This includes Scene Eleven in its entirety.

As a result of her total disappointment and defeat, Blanche's mind has become unbalanced, and even Stella must free herself from this burden. Only Stella and Mitch are truly affected as she is taken away.

A lady to the end, Blanche responds to the doctor's kindness, even though this is merely his simple way of handling her. After this brief interruption the poker game continues.

Opening

There would be no particular advantage in beginning the play before Blanche's arrival in New Orleans, since this is the story of the forces that destroy her, and the agent of her destruction is Stanley. Her loss of the plantation, her affair with the high school student, her promiscuity, all can be put to better use as exposition (since they become tools in Stanley's hands) than they would if we saw them acted out. The author has chosen the right moment in the over-all story to begin his dramatization.

Unity

While the unity of time is disregarded, unity of place and action are observed. It is the latter that is primarily responsible for the tightness of the structure that we feel. There is nothing in the entire work that does not bear on the story of Blanche's downfall.

Exposition

The early exposition is handled by the simple and reliable device of placing one of the characters in unfamiliar surroundings, so that explanations are in order. There is a brief scene between Blanche and Eunice. It is without conflict, but Blanche is obviously so out of place in this environment that we are curious to know more about her. The same is true during the first part of the scene with Stella.

We sense the potential of conflict in everything the two women say to each other. We also suspect that Blanche isn't all she pretends to be. (She goes after a second drink when she has already had one surreptitiously, tells Stella that one is her limit, and then has a third.) Her long account of how Belle Reve was lost is gripping because of her emotional defensiveness, the importance of the information to Stella, and the fact that it nearly leads to a quarrel between the sisters.

Blanche's telling Mitch about her marriage (Scene Six) is absorbing exposition not only because it is so hard for her to talk about it, but because of the effect it is having on Mitch.

Stanley's revelations about Blanche's past hardly seem like exposition at all, though they are. As in *Oedipus the King* and *Ghosts*, exposition of past events is used here to drive the story forward. We are held and moved by it because we know what this knowledge in Stanley's hands can do to Blanche. Stella reflects our own fears.

Characterization

It would be hard to find more sharply drawn and contrasting characters than the four principals in the play. Blanche and Stanley both, in their mannerisms, dress, and speech, are so antithetic that one can sense the inevitable clash even in Scene One.

Stella is balanced between the two. Her speech reflects the more cultivated background in which she has grown up, while her actions reflect her divided loyalties. Mitch's small talk and his actions are equally revealing. He doesn't want to remove his coat because he perspires. His amorous attempts are awkward and fumbling. He speaks tentatively, afraid of hurting and afraid of being hurt.

There is hardly a line spoken by one of the four principals that, taken out of context, couldn't be immediately identified with the character.

Development

We have already examined Blanche's objective, since she is the protagonist of the entire play.

Stanley's objective is to protect his marriage and his way of life. He is often the protagonist of incidents when he is attacking

Blanche. In Scene Eight, for example, his objective is to order Blanche to leave. Obstacles are his reluctance to open up the subject during the party, and Stella's disapproval. The climax is his giving Blanche the bus ticket, and the resolution, his assurance to Stella that all will be well once Blanche is gone. The beginning of Stella's labor is incidental, and not a part of this substructure.

Stella's objective is to find a way of protecting her sister while preserving her own marriage. Mitch's is to find a companion in his loneliness.

Most of the scenes are made up of two or more incidents, all related to the underlying structure of the entire play. Some of the incidents are built in the conventional manner. Scene Six, which contains but one incident, has Blanche as its protagonist. Her objective is to lead Mitch to a proposal of marriage. The obstacle is Mitch's reticence and shyness. The climax is his embrace after Blanche has told him the story of her marriage. The resolution is her relief and gratitude.

Dramatic Irony

The device is used extensively in the play. The first time is Blanche's pretending not to know where the liquor is (Scene One). She has already found it. Later she says that one drink is her limit, and then that she seldom touches it.

In Scene Two we are already aware of Stanley's anger and suspicions about the loss of the plantation when Blanche comes out of the bathroom and tries to be flirtatious.

In Scene Three we know that Blanche is lying to Mitch about her age, and in general misrepresenting herself and her position there.

In Scene Four we know that Stanley has overheard Blanche's attack on him. The two women do not.

In Scene Six those who understand French know what Blanche is really saying to Mitch. And we know she doesn't have the ideals to which she pretends.

During most of Scene Seven and all of Eight we know that Stanley has learned the truth about Blanche; then we learn that he has already told Mitch, so we know why Mitch does not come to the party. The use of this particular irony continues into Scene Nine, and ends when Mitch tells Blanche that Stanley has revealed the truth about her past. Now Blanche knows what we know.

In Scene Ten we know that Blanche is merely pretending there has been a wire from Shep Huntleigh, and that Mitch did not return and apologize.

In Scene Eleven we know, as Blanche does not, that Stella has had her committed. We also know that Blanche's story of the rape, which Stella refuses to believe, is true. Finally, unlike Blanche, we know who the doctor is, and what motivates his kindness to her.

Preparation

Mitch's tearing the paper shade off the lamp so that he can look closely at Blanche is carefully planted. In Scene One Blanche tells Stella to turn off the light, she won't be looked at in this glare; in Scene Three Blanche asks Mitch to put the shade over the light bulb. There is another reference to it in Scene Five.

Stanley's ability to check on the reports of Blanche's past is planted in Scene Five when he tells her that a man named Shaw goes in and out of her home town.

Activity

There is a lot of physical activity in the play, and all of it is significant. One very important point is made by activity alone, without dialogue, and it is tremendously effective. At the end of Scene Four Stella, after listening to Blanche's diatribe against Stanley, runs to embrace him, as Blanche watches.

Stanley's crudeness and bad temper are demonstrated several times in physical movement: he pulls her clothes, jewelry, letters, out of her trunk (and Blanche snatches the letters back); he tosses the radio out the window; he throws his supper dishes on the floor before stalking out of the kitchen; he chases Stella and hits her; and, of course, the rape is the most significant business of all, symbolizing as it does his complete triumph over Blanche.

There are equally revealing bits of business for Blanche: she asks Stanley to button up her dress; she kisses the paper boy, a complete stranger. Her state of mind is revealed in her frantic efforts to phone Shep Huntleigh; and, in Scene Ten, after she dresses in her finery she smashes the mirror.

The empty place at the birthday party dramatizes Mitch's absence. And no one who has ever seen a good production of the play will ever forget Mitch's tearing the shade off the light and searching Blanche's face in its glare.

The matron forcing Blanche to the floor and the doctor lifting her up are also very effective pieces of business.

On the street outside, activity is used to help establish the atmosphere of the quarter, and, particularly in the climactic Scene Ten, to complement the action in the flat.

Dialogue

Although the mood of the play is poetic, dialogue throughout is realistic. Even Blanche's poetic flights, such as her reference to the Pleiades' going home from their bridge party, are realistic in the sense that they are natural speech for Blanche—the kind of things such a woman would say. The poetry of the play is achieved not by formal poetic speech, but by a combination of many different factors (and this is Tennessee Williams' magic, a quality that is perhaps not subject to cold analysis).

Effects

Williams has never been afraid to employ highly theatrical effects, and this play is no exception. The mood is reinforced time and again by such devices as the sound of a blues piano and other kinds of music, the roar of a locomotive and the glare of its head lamp, thunder, cries of street venders.

There are other effects, not to be accounted for in strictly realistic playwriting. The walls of the flat become transparent, for example. And we go into complete subjectivity as Blanche's mind gives way. Inhuman voices, like jungle cries, are heard; shadows and reflections move like flames along the walls.

Plausibility

As with all fine plays, characterizations and motivations are so balanced and locked together that the course of events seems utterly logical. Blanche is doomed from the moment she sets foot in Stanley's home. One of them has to destroy the other, and Stanley is the stronger.

ARTHUR MILLER

Death of a Salesman

1949

We need not be too concerned here over the debate this play has aroused: whether a "common man" (one who, furthermore, is misguided, inarticulate, and incapable of tragic insight) can be the subject of a true tragedy. This is for the theoreticians to argue; we are concerned with structure. *Death of a Salesman,* which has enjoyed great popular success, is one of the most important plays of the mid-century and an extraordinary technical achievement. In the author's words, he resolved "not to write an unmeant word for the sake of the form but to make the form give and stretch and contract for the sake of the thing to be said." And John Gassner comments that Miller's flair for tight construction "becomes a virtue . . . because it gives the author both the assurance and the skill to break the conventional mould of realism."

Arthur Miller tells us that his original conception of the work envisioned everything taking place inside Willy Loman's head, the past and present existing all together without sequential boundaries of time or place. Structurally the play would simply draw up Willy's memories "like a mass of tangled roots without end or beginning" until the memories overwhelmed him and he destroyed himself.

But the play did not develop quite like that. A good deal of it does consist of Willy's memories and his imaginings, but many of the scenes are written in a straightforward, realistic manner, moving forward chronologically. These scenes will be referred to here as "actuality episodes." The others, which move freely back and forth through time, will be designated as "memory" and "hallucination" episodes.

The play was written for the proscenium theatre.

Premise

Willy Loman, a salesman in his early sixties, returns to his home shortly after starting out on a selling trip. He is working on straight commission, and not making enough to meet expenses. Today he is unable to drive his car safely; his mind is wandering; he is an exhausted, bewildered man. He is haunted by a sense of unfulfillment, of something desperately wrong in the way he has ordered his life and in his relationship with his sons.

His wife Linda is sympathetic and understanding. His older son, Biff, a man of 34, has just returned home after a long sojourn in the West. He appears to be a failure at everything he has attempted. A second son, Happy, holds an unimportant job in a store. Happy has his own apartment, and his thoughts are almost entirely of his sexual conquests. Willy has always had great hopes for his two sons, especially Biff, and has tried to imbue them with his own philosophy— that it is the impression one makes on others, and whom one knows, that determines success or failure in the business world, and thus in life.

Facts antecedent to the play, all of whose forward action takes place within twenty-four hours, are primarily psychological. Of primary significance is the fact that Willy has given his two sons, especially Biff, such an overriding sense of their own potential and importance that they are unable to adjust to the world realistically. He has indoctrinated them with the same set of false values by which he has lived himself.

Synopsis

The author employs many theatricalist devices. The setting, like the work itself, mingles realism, symbolism, and expressionist elements. What we see is the outline of a wooden frame dwelling, set among towering apartment houses, with certain of its rooms open to view— principally the kitchen and two bedrooms. During the actuality episodes the actors observe the convention that the house has solid walls, and can be entered only through a door. However, in the episodes that reflect Willy's memory or his hallucinations, they ignore the convention and step through the "walls," frequently onto the forestage, where much of the action takes place. Lighting plays a very important part in the play's presentation, and at times during the nonrealistic episodes a pattern of leaves is projected on the set.

The play is in two acts, followed by a Requiem; except for one intermission it is played without interruption. The episodes are numbered purely for convenience in this analysis. They are not numbered in the text. The action flows continuously, episodes often blending into each other, with no definite point at which one ends and another begins.

ACT ONE

[] *Episode One*

Actuality. It is evening. Willy Loman, carrying his sample cases, returns home unexpectedly. When his wife, Linda, questions him he says that he kept driving his car off the road. He is very tired and confused. He decides that in the morning he will ask his boss, Howard, to take him off the road and give him a job in New York.

Both his sons are in the house, asleep. That morning Willy had asked Biff, who has just returned from a long absence in the West, whether he was making any money. Biff apparently resented this and a quarrel developed. Willy finds it hard to understand how a man of Biff's potential can be a failure. He hopes to help Biff get a job as a salesman. Biff's attractive personality should insure his success in selling, Willy thinks.

Willy feels shut in. The apartment buildings that have risen around the house shut off light and air. Nothing will grow in the garden any more. Linda tries to comfort and reassure him. In the upstairs bedroom Biff and Happy wake up and listen. Willy reminisces about happier days. He recalls the flowers in the yard, and how thoroughly Biff used to polish the car. Then he goes into the kitchen to get something to eat.

[] *Episode Two*

Actuality. The lights come up in the boys' bedroom. Occasionally we hear Willy muttering below. Happy tells Biff that their father can't keep his mind on his driving. He'll lose his license. There is a reference to the ill feeling that exists between Biff and his father; then the boys laughingly recall various sexual adventures. The talk returns to Willy's condition. Happy says he talks to himself, often about the fact that Biff hasn't settled down. Biff hints darkly that this isn't all that is bothering Willy.

Happy questions Biff about his future, and Biff confesses that he doesn't know what he wants. He has been working mostly as a ranch hand and he loves the open country, but that kind of life doesn't lead anywhere. That's why he came home. But now that he's here he is still perplexed. His life so far has been wasted. Happy is not content either. He has his own apartment, a car, and plenty of women, but he isn't getting anywhere. Biff suggests that they both go out West and buy a ranch. Happy is attracted to the idea at first, then cools as he reflects that it would probably mean less money and fewer girls. Furthermore, he wants to make good at the store, to "show them" that he is as good as the men over him. Happy says rather proudly that the girl he was with that night is engaged to marry an executive of the store. He also confesses that he takes bribes from manufacturers to throw orders their way.

Biff recalls that a man he worked for before he went West, Bill Oliver, told him that if ever he needed anything to come to him. Biff will go see him in the morning and ask to borrow some ten thousand dollars to buy a ranch. Happy is enthusiastic, and tells Biff that Oliver always liked him. Biff wonders whether Oliver still thinks he stole a carton of basketballs from the firm. Happy is sure that Oliver will have forgotten all about that.

We hear Willy in the kitchen congratulating Biff on the great simonizing job he has done on the car. Happy pleads with Biff to stay here and help him handle this situation, for Willy lives increasingly in the past. Biff is indignant that Willy carries on this way, talking to himself, where Linda can overhear. The boys decide to go to sleep. The lights dim on the bedroom and come up on the kitchen.

[]   *Episode Three*

The episode begins as actuality. Willy gets a glass of milk and addresses the boys, telling them the best way to polish the car and offering some fatherly advice about girls. He envisions swinging a hammock between two elms in the back yard. The two boys appear, now of high school age, and we are in a memory scene. Willy has brought his sons a punching bag. Biff shows Willy the football he is practicing with, and admits he "borrowed" it from the locker room. Willy laughingly tells him it should be returned, but says the coach would probably congratulate him on his initiative. There'd be trouble if anyone else had taken the ball.

Someday, Willy says, he will have his own business—bigger even than that of his next-door neighbor, Uncle Charley; for, though Charley is liked, he is not well liked. Willy tells the boys about the fine cities in New England, and how well known and well liked he is everywhere up there.

Biff is the captain of the high school football team, and next Saturday is an important game. Bernard, Uncle Charley's son, a studious and conscientious boy, enters to remind Biff that he is supposed to study with him for the Regents examination next week. If Biff doesn't pass he won't graduate. Because of his football prowess Biff has been offered a scholarship at the University of Virginia. Willy ridicules the idea that Biff could be flunked, and Bernard returns home. Willy observes that Bernard is not well liked, and that, for all his studying, it's Biff and Happy who will make their mark in the business world, for they have the appearance and people like them. Willy is well liked, too—he never has to wait in line to see a buyer.

Linda enters, and, as the boys cheerfully undertake various household chores, Willy admits that he hasn't made over seventy dollars on his last trip, and there are payments due on the refrigerator, the washing machine, the vacuum cleaner. Actually the family is very sorely pressed. Although Willy is naturally optimistic, doubts assail him. He feels that people are laughing at him, that he talks too much, that he is not dressing to create the right impression. Loyally Linda tries to bolster his self-confidence.

[]   *Episode Four*

Another memory. The locale shifts to Willy's hotel room in Boston, where a woman, about to go, is laughing and primping. Willy tells her that he'll be back in about two weeks. She says she'll put him right through to the buyers, and thanks him for a gift of stockings. Willy kisses her roughly.

[]   *Episode Five*

It is still the past as Willy remembers it, and we are back in the kitchen. Linda is mending a pair of stockings. This disturbs Willy, who tells her to throw them away. Bernard rushes in, saying that Biff must study his math. He won't be able to give Biff the answers on a Regents examination. Gently Linda urges Willy to talk to Biff, but Willy explodes. There is nothing the matter with Biff. Unlike that worm Bernard, Biff has personality.

[]   *Episode Six*

Actuality. Happy, in pajamas, comes down and tries to persuade Willy to go to bed. Willy muses about his brother Ben, who as a youth urged him to go with him to Alaska. According to Willy, Ben ended up owning diamond mines, rich at the age of twenty-one. Happy says he'll help Willy financially, but Willy ridicules and re-bukes Happy for the way he lives and for his lack of concern.

Charley, Bernard's father, comes in from next door, saying that he couldn't sleep. He suggests a card game, and the two men play. Charley offers Willy a job, which is indignantly refused. It is obvious that Charley knows the true situation and wants to help, but Willy's pride won't let him work for Charley. Suddenly the brave front cracks open. Biff will go back to Texas. Why? What has Willy done wrong? Charley tells him to forget Biff. Willy tries to salvage his pride and put Charley down by bragging about the new ceiling he put up in the living room.

[]   *Episode Seven*

This episode starts as a continuation of actuality, but, with the ap-pearance of Willy's brother Ben, it begins to evolve into a scene of Willy's hallucination. After Charley's exit everything that occurs is in Willy's mind.

Willy and Charley are still playing cards. Ben, a prosperous man in his sixties, appears. He is, of course, unseen by Charley. Willy tells Charley they have heard from Ben's wife in Africa that Ben has died. There will be no money—Ben had seven sons. Willy lost his great opportunity with Ben when he didn't accompany him to Alaska.

Ben asks Willy about their mother and father, and Willy, his mind half on the cards, briefly tries to answer Ben's questions. Charley is puzzled by Willy's words, and soon they are quarreling. Disgusted, Charley goes home.

Willy now approaches Ben and they shake hands. Linda enters, meets Ben, and listens as the men talk. Willy wants to know the secret of Ben's success. He calls young Biff and Happy to listen, but Ben offers little in the way of enlightenment. He walked into the jungle at seventeen, and four years later walked out rich. Ben tells Biff to punch him in the stomach, and for a moment they spar. Then Biff is on the ground, with the tip of an umbrella pointed at his eye. Laughingly Ben tells the boy never to fight fair with a stranger.

Biff and Happy run off to get some sand from the nearby apartment construction site—they'll build a front stoop right now. Charley comes on, warns that if the boys steal any more building materials the watchman will call the police. Ben and Willy consider this kind of petty thievery very enterprising. Bernard runs in to say that the cops are chasing Biff, and Linda leaves, alarmed.

Willy urges Ben to stay—he needs moral support, and advice. Ben congratulates Willy on the way he's bringing up his sons, and disappears. Willy is reassured. To walk into the jungle and come out rich—that's what he wants for his sons.

[]   *Episode Eight*

Actuality. Willy is in the yard, still speaking to Ben, as Linda, in night clothes, comes looking for him. But Willy goes for a walk, and Linda sits in the kitchen, mending his jacket. Biff and Happy come down, wakened by Willy's talking to himself. Biff is shocked, and Linda rebukes him for not having kept in touch. She is puzzled that Biff and Willy don't get along as they used to. She insists that Biff try to show some respect and affection for his father. It is clear, however, that Biff knows something about Willy that he won't talk about.

Linda says that Willy is exhausted. He is now working on straight commission instead of salary. He constantly borrows money from Charley and pretends it's his earnings. Linda rebukes both boys for their lack of understanding. Happy is a philandering bum, and Biff—what happened to the love he and his father once shared? Biff tells her he'll get a job in New York and turn over half his pay. But he knows that Willy is a fake.

Linda decides to tell them the worst. Willy has been trying to commit suicide. His recent car accidents have been deliberate. She has also found a length of rubber hose near the gas heater that Willy could use to kill himself. But Linda cannot bring herself to humiliate him by removing it.

Biff is remorseful. He renews his pledge to stay home and help. Happy criticizes Biff for not conforming to the business world's behavior patterns.

Willy returns from his walk, and there is more evidence of the ill feeling between him and Biff. Then Happy breaks in to tell his father that Biff intends to see Bill Oliver tomorrow, hoping to be staked in a business venture. Willy is interested but still somewhat contemptuous until Happy suggests that he and Biff go into partnership in selling sporting goods. Both boys are athletic, and they could promote their business by organizing exhibition matches and games. Willy, Biff, and Linda all respond to the idea enthusiastically. Biff says that this is the proposal he will outline to Oliver, and Willy immediately begins telling him how to approach Oliver and how to act in his office. There is another near quarrel with Biff when Willy starts barking impatiently at Linda, but he goes into the house, and she follows.

Outside, Biff and Happy talk hopefully of the proposed sporting goods store. In the bedroom Willy tells Linda that Oliver will welcome Biff. The boys come in to bid their father good night, having been prompted by Linda, and Willy is again full of advice for Biff, who has some trouble keeping his exasperation under control.

Linda starts to sing Willy to sleep, and he recalls the glorious days when Biff was a high school football hero. Timidly Linda asks Willy what it is that Biff holds against him. Willy avoids answering, but agrees that in the morning he will ask Howard, his employer, to take him off the road and give him a job in New York. Biff, in the kitchen, finds the rubber tubing near the gas heater, and confiscates it.

[]   *In Brief*

Willy's malaise, as he himself dimly realizes, goes far deeper than his financial problem, though this is serious enough. His sons, for whom he had such hopes, are failures, and his favorite, Biff, even hostile. It is soon clear that neither Biff nor Happy is capable of rescuing the drowning Willy. Linda partially understands what is happening to him, but she is helpless too.

Gradually Willy's standards are revealed, the values he has given his sons and by which he has lived himself—values that will not sustain them now. We are shown the falsity of these standards chiefly in the memory and hallucination episodes, which also serve to dramatize Willy's despondency and his increasing desperation.

The family seizes on the totally impractical and delusory plan to borrow money to open a sporting goods store as a solution to the boys' difficulty, and Willy decides to ask to change his job. The act ends with all of them placing too much hope on these doubtful prospects. We can see that the kind of people Willy and the boys have made of themselves dooms them to failure.

ACT TWO

[]   *Episode One*

Actuality. The time is the following morning. The boys have already
left the house. Willy and Linda are finishing breakfast. Willy is in a
state of feverish excitement. Today may be the turning point in their
lives—Biff has gone to see Oliver and Willy is going to see Howard.
As Willy talks, Linda tries to help him into his jacket, but he keeps
slipping out of it. He speaks of getting a little place in the country,
but there are immediate financial problems to be faced, installment
payments to be met.

Linda tells Willy that the boys are taking him to dinner tonight, in Manhattan, and this pleases him greatly. With a final rebuke
to Linda for mending her stockings he leaves the house.

The phone rings. It is Biff, waiting to see Oliver. Joyfully
Linda tells him that the rubber tube by the gas heater is gone, but
Biff tells her that he, not Willy, removed it. Linda tells him to make
a good impression on Oliver and to be very nice to Willy tonight.
Perhaps Willy will have good news too—a New York job.

[]   *Episode Two*

Actuality. The scene is Howard's office. A man of 36 and present
head of the firm, Howard has a new toy—a wire recorder, which he
has taken home the night before and now insists on demonstrating.
Howard's family whistles and recites on the machine as Willy pretends to be interested, vainly trying to focus Howard's attention
on himself.

It occurs to Howard that Willy was scheduled to be in Boston
today, and Willy broaches the subject of a job here in New York. He
speaks of his long service with the firm and his friendship with
Howard's father. Howard maintains that there is no place for him
here, and Willy begins to argue frantically. Howard is adamant and
finally leaves the room, telling Willy to pull himself together.

Imagining that he is appealing to Howard's father, Willy leans
on the desk and accidentally switches on the recorder, which starts
burbling its inanities. Howard rushes back in, and Willy, thoroughly
shaken and demoralized, says he'll go to Boston. But Howard has had
enough, and tells Willy that he doesn't want him to work for them
any more. When Willy protests, Howard asks why his sons can't give

him a hand. As Howard leaves the office he tells Willy to stop by later in the week and leave his samples.

[] *Episode Three*

This episode is hallucinatory, later blending with memories. Ben appears, about to leave for Alaska, and urges Willy to accompany him. Fortunes are to be made. Willy is tempted, but a youthful Linda opposes the move. Willy has a good job here, and is building a future with the firm. Biff and Happy, as high school students, come on. Willy, with the boys in mind, says that fortunes and futures can be achieved right here, on the basis of being liked.

Biff is playing an important football game today. Thousands of people will be watching and cheering and loving him. Young Bernard has appeared, and he and Happy vie for the honor of carrying Biff's helmet. Willy is beside himself with pride and anticipation, and, when Charley enters and pretends not to know what all the excitement is about, Willy is not amused.

[] *Episode Four*

Actuality. We are in the reception room of Charley's office. Bernard, with coat, bag, and tennis rackets, is waiting to say good-bye to his father. Willy can be heard shouting outside—a continuation of the last episode. Charley's secretary asks Bernard to go out in the hall and head Willy off, for his father is very busy. But Willy enters the room, and learns that Bernard is just leaving for Washington, to plead a case. Willy is obviously impressed and jealous of Bernard's success. He brags that Biff is working on a big deal with Oliver, the sporting goods man; that it was Oliver who sent for Biff to come back East. Suddenly Willy's bravado crumbles. What is Bernard's secret? Why hasn't Biff made it? Bernard replies that Biff never trained himself for anything, and then he begins to ask questions that Willy can't or will not answer. Why, after Biff flunked math in high school, didn't he make up the course during the summer? Bernard remembers that Biff went to Boston to see his father, and when he came back he had given up the idea of going on to college. What happened in Boston? Willy senses that he is being blamed for Biff's decision and subsequent failure, and he becomes angry.

Charley enters, and proudly says that Bernard's case is being tried before the Supreme Court. Bernard leaves. Unasked, Charley pulls out fifty dollars, but Willy needs a hundred and ten. Willy protests that it will all be repaid. Charley is exasperated. Why won't Willy take the job he offers him? Willy says he has a job, then admits he has just been fired. Charley tries to puncture Willy's illusions about the path to success, and again urges him to take the job, but Willy simply can't work for him. Charley resignedly hands Willy the money he needs. Willy muses that, after all the years of working, one ends up worth more dead than alive. Charley is his only friend, he says as he goes.

[]   *Episode Five*

Actuality. Happy is the first to arrive at the restaurant. The waiter, who knows Happy's habits, puts him in a back room. A young woman comes in and sits at the next table, and within moments Happy is talking to her. Biff enters, and Happy introduces him as a quarterback with the New York Giants, refers to himself as a West Pointer. Biff is troubled and preoccupied, but Happy blithely arranges a double date, and the woman goes off to call a friend.

Biff appeals to Happy to help explain matters to Willy. Biff had waited six hours, then saw Oliver momentarily as he was leaving his office. Oliver didn't remember him at all, and Biff realized that he had been only a shipping clerk there, never a salesman. In panic he had then taken Oliver's fountain pen from his desk and run from the building. Biff believes that he must convince his father that he is not the man Willy thinks he is, certainly not the kind of person to whom people lend large sums of money. Happy insists that Biff can't tell such a story to Willy now, and says they must dissemble, pretending that Oliver is thinking over Biff's proposition and then let the whole matter gradually die.

Willy comes in, sits with the boys, and immediately wants to know how Biff got along with Oliver. Gently Biff tries to tell him, but Willy is in no mood to hear of anything but success. When Biff gets as far as convincing him that he was no more than a shipping clerk in the firm, Willy bursts out that he doesn't want to be lectured, that he was fired today, and he needs some good news for Linda. Biff is so shocked by this disclosure that he can hardly bring himself to continue. Further, Willy interprets everything he says as an account of progress, and Happy encourages this delusion. When Willy begins to suspect that something is wrong, he accuses Biff of not seeing Oliver at all. Biff feels utterly discouraged and frustrated.

[] *Episode Six*

This flows right on as a continuation of the preceding episode, but with memory elements intruding into actuality from time to time as Willy's mind roams the past for an explanation of his failures.

As Biff once more tries to explain the situation, young Bernard comes to see Linda to tell her that Biff flunked math and has gone to Boston to see his father. Linda hopes that Willy can intercede with the teacher.

Then Willy snaps back to reality, and realizes that Biff stole Oliver's pen. He is appalled. But the night of Biff's arrival in Boston begins to intrude on his consciousness. We hear a switchboard operator's voice trying to reach Willy in his hotel room, and Willy, in the restaurant, shouts that he is not there. Biff is puzzled and alarmed by his father's behavior, and tries to assure him that he will still make good. Finally Biff starts pretending that his interview with Oliver was successful. It's a bluff he can't carry on, however, and a quarrel quickly ensues between the agonized father and son. As Willy's mind wanders again, the girl in the restaurant returns with her friend for the double date. The woman in Willy's hotel room is heard urging him to answer the door. Willy leaves this area of the restaurant.

Biff appeals to Happy to help his father, but Happy is concerned now only with the girls. Desperately Biff pulls the rubber hose from his pocket, and tells Happy that Willy is trying to commit suicide. Biff believes that he can no longer help Willy, but that Happy could. Overcome with emotion, Biff hurries away.

Happy gathers up the two girls and starts off in pursuit of Biff as we hear Willy, in the hotel room, begging his companion not to answer the door.

[] *Episode Seven*

Memory. This is the hotel room. The woman, preparing to leave, urges Willy to see who is knocking. Willy finally agrees to do so if she will hide in the bathroom. She does, and Willy admits Biff, who has come to beg his father to intercede with his math teacher, for without the credits he needs to graduate he can't go on to college. Willy agrees to return to New York at once, and, as the delighted Biff tells how he incurred the teacher's enmity when he was caught imitating his lisp, the woman comes out of the bathroom. Willy tries to pretend that her presence in the room is innocent, but Biff is horrified. Willy pushes her out, as she protests that she wants the stockings he promised her.

After she goes, Willy makes light of the incident and prepares to accompany Biff back home. Biff tells him not to bother; he doesn't want to go on to college, nor will he enroll in summer school to make up the math credits. Willy is angered. Biff calls his father a fake and a liar, and says he gave the woman his mother's stockings. He walks out, leaving Willy on his knees, shouting after him.

[] *Episode Eight*

Actuality. The locale of the setting shifts back to the restaurant. Stanley, the waiter, enters, finds Willy on his knees, and helps him up. Willy asks where he can buy some seeds. Nothing is planted yet. He hurries out.

[] *Episode Nine*

Actuality. We are in the kitchen as the boys return home very late. Happy brings a bunch of flowers for Linda. Knocking the flowers to the floor, she accuses Biff of not caring whether Willy lives or dies, and orders both boys out of the house. They invited Willy to dinner and then deserted him for a couple of whores. Happy goes to his room, but Biff is full of self-loathing and reproach. When he finds that his father is out in the yard, planting seeds, he determines to talk with him, even though Linda forbids it.

[] *Episode Ten*

This begins with the actuality of Willy planting seeds by flashlight, but quickly involves the hallucinatory figure of his brother Ben.

Willy is contemplating suicide. His insurance policy would pay Linda twenty thousand dollars. He asks Ben's opinion. Ben is intrigued, but dubious. Willy visualizes his funeral, with buyers coming from all over New England to pay their respects. That's something that would impress his son. Biff would see what a power Willy really was. Ben wants to think the matter over before advising him.

[] *Episode Eleven*

Actuality. Biff comes into the yard to say good-bye to Willy. He intends to leave home for good. Willy still wants to know if he is going to see Oliver the next day. Biff doesn't try to explain any more, just urges Willy to come inside. In the kitchen Biff tells Linda that he's leaving. She agrees that this is best, and Biff goes to shake hands with his father. Willy says there's no need to mention the pen to Oliver, then turns on Biff and accuses him of leaving just for spite. When Biff is down and out he needn't blame his father. Biff, he says, is just trying to put the knife in him. Happy appears on the stairs, listening.

Pulling the rubber hose from his pocket, the furious and exasperated Biff confronts his father with it, and announces that for once the truth will be spoken in this house. Biff had no address for three months while out West because he was in jail—for theft. Willy had always blown him so full of hot air that he couldn't take orders from anybody. Willy counters that Biff is just trying to spite him. Biff continues that today, as he was running out of Oliver's building, he realized what he was and what he really wanted—a simple outdoor job. Biff is not a leader of men, and neither is Willy. Biff is a dollar-an-hour laborer, and Willy a drummer who has landed on the scrap heap. And the family can stop waiting for Biff to bring home the prizes.

Willy is raging under this attack on the standards and ideals by which he has lived, but Biff's fury is spent, and he breaks down, sobbing and holding onto his father. Willy suddenly realizes that Biff loves him. If only Willy would give up his dreams for Biff, expectations that Biff cannot possibly fulfill! Biff goes upstairs.

Willy, shaken and nearly overcome by the realization of his son's true feeling for him, says the boy is going to be magnificent.

[]   *Episode Twelve*

This is a mixture of actuality and Willy's hallucination. Ben appears, and suggests that Biff would have an outstanding career with Willy's life insurance money backing him. Meanwhile, Happy promises to change his ways, kisses his mother, and goes upstairs. Ben's image continues to entice Willy toward suicide. Linda urges Willy to come to bed, but he begs her to go ahead—he wants to be alone for a few moments. Linda leaves. Willy is exultant, now that he knows how to realize his dreams for Biff. Ben goes on ahead, as Willy addresses the absent Biff, telling him, in football terms, of the important people watching him and that he must win. We hear Linda calling from the bedroom, and Willy rushes off after Ben.

As Linda, Biff, and Happy all get up to investigate, we hear

the sound of the car starting, driving off, and, musically, the crash
that kills Willy.

[]   Requiem

Linda, Biff, Happy, Charley, and Bernard stand at Willy's grave.
Linda is puzzled that no one else came to the funeral—none of his
many friends. And there is irony in that they were nearly out of debt,
after thirty-five years. Biff remembers good times they had, but his
father's dreams were wrong, all wrong.

Charley says a salesman rides on a smile and a shoeshine—he
has to dream. Biff suggests that Happy come West with him, but
Happy is going to climb to the top right here. Willy had the right
dreams, and Happy's going to prove it.

Alone at the grave for a moment, Linda says she can't understand why Willy did it. She made the last payment on the house
today. They're free and clear.

[]   In Brief

The act begins with a reminder of the high expectations with which
the preceding one closed. Willy's first disillusionment comes when,
instead of being transferred to a New York job, he is fired. The code
by which he has lived avails him nothing.

In Willy's memory we see his expectations for Biff, and then,
in actuality, when Willy goes to Charley's office to borrow money,
the contrast between Bernard's success and Biff's failure. In the restaurant episode we see how Biff has been betrayed by Willy's
standards, and, in the hotel room scene that follows, how Biff's respect for his father was shattered. (A number of critics have objected
that Biff's discovery of Willy's philandering could be a contributory
cause of the boy's turning against him but hardly the pivotal point
of their relationship that the play indicates.)

In justifiably upbraiding Biff and Happy for deserting Willy
at the restaurant, Linda nevertheless fails to indicate that she has any
understanding of what made the boys the way they are. Willy, his
world collapsing, contemplating suicide, cannot give up the idea that
Biff is a leader. But Biff knows the truth about himself and about
them all. Through all his bitterness and disillusionment, however,
his love for his father comes through, and in this Willy finds the
justification of his hopes for Biff, and in his own eyes a valid reason
for his suicide. The money will stake Biff in his career.

The Requiem comments on Willy from the point of view of the other principals.

Protagonist and Objective

Willy is the protagonist. In his extremity the values by which he has ordered his life and which he has inculcated in his sons appear to fail him, and proving their validity becomes a pathological need. Biff is, in a sense, an extension of Willy himself, and his success would be the verification and crowning achievement of Willy's whole philosophy. Hence Willy's rage at Biff's failure and his frantic attempt to help his son toward what he considers to be success.

John Gassner points out that in making the struggle between Willy and Biff the main feature of the play "the pathos of failure is pitched higher than the sociological level." Willy is "a father for whom the love and success of his favorite son is a paramount necessity and a consuming passion." But Biff's success is to be achieved by guiding him in the hollow principles of success worship that Willy espouses. That these false values are in conflict with the love he seeks is the factor that makes the play so penetrating.

The author himself speaks of "Willy's desperation to justify his life," and this must be considered the objective, for it embraces both the need for Biff to succeed and the validation of Willy's philosophy.

Willy goes to his death believing that his insurance money will bring Biff the success that each has sought so long. But we know that the suicide is merely another sacrifice on the altar of false gods. It must be said that Willy fails to achieve his objective.

Obstacles

Since Willy seeks to validate the principles by which he has lived, to "justify his life," the chief obstacle is simply the fact that the principles are worthless. In an emergency they cannot sustain him philosophically or practically. We see the results of this failure in all of Willy's relationships, but chiefly with Biff. The play's main externalized conflict is between Willy and Biff, for Willy's system of false values has ruined his son. (Willy fails to comprehend that he himself is responsible for it.) The antagonism between Willy and Biff is due not only to Willy's resentment of his son's failure; it is compounded by Biff's disillusionment over his father's philandering, and—as Biff acquires insight—over Willy's delusory success worship. Biff's failure, therefore, and his attack on Willy's standards can both be seen as obstacles to Willy's objective.

Major Crisis and Climax, Theme

As in *Ghosts*, the crisis occurs long before the opening of the play, for Willy's downfall was set in motion when he first embraced a system of false values. Within the framework of the situation as Miller presents it, what follows is the inevitable result.

The climax is a rather extended one. Biff's outburst in II-11, as he strips away the pretenses and illusions by which they have lived, destroys Willy's whole philosophy. But Willy cannot face the truth, and when Biff breaks down, and Willy realizes that his son does love him in spite of their differences, he seizes upon this as justification for his suicide. Killing himself becomes the ultimate assertion of belief in his own values, for its purpose is to provide Biff with the means of making a success of his life, a success built on the same principles that have governed Willy in his lifetime.

Willy's failure is a personal failure, not that of a materialistic society. (Charley, functioning within that society, is no failure, nor, on Willy's terms, is Howard.) Willy fails because the standards he embraces fail him. And they fail Biff, even to the point of driving underground his natural love for his father. Thematically the play condemns the values by which Willy has ordered his life, and which he has imparted to his sons.

Resolution

This follows Willy's realization that Biff loves him, and includes his decision, prompted by Ben, to kill himself, the car crash, and the section marked "Requiem," in which the principals comment on Willy.

Opening

Miller begins the play at a moment when Willy's world has begun to come apart. Although many of the events that occurred much earlier are staged for us, they are presented as part of Willy's memories and thus serve as a kind of dramatized exposition, driving the story forward by what they reveal. There would be no more point in presenting the memory sequences first than there would be in beginning *Oedipus the King* or *Ghosts* earlier.

Unity

The play is presumed to take place within some twenty-four hours, and the memory and hallucination episodes, though separated from the present action by years, do not affect the impression that the unity of time is being observed, for they reflect what is going on in Willy's mind at present. Unity of place is disregarded, but this is of little consequence.

The unity of action may be questioned. By far the greater part of the play does deal with Willy's attempt to affirm the validity of his beliefs. But is Willy's unfaithfulness to Linda entirely pertinent? It is true that Biff's learning of his father's philandering turns him away from completing his education; but would an educated Biff have turned out any better? This is debatable.

Exposition

The first episode in Act One, between Willy and Linda, is almost entirely expository. It is not conflict that carries the exposition, but our realization that something serious and perhaps tragic is happening to this man. We have a growing feeling of apprehension. The same may be said of the exposition in I-2, between Biff and Happy.

As John Gassner has noted in *The Theatre in Our Times,* the question we ask ourselves as the play proceeds is not the usual "What is going to happen next?" but "What is really the matter, and why?" The various memory and hallucination episodes are a kind of dramatized exposition whose pieces fit together like those of a jigsaw puzzle to answer the question "Why?" Obviously we must care deeply about Willy and what is happening to him to be interested in the answer. It should also be noted that these expository reminiscences, often employing conflict within themselves, are invariably bracketed by scenes of conflict in the actuality episodes.

Characterization

Though Willy does not remotely approach the qualifications of a tragic figure as defined by Aristotle and followed by many dramatists since, he does attain a kind of tragic stature by the intensity of his faith. Though his dream may be worthless, he pursues it with heroic passion, and his failure is a mighty one, because he feels it mightily. His suicide, in fact, is yet another assertion of his faith. That Willy never understands the true nature of his dream is perhaps the most tragic thing about him.

Biff is more complex than Willy, and in some ways a more interesting character. Not only does the intensity of his emotion match that of his father, but he is the only one to arrive at self-knowledge during the play—an occurrence normally experienced by the protagonist himself.

Linda is presented as a completely loyal wife, defending Willy even against their sons, but she has neither the understanding nor the resources to sustain him in his distress. At his grave Linda is still bewildered. Happy is sharply but conventionally drawn in his profligacy.

Charley has made a success in the business world, the same world in which Willy has striven so hard, and Charley has raised a son who is also a success. It would seem that Willy's conception of the road to success, and not the system itself, is responsible for Willy's predicament.

Development

The author has said that friction, collision, and tension between the past and the present are at the heart of the play's construction, and in the same essay (Introduction, *Collected Plays*, Viking Press, 1958) that the various scenes represent a mobile concurrency of past and present, for Willy has destroyed the boundaries between then and now. This unconventional structure obviously works as an over-all plan because we do want to know why.

Some individual scenes are built in the conventional way. II-2 is an example. Willy is the protagonist; his objective, to persuade Howard to transfer him to a job that will eliminate the traveling. There are several obstacles: first, Howard's preoccupation with the wire recorder, then his indifference to Willy's problem, then Willy's own inept handling of the situation, which only increases

Howard's resistance. The climax is Willy's being fired; the resolution, his shock, culminating in an hallucination.

The hotel room scene, II-7, is similarly built. Willy is the protagonist; his objective, to conceal from Biff that he has a woman in the room. The obstacles are Biff's persistence in getting into the room and the woman's lack of concern. The climax is Biff's seeing the woman; the resolution, his turning against his father.

Dramatic Irony

A subtle use of dramatic irony pervades a large part of the play. It begins when we realize that Willy's own standards are, at least in part, what has brought him to a dead end. Willy's failure to see what is apparent to the audience arouses our pity and anxiety.

There are other more specific uses of the device. In the memory scenes that show Willy's high hopes for Biff, we already know that these hopes are not to be realized. (Reversing the chronology of events automatically creates dramatic irony. Cf. Kaufman's and Hart's *Merrily We Roll Along.*)

In I-4 Willy is thanked by the woman in the hotel room for a gift of stockings. We know then, as Linda does not, why it so disturbs Willy to see her mending her own stockings. In the restaurant scene (II-5) we know, as the boys at first do not, that Willy has been fired. We also know, as Willy does not, that Biff has not been successful with Oliver. In the hotel scene (II-7) we know long before Biff does that Willy has a woman in the room.

Preparation

The hotel room scene (II-7) is foreshadowed in I-4; and the fact that Biff knows something discreditable about Willy is planted several times. He himself hints at it in I-2 and I-8; Linda asks Willy what Biff holds against him in I-8; and Bernard questions Willy about it in II-4. We are thoroughly prepared for the disclosures of the hotel room scene when it occurs.

Biff's habit of stealing is shown in I-3, when he "borrows" the football, and in I-7 when he takes the building material from the apartment site. We are not surprised that he takes Oliver's pen.

In II-4 Willy muses bitterly that a man ends up worth more dead than alive. This foreshadows his suicide.

Activity

In this play there is a greater dependence on dialogue and less on significant activity than one might expect. However, certain activities are worth noting.

The card game (I-6 and I-7) helps to dramatize the relationship between Willy and Charley. Ben's sparring with Biff and the business of pointing the umbrella at Biff's eyes are highly effective (I-7).

Linda's mending clothes—Willy's jacket and her stockings—is revealing, and there is a very telling piece of business in II-1 when Linda tries to help Willy into his jacket and he keeps walking out of it.

The use of the wire recorder as a symbol of Howard's preoccupation and indifference is brilliant. The device is especially effective when Willy inadvertently turns it on after Howard has left the room (II-2). The play could have used other significant activity to advantage.

Biff's pulling the rubber hose from his pocket when he confronts Happy in II-6, and Willy in II-11, is excellent stage business, as is Linda's knocking the flowers to the floor in II-9.

Dialogue

The dialogue throughout, though realistic in the sense that it simulates everyday speech, is marked by an intensity of feeling and a kind of forcefulness that is probably far beyond what we would hear in real life. However, the effect is the desired one—that of poorly educated and semiarticulate people under great emotional stress. It is doubtful whether the same intensity and clarity could have been achieved had Miller striven for greater verisimilitude to common speech.

Effects

Music and lighting (especially the pattern of leaves thrown over the entire setting) are used throughout to reinforce mood. They are particularly useful in the transitions between actuality and memory or hallucinations. The actors' disregard of the supposedly solid walls of the house in the latter types of scenes also helps to set them apart from the actuality episodes.

The outline of the apartment buildings surrounding the house contributes a claustrophobic effect.

Plausibility

To most people Willy is a totally believable character and, with the exception of Ben, the others are too. Ben is vaguely drawn, and one is at a loss to know how much of his legend to believe. This uncertainty about Ben is undoubtedly deliberate: he is presented as the hallucination of a desperate and exhausted man. Even so, it may be questioned whether he would be a more effective figure if he were as solidly established a character as Charley, for example.

Although there is a definite feeling of inevitability about the course of events in the play (with the possible exception of Biff's sudden and violent change of attitude when he discovers his father's unfaithfulness), most critics have felt that the work falls short of the highest form of tragedy. This may be due less to the fact that Willy is a "little man" than because his experience fails to enlighten him in any way. He is the same man at the end that he was at the beginning.

SAMUEL BECKETT

Waiting for Godot

1952

Note: This chapter was written by Richard Mansfield, formerly one of my students. Among Mr. Mansfield's several excellent plays is one, relating to Beckett's masterpiece, entitled *The Arrival* (*Variations on a Theme*).
—E. M.

In order to understand a play's construction one must understand the playwright's vision. For it is his vision which has formed and shaped his play. The playwright's vision is the play's content; the play's form is the structure assembled to express this content. When completed, form and content become one and the same thing, but in the creation of a work of art content precedes form; form shouldn't precede content. When it does, art becomes a preconception—a cliché—rather than an exploration into the unknown waters of the human soul. One does not need to seek new forms for the theatre, but new visions.

    Waiting for Godot is a vision of human existence. Its incomprehensibility for so many people, for so many years, had little to do with a misunderstanding of the play's theatrical form. It had to do with an unwillingness to face up to a vision of life which says that we spend our lives waiting; that we never really live our lives, but that our lives are lived for us out of habit; that we wait for Godot and Godot never comes. In this sense Godot is death; Godot is tomorrow; Godot is everything that separates a human being from himself, from his own nature, from a confrontation of himself with himself. If we conceive of time as a focal point on a globe, and the development of the action as meridians leading away from this focal point, a study of the play's structure shows that all the action leads back to its beginnings, in a circular route. The *form* of the play is circular because the *content* of the playwright's vision is circular.

Premise

On a country road by a tree two tramps, Vladimir and Estragon, wait for a Mr. Godot.

Facts antecedent to the play: yesterday Vladimir and Estragon met to wait for a Mr. Godot; he didn't come. The antecedent facts are exactly the same as the basic circumstances which surround the opening of the play, except for one thing: time has passed, is passing, will continue to pass. As Martin Esslin points out in his excellent book *The Theatre of the Absurd*, instead of telling a story, the play explores a static situation.

Synopsis *

The setting is a country road, with a tree. It is evening. The play is in two acts.

Most plays tell a story. A story is a narrative or recital of an event or series of events. In the theatre these events are told through action. The action forms the plot. Aristotle defined plot as a series of events which when linked together form a beginning, middle, and end. The beginning contains the premise or basic situation, the middle contains the conflict which arises out of the basic situation, and the end contains the resolution to the conflict. Plot, defined in these terms, is linear. When writing a synopsis of a linear play, one describes the premise and then picks out the action which develops the plot to its logical conclusion. But *Waiting for Godot* does not have a linear development. It therefore has no plot. The play is plotless, but not formless.

A number of contemporary dramatists have broken away from the linear form, Beckett being one of them. They have replaced plot with a series of poetic images which when presented in their entirety

---

* *Waiting for Godot*, perhaps more than any other play examined in this volume, requires a familiarity with the complete text in order fully to comprehend its structure.—E. M.

express the author's feeling about the human condition. This difference in form comes out of a profound revaluation of art and life itself. These coeval dramatists are much more concerned with what is happening than with what's going to happen next.

The following is a description of the action as it evolves out of a flight from the nucleus of time.

ACT ONE

Estragon, sitting on a low mound, is trying to take off his boot. Enter Vladimir. Estragon, with the first line of the play, states their dilemma—"Nothing to be done." Estragon has spent the night in a ditch, was beaten up, but does not know by whom, and Vladimir expresses his surprise and pleasure at seeing him again. Vladimir muses that but for him, over the years, Estragon wouldn't be here at all. They should have ended it all a long time ago in a suicide pact by jumping off the Eiffel Tower. Now they are so disreputable the powers that be wouldn't even let them go up there.

Estragon continues to pull at his boot. Vladimir meditates on "the last moment. . . . Hope deferred maketh the something sick," but can't recall the correct quotation or its source. He removes his hat, shakes it and knocks on it to dislodge any foreign body, puts it on again, and expresses his increasing alarm over the situation. Estragon plays with his toes.

Vladimir then gets into a protracted discussion about the two thieves who were crucified at the same time as their Savior. One of the two thieves was supposed to have been saved from death, the other damned. There were four Evangelists, but only one speaks of a thief's being saved. Of the other three, two do not mention any thieves at all, and the third says that both thieves abused the Savior because he wouldn't save them from death. Everybody accepts the interpretation of the thief being saved and ignores the other three versions. Estragon says people are ignorant, and dismisses them contemptuously.

Estragon rises, looks off into the distance, and suggests to Vladimir that they go. Vladimir reminds Estragon that they can't leave because they are waiting for Godot. The two tramps are confused as to what day it is and whether they've come to the right place to wait. Fearing that perhaps they've missed him, that he has already come and gone, Vladimir and Estragon fall into silence.

Vladimir paces back and forth. Estragon falls asleep immediately. Vladimir quickly awakens his friend because he feels lonely.

Estragon wants to tell his dream, but Vladimir refuses to listen. Estragon suggests that they hang themselves. Not trusting the strength of the tree, they try to determine which of them is the heavier. The fear is that, if one of them is hanged and the bough breaks, the other will be left alive and alone. They decide to do nothing.

Their thoughts turn again to Godot. They are not sure what they asked him for. Apparently their request was an indefinite sort of prayer, which Godot said he'd have to consider at some length and in consultation with others. Any rights they had they got rid of, Vladimir maintains.

Estragon complains that he's hungry, and Vladimir offers him a carrot. Estragon asks if they are tied to Godot, and is told that they are indeed, at least for now. They are not certain, however, that Godot's name is really Godot. Estragon complains that the carrot tastes worse the more he eats of it, whereas Vladimir finds the reverse to be true. Both men recognize their helplessness in the situation.

A terrible cry is heard. Pozzo and Lucky enter. Pozzo drives Lucky by means of a rope passed around his neck. Lucky carries a heavy bag, a folding stool, a picnic basket, and a greatcoat. At the sight of Vladimir and Estragon, Pozzo stops short, causing Lucky to drop all the baggage. Estragon mistakes Pozzo for Godot. Pozzo is surprised and offended that neither Vladimir nor Estragon has heard of him. He is indignant that the two tramps are waiting for Godot on his land, but there is nothing he can do about it since the road is free to all. Pozzo informs Vladimir and Estragon that he has been traveling for six hours on end, without a soul in sight, and wishes to dally a moment before he ventures any farther. He then proceeds to seat himself with the help of Lucky. Pozzo unpacks his picnic basket and begins to eat.

Vladimir and Estragon circle Lucky, inspecting him up and down. Vladimir notices a running sore on Lucky's neck. He and Estragon speculate that Lucky is, perhaps, a half-wit or a cretin. Pozzo finishes his meal and lights his pipe. Estragon asks if he may have the leftover bones from the chicken Pozzo has eaten. Vladimir is scandalized. Pozzo tells Estragon that in theory the bones go to the carrier. Lucky refuses the bones and Pozzo awards them to Estragon.

Vladimir explodes with indignation because Lucky is treated so badly. Pozzo says that he must be going, but then decides to sit down and smoke another pipe of tobacco. Vladimir wants to leave. Pozzo tries to detain them. He suggests that he, being not especially human, may be responsible for Vladimir's desire to go. Estragon asks Pozzo why Lucky doesn't put down his bags. Pozzo says that Lucky has the right to set the bags down, but doesn't want to. The purpose of Lucky's action, or inaction, is to impress Pozzo so that Pozzo won't sell him at the fair. Lucky begins to weep. Estragon approaches Lucky to wipe away his tears, but Lucky kicks him violently in the shin. Pozzo notes that, as Lucky stops crying, Estragon, who is in pain, starts to cry. "The tears of the world are a constant quantity. For each one who begins to weep, somewhere else another stops." Estragon, furious with Lucky, spits on him.

Pozzo, turning to Vladimir, says it was Lucky who raised his thoughts from the ordinary to the beautiful. Vladimir, who finds Pozzo's maunderings intolerable, wishes the night would come. Estragon and Vladimir berate Pozzo for turning Lucky out. Pozzo, in self-defense, says that he can no longer endure the way Lucky goes on about things. He'll drive Pozzo insane if he keeps him. Vladimir and Estragon, almost in the same breath, then turn on Lucky and denounce him for causing Pozzo to suffer. Pozzo tries to deny that he's the kind of man that can be made to suffer. Vladimir and Estragon comment sarcastically on the delightful evening they are having.

Pozzo seems to have misplaced his pipe. Time, Vladimir believes, has come to a stop, but Pozzo is skeptical. Vladimir suggests to Estragon that they go. Pozzo, with great verbosity, describes the sky. He demands the unremitting attention of Vladimir, Estragon, and Lucky. When he's finished he asks the two tramps how they found his performance. They reply with words of encouragement. Silence. Estragon, in despair, says that meanwhile nothing is happening.

Pozzo, pleased with the response to his performance, wonders if he might not be able to do something for the two tramps. He asks them if they would like Lucky to dance, sing, recite, or think. Vladimir and Estragon decide that they would like to have Lucky both dance and think. Pozzo tells the tramps that Lucky used to be able to do many dances, but that all he can do now is a dance he calls "the net." Lucky dances—clumsy movements as of a man trying to escape from a net.

Pozzo has misplaced his vaporizer, which he now refers to as his "pulverizer." Vladimir tells Pozzo that he wants Lucky to think. What follows is a torrent of disjointed language, spoken by Lucky, expressing philosophic, religious, and scientific thought. The speech is a remarkable illustration of the disintegration of language as a result of the inability of the intellect to cope with the reality of being.

During the course of Lucky's tirade Pozzo reacts with disgust and agitation. Vladimir and Estragon gradually object and then protest violently. Finally all three of them throw themselves on Lucky, who struggles and shouts the last few words from the ground. Vladimir seizes Lucky's hat and Lucky falls silent. With a great deal of effort Lucky is finally put back on his feet. Pozzo is suddenly aware that he has misplaced his watch. He determines that he must have left it at home. Pozzo prepares himself for his departure, but finds it difficult to leave. Estragon comments that life is that way. Pozzo and Lucky exit. Estragon suggests to Vladimir that they go too. Vladimir replies that they can't because they're waiting to keep their appointment with Godot.

A boy enters. He tells Vladimir that he has a message from Godot: he will not be coming tonight, but will come tomorrow for certain. Vladimir questions the boy. He is a native of the surrounding area and works for Mr. Godot. He tends the goats and his brother tends the sheep. Mr. Godot is good to him, but beats his brother. The boy gets enough to eat, and he and his brother sleep in the hayloft. Vladimir asks the boy if he's happy, but the boy doesn't know. He asks what he should tell Godot. Vladimir hesitates and tells the boy to tell Godot that he has seen them. The boy turns and runs off.

Night falls very suddenly, and the moon comes up. Estragon decides to leave his boots here for someone with smaller feet. Vladimir tells him that things will be better tomorrow—the child said that Godot was sure to come. Vladimir suggests that they take shelter for the night. Estragon halts before the tree and asks Vladimir to remind him to bring some rope tomorrow, so they can hang themselves if Godot doesn't come. The two tramps talk about separating for good, but decide that it's not worth the trouble now. Estragon suggests that they go. Vladimir agrees. They do not move.

[] *In Brief*

The play opens with the reunion of Vladimir and Estragon. The first important image to emerge in the play is   story of the two thieves. It reveals Vladimir's preoccupation with salvation. As the action progresses it becomes apparent that time hangs heavy on their hands. They are waiting for a Mr. Godot to arrive, with nothing to do in the meantime. The two tramps are confused as to whether they have come to the right place to wait, what day it is, and what they have asked Godot for. They are not even sure that Godot's name is

Godot. The waiting becomes unbearable and they contemplate suicide, but reject the idea for fear one of them will remain alive and, therefore, alone.

The entrance of Pozzo and Lucky is a relief for the two tramps, for they now have two more people present to help them pass the time. Outwardly Pozzo appears to be quite self-assured, but, as the action progresses, it becomes quite clear that he suffers without the aid of others. He continually loses his personal possessions, as if in some way he wished to rid himself of the very things he feels are so important. Pozzo and Lucky are involved in a master-slave relationship. Lucky has taught Pozzo all the finer things in life. He does a dance which he calls "the net," because he feels entangled in a net. Lucky's disjointed speech expresses, among other things, the inability of his intellect to cope with life. The speech also reveals Lucky, of all the characters in the play, to be the most aware of his situation.

Pozzo and Lucky depart and the boy enters. He tells Vladimir that Godot has postponed his arrival until tomorrow.

Vladimir and Estragon talk of parting. They decide to remain together and to return tomorrow to wait for Godot. When Estragon suggests that they go, neither moves.

ACT TWO

It is the next day, same time and place. The tree has sprouted a few leaves.

Vladimir enters. He sings a song to himself, telling of a dog who stole a crust of bread and was beaten to death by the cook. Then all the other dogs came and dug a tomb for the dead dog. On the tombstone they wrote the story of the dog who was beaten to death by the cook. The song is repeated.

Estragon enters, barefoot. Vladimir questions him, asking where he spent the night and if he was beaten up. Estragon, tired of the same questions, the same routine, exclaims: "Don't touch me! Don't question me! Don't speak to me! Stay with me!" The two tramps are happier by themselves, but are unable to remain separated. Estragon admits to having been beaten up again during the night by a company of ten. Vladimir insists that if he had been present he would have kept Estragon from doing whatever it was that provoked the ten to beat him up. Estragon protests that he was doing nothing. Vladimir says it's how one does nothing that counts, if one wants to live.

Vladimir notices that things have changed since yesterday. He refers to the tree. Estragon isn't sure whether the tree was there yesterday or not. He either forgets things at once or not at all. He has crawled around in the muck and mud all his life, and is not particularly interested in the scenery. Vladimir says that their present location certainly is very different from the Macon country. Estragon replies that he's never been in the Macon country, that he's spent his miserable life here in the Cackon country. Vladimir insists that the two of them were in the Macon country picking grapes for a man, whose name he can't recall, at a place whose name escapes him also. Estragon concedes that he might have been there.

Vladimir tells Estragon he's a difficult man to get along with, but they might as well talk together calmly since they can't keep silent. In a poetic passage of great beauty he explains that they must converse to keep themselves from thinking, or listening to the dead voices talking about their lives. It isn't enough for the dead to have lived; they must continue to discuss it too. A long silence. The two tramps try to get a conversation going. Vladimir says that they are no longer in any danger of thinking, but there are worse things. To have thought and then to remember one's thoughts is worse. Estragon says they don't have to look back. Vladimir replies that one can't help looking back. Another silence.

Again, Vladimir and Estragon are faced with having to engineer a new conversation. Vladimir remarks that the tree was bare yesterday, but now it has leaves. Estragon says they were somewhere else yesterday, not here. Vladimir asks Estragon what they did yesterday evening if they weren't where they are now. Estragon replies that they spent the evening chatting about nothing in particular, as they have for fifty years. But he can hardly remember Pozzo and Lucky, and Vladimir jogs his memory by pointing to the wound on his leg where Lucky kicked him.

Vladimir suggests to Estragon that he try on his boots, which are on the ground where he left them the night before. Estragon doesn't think they're his boots. He wants to go, but Vladimir says they can't—they are waiting.

To pass the time Vladimir helps Estragon to try on the boots. They fit. Estragon observes that they always find something to do to reassure themselves of their existence. He walks about in the boots, then lies down and tries to sleep. Vladimir hovers over him, singing softly, then takes off his coat and puts it over his friend. Estragon wakens suddenly and says he dreamt he was falling. Vladimir reminds him, when he wants to go, that they can't. They are still waiting.

Vladimir spots Lucky's hat on the ground. He picks it up, puts it on, and hands his hat to Estragon. What follows is a vaudeville routine that involves an exchange of putting on and taking off three hats. Next they play a game of impersonating Pozzo and Lucky. Estragon becomes bored and exits. He immediately returns, exclaiming that he is under a curse. "They" are coming. Vladimir says that it must be Godot at last! Estragon goes off in the opposite direction, but re-enters at once. "They" are approaching from that direction too. He tries to hide, but there is no place. Bored again, he and Vladimir play a game of insults and reconciliation.

Pozzo and Lucky enter. Pozzo is blind; Lucky, with a rope around his neck, leads him. On seeing Vladimir and Estragon, Lucky stops. Pozzo bumps into Lucky and they both fall to the ground. At first the two tramps think that Godot has come, but Vladimir finally identifies Pozzo, who cries out for assistance. The tramps debate at some length whether as compassionate creatures they should help a fellow being. Estragon asks Pozzo how much his help is worth. Pozzo offers him two hundred francs. Vladimir attempts to help Pozzo up, but falls to the ground. Next Estragon tries to help Vladimir up, but he also falls. Estragon calls out to Pozzo, using the name Abel. Pozzo responds. Estragon calls out to Lucky, using the name Cain. Again Pozzo answers. Estragon concludes that Pozzo is the whole human race.

Vladimir and Estragon finally get up and help Pozzo to his feet. Pozzo states that he is blind and asks the two tramps if they are friends or robbers. Vladimir asks when it was that Pozzo went blind. Pozzo says that the blind have no conception of time. He asks the tramps to check on Lucky to see if he is all right. Estragon crosses to Lucky and kicks him violently. In the process he hurts his foot. Estragon sits and tries to remove his boot. He soon gives that up and falls asleep.

Vladimir attempts to establish the fact that Pozzo and Lucky were the same two people who were present yesterday. Pozzo doesn't remember anything about yesterday; tomorrow he won't recall what happened today. He calls out to Lucky and tells him to rise. Lucky gets up, gathers up his burdens, and gives Pozzo the whip. Vladimir requests that Pozzo have Lucky think before they depart. Pozzo says that Lucky is dumb. Vladimir asks him when this came about. Pozzo, in a burst of fury, denounces Vladimir for harassing him with questions about when things happened. Birth and death are no more than an instant apart. Pozzo and Lucky leave.

Vladimir crosses to Estragon and wakens him. Estragon asks him if Pozzo is Godot. Vladimir says "no," but upon reflection isn't quite sure. He doesn't know what to think any more. He questions whether he was sleeping while other men suffered. Perhaps he is sleeping now. He glances at Estragon, who has fallen asleep again, and comments that when Estragon wakes up he'll remember nothing. Vladimir, in despair, exclaims: "Of me too someone is saying, He is sleeping, he knows nothing, let him sleep on. I can't go on! What have I said?"

The boy enters. He addresses Vladimir as Mr. Albert. Vladimir asks the boy if he recognizes him, but the boy says he doesn't. Vladimir, already anticipating the answers, questions the boy about Godot. The boy affirms that Mr. Godot won't be coming this evening, but certainly tomorrow. Vladimir asks what Godot does, and is told that he does nothing. We learn that Godot has a white beard. The boy asks what message he should give to Godot. Vladimir tells the boy to tell Godot that he has seen them. Vladimir advances toward the boy with sudden violence, saying that he wants to make sure the boy sees him, that he won't return tomorrow saying that he never saw him before. The boy runs off.

The day ends and the moon rises, as before. Estragon wakens, takes off his boots, and places them in the same spot as before. Vladimir tells Estragon that Godot won't be coming this evening, that they'll have to take cover for the night and come back again tomorrow. Estragon suggests that they drop Godot. Vladimir replies that if they did Godot would punish them. As in Act One, the two tramps contemplate suicide. They test the rope Estragon uses for a belt, but it breaks. All that is left for them to do is to return tomorrow. Vladimir suggests that they go. Estragon agrees. They do not move.

[]   *In Brief*

The second act begins with Vladimir singing. The song, like the play, repeats itself. The tree has grown leaves overnight, which suggests the passage of time. Estragon enters, and the two tramps are reunited. They admit to getting on better without one another, but are unable to remain apart. Vladimir tries to remind Estragon of yesterday, but Estragon remembers nothing. When one waits, each day becomes like every other day. Estragon states that they can't keep silent—it's so they won't think or hear all the dead voices, the voices from the past that resurrect themselves and leave Estragon and Vladimir unable to rest in the present.

Again, as in Act One, the two tramps find difficulty in passing the time. They play at being Pozzo and Lucky, do their exercises, curse at each other, and exchange hats. Estragon comments that they always find something to do to give themselves the impression that they exist. Thinking that he spots Godot approaching, Estragon runs off in the opposite direction. He quickly returns, exclaiming that they are surrounded and that he is in hell. Estragon's behavior indicates two things: he dreads a confrontation with Godot, and the image of Godot cannot be eluded, no matter what direction one chooses in life.

Pozzo and Lucky enter. Their condition has deteriorated. Pozzo is blind and Lucky is dumb. Vladimir attempts to establish time as a point of reference. When he asks Pozzo when he went blind, he is told that the blind cannot comprehend time. Pozzo has been unsuccessful in getting rid of Lucky at the fair, and all that remains for the two of them is to go on. Pozzo and Lucky leave. Vladimir, reflecting upon his situation, realizes that he too is asleep, that he knows nothing. For a moment he becomes conscious of the futility of "the wait" as a means of salvation.

The boy enters, and Vladimir, already anticipating the answers, questions the child. He learns that Godot won't be coming this evening, but surely tomorrow. The boy leaves.

As in Act One, the two tramps talk of parting and contemplate suicide. When Estragon suggests that they drop Godot, Vladimir replies that Godot would punish them if they did. So, unable to part, unable to commit suicide, unable to give up the hope of salvation, the two tramps decide to take cover for the night, only to return tomorrow to act out the abomination of their existence.

Protagonist and Objective

Actually, Vladimir is the protagonist. His objective is to wait for Godot. To achieve this objective all he must do is wait. But Vladimir is either unable or unwilling to face "the wait" alone. Waiting produces anxiety and boredom because nothing changes; no one comes or goes. He needs Estragon in order to make the waiting tolerable. Moreover, Estragon finds it difficult to exist without Vladimir. He's pulled into "the wait" along with Vladimir. The two characters share the same basic situation, with a common objective— to wait for Godot. The play, therefore, has a double protagonist. It is quite possible that Vladimir and Estragon are but two aspects of the same personality in opposition—Estragon representing the physical and sensual nature of the individual and Vladimir the striving of the intellect toward a higher degree of consciousness.

Obstacles

The major obstacle in the play is time. Again and again the movement of the play leads the two tramps back to their beginnings: silence, nothing to be done. The difficulty Vladimir and Estragon face is to fill up time with action, *any* action that will help them to escape a confrontation of themselves with time. To experience "the wait" with nothing to do is to experience time stripped of action. Time is a measure of human existence, comprising the past, present, and future. But time is relevant only in relation to death. For, if death did not exist, time would be infinite and therefore meaningless. Time is a concept devised by man to measure his own mortality. Vladimir and Estragon don't want to experience time stripped of action, because they don't want to be aware of their own mortality. Action becomes a vehicle of escape. Since the two tramps can't escape their own mortality, their actions become meaningless, performed to reassure themselves that they exist, and to create an illusion of being. They bide their time in the hope that Godot will come and save them from the human condition. But to *be* is to exist without hope; to hope is to exist without being. The two tramps can't face death; therefore they can't face life.

Major Crisis and Climax

The major crisis and climax each occur *twice*. The play is constructed as if it were two one-act plays, rather than a play with two acts. With minor variations the action of the first act repeats itself in the second act. The basic situation in both acts is the same and the objective of the play's protagonists remains the same.

The major crisis in each act occurs with the entrance of the boy, for he has the information which shifts the dramatic action of the play. The climax occurs when Vladimir learns that Mr. Godot will not be coming that evening, but surely tomorrow.

Theme

Beckett, in writing *Waiting for Godot*, sees humanity waiting to be saved. Salvation takes the form of a Mr. Godot. Godot has many faces, and for each individual this face may be different. But *who* or *what* Godot is is not important. What is important is the effect the image of the face has upon the people who are waiting.

Vladimir and Estragon want to be saved from the human condition: the consciousness of being, followed by the awareness and inevitability of death. Godot's function is to keep the two tramps unconscious of their condition. He is the illusion they erect in order to escape facing up to the reality of their existence. Beckett has created a play which reveals the wish to escape from the reality of being by believing in and hoping for salvation. He refuses to take sides or draw conclusions, but merely presents a state of affairs as he sees it. He will not substitute one illusion for another, for this is precisely the illness, not the cure.

Resolution

The resolution to *Waiting for Godot* is that there is no resolution. The play is open-ended. It will repeat itself ad infinitum. (Cf. Sartre's *No Exit.*) Toward the end of each act two alternatives are contemplated—suicide and separation. Both are rejected for one reason or another, and "the wait" continues.

Opening

The play begins with a basic situation or premise which presents a *state of being*. It is an exploration in depth of the human condition. It is not a play which contains circumstances and events from the past, selected by the playwright, to characterize the development of a given situation to its logical conclusion within the framework of a larger story. This latter approach presupposes the importance of individual character, circumstances, and events within a sequential time order. But Beckett is dealing with a problem of *existence*, which makes sequences in time and individual character irrelevant. He strips action down to a state of being where *all* men, at any given moment of their lives, are faced with the same problem or choice: to accept one's own mortality and experience life through all of our senses, or to escape the reality of what we are through habit. *Waiting for Godot* is a microcosm of this conflict.

Unity

Unity of time and place are observed. A first encounter with the play might suggest that much of the action is irrelevant. Upon deeper examination, however, it becomes clear that, if all the action is understood as a flight from the nucleus of time, all the irrelevancies become relevant. Action becomes the means of escape used by Vladimir and Estragon to avoid the reality of being.

Exposition

We find upon careful examination that Samuel Beckett is not using exposition to reveal the individual backgrounds of his characters. In fact, the outstanding characteristic of antecedent material that emerges from time to time during the course of the play is that nothing is certain. The characters are constantly calling into question the validity of past events and circumstances that affect their lives. For example: Vladimir and Estragon are not sure that they have come to wait for Godot at the same place as yesterday. They are not even sure who Godot is, what he looks like, or what he promised them. The only thing they are sure of is that they are waiting for Godot to come, and that if he doesn't come today, they'll return tomorrow to wait for him. This amnestic quality calls into question the difficulty of defining one's own identity. It is Beckett's view that who or what we are from one moment to the next in our lives is always in constant flux. Again, it becomes clear that a deviation in structural form takes place because the artist's viewpoint of life differs from that of his predecessors.

Characterization

A character's behavior in a play is determined by his over-all objective within the framework of the play.

As has already been mentioned, Vladimir and Estragon share the same objective—to wait for Godot. Their problem is what to do while waiting. They are dependent upon each other to fill up "the wait" with action. This puts the two tramps in the absurd position of waiting around to be saved, with nothing to do in the meantime. When a situation is absurd it becomes humorous. For Vladimir and

Estragon, humor is the expression of a conscious anxiety which recognizes the absurdity of one's own actions in the face of death. It raises the tramps, as characters, from the level of the tragic to that of the absurd. What is tragic about a character is his blindness and unwillingness to face up to the inevitability of what he is in relationship to the circumstances that surround his life. Humor becomes the escape valve which allows Vladimir and Estragon to express their *awareness* of the absurd situation in which they find themselves.

Pozzo, in the first act of the play, states his objective—to get rid of Lucky by selling him at the fair. In the second act he returns, defeated. He has not been able to rid himself of Lucky, and now he's blind. All that remains for Pozzo is to go on.

Lucky's objective is to remain with Pozzo. He functions as Pozzo's menial in the hope that Pozzo will keep him and not get rid of him by selling him at the fair. In the second act Lucky achieves his objective. But, like Pozzo, Lucky's physical condition has deteriorated—he is now dumb. He continues to play the role of slave to Pozzo's role of master. Lucky and Pozzo condemn themselves to act out their charade of life in order to survive.

The boy's function in the play can be compared to that of the messenger in the classic Greek theatre who alters the course of the action. The boy's objective is to deliver Godot's message to Vladimir and Estragon. It is not clear to Vladimir whether the boy in the first act is the same boy who appears in the second act or, possibly, his brother. In any case the boy, whether the same or not, serves the same function in the play. His message answers the question of whether Godot will come.

Development

The structural pattern of this play represents a flight from the nucleus of time. The action is centrifugal, but inevitably Vladimir and Estragon are led back to their beginnings—nothing to be done. This mode of behavior is repeated again and again up to the entrance of the boy. When the tramps learn that Godot will not be coming that evening, all that is left for them to do is take cover for the night. Tomorrow they will return to wait for Godot and act out the same patterns of behavior, with variations, until Godot arrives.

Dramatic Irony

In *Waiting for Godot* the audience is as much in the dark about the situation in which Vladimir and Estragon find themselves as the tramps themselves. There is, however, an interesting use of dramatic irony that deviates from the conventional definition. There are moments in the play when Vladimir and Estragon become conscious of the futility of their actions. When this occurs the characters step outside of their situation and perceive their actions with the same awareness as does the audience. At these moments the characters become an extension of the audience's consciousness. We, the audience, see the characters perceiving themselves. The irony that is created is the awareness that the characters see themselves as we perceive ourselves in our own daily lives. Brecht called this effect "alienation." Many contemporary works of art are not trying to create an *illusion of reality,* but are rather trying to reveal that *reality is the illusion* we create for ourselves.

Preparation

In a play with a linear plot (beginning, middle, and end) a number of facts and circumstances are often revealed to the audience which are made to pay off later in the play. Beckett, like Harold Pinter, reveals very little of a character's past life. This creates a new and different kind of suspense—a suspense that does not derive from what is going to happen next, but from what is happening now. Godot's arrival is anticipated, but Vladimir and Estragon are not even sure what Godot looks like. Nothing is sure in the play. Its progression is developed from *not* knowing—a condition that affects all of us in our daily lives. This use, or lack of use, of preparation is not necessarily thought out by the playwright in advance, but an inevitable outcome of the situation and the playwright's point of view.

Activity

It is evident from the activity in the play that Vladimir and Estragon resemble clowns. There are many examples of this: pratfalls, hats being put on and taken off, pants falling down about the knees, boots that are too tight to put on, a tug at a rope which breaks, et cetera.

The two tramps become clowns because they, along with us, are aware of the absurdity of their condition. The clown ideally expresses the struggle of all human endeavor on the level of the absurd.

Pozzo plays the role of "the actor" in order to entertain himself and others. He behaves like a ringmaster in a circus. He wants to make sure that everyone is looking at him and listening to what he has to say. He milks every activity for all it's worth. The simple act of rising and seating himself becomes a long drawn-out affair. The way in which Pozzo eats, drinks, and snaps his whip at Lucky characterize him explicitly. Pozzo also has a tendency to lose objects such as his pipe, watch, and vaporizer. For all his seeming self-confidence, Pozzo is quite helpless without the assistance of others. This fact is painfully underlined in Act Two when we see that he is now blind.

Lucky attends to Pozzo's every need. He carries a heavy bag, a folding stool, a picnic basket, and a greatcoat. Instead of sitting down to rest he remains standing. There is a running sore produced by the chafing of a rope tied around his neck. He even carries in his mouth the whip with which Pozzo beats him. All his actions dramatize the master-slave relationship with Pozzo. Lucky does a dance called "the net" because he thinks he's entangled in a net. Although intellectually superior to Pozzo, Lucky is contained within the net of their relationship and the net of his life.

Dialogue

Beckett's dialogue exists on three levels: the stand-up, comedic routines of Vladimir and Estragon, the bombastic utterances of Pozzo, which at times turn into poetic imagery, and the disintegrated cogitations of Lucky.

At the beginning of Act Two Vladimir sings a song that repeats itself. The song is an epitome of the dialogue and the over-all structure of the play. Vladimir and Estragon make up word games in order to drown the silence. They try to expand seemingly meaningless banter into major proportions, but inevitably their words break down. The dialogue becomes funny because words are used to fill up time rather than to communicate ideas or feelings. Words become one of the tools used by the two tramps to escape the situation in which they find themselves.

Pozzo, like Vladimir and Estragon, stretches words out to their limit, but for an entirely different reason. His grandiloquent phraseology is used to gain the attention of others. More than anything else, Pozzo's dialogue reveals the pomposity of his existence. Only toward the end of Act Two, when his physical condition has deteriorated, does Pozzo's magniloquence break down into truly poetic language. Faced with what he is rather than what he would like to be, Pozzo expresses the reality of his condition.

Lucky's speech is Beckett's tour de force. The speech, in essence, expresses the disintegration of thought and language when they are confronted with the human condition. When one takes everything into consideration (all philosophic and religious thought, et cetera), life still seems to add up to an absurdity when it is confronted with death. Lucky's speech expresses the impossibility of the intellect to solve the problem of time and being.

Effects

Beckett has decorticated the stage to its bare minimum. All extraneous theatrical effects have been eliminated. The simplicity of the setting gives the play a universality: a country road, a tree. The costumes create a recurrent character in Beckett's works—the tramp. Aside from off stage sounds of baggage being dropped, Pozzo and Lucky rising or falling, there is no use of sound effects. No music is used except for the song Vladimir sings to himself at the beginning of Act Two. The simplicity of stage properties (the whip, the rope, the folding stool, the picnic basket, the greatcoat, the hats, the turnips, the carrots) intensifies the microcosm of existence Beckett is exploring.

Two additional effects, which are interrelated to the passage of time, are of particular interest. First, the light fades in an instant: suddenly it is night, and the moon rises. Vladimir and Estragon now know that Godot will not be coming that evening. The major dramatic question has been answered. Beckett turns day into night in an instant because the realistic passage of time that it would take to turn day into night is irrelevant to the dramatic situation. All that is left for the two tramps to do is to take cover for the night and return again tomorrow. Second, in Act Two, the tree has sprouted leaves overnight. Since each day seems like every other, the passage of time becomes meaningless. Beckett underlines the fact that habit numbs us to the reality of being. Whether one waits one day or a thousand days the result is the same—emotional paralysis.

Plausibility

Given the situation in which Beckett has placed his characters, their actions are entirely plausible. Vladimir and Estragon are unable to give up the hope that Godot will come and save them. They are inevitably condemned to fill up time with action day after day till Godot arrives. The circle cannot be broken unless Godot arrives, they give up the hope of his arrival, or death overtakes them. Similarly Pozzo and Lucky have not found a satisfactory solution to their existence. Neither Pozzo's wealth nor Lucky's intellect has saved them. In Act Two, when Pozzo has gone blind and Lucky dumb, they have no alternative but to go on. They no longer can survive alone, but each is dependent upon the other's co-operation.

And Finally

Samuel Beckett is one of the giants of the contemporary theatre. His genius lies not only in his intellect, but in his courage to face the human condition without hope. He is not a nihilist, but a man who refuses to build illusions in order to avoid the reality of being. *Waiting for Godot* was first presented in Paris in 1952. It has taken a good portion of the world almost twenty years to catch up with the playwright's vision.

ALAN JAY LERNER

My Fair Lady

1956

The book and lyrics of *My Fair Lady,* considered as a play, represent a considerable diminution and coarsening of the brilliant original from which it derives, Shaw's *Pygmalion.* Naturally one expects that a play, in the process of conversion to a musical comedy, will be condensed in order to make room for the music. And the enormous commercial success of *My Fair Lady* attests to the pleasure the conversion has given millions of people. The incontestable diminution (both quantitative and qualitative) is compensated, of course, by the elements that have been added—the music and lyrics, the dances, and the spectacle of lavish settings and costumes.

The synopsis and analysis that follow assume a familiarity with the original play.

Premise

This is identical with that of *Pygmalion,* with one exception: there is no hint that Higgins is psychologically incapable of a romantic interest in women.

Synopsis

As is usual with popular musical plays, there is but one intermission, and each of the two acts consists of many separate scenes. The various scenes and musical numbers are arranged to use the full stage and the forestage, more or less alternately, in such a way that the scenic demands can be met without interruption. In other words, scenes that require only a shallow set or backdrop are performed while the big sets are being changed.

ACT ONE

[]   Scene One

The setting is the portico of the Royal Opera House, Covent Garden.

The scene begins with some street entertainers dancing and performing acrobatic stunts as the audience comes out of the opera house, hoping to find taxis on this cold and rainy night.

Mrs. Eynsford Hill and Freddy come through the crowd and, in a collision, Eliza's violets are knocked into the mud. Freddy apologizes and runs off to hail a taxi, followed by his mother. (The role of Clara in Shaw's original play has been eliminated.) Colonel Pickering appears, and Eliza urges him to buy a flower. He gives her some small change; a bystander warns her to give him a flower for it, as there is a man nearby writing down every word she says. As a crowd collects, Higgins comes into view, shows her what he he wrote, and imitates her speech.

Higgins then, as in the original play, identifies Pickering and some of the bystanders by their speech. He explains to Pickering that phonetics is his profession and that people pay him to have their speech habits corrected. This leads into Higgins' song "Why Can't the English?," in which he deplores poor speech and explains how, by indelibly branding a person of poor education and background, it can keep him from rising to a higher social or economic level.

After the song Higgins remarks that he could turn the flower girl into a lady in six months' time. Pickering and Higgins find that they know of each other's work, and Higgins invites the colonel to stay at his home. Eliza overhears the address.

As the two men leave, Higgins gives her a handful of change, to her great delight. She feels rich, and begins to dream of the comforts that money can buy. The scene ends with her song "Wouldn't It Be Loverly?," accompanied by the costermongers, who pantomime having dinner in a fine restaurant and driving home afterward in a taxi.

[]   *Scene Two*

The setting is a shabby back alley, with a small public house at one side.

The bartender throws the impecunious Doolittle and two of his friends out of the pub. Doolittle expresses his belief that his daughter owes him half a crown now and then. Eliza enters, and refuses him money even before he asks for it. He maintains that he can't go home and face her "stepmother" without a drink. He's willing to marry the woman, he says. He's a slave to her just because he's not her husband. In view of her own windfall, Eliza relents and gives him some money.

Doolittle, overjoyed, tells his two drinking companions of his good luck. This leads into a song-and-dance number, "With a Little Bit of Luck," sung by Doolittle with the other two men chiming in. The song celebrates a lucky man's escape from such trials as work, temperance, marriage, the obligations of Christian charity, and retribution for wrongdoing. Sleeping residents of the alley, wakened by the uproar, shout angrily, and the men cheerfully go into the pub.

[]   *Scene Three*

The setting is Higgins' study, the same as Acts Two and Four of *Pygmalion*.

Higgins and Pickering are listening to speech recordings when Mrs. Pearce ushers Eliza into the room. Higgins says he has enough recordings of her kind of speech and impolitely orders her to go. But Eliza has come to take speech lessons, and will pay for them, she says. Higgins is affronted, but the naturally courteous Pickering draws her out. She wants to be a lady in a flower shop, but knows that she will not be hired unless she learns to speak correctly. Pickering, addressing her as Miss Doolittle, asks her to sit. Eliza offers to pay a shilling a lesson, which Higgins correctly regards as munificent, considering the girl's income. Pickering reminds Higgins of his boast, and says he will pay for the lessons. Higgins accepts the challenge, and tells Mrs. Pearce to take the girl, scrub her, burn her clothes, and order new ones. The housekeeper protests this high-handedness. Eliza is frightened, but it develops that her father kicked her out, and thus she "belongs to no one." Mrs. Pearce demands to know what is to become of the girl afterward, to which Higgins replies that they can simply throw her back where she came from. Eliza starts to leave, but Higgins tempts her with chocolates, eating half of one himself to show it isn't poisoned. In a burst of ironic eloquence he persuades Eliza to stay and overrides the qualms of the other two. Mrs. Pearce leads Eliza out.

Pickering wants reassurance that no advantage will be taken of Eliza's position, and Higgins states his own unflattering view of women. He is a confirmed bachelor, and likely to remain one. This leads into his solo, "I'm an Ordinary Man," a preposterously one-sided view of the many masculine virtues and feminine deficiencies. He hasn't any intention of ever letting a woman turn his life into a hell. He switches on one recording machine after another, at accelerated speed, to illustrate women's chatter. As the noise becomes unbearable he suddenly turns the machines off and sinks contentedly into a chair.

[] *Scene Four*

The setting is the back alley and pub, the same as I-2.

Again the bartender throws out Doolittle and his two cronies. A woman neighbor informs Doolittle that Eliza has moved in with a swell. She has asked the neighbor to send her possessions, all except her clothes, in care of Professor Higgins, 27-A Wimpole Street.

Doolittle is delighted. He sees the prospect of his daughter now supporting him. He and his friends burst into a reprise of "With a Little Bit of Luck."

[] *Scene Five*

The setting is again Higgins' study.

Mrs. Pearce protests that Higgins is working Eliza too hard, but he isn't interested. Nor does he care to see his mail. She continues that there is still another letter from the American millionaire asking Higgins to lecture for his Moral Reform League. Impatiently Higgins tells her to leave the letter on his desk; he will answer it.

The butler announces that Alfred Doolittle wishes to see Higgins about his daughter. Pickering, who has been reading, looks up in alarm, but Higgins says that, if there is to be any trouble, it will be Doolittle's with him.

Doolittle is shown in, and demands his daughter. Higgins tells him to take her away at once. This isn't the response that Doolittle had anticipated, and he quickly backtracks. Higgins accuses him of attempted blackmail, and moves to phone the police. Doolittle protests that he hasn't asked for money, but it's plain that that is what he wants. Eliza had sent for her things, but not her clothes; and what is a parent to think? Higgins tells Mrs. Pearce to fetch Eliza and send her off with her father. But Doolittle insists on further discussion, and Mrs. Pearce leaves the room.

Doolittle asks five pounds. Pickering says that Higgins' intentions are honorable, to which Doolittle replies that if they weren't he'd ask fifty. Pickering and Higgins are shocked, but Doolittle explains that he can't afford morals. He is one of the undeserving poor, up against middle-class morality. His needs are greater than those of the deserving, but he is always refused charitable assistance. He intends, however, to go on being undeserving.

Higgins, delighted with this unorthodox philosophy, offers him ten pounds, but Doolittle turns it down. He and his missus wouldn't feel free to spend so much. They'd put it by, and then farewell to happiness. Doolittle admits that he has never been married, not even to Eliza's mother.

Higgins gives him a five-pound note as Eliza, clean and properly dressed, comes in with Mrs. Pearce. Eliza is protesting that she won't say her vowels one more time. At first Doolittle doesn't recognize her, then expresses his pleased surprise that she has cleaned up so good-looking. Telling Higgins to apply the strap if she gives him any trouble, Doolittle leaves.

Gleefully, Higgins tells Mrs. Pearce to write the American millionaire to get in touch with Alfred Doolittle if he wants a lecturer. Mrs. Pearce says she will, and goes. Eliza demands to know what her father is doing here. Higgins ignores this, and orders her to say her vowels. Eliza rebels—she knows her vowels. Higgins becomes angry and dictatorial; Pickering gently urges her to obey. As the two men leave, Higgins threatens that there will be no lunch or dinner till she can say her vowels correctly.

Alone, Eliza sings "Just You Wait." In it she imagines various kinds of punishment to be inflicted on Higgins in retaliation for the way he is treating her. Revenge is sweet. The lights black out and come up again on the same scene.

Higgins, with Pickering looking on, is trying to teach Eliza to pronounce her *A*'s properly in the sentence "The rain in Spain stays mainly in the plain." She can't do it, and he skips to another exercise— a line in which most of the words begin with the letter *H*. He lights a gas flame that will waver as her breath is expelled, but she can't do the *H*'s either. Finally he simply has her say "ha-ha-ha-ha" again and again over the flame, then forgets about her in discussing speech peculiarities with Pickering. By now Eliza is gasping, but Higgins tells her to continue. With a final "ha" she blows out the flame, and the lights go out.

Six servants appear in a spotlight, and sing about "Poor Professor Higgins"—the way he slaves at this task without rest. There isn't a word in the song about Eliza's slaving.

When the lights come up Pickering is seated at a tea table eating strawberry tarts, and Eliza is trying to accent phrases properly as Higgins illustrates the emphasis on a xylophone. Eliza is hungry, and her eyes and mind are on the tarts. Higgins helps himself to a morsel from the tea tray while coaching Eliza, and he and Pickering discuss how delicious everything is. There is one tart left, and Higgins says he knows who'd like it—whereupon he gives it to the canary. Eliza shrieks and the lights black out. The servants appear again and sing about the ordeal of poor Professor Higgins, working on and on into the night.

The next incident finds Eliza trying to speak with marbles in her mouth. Ultimately she swallows one. In the spotlight the servants themselves are beginning to rebel, hearing nothing but speech exercises all day long. They urge their employer to give up.

As the lights come up Eliza is back at the "rain in Spain" exercise. She is very tired, and Pickering urges Higgins to do no more tonight. But Higgins is determined that the girl will succeed, and he speaks sincerely and movingly on the grandeur and majesty of the English language. Once more Eliza tries the exercise, and this time the A's are sounded correctly—"the rain in Spain stays mainly in the plain." Higgins and Pickering are incredulous at first, then begin to dance and sing with joy as Eliza sounds her H's and accents phrases properly. This leads into the exhilarating and climactic song and dance, "The Rain in Spain," celebrating Eliza's accomplishment and Higgins' victory. As Pickering does flamenco steps, Higgins tangos with Eliza, then all collapse in laughter.

Mrs. Pearce and two servants appear, wakened by the noise. Higgins decides to test Eliza by introducing her at the races. His mother has a box at Ascot. He and Pickering will buy her a suitable outfit in the morning. The men go off to bed. Mrs. Pearce tells Eliza to get to bed too, but she is too excited for sleep. She sings "I Could Have Danced All Night." It is more than learning to speak properly that has thrilled her, however—she has been in Higgins' arms, and danced with him. The servants, joining in the song, urge her to lie down and sleep, but Eliza throws off the comforter that Mrs. Pearce has put over her, and continues to sing and dance.

[]   *Scene Six*

The setting is Ascot, before the club tent.

Colonel Pickering informs Mrs. Higgins that her son is there at the races today. Her displeasure at this intelligence is not lessened when she learns that, furthermore, he has brought along a flower girl he has been training in speech and deportment. Mrs. Higgins informs her chauffeur to stay nearby; she may be leaving abruptly.

[]   *Scene Seven*

The setting is inside the tent, from which the track can be viewed.

A fashionably attired crowd watches the running of a race. With expressions of utter boredom that reflect not the slightest concern or emotion they sing the "Ascot Gavotte," the words of which describe the frenzied, pulse-pounding excitement of the spectacle they are watching. As the race ends they drift off.

Mrs. Higgins enters, followed by her son. Higgins tries to reassure her that the flower girl knows how to behave. She has been told to confine her comments to the weather and people's health. Mrs. Eynsford Hill and her son Freddy come in, with another couple. They are followed by Pickering, escorting Eliza—beautiful and exquisitely gowned. Eliza is introduced and, in spite of some over-articulation, manages to respond correctly. Freddy is instantly captivated. To Mrs. Higgins' polite query as to whether it will rain, Eliza replies that the rain in Spain stays mainly in the plain. Then the scene follows, in condensed form, the similar one in *Pygmalion*. Eliza describes her aunt's illness, the quantities of gin that were poured into her, and the possibility that she was done in for her new straw hat. Freddy is greatly amused at the "new small talk," as Higgins calls it, and Mrs. Higgins, who, of course, knows the truth about the girl, is quite taken with her.

It is time for the next race, and Freddy, who has placed a bet on a horse called Dover, gives the ticket to Eliza. The fashionable crowd returns, and everyone lines up to watch the race. There is a brief reprise of the "Ascot Gavotte," with everyone except Eliza maintaining the same stony-faced demeanor. To the others' dismay and shock, Eliza begins to shout encouragement to Dover. But Dover apparently falls behind, and, as her excitement mounts, the flower girl begins to scream real gutter language at him, as several ladies faint.

[]   Scene Eight

The setting is the exterior of Higgins' house.

Freddy appears, checks the address with a policeman, and buys a nosegay from a passing flower girl. He knocks at the door, and while waiting sings briefly and romantically of his meeting with Eliza at Ascot. Mrs. Pearce comes to the door, and Freddy asks if Miss Doolittle is at home. Mrs. Pearce takes the nosegay and disappears. Freddy sings "On the Street Where You Live," a sentimental ballad.

Mrs. Pearce returns to say that Miss Doolittle does not want to see anyone ever again. Freddy says he will wait for her out here— even though it might be weeks. Mrs. Pearce goes back in, and he sings a short reprise of "On the Street Where You Live."

[]   Scene Nine

The setting is Higgins' study.

This is the night of an embassy ball, at which Higgins and Pickering plan to introduce Eliza. Though Higgins puts on a show of confidence, Pickering is extremely nervous. Mrs. Pearce reports that the car is outside and that she is helping Eliza dress. After a further discussion of the importance of tonight's event and the possibility that the deception will be found out, Eliza appears. She is magnificently gowned and jeweled. The three leave for the ball.

[]   Scene Ten

The setting is a promenade outside the embassy ballroom.

A footman is announcing the guests as they arrive. Mrs. Higgins is chatting with friends. A fiercely bewhiskered Hungarian, Professor Karpathy, enters. He is followed by Pickering, who tells Mrs. Higgins that Eliza has quite captivated the ambassador's wife. Higgins appears, and Karpathy runs to him, identifies himself as a former pupil, and says that he is here as a translator for those who do not speak English. Further, because of his knowledge of phonetics, he is able to detect impostors. Pickering and Mrs. Higgins, who has grown fond of Eliza, are alarmed, but Higgins is confident. Eliza enters, and Karpathy asks to be introduced. A royal couple make their entrance, and the crowd moves into the ballroom.

[] *Scene Eleven*

The setting is the ballroom.

This is a spectacular scene of the ball itself, with no audible dialogue. Higgins is dancing with Eliza. Karpathy, deliberately changing partners during a waltz, manages to dance with Eliza. Pickering frantically signals Higgins to interrupt them, but Higgins merely stands watching. The curtain falls.

[] *In Brief*

These eleven scenes in the first act correspond to the first three acts of *Pygmalion*. In the interest of providing opportunities for scenic and costume display, for dancing and production numbers, and a somewhat broader kind of comedy than is found in the original, a number of scenes have been interpolated. (And a good deal of the original play has been dropped, of course, to make room for the new material.)

We now meet Doolittle in his own environment (I-2), and a bit later we see Doolittle get the news of Eliza's move to the Higgins house—an incident covered by a rather awkward piece of exposition in the original play. The actual training of Eliza, almost entirely slighted by Shaw, is shown in the several episodes of I-5. These, though comic in effect, are full of hard work and discouragement for both pupil and teacher, and they enhance by contrast the breakthrough, when it comes, in the triumphant "Rain in Spain" number. Eliza's exhilaration and growing fondness for Higgins are indicated by "I Could Have Danced All Night." The reasons for substituting Ascot for Mrs. Higgins' drawing room in a big and gaudy musical show seem obvious, and quite justified.

Freddy's "On the Street Where You Live" (I-8) merely adds a more conventional romantic element, set against the highly unconventional romance toward which the musical version is heading. The number also makes it possible to change the setting from the Ascot tent to Higgins' study, just as the promenade (I-10) facilitates the change from the study to the ballroom. This is a practical aspect of writing for the musical comedy stage that must be kept in mind.

The entire episode at the embassy is suggested by Shaw's interpolated scene at the end of Act Three in *Pygmalion*, but is normally covered only by exposition (Act Four) in the version of the play usually staged. The fact that this episode is climactic to the winning of Higgins' bet, as well as offering an opportunity for a splendid production number, makes it an ideal close for the first half of the musical version.

Nearly everything in *My Fair Lady* stems from the Shaw text, either directly or from its implications, and most of the comments made about the structure of *Pygmalion* apply equally to *My Fair Lady*. The one important change is the linking of Higgins and Eliza romantically at the end. Higgins' song "I'm an Ordinary Man" is so preposterously antifeminine that one almost expects him to follow the dramatic cliché right then and there—swallow his words and fall down and worship the next female he encounters. One suspects that G.B.S. would not have been entirely happy with the obviousness of this song, nor with the sentimentality of "On the Street Where You Live," but these are small matters in a generally fine adaptation of the tale from one medium to another.

ACT TWO

[] *Scene One*

The setting is Higgins' study.

The servants are asleep about the room as the curtain rises. The clock strikes three, and Mrs. Pearce enters to awaken them. Higgins and Pickering come in, followed by a very tired Eliza, to whom no one pays the slightest attention. Pickering congratulates Higgins on his achievement, but Higgins seems bored and indifferent about the whole affair.

Pickering begins the song "You Did It," but Higgins insists that much of the credit should go to Pickering. Still singing, they recount the events of the evening to Mrs. Pearce and the servants, and soon the latter, too, are joining in the hosannas for their employer. It never occurs to anyone that Eliza has contributed anything to Higgins' triumph.

Higgins thanks God that it's all over at last. The servants leave. Higgins, turning to Eliza, asks her to leave a note for Mrs. Pearce about breakfast, and wonders where his slippers are. Eliza picks them up and throws them at him. She has won his bet for him, she says, but she doesn't matter. Higgins, genuinely startled, wants to know the reason for this behavior. She attacks him ferociously, then subsides in tears. What is to become of her? Higgins replies that it doesn't matter what becomes of her; then he patronizingly tries to reassure her. But she will not be comforted. Where is she to go, and what is she to do? What has Higgins left her fit for?

Higgins suggests that she marry. Doubtless his mother could find some chap or other who'd be suitable. Eliza replies that as a flower girl she was above selling herself. Higgins has another idea—perhaps Pickering would set her up in a flower shop. He starts off to bed.

Eliza asks if her clothes belong to her, then turns the jewelry she is wearing over to Higgins for safekeeping. She also removes a ring he had bought for her in Brighton. He throws it across the room, and towers over her so threateningly that she cries, "Don't you hit me!" Furious, he again starts to go. Eliza tells him to leave his own note for Mrs. Pearce. Damning everyone and everything, Higgins stomps off, tripping on the steps and inadvertently turning on the recording machine. Violently he switches it off and slams the door behind him. Eliza sings a reprise of "Just You Wait," and ends sobbing.

[] *Scene Two*

The setting is the exterior of Higgins' house.

Freddy is still at his post, and he sings a reprise of "On the Street Where You Live." Eliza, dressed in street clothes, comes out carrying a suitcase. Astonished, she asks what he is doing here, and he declares his love, continuing the song. Suddenly Eliza turns on him with a song in a very different mood, "Show Me." She is tired of words—endless words from Higgins, now words from Freddy. If he loves her he should show her, not tell her about it. She crowns him, finally, with her suitcase, and marches off. He follows, as much in love as ever.

[] *Scene Three*

The setting is the flower market at Covent Garden.

Costermongers, warming themselves around a fire, sing a reprise of "Wouldn't It Be Loverly?" Halfway through the song Eliza enters. Two flower girls seem to recognize her, then decide that the well-dressed lady merely resembles the girl they knew. The same thing happens with the men around the fire. They move away from her. Eliza, picking up a bunch of violets, continues the reprise of "Wouldn't It Be Loverly?"

Suddenly Doolittle comes out of a nearby pub. He is resplendently dressed, as for a fashionable wedding, and the bartender bids him a respectful good night. Doolittle tips him generously.

Eliza is astonished to see her father thus transformed. Resentfully Doolittle explains that Higgins has delivered him into the hands of middle-class morality. The American millionaire to whom Higgins wrote has bequeathed Doolittle four thousand pounds a year. Now Eliza's "stepmother" insists that they marry. She wants to be respectable too. Doolittle sadly admits that he hasn't the nerve to refuse the money.

Freddy appears. He has been waiting for Eliza in a taxi. Doolittle invites his daughter to the marriage ceremony later in the morning, but Eliza declines. She tosses away the violets, wishes her father good luck, and leaves with Freddy.

Doolittle has but a few more hours of freedom. He intends to make the most of them, getting drunk and chasing girls; but he urges his friends, in song, to "Get Me to the Church on Time." The number ends with an exuberant dance.

[]   *Scene Four*

The setting is a hallway in Higgins' house.

Higgins pounds on the door of Pickering's room. Eliza has gone and has taken her clothes. Mrs. Pearce wants to know whether either of the gentlemen frightened her last night. On the contrary, they hardly said a word to her, and suddenly and inexplicably she lost her temper.

Pickering phones the police, and has some difficulty explaining the missing girl's position in the household to an obviously suspicious inspector. As Pickering makes a second call to the Home Office, Higgins sings "A Hymn to Him," in which it appears that the male sex has a monopoly of the virtues, and in a more perfect world women would be more like men. Pickering makes an appointment with a friend at the Home Office and leaves, as Mrs. Pearce comes in with coffee for Higgins, who continues to sing. If only women could be like him!

[]   *Scene Five*

The setting is the conservatory in Mrs. Higgins' house.

Eliza has been telling Mrs. Higgins of her success at the ball and the subsequent events on returning home. Mrs. Higgins says she would have thrown the fire irons, not the slippers. Higgins arrives, and is astonished to find Eliza having tea with his mother. He orders the girl to come home at once, but Mrs. Higgins tells him that if he doesn't behave she will have to ask him to leave. She wonders how Eliza ever learned manners from her son. Eliza explains that she never would have, except for Colonel Pickering. The difference between a lady and a flower girl isn't how she behaves, but how she's treated. The colonel had always treated her as a lady. As a caller arrives, Mrs. Higgins, advising her son to stick to two subjects, the weather and his health, leaves the room. Higgins and Eliza are alone.

Higgins tells her that if she comes back she will be treated exactly as before. He cannot change his nature or his manners. Eliza replies that she doesn't mind his swearing at her, but she will not be passed over. She can get along very well without Higgins. He answers, with rather unexpected humility, that he will miss her. Eliza says he has her voice on the phonograph, and it has no feelings to hurt.

He urges her to return for the fun of it, just as he took her on, with either one free to break off the relationship at will. Perhaps she'd like to marry Pickering. Angrily Eliza says she wouldn't marry Higgins, who is nearer her own age. She might marry Freddy, though. Higgins snorts that she evidently wants him to be as infatuated with her as Freddy is. No, what Eliza wants is a little kindness and friendliness. Higgins rudely tells her to go find some sentimental hog to kiss and kick her—that's all she can appreciate.

Eliza, near tears, says she'll marry Freddy, who loves her. She'll support him by teaching phonetics. She can be an assistant to that brilliant Hungarian. At this Higgins explodes, and Eliza suddenly realizes that she is the victor in this duel. She no longer need care a snap for his bullying. She sings "Without You," a celebration of Higgins' insignificance in the wider scheme of things and a declaration of her own independence.

Higgins, for his part, realizes that he has created a real woman, and he likes her in this mood. Coolly, Eliza bids him farewell and leaves the room. Mrs. Higgins enters. Higgins is now deeply disturbed, but he declares his independence too. He can get along without Eliza. He has his own spark of divine fire. As he goes, Mrs. Higgins applauds, and murmurs a bravo for Eliza.

[]   *Scene Six*

The setting is the exterior of Higgins' house.

Higgins arrives at his home. The entire scene consists of the song "I've Grown Accustomed to Her Face." Eliza's proposed marriage to Freddy has put him in a jealous rage, and it is apparent, even though he would not acknowledge it, that he is in love with the girl.

[] *Scene Seven*

The setting is Higgins' study.

Higgins enters, disconsolately turns on the recording machine, and we hear Eliza's voice on the day of her arrival as she asked for lessons, and Higgins' heartless comments to Pickering about her. Eliza herself enters, turns off the machine, and continues speaking in the character of the flower girl. Higgins, no man for an outward show of emotion, settles back comfortably and asks where the devil his slippers are. Eliza understands.

[] *In Brief*

Acts Four and Five of *Pygmalion* form the basis for the second act of *My Fair Lady*. Where Shaw's climax consisted of Eliza's blossoming forth as a real woman of spirit and independence (the corresponding development in the musical version is Eliza's song "Without You"), *My Fair Lady* must convince us that Higgins and Eliza are really in love, and that only a reconciliation will provide a satisfactory ending. The effort to steer the original material off in this new direction sometimes makes for rather rough going.

Higgins' thoughtless treatment of Eliza after the ball is underscored by the song "You Did It," and her resentment by the reprise of "Just You Wait." Then she runs into Freddy outside the house. It would seem that her natural reaction would be to respond to Freddy's adoration with relief and gratitude. She has ample reason to be angry with Higgins, but Freddy appreciates her. The adapter, however, cannot permit Eliza to show any affection for Freddy, for, unlike Shaw, he wants the girl to wind up with Higgins. A new and almost completely irrelevant issue is obliged to do service at this point: Eliza doesn't want to be told that she is loved, she wants to be shown. This has certainly not been a matter of concern up to now, and "Show Me," whatever its merits as a song, seems forced and wrong in the context of the story. One would have expected a musical number at this point to deal, perhaps, with the warmth of her feelings toward Freddy, even though she doesn't truly love him.

II-3, the episode at the flower market, however, is a valid addition and expansion of the original story. Whereas Shaw, without such a scene, can tell us only that Eliza can't go back, here we see that she can't, and we feel her emotion as she fails to establish contact with her former friends.

Doolittle, as extraneous to the main plot line as ever, appears in the flower market more logically than in Mrs. Higgins' drawing room, as in the original. His explanation of what has happened to him suffers a bit from not having Higgins there to bear his reproaches, but on the whole the changed locale works satisfactorily.

"A Hymn to Him," like "I'm an Ordinary Man" in the first act, builds Higgins' male self-sufficiency and vanity, so he will have farther to fall when he is finally obliged to capitulate to his natural needs and desires. "I've Grown Accustomed to Her Face" is, of course, a recognition that he loves Eliza, and prepares us for her return at the end.

Protagonist, Objective, Obstacles, and Crisis

All are similar to the source material, and may be studied by referring back to *Pygmalion*.

Climax

There is a similarity to *Pygmalion* in *My Fair Lady*'s climaxes, but with one important difference. By the use of songs—"I'm an Ordinary Man," "I Could Have Danced All Night," "A Hymn to Him," "Without You," and especially "I've Grown Accustomed to Her Face"— the Higgins-Eliza relationship is romanticized, and the audience led to want these two proud and prickly people to come together. Hence a new element has been added to *Pygmalion*'s major climax. (Eliza's declaration of independence and Higgins' realization that he has created a real woman.) This additional element extends the dramatic question beyond the corresponding point in *Pygmalion,* and places the major climax of *My Fair Lady* in the final scene. Higgins now wants Eliza for himself ("I've Grown Accustomed to Her Face" indicates his jealousy of Freddy), and the story will not be over until he gets her.

Theme and Resolution

Though considerably diluted by the unavoidable cutting and condensation of Shaw's original, the play's thematic implications are present also in the musical version. By the gratuitous addition of the Higgins-Eliza romance, however, we may also infer that "love will find a way"—a none-too-startling insight.

As the climax occurs at the final curtain, the resolution is left to our imagination.

Opening, Unity, and Exposition

All are similar to Pygmalion. "Why Can't the English?" and "Wouldn't It Be Loverly?" not only characterize the two principals in the first scene, but carry, by implication, a good deal of exposition. Both songs serve their purposes admirably.

Characterization

Perhaps unavoidably, in view of the need for condensation, characterizations are not nearly so sharp and penetrating as in Shaw's original. Eliza's characterization flies right off the track with "Show Me." The transformation of Higgins from the pugnacious bachelor to a man reluctantly recognizing that he is in love is accomplished almost entirely by the song "I've Grown Accustomed to Her Face," and it works.

Development

The comments made on the progression of scenes in Pygmalion generally apply also to My Fair Lady. The latter, however, contains many scenes either not found in Pygmalion, or transferred to a different locale. On the whole these dovetail satisfactorily with the scenes that are derived more directly from the original.

The introduction of Doolittle in I-2 is unnecessary to the plot (as is Doolittle himself). It doesn't move the story forward, but it certainly does no harm, for the amusing characterization of the man, his relationship to his daughter, and the exuberance of "With a Little Bit of Luck" combine to hold our interest.

I-4 occupies a somewhat more organic position in the plot line, for it shows us how Doolittle knows where Eliza has gone and, as has been noted earlier, eliminates some awkward explanations and exposition.

I-6 and I-7 are solidly based on Pygmalion's Act Three, the

testing of Eliza before people who don't know who the girl is. The introductory material has been put into a separate scene (I-6) merely to permit the change of setting from the study to the interior of the tent.

I-8 establishes Freddy's infatuation in a conventionally built episode. Freddy, the protagonist, wants to meet Eliza again. The obstacle, none too well motivated, is her disinclination to "see anyone ever again." Why? We don't know. Freddy fails to achieve his objective, and the scene's resolution is that he will wait there until she comes out.

I-9, I-10, and I-11 are substantially new, and are structurally a single scene. Higgins is the protagonist; his objective: to pass off Eliza as an aristocrat. The chief obstacle (aside from Eliza's own insecurity) is the Hungarian's ability to detect impostors. The act ends without reaching a climax, which leaves the audience in suspense during the intermission.

II-2, as has already been noted, is not only irrelevant, but the song "Show Me" lacks proper motivation. II-3, on the other hand, works beautifully. Eliza is the protagonist; her objective: to learn whether she would be accepted by her old friends in the market. The obstacle is the same gulf that prevented her moving into a different social class before. Now it bars her way back. Through this pattern is woven the secondary story of Doolittle's rise to eminence. "Get Me to the Church on Time" is more of a music-hall turn than an integral part of the story, but it is such a rousing song that we don't notice that the play has halted for it.

II-6 and II-7 are structurally one scene. Though Higgins is the protagonist, he is entirely passive now, making no effort to bring back the Eliza he misses. She does return, small thanks to him, and, were it not for the fact that we sense his joy and deep relief (carefully prepared by the song "I've Grown Accustomed to Her Face" and his business with the recording machine), the ending would be flat indeed.

Dramatic Irony

Most of the situations employing this device in *Pygmalion* are represented in *My Fair Lady*. And Eliza's return to the flower market (II-3) depends for its effectiveness not only on our knowing that the well-dressed lady is the former flower girl, but on our sense of what it would mean to her if she could be accepted there again.

In addition it might be noted that the songs "I'm an Ordinary Man," "You Did It," and "A Hymn to Him" owe their pungency to our awareness that the sentiments expressed are wild distortions of the truth.

Preparation

Again, we can refer back to *Pygmalion* for comments on preparation. However, Eliza's vulgar outburst at the races is so entirely natural under the circumstances that no preparation is necessary. (In the play, Mrs. Pearce asks Higgins not to use the word "bloody.")

My Fair Lady has a valid bit of preparation neglected by Shaw. Mrs. Pearce brings in a letter from an American millionaire, and we see how contemptuous Higgins is of the American's request that he lecture. It becomes far more plausible, then, for Higgins to recommend Doolittle for the job.

Activity

There are quite a number of significant pieces of business to be found in *My Fair Lady* in addition to the ones supplied by the original author.

In I-3 Higgins turns on several recording machines at high speed to illustrate how women's chatter sounds. The teaching episodes in I-5 give us a gas flame that wavers when an *H* is sounded properly, a strawberry tart that is offered to a canary while Eliza is longing for it, and an attempt to speak with marbles in her mouth.

Since a race track is a place where one expects highly expressive and uninhibited behavior, the stony-faced and impassive demeanor of the society folk at Ascot becomes a comment on British imperturbability. (A lack of activity when we expect movement can be significant too.)

Karpathy's deliberately changing partners during the ball in order to dance with Eliza is effective; so is Higgins' tripping on the steps and inadvertently turning on the recording machine when he is trying to make a dignified exit after his quarrel with Eliza (II-1).

Eliza's tossing away the violets when she leaves the flower market (II-3) may be a little obvious. Far better is Higgins, in II-7, turning on the record of Eliza's voice when she first arrived—and hearing his own jeering comments echoing back at him.

Dialogue and Plausibility

Since most of the dialogue is Shaw's, it is fine, though greatly diluted. As for plausibility, the comments on *Pygmalion* will serve here too, though it must be admitted that the ending of the play was far more logical and astringent than "the mineral oil of the musical's denouement," as John Gassner put it.

The Songs

Unlike the early musical comedies and operettas, whose story lines often ground to a halt whenever it came time for a musical number, the modern musical theatre insists that its songs pull their own dramatic weight. "The Rain in Spain" and "Without You" each carries a whole dramatic climax. Other songs serve primarily to characterize ("Wouldn't It Be Loverly?", "With a Little Bit of Luck," "I'm an Ordinary Man," and "A Hymn to Him"). "Why Can't the English?" and "You Did It" actually carry the story. "I Could Have Danced All Night" and "I've Grown Accustomed to Her Face" signal a change of attitude on the part of the singer. Ideally, songs occupy the peaks of the action rather than, as in the old days, the valleys.

HAROLD PINTER
The Birthday Party

1958

A characteristic of Pinter's plays is the deliberate withholding of motivations and background material that are normally found in more conventional works. The author has said that there are no hard distinctions between the real and the unreal, the true and the false, and that a character whose behavior is unexplained can be as worthy of attention as any other. Thus his plays, lacking in logical explanations, superficially appear to be exercises in mood alone—dread, menace, terror. But they can be interpreted in many different ways, often on several levels of meaning at the same time. Pinter is a poet as well as a playwright, and perhaps the soundest approach to his plays is to view them as poetic imagery.

On a literal level nothing could better illustrate what happens to a play when motivations are inadequate or totally neglected. Though their omission may help the author toward the distillation of a particular mood, the result can nevertheless be extremely puzzling, and not entirely satisfactory to the average audience.

Pinter's plays have undoubted dramatic power, in spite of their obscurity, and the author must be accounted a major dramatist. His plays are usually considered as belonging to the Theatre of the Absurd.

Premise

Stanley, a young man in his late thirties, is the only boarder in a house presided over by Meg, a slovenly woman who displays a suffocating and somewhat erotic motherly concern for him. Meg's husband, Petey, is dull-witted but harmless. Stanley himself is an idler, though at one time he had a job playing the piano at a local seaside pier. Apathetic now, he appears to have found a refuge from the outside world in Meg's boardinghouse. Two representatives of that outside world, who represent some kind of threat to Stanley, are searching for him.

Facts antecedent to the play are cloaked in equivocation. Stanley in some way may have betrayed or aroused the ire of "the organization," but much depends on what interpretation we put on subsequent events, or whether we are even willing to accept such ambiguity at all.

Synopsis

The setting throughout is the living room of a shabby boardinghouse in an English coastal town. Setting, costumes, and physical activity are all realistic.

The play is in three acts.

ACT ONE

Meg is serving breakfast to her husband, Petey. Their conversation is so stupifyingly dull that it becomes very funny indeed. These two are bored with each other, but amiable. Stanley, their boarder, hasn't yet come downstairs. Petey remarks that he has met two men on the beach who have inquired about renting a room. Meg says she can accommodate them, and goes up to waken Stanley. He comes down for his breakfast, and Petey, a deck-chair attendant, goes off to work.

Stanley is unshaven and unkempt, but he is very attractive to Meg, who fusses over him dotingly. He rather contemptuously tolerates her attentions, and his occasional thrusts of ridicule are lost on her. When Meg mentions that she is expecting two gentlemen to rent a room, he appears vaguely alarmed. Then he tells her he has been offered a job playing the piano on a round-the-world tour. Next he describes a successful concert he once performed; then says he found the hall shuttered and deserted when he went to play a second concert. Changing the subject, he tells Meg, portentously, that "they" are coming today in a van, bringing a wheelbarrow. "They" are looking for someone.

There is a knock at the front door, and a voice tells Meg that "it" has come. As Meg leaves to shop, her friend Lulu enters with a large package which she places on the sideboard. Lulu is a flirtatious girl in her twenties. She warns Stanley not to touch the package, and suggests that he wash and shave. They discuss the possibility of going out together, but Stanley maintains there is nowhere to go. Suddenly he demands to know whether Meg had many boarders before he came here. He seems to be worried about the two men who are expected. Lulu leaves, and Stanley goes into the kitchen to wash.

Goldberg and McCann, carrying suitcases, open the door and come into the room. Unnoticed, Stanley slips out of the house. Goldberg is urbane, talkative, full of a false geniality. McCann, a burly Irishman, is somewhat sullen. The men sit, and Goldberg reminisces sentimentally about seaside holidays in his youth and about his family. McCann seems nervous about being here, but Goldberg assures him that they have come to the right house. He goes on to say that, when this job came up, he asked particularly for McCann as an assistant. McCann wants to know whether the job is like anything they've done before. Goldberg reassures him without really telling him anything.

Meg returns from shopping, meets the men, and pleasantries are exchanged. Goldberg finds an excuse to send McCann from the room, then questions Meg about her boarder. She tells him about Stanley and his piano-playing. She wishes that Stanley could have played tonight, for today is his birthday. Goldberg then suggests that they have a party to celebrate. McCann returns, hears about the party, and Meg says she will invite Lulu also. Meg will put on her party dress; Goldberg will bring refreshments. Meg takes the two men upstairs to their room.

Stanley returns to the house, listens, and looks about nervously. Meg comes downstairs, and tells him the two gentlemen have taken the room. Stanley queries her about them, but she can barely remember their names. "Goldberg?" he asks. He seems too terrified to move, or, momentarily, even to speak. Trying to cheer him, Meg gets the package from the sideboard and tells Stanley it's his birthday present. He protests that this is not his birthday, but he opens the package. It is a toy drum. Meg demands a kiss. Stanley begins to beat the drum savagely, in mounting panic.

[] *In Brief*

Stanley, whatever his background or career, appears to have found safety from the outside world in this shabby refuge. (His finding the hall deserted when he went back to play a second concert might be interpreted as a rejection by the outside world; his telling Meg that "they" are coming in a van and bringing a wheelbarrow may be a metaphor for a hearse and coffin.)

That Stanley fears some threat from the outside world is evident from the moment Meg tells him that two men are looking for a room. When the men arrive he temporarily flees. Since it is obvious that Goldberg and McCann are pursuing Stanley, their superficial amiability makes them particularly sinister. Unable to stay away from the house, Stanley returns. His worst fears seem to be confirmed, and he is in utter terror. Our curiosity and apprehension aroused, we wait to see what Goldberg and McCann will do to him. (Meg's giving Stanley a toy drum suggests—though this is by no means the only interpretation—that to her Stanley is still a child.)

ACT TWO

It is evening. McCann sits tearing a newspaper into long strips. Stanley comes in, gets a drink of water, and starts to leave again when McCann intercepts him and introduces himself. Stanley would like to go, but McCann says that a birthday party is being held for him there tonight. Stanley considers this unfortunate—he isn't in the mood for a party. However, he sits and asks McCann if they haven't met before. McCann doesn't think so. Stanley says he'll be moving back home soon. He had a small business that required him to leave home for a while, but now he wants to return. He becomes increasingly nervous in McCann's company. When he grips the Irishman's arm, McCann hits him. Stanley protests that he has never caused any trouble, then tries flattery to see what he can learn about McCann and his friend.

Goldberg enters with Petey, who introduces him to Stanley. Goldberg talks sentimentally of his "old mum" and his boyhood. Petey can't stay for the party, he says—this is his chess night—and he leaves. McCann also goes, to get liquor.

Stanley, saying that he is the manager of the house, tells Goldberg that his room is engaged, and that he and McCann will have to leave. Goldberg ignores this and congratulates Stanley on his birthday. He compares birth to getting up in the morning. McCann returns with liquor, and Stanley orders him out. McCann puts the bottles on the sideboard. Stanley tells Goldberg that it's no good starting trouble, and insists that they go. After some argument they all sit at the table, and Goldberg and McCann start quizzing Stanley, giving him little or no chance to answer. Many of the questions are weirdly nonsensical and based on contradictory assumptions, though McCann at one point does ask him why he left the organization, and a bit later says that he betrayed the organization. Stanley is being browbeaten in a torrent of uncommunicative language.

McCann takes Stanley's glasses, without which he is fairly helpless, and the questions come more furiously than ever, until Stanley, thoroughly brainwashed, is unable even to speak coherently. He kicks Goldberg in the stomach, and McCann is threatening to bring a chair down on his head when Meg comes into the room, in evening dress, with the drum and sticks.

Meg's dress is admired, and Stanley gets his glasses back. Drinks are poured, and Goldberg suggests that they toast Stanley on his birthday. McCann turns out the lights and shines an electric torch on Stanley's face. Meg proposes the toast—a maudlin tribute to Stanley, her "good boy."

As the lights are switched on again, Lulu arrives, and Goldberg makes a preposterously sentimental speech about finding evidence of love and true affection in this house. He congratulates Stanley again, the lights are switched off, and again McCann shines the torch on Stanley's face. They drink another toast to him before switching on the lights.

The drinking continues, with Stanley almost entirely still and withdrawn. Lulu sits on Goldberg's lap. Meg asks Stanley to dance with her, but he is indifferent. Goldberg talks of his deceased wife, and he and Lulu embrace. Meg tells McCann about her childhood, and he sings an Irish ballad.

Now Meg wants to play blindman's buff. She is the first to be blindfolded, then McCann, then Stanley, who has reluctantly joined the game. Lulu and Goldberg kiss. McCann, who has taken Stanley's glasses, now deliberately breaks them, then places the drum in Stanley's path. Stanley's foot goes through it, and, dragging the drum along, he reaches Meg and starts to strangle her. Suddenly the lights go out.

In the darkness there is general panic, and McCann drops his torch. They all search for it. Lulu screams and faints. McCann finds the torch, and reveals Lulu spread-eagled on the table, with Stanley bent over her. Stanley begins to back away, giggling, as Goldberg and McCann converge upon him.

[] *In Brief*

The act traces a rising level of torment for Stanley, beginning with just a hint of animosity on the part of the visitors, then moving irregularly toward open malevolence. Stanley's attempt to order the men out of the house is his only open defiance, and it is short-lived. From that point on he is a helpless victim. They torture him, almost playfully, until Meg's entrance, when they relax their pressure. But, as the drunken party proceeds, the pressure quickly climbs to overt sadism. (Stanley's foot going through the drum might indicate the end of his career as a musician, or perhaps the end of his status as Meg's child.)

Meg and Lulu, the two people who might conceivably have helped Stanley, are rendered ineffectual by liquor and sex.

ACT THREE

It is the following morning, breakfast time. Meg and Petey engage in the same kind of vapid conversation as at the start of Act One. There is nothing left in the kitchen for breakfast, but Meg plans to go shopping. Meg is hung over, and, finding the broken drum, doesn't remember how it happened. Stanley hasn't yet come down. Meg took his tea up to him, but was met at the door of his room by McCann, who said he'd already made tea for Stanley. Later both Goldberg and McCann came down to breakfast. Meg asks her husband about a big car standing in front of the house, and whether there is a wheelbarrow in it. He replies that it's Goldberg's car, and that he doesn't see any wheelbarrow. (It seems probable that Petey knows something of what happened during the night, but is sparing Meg.)

Goldberg comes downstairs and sits at the table. Meg speaks of the car. He praises it, says there's room in the front and the back, and that it has a beautiful boot—just room for the right amount. Meg leaves to go shopping.

Petey inquires about Stanley. Goldberg says he thinks Stanley is better this morning, but that the birthday celebration brought on a nervous breakdown. Petey tells of having come home last night to find all the lights out. He put a shilling in the slot, however, and all the lights came on again. Then he went upstairs and McCann told him about Stanley's collapse. Goldberg says that Stanley's recovery is a possibility. Petey suggests calling a doctor, but Goldberg says that has all been taken care of. Petey's efforts to help Stanley are feeble and ineffectual.

As Petey goes into the kitchen McCann comes in. He tells Goldberg that he's not going up to Stanley's room again. Goldberg can go himself next time. Petey, returning, hears McCann say that he'd given Stanley his broken glasses, and Petey offers to mend them with tape, but Goldberg doesn't encourage this. He says he's taking Stanley very soon, to Monty, a doctor.

McCann questions Goldberg about a girl in the house—presumably Lulu—who had nightmares during the night. Goldberg replies that the girl was merely singing and that he had joined her in song. Petey goes out to the garden, asking Goldberg to let him know when Stanley comes down.

McCann sits and begins tearing a newspaper into strips. This annoys Goldberg, who tells him it's pointless and asks him to stop. Goldberg seems older and drained of energy. McCann wants to get the job over with and get out of here. When he calls Goldberg Simey, a name Goldberg had earlier remarked that his mother had used, Goldberg attacks him viciously. Then Goldberg asks McCann to look into his mouth. He has never lost a tooth, has always kept himself physically fit, and stayed tops in his subjects at school. He followed his dear, dying father's advice to forgive and let live. Goldberg wheezes involuntarily, and McCann depresses his tongue with a spoon, pronounces Goldberg in perfect condition. McCann takes a chest expander from a suitcase; Goldberg exercises with it and breaks it.

Lulu enters and McCann goes out, leaving her alone with Goldberg. Apparently they had spent the night together, and she upbraids him, in cliché terms, for defiling her. McCann returns and tells the girl to confess. Goldberg says McCann is an unfrocked priest. Lulu beats a hasty retreat.

McCann fetches Stanley, who is clean, shaved, and immaculately dressed in striped trousers, black jacket, and a bowler hat. Stanley sits, motionless, seemingly unaware of anything or anyone around him. Goldberg and McCann question him, tell him he needs a change and that they can save him. They will care for him, make him a rich and successful man. Asked at last for his opinion on all this, Stanley tries to speak, but can utter only meaningless sounds and clutch his broken glasses.

As Goldberg and McCann start to take Stanley outside, Petey

comes back in. Goldberg says they're taking Stanley to Monty. As Petey objects, Goldberg threatens to take him along too. The three men leave, and we hear the car drive off.

Petey sits, picks up the newspaper with its torn strips. Meg returns. Petey tells her that Goldberg and McCann have gone, but he cannot bear to tell her the whole truth, and says that Stanley is still asleep. She, on her part, is subconsciously aware of the truth, but her mind goes back to the party and the lovely time they had last night. She was the belle of the ball.

[] *In Brief*

Since we don't know for some time what has happened to Stanley, we wonder about him and fear for him. Our fears are hardly lessened by the talk of there being "enough room" in the car, by Goldberg's announcement that they are taking Stanley to Monty, and by the near quarrel that develops between Goldberg and McCann.

Goldberg's scene with Lulu, after what was apparently a night of debauchery, is wonderfully comic, and, while it is tangential to the main story line, the scene holds because we are still waiting to learn what has happened to Stanley.

With Stanley's entrance we see the result of what was done to him, but no further part of the action that has destroyed him. (Stanley's dress and physical condition suggest a corpse prepared for burial.) After another sadistic bullying, in which Stanley's captors test the effectiveness of his collapse, they take him away. Meg, who has been so protective, cannot face the reality of Stanley's fate.

Protagonist and Objective

Stanley is the protagonist. His objective: to escape the fate that is pursuing him.

Obstacles

The chief obstacle is the skill and determination of Goldberg, assisted by McCann. There appears to be another obstacle within Stanley himself—his unwillingness or inability to flee his pursuers. When he first sees them, he runs out of the house, but before the act is over he has come back, and he makes no further attempt to leave, even when Meg confirms that the name of one of the men is Goldberg. We must interpret for ourselves this aspect of Stanley's behavior. Perhaps he knows the futility of trying to escape.

Major Crisis and Climax, Theme

If one accepts that Stanley could have evaded the men by leaving the house and hiding, then the crisis occurs when he is drawn back again at the end of Act One, for from then on his fate is sealed. A less literal interpretation of the play suggests that Stanley's flight would be useless, that he would be found sooner or later. In this case the crisis may be said to have occurred before the play starts, when Stanley "betrayed the organization," either figuratively or literally.

The climax is Stanley's destruction. We see this pursued through the greater part of Act Two, and it reaches the peak of its intensity at the end of the act. Technically that is the climax, so far as it is dramatized. The fact that more was apparently done to Stanley during the night might be compared to the rape of Blanche Du Bois—once we know that the victim has lost, it is unnecessary to carry the action farther. There is this difference, however—we know what happened to Blanche. We're not at all sure what else is going to happen (or did happen) to the protagonist of *The Birthday Party*.

The withholding of so much information in the Pinter plays leaves them open to wide thematic interpretation. What we supply by way of explanation determines what the plays mean.

Who are Goldberg and McCann, from whom there is no escape? Representatives of a Mafia-like organization that Stanley has betrayed? The theme obviously would be a shallow one, on the level of a gangster movie. Are they forces of the outside world that Stanley has rejected? The agents of Philistinism forcing a Bohemian into conformity? Or perhaps the pressures of worldly necessity that drive a child from the warmth and security of his home into the responsibilities of adulthood? Perhaps they are emissaries of Fate, in the Greek sense—ominous forces of destiny, death pursuing life, with Goldberg a surrogate for Jehovah, McCann for Lucifer. Or could they be the reflections of Stanley's own conscience, come to haunt him for some unnamed crime? These various metaphors don't necessarily exclude one another. Many wheels are turning here.

Resolution

Whether we regard the end of the second act as the climax, or consider that it occurs off-stage between Acts Two and Three, the entire third act must be looked upon as resolution. (*The Cherry Orchard* also devotes an entire last act to resolution.)

Goldberg and McCann have apparently accomplished the purpose for which they came, but we want to see Stanley for ourselves. Wisely, the author delays bringing him before us until late in the act, and this enables him to hold our attention during such matters as Goldberg's farewell to Lulu and the various other implications of what went on during the night. Once we have seen that Stanley has indeed been broken, the play must end quickly. It does so on the ironic note of Meg's ignorance of what has been done to her precious boarder under her very nose.

Opening

Since the play deals with Stanley's destruction, it begins with the coming of the forces that are to destroy him. We hear of Goldberg and McCann's arrival soon after the curtain rises. Since we are not concerned with what led to Stanley's destruction, there would be no point in starting the play earlier, while beginning it later would cause us to miss a great deal of its mounting tension and terror.

Unity

Unity of time and place are observed. Whether there is unity of action must be determined by how much of the play's content we regard as pertinent to the main story line, and how much immaterial. In this aspect, as in so many others, we see the modern drama's departure from the older, more rigid forms, into a far more permissive structure.

Exposition

Since the play ignores the reasons for the events it depicts, astonishingly little exposition is required. It is true that Stanley talks about his experiences as a pianist, and Goldberg about his youth and his family, but these scenes are not presented in conflict or by any of the other methods commonly used to carry exposition. They are straight narrative. Stanley's words hold our interest because what he says is so bizarre; Goldberg's, because of the contrast between his sentimentality and his sinister character.

Characterization

Though we are given no clues as to the background of these people, each is distinctly characterized by his attitudes and manner.

Stanley, though a refugee from a wider and frightening world, dreams of a global tour as a pianist. He is caught between his fears and his self-delusions, and is without defenses. Goldberg, authoritative and sentimental in relaxed moods, is seen in action to be brutally cruel. The taciturn McCann lacks Goldberg's self-confidence, but appears to enjoy torturing his victim quite as fully as does his chief. Meg is dull-witted, silly, and possessive to the point that Stanley resents and ridicules her. Petey is well-intentioned, but stupid and ineffectual. Lulu, a shrewd and calculating trollop, pretends to a nonexistent virtue. These are very real people, even if we don't fully understand their motives or what made them the way they are.

Development

While the play's basic structure sets a pattern that controls its progress from one scene to the next, the individual scenes are hardly built in the conventional sense at all. Consider the scene between Goldberg and McCann in the last act. It begins with McCann rebelling against going up to Stanley's room again, continues with Goldberg's refusal to have Stanley's glasses repaired, goes on to a bit of exposition about a girl having had nightmares during the night, and is followed by a quarrel over McCann's tearing up the newspapers and his calling Goldberg Simey. The quarrel evaporates as quickly as it began, and soon Goldberg is having his teeth examined and is reminiscing about his father. The scene ends with his breaking the chest expander.

Such seemingly directionless writing can be very puzzling and irritating, but many people accept it in Pinter, in part because the basic structure of his plays is sound, and thus he has captured their interest.

Dramatic Irony

One small bit of humor in the first act depends on our knowing, as Meg does not, the meaning of the word succulent. But there is no significant use of dramatic irony until the end of the play, when Meg is told that Stanley is still upstairs asleep.

Preparation

The arrival of Goldberg and McCann is prepared by Petey's mention of having encountered them, then by Stanley's alarm when Meg speaks of them, later by his questioning Lulu about other boarders. The quarrel that is sparked by McCann's calling Goldberg Simey is planted earlier when Goldberg is talking about his mother. Goldberg's final scene with Lulu is anticipated by McCann's asking him about the girl with nightmares.

Activity

There are a number of extremely effective bits of stage business. Stanley's banging on the drum at the end of the first act conveys his terror better than words could do. Taking Stanley's glasses away from him and later breaking them suggests the sadism and relentlessness of the men, as does turning the torch on Stanley's face, the game of blindman's buff, placing the drum where Stanley will stumble into it, and Stanley's attempt to walk with his foot through the drum. His attempt to strangle the first person his hands touch indicates his panic and demoralization.

Dialogue

Pinter's handling of dialogue is unique and quite extraordinary. Instead of the characters' following each other's thoughts and reacting with logic and understanding (as they do in Shaw's plays, to cite an outstanding example), their speech veers off on tangents in a manner that is still uncannily lifelike and true to the character being portrayed. There are the fumbling reactions of the slow-witted, and the pauses when we can fairly hear the grinding of their mental machinery.

There are the irrelevant comments, the repetitions, the gropings, the inability to formulate a logical thought or sentence, that are all characteristic of common speech. Pinter himself has said that people are frightened of communication; hence they take refuge in cross talk, and speak of things other than what is on their minds. Thus their thoughts and their words sometimes work at cross-purposes, or the words are used to conceal their thoughts. Pinter's ear for ordinary speech is very accurate.

Effects

In contrast to the content of The Birthday Party, its setting, costumes, properties, and stage movement are all realistic. There is no dependence on atmospheric lighting, music, or sound effects to reinforce mood. Even the sudden failure of the lights at the end of Act Two is explained later when Petey reports putting a shilling in the slot.

The contrast between what is said and done on the stage and the banality of the environment accounts for a large part of the play's sense of terror. All this is happening, not at midnight in a bat-infested castle, but in a commonplace boardinghouse.

Plausibility

Without motivations for the actions of the characters, speculating on the logic or inevitability of the course of events is a fruitless exercise.

EUGENE IONESCO
Rhinoceros

1959

One of the most distinguished and frequently-performed dramatists of the *avant-garde*, Ionesco uses the theatre to explore his principal philosophic concerns. As Martin Esslin suggests in *The Theatre of the Absurd*, these concerns are the isolation of the individual and his difficulty in communicating with his fellow creatures, as well as his subjection to both internal anxieties and the external pressures imposed by a society that demands conforming standards of behavior.

While Ionesco professes to build his plays on a pattern of states of consciousness or situations that "grow more and more dense, then get entangled, either to be disentangled again or to end in unbearable inextricability," it will be seen that in *Rhinoceros*, at least, we have a more or less conventional structure based upon a fanciful and highly symbolic premise. Once the audience accepts the proposition (as they will) that a man can turn into a rhinoceros, the rest of the work can proceed logically to a satisfying conclusion. Most of the author's shorter works are less conventionally constructed.

One cannot escape the feeling that *Rhinoceros* would have been more effective if it had been planned as a short play instead of being stretched to a full evening's length. Both dialogue and action are repetitious, with the result that the whole tempo of the work slows down, at times, almost to the point of ennui.

The play was written for the proscenium theatre, with some incidental action occurring in the orchestra pit.

Premise

A provincial French town is afflicted with an epidemic that finds people, under social pressure and the impulse of the individual to conform, turning into rhinoceroses. One ordinary and otherwise unremarkable man determines to resist these pressures and remain a human being. (It may be noted that the premise is not disclosed until well into the play.)

Synopsis

Realistic settings are called for, with some fanciful or expressionist elements, such as rhinoceros heads appearing on the walls, entering into the decor late in the play.

There are three acts, the second being divided into two scenes.

ACT ONE

The scene is the town square. A café and terrace, set with tables, and a grocery store are visible. It is near noon on a Sunday in midsummer.

A housewife carrying a cat and a basket of provisions crosses the stage, to the annoyance of the grocer's wife, for the woman has done her shopping elsewhere. Then two men enter from opposite sides, meet center. They are Jean, impatient and dictatorial in manner and fastidiously dressed, and Berenger, unshaven and unkempt, half asleep, and suffering from a mild hang-over. Both are of indeterminate age. They have an appointment.

Berenger is late, but Jean, knowing Berenger's habits, came late deliberately. Jean, as a faithful but highly disapproving friend, criticizes Berenger severely for his slovenly dress and deportment, and for his drinking. Berenger accepts all these captious remarks in a docile and apologetic manner. The noise of a large, heavy-breathing animal is heard galloping across the square. Jean and others who have come outside identify it as a rhinoceros. As the dust settles and the animal disappears, the event is regarded as extremely peculiar, but not alarming. It is discussed by a number of people, including a logician, another old gentleman, the housewife with her cat, the waitress and the proprietor of the café, and the grocer and his wife. The old gentleman helps the housewife pick up things she has dropped in her fright, Jean and Berenger order drinks, and gradually the others drift off.

Though Berenger is inclined to think the rhinoceros escaped from a zoo or a circus, and to dismiss the incident as of no importance, Jean is worried, and berates his friend for regarding the matter so lightly. Berenger protests that a stupid and ferocious animal is not worth quarreling about, and tries to change the subject, at which Jean takes offense. Berenger lifts his glass to drink when Daisy passes by, a young typist to whom he is attracted. Not wanting Daisy to see him in his unkempt condition, he rises and inadvertently spills his drink on Jean's trousers. Jean is furious, and talks to Berenger as though he were a hopeless alcoholic.

The old gentleman and the logician are passing at the moment, and, flailing his arms about, Jean accidentally hits one of them. There are apologies, and the two older men sit at another table on the terrace. There follows a curious double conversation in which the remarks made by Jean and Berenger on the one hand, and by the old gentleman and the logician on the other, run parallel and often complement each other. It is a highly amusing tour de force, though not essentially dramatic.

In this scene Jean brags of his physical and moral strength in contrast to Berenger's alleged weakness and general incompetence. When Daisy's name comes up Berenger admits that he cannot hope to compete for her affections with Dudard, an office colleague. Jean urges Berenger to put up a fight, try to get ahead in the world, stop drinking, dress properly, develop his mind—for example, by attending the plays of Ionesco. Berenger apparently takes all this advice to heart and resolves to do better. At the same time the logician is demonstrating syllogisms to the old gentleman: a cat has four paws, Isadore (a dog) has four paws, therefore Isadore is a cat. The "logic" grows more and more nonsensical as the scene progresses, and the two couples are frequently saying the same thing at the same time.

Another rhinoceros—or perhaps the same one—is heard tearing through the square. Again various people appear, attracted by the commotion, and then the housewife, bearing the bloody corpse of her cat, which the beast has trampled. She is inconsolable, though she drinks some brandy. Jean and Berenger begin arguing as to whether the rhinoceros had one horn or two, and whether the African rhinoceros has one horn and the Asian two, or vice versa. The dispute grows heated, with the spectators taking sides and Jean and Berenger hurling insults at each other. The housewife, bemoaning the death of her cat, is led into the café. Jean, in a fury, finally leaves, and Daisy tells Berenger he shouldn't have angered Jean. Berenger seems to regret the quarrel, and muses that Jean really has a heart of gold.

As the crowd begins to disperse they are all still arguing about which breed of rhinoceros has two horns. The logician presents his card to Berenger, and says they must formulate the fundamental question, which is whether the second rhinoceros was the same as the first, or another one. Even if it could be established—which it evidently can't—that the first rhinoceros had two horns and the second only one, it could still be the same animal, if it had lost one horn in the interim. The logic of the matter proceeds in this fashion without their drawing any reliable conclusions.

The logician and the old gentleman leave as the housewife reappears from the café, where she has been given a box in which to bury her cat. Daisy and the waitress follow, as in a funeral procession. The café proprietor, the grocer, and his wife all declare that they aren't going to stand for their cats being trampled to death by rhinoceroses.

Berenger calls for a brandy. He is sorry he quarreled with Jean, and tells himself that he is much too upset to begin any program of self-improvement today.

[]   *In Brief*

Act One carefully establishes the characters of Berenger and Jean, and the fact that at least one noisy and dangerous beast has mysteriously appeared in the neighborhood. The carping and disagreements between the two men provide conflict for the purpose of characterizing them, but the quarrel itself isn't essential to the story line. In fact, Jean will later drop out of the play entirely.

The premise and objective have not yet been given to us, and this is the reason for a certain feeling of aimlessness in the first act. Brilliant verbal fireworks compensate to some degree.

ACT TWO

[]   *Scene One*

The setting is an office. Visible is the head of the stairway that leads up to it, and a window overlooking the street.

Present as the curtain rises are: Papillon, supervising head of the office; Dudard, about 35, competent and attractive; Botard, about

60, another employee, very opinionated; Daisy, the typist. They are all discussing whether there is a rhinoceros at large in the town.

Botard is very skeptical, but Daisy insists that she saw the beast herself, and Dudard and Papillon find that the death of a cat has been reported in the newspaper. Still Botard doesn't believe it.

Berenger climbs the stairs, signs the time sheet, and the day's work begins for them all, though the argument continues. Berenger says he saw the rhinoceros too, and Botard makes a sign to the others that Berenger drinks. Papillon tries to end the discussion and goes into his office. Work proceeds desultorily, and soon the argument bursts forth anew. Botard regards the whole story as a hoax. Papillon reappears and asks why a Mr. Boeuf has not reported for work. At this moment Mrs. Boeuf climbs the stairs. She says that her husband, visiting relatives for the weekend, came down with the flu, according to a telegram she has received. She sits, breathing heavily, and explains that she was chased all the way from her house to the office by a rhinoceros. In fact, she says, the animal is at the foot of the stairs right now, trying to come up.

There is a trumpeting below, and the stairway collapses in a cloud of dust. They all rush to look, and describe the creature as spinning around and around. There are two horns, but Berenger isn't sure whether this means the African or the Asiatic breed. It occurs to Papillon that with no staircase they can't get out. Mrs. Boeuf, with a horrified cry, recognizes the rhinoceros as her husband, and faints. Regaining consciousness, she claims that the trumpetings they hear are Mr. Boeuf calling her. She runs to the landing and jumps, apparently landing on the animal's back, and we hear it galloping away.

Daisy, meanwhile, has been phoning the fire department to come and rescue them. She says they are busy trying to meet various emergencies all over town. Thirty-two rhinoceroses have been reported so far. But the firemen are on their way.

Papillon says that under the circumstances Boeuf will have to be replaced, and Botard, bristling, says that such a dismissal is against union rules and that he will report it. He hints that the whole rhinoceros phenomenon is part of a sinister plot by "traitors," but against what or whom he is somewhat vague.

The firemen arrive and place a ladder against the window. As Papillon warns everyone that work is to be resumed as soon as possible, Daisy is carried down to the street. Papillon goes down, then Botard, protesting that he intends to get to the bottom of this mystery. He is followed by Berenger and Dudard, each politely urging the other to go first.

[] *Scene Two*

We are in Jean's house. Doors lead to the outside stairs and to the bathroom. Also visible is the door to a neighbor's flat.

Berenger knocks at Jean's door, and the neighbor appears at his, reporting that Jean was in a bad temper last night. Berenger knocks again, and Jean, rousing from sleep, lets him in. Jean is taciturn and his voice is hoarse. Berenger apologizes for his part in their quarrel. Jean accepts the apology rather ungraciously, and complains that he doesn't feel well. His forehead pains him. He can't recall having bumped his head, but there is a swelling there. He goes into the bathroom to look in the mirror; when he returns his skin has turned a bit green. His breathing is heavy, and his flesh seems to be hardening. Although Berenger urges it, Jean refuses to see a doctor.

Pacing the floor, he becomes more and more disagreeable and misanthropic. If people get in his way, he says, he'll run them down. His voice grows hoarser, and presently he begins to make strange noises.

Berenger tells him that Boeuf turned into a rhinoceros. At first this news makes no particular impression on Jean, and he goes into the bathroom again. Berenger tries to phone a doctor, but Jean returns before the call can be completed. He throws off his pajama top; his body is quite green. They discuss Boeuf and his wife, Jean reacting testily to Berenger's comments. He argues that Boeuf may have chosen voluntarily to change form, and that rhinoceroses aren't necessarily a lower form of life. Jean believes it might be advantageous to substitute the laws of the jungle for civilization's moral standards. Berenger listens in disbelief. Can it be that Jean wouldn't mind being a rhinoceros himself? Jean replies from the bathroom that he is all for change, and as he reappears he is remarkably changed himself. He tosses the bedclothes about, and begins crying for the swamps. He makes a lunge at Berenger, who dodges and then succeeds in locking Jean in the bathroom. The door is pierced by a horn, and we hear loud trumpetings and the sounds of falling objects and shattering glass.

Berenger, in panic, runs into the hall and knocks at the door of the neighbor's flat, shouting that there is a rhinoceros in the building. Then he stops at the porter's door, and a rhinoceros head appears. As he passes the neighbor's door on his way back to the flat, two more such heads peer out at him. Back in the flat he tries to climb out of the window, but sees a procession of rhinoceroses crossing below. (Heads are carried across the orchestra pit.)

The bathroom door shakes under the impact of repeated lunges, and Berenger finally manages to escape through the hall, crying: "Rhinoceros! Rhinoceros!"

[] *In Brief*

In a manner more closely resembling the documentary form than the dramatic, II-1 continues the account of a town where men are turning into beasts. The play hasn't yet come quite into focus. Berenger's reactions to the events in this scene are no more important than those of anyone else. The material is so bizarre, however, and the mixture of comedy and horror so skillful, that our interest is still held.

II-2 provides an opportunity for bravura performing, and the right actors can make the scene absolutely spellbinding. (Zero Mostel and Eli Wallach played the roles of Jean and Berenger in the Broadway production.) As Berenger's behavior suggests that he will resist turning into a rhinoceros, we at last identify an individual to whom we can have an emotional reaction, whose problem permits our sympathies to be engaged.

ACT THREE

The setting is Berenger's flat. As in the preceding scene we also see the hall outside, with another door at the landing.

Berenger lies asleep, a bandage around his head. From the street comes the sound of a herd of rhinoceroses rushing by. Berenger wakens from what is apparently a bad dream, goes to a mirror, lifts the bandage, and examines his forehead. More animals thunder past, and he takes a drink, then coughs. The cough worries him.

Dudard, his young associate at the office, knocks and Berenger receives him politely. Berenger wonders whether his voice has changed in any way, and Dudard assures him that it hasn't; nor is there any bump on his forehead. Berenger admits that he is frightened of turning into "someone else," and Dudard tries to calm him. They talk about Jean's changing into a rhinoceros. This has been a traumatic experience for Berenger, and he reiterates that he wants to remain as he is. Dudard regards the transformations as a disease, like influenza, which the majority of the population doesn't catch even during an epidemic.

More rhinoceroses gallop by. Dudard shuts the window and tells Berenger to ignore them. Thinking that perhaps alcohol kills the microbes of rhinocerositis, Berenger pours a drink for himself. He coughs, and asks Dudard if it's a human cough. Dudard grows impatient, tells him he's getting neurotic; the rhinoceroses aren't nearly so bad as they're painted. All you have to do is keep out of their way and they ignore you, he says. Dudard is already beginning to get used to them.

A herd passes by again, and Berenger cries that he'll never get used to them. He will write to the newspapers, complain to the authorities. Evil must be attacked at the source. Dudard protests: it's nobody's business if others want to change their skin and manner of life.

Changing the subject, Dudard reports that the office considers Berenger to be on sick leave. Work has not been resumed there in any case. The fact is that Papillon resigned—he turned into a rhinoceros. Berenger is appalled. Papillon would never let that happen to him if he could help it. It must have been involuntary. And if that is the case, it could happen to Dudard—or to Berenger himself.

What did old Botard think of Papillon's behavior? Botard, Dudard replies, was outraged. For once Berenger agrees with Botard, whereas Dudard feels that Botard has always been intolerant of others. One has to keep an open mind, try to understand why people behave as they do. Who can say what is normal and what is abnormal behavior? The argument grows, with Berenger deploring Dudard's tolerance, under the circumstances, and Dudard his friend's narrow-mindedness.

Berenger promises to introduce Dudard to the logician, who, being a philosopher, can perhaps enlighten him. The conversation is drowned out by the noise of the beasts below. Berenger shakes his fist and cries out against them. Just then the logician's hat, worn over a horn, passes by in the orchestra pit. Berenger is in despair. He shouts that he will never become one of them.

Daisy, carrying a basket, knocks at the door. Dudard and Berenger both welcome her. She says that Botard has become a rhinoceros. Berenger finds this hard to believe, but Daisy says she saw him do it. He wanted to keep up with the times.

Dudard is clearly enamored of Daisy himself, but Berenger is too shocked by Botard's transformation to pay much attention to either of them. He tries to rationalize Botard's behavior. Daisy reports that even the great and famous are now turning into rhinoceroses. She takes food from her basket and begins setting out a meal. Dudard is invited to share it. A hint of jealousy creeps into his attitude.

Suddenly, with a great crash and amid clouds of dust, the nearby fire station is demolished by the rhinoceroses. As the three humans peer out of the window it develops that the deed was done by the firemen themselves, all of whom have been transformed. People turning into beasts appear in the hallway, and rush outside.

Daisy urges the men to come and eat, but Dudard protests that he feels more like going outside and dining on the grass. Berenger, alarmed, urges him to stay. Daisy says that Dudard must choose for himself. Dudard rationalizes that he must stick by his employers and his friends, and not cut himself off. Berenger says that his duty is to oppose the rhinoceroses, but by now Dudard is running around the room in circles. He dashes outside, as Berenger calls after him despairingly.

From the window Berenger and Daisy can't identify Dudard from the other animals milling about below. There isn't a single human being to be seen. Half the beasts have one horn, half two—the only distinction. Berenger tells Daisy that she should have persuaded Dudard not to transform—after all, the man was in love with her. Berenger declares his own love, and asks if he may kiss her. On the back wall of the room, stylized rhinoceros heads begin to appear and disappear, but become more numerous as the act progresses.

Daisy responds to Berenger's love-making, and they talk about their future together. She allows him a small drink of brandy, then removes his bandage and tells him his forehead is smooth as a baby's. He speaks of Papillon: perhaps Daisy shouldn't have spoken so sharply to him; that may have influenced his decision. Berenger reproaches himself for his own quarrel with Jean. Daisy urges him to forget the past. There is no need for self-reproach; neither of them has as many faults as the average person. Berenger responds happily in the warmth of her love.

The telephone rings. At first Berenger is afraid to answer, but decides that it may be an appeal for help. When he lifts the receiver nothing but trumpetings are heard. Indignantly they assume that others are making fun of them. The phone rings again, but instead of answering they switch on the radio, which produces nothing but trumpetings. Daisy is frightened. Can it be that they are the only two people left? Are they alone in the world? Berenger says that's what she wanted; she says it's what he wanted. Noises fill the room, and more rhinoceros heads crowd the back wall. The beasts are heard crashing about on the floor above, and the trampling, breathing, and trumpeting sounds become rhythmical. Daisy, maintains that they must try to understand the rhinoceroses, learn their language, and get along with them. Berenger says that he and she are like Adam and Eve, and their children will save the human race. But Daisy doubts whether it's worth saving. Perhaps they are the abnormal ones, and the rhinoceroses are the real people. As for love, how can that compare with the energy of the creatures outside? Berenger slaps her, then apologizes. She forgives him and tells him she will help him resist.

But the rhinoceros sounds have become melodic, and to Daisy they are a siren call. She looks out and says the animals are dancing. Berenger is repelled, and tells her they can't live together. Calling him not a nice man, she slowly goes down the stairs to join the herd.

At first Berenger tries to call her back, then locks the door and closes the windows. He tells the rhinoceros heads on the wall that he is human, and intends to remain so. The sounds from outside assail him. He plugs his ears with cotton and goes to the mirror.

Can the rhinoceroses turn back into men, he asks. To convince them he would have to learn their language, or they his. Can it be, as Daisy said, that they are the ones in the right? He finds some photographs and hangs them on the wall, shouting, "That's me!" They are not pictures of Berenger, but of other human beings, and very ugly. By comparison the rhinoceros heads on the wall appear beautiful.

Now Berenger himself begins to crack. He pulls the pictures down angrily. He wishes he had a horn like the others, that his skin would grow rough and turn that wonderful dark green. He tries to trumpet, but what emerges is merely a howl. Alas, it is too late to transform. He is the monster now, and he is ashamed. One should never try to maintain one's individuality.

Suddenly he reverses himself again. He will put up a fight. He may be the last man in the world, but he will not surrender.

[]   *In Brief*

We are at last deeply concerned for Berenger, his struggle and his fate, and Act Three moves straightforwardly through to its climax and resolution in terms of a leading character capable of arousing our emotions. Stylistically the play seems to alter somewhat with the introduction of purely expressionist elements.

Protagonist and Objective

Berenger is the protagonist, his objective being to avoid turning into a rhinoceros.

Obstacles

The obstacles consist of the various social and emotional pressures to conform. Berenger's employer, his friends, and acquaintances all accede to these pressures and leave him alone in his defiance. Finally even his own reason tells him to surrender.

Major Crisis and Climax, Theme

The crisis comes very close to the end of the play. It is Berenger's loss of will power, his wishing that he too were a rhinoceros. The climax follows at once, and rather unexpectedly, when his determination to remain human reasserts itself (or when he rationalizes his failure to turn into a beast, depending on one's interpretation of the work).

Thematically one can read into the play either the plight or the heroism of the individualist in a world pressing him to conform. It should be noted that Berenger's final defiance at the end can quite easily be interpreted by the actor as "sour grapes." On the other hand, if the final lines are considered heroic, we may well ask what changed Berenger's mind at the last moment. *Rhinoceros* can be a profoundly pessimistic play.

Resolution

Had the author chosen to write one, a resolution might have solved the ambiguity noted above. Ionesco preferred to end the play at its somewhat equivocal climax.

Opening

From a structural standpoint this play could just as easily, with a few minor changes, begin with II-1 and drop the first act entirely. This is not to ignore the many virtues of Act One, but merely to note that it takes too long to get the story moving and our emotions involved—an indication that too early a point in the over-all story has been chosen for beginning the play.

Unity

All three unities are ignored, not only the relatively unimportant time and place, but the critical one of action. Scene after scene is included for certain theatrical values inherent in the scene itself, but with little bearing on the main story line, and therefore dispensable. Certainly there is no dramatic law that says one can't include such scenes, but there is a price to be paid for them. They must be so intrinsically interesting that the audience will enjoy them even though they lie outside the play's main thrust. *Rhinoceros* contains several such independently rewarding scenes, notably the parallel conversations (Berenger-Jean, logician-old gentleman) in the first act.

Exposition

The play, with its very early opening, requires practically no exposition of antecedent action. A good deal of the rhinoceros action, which, of course, can't be staged, is reported by eyewitnesses, and technically this is exposition. But, like the Greek messengers who bring bad tidings, they have something to say that is newsworthy; hence we listen.

Characterization

Berenger (who appears in other Ionesco plays as well) is a well-rounded character—friendly, modest, considerate, but apparently not a strong or determined person. Because he has been drawn so carefully in the early portions of the play, we believe in his plight and admire his growing courage; since he has been presented so sympathetically, we identify with him.

But Berenger is the only one conceived in three dimensions. The others, even Jean, have one or two boldly sketched characteristics and that is all. Papillon, Botard, Daisy are all made of cardboard.

Development

Rhinoceros is episodic in construction—a series of scenes that, while they follow one another chronologically, do not, on the whole, grow out of preceding scenes. The play is more a collection of incidents than an organic growth.

The one clearly discernible thread that binds the work together is the psychological change in Berenger, from his almost contemptuous dismissal of the danger in the beginning to his panic and desperation at the end.

Dramatic Irony

Except for the fact that we are aware that Jean, Dudard, and Daisy are transforming before Berenger becomes aware, no use is made of dramatic irony.

Preparation

There is hardly a plant in the entire play. The episodes simply unfold as they are presented, without preparation.

Activity

In this area Ionesco is inventive indeed. From the moment the housewife appears with her cat and her basket of food, right through to Berenger's hanging pictures of human beings on the walls of his room and then throwing them down, business and properties are used with force and meaning.

The sounds of the rhinoceroses—their galloping, breathing, trumpeting—make us feel the presence of the animals. Berenger sees Daisy and spills his drink on Jean. The housewife brings in the carcass of her cat, killed by a rhinoceros; later the cat is put in a coffin and there is a funeral procession. In II-1 the office stairway collapses, and firemen carry the employees out through a window. Jean's turning into a rhinoceros before our eyes is one of the most extraordinary pieces of business ever invented for an actor.

Berenger's coughing and the bandage around his head in Act Three express his fear of being transformed; the trumpetings heard over the radio and telephone dramatize what is happening outside. There are many other instances of the effective use of the stage and its resources in this highly imaginative work.

Dialogue

For realistic speech the dialogue seems rather stiff. It is certainly repetitive. Points are belabored that could have been made in half the time and length.

Effects

Up until the rhinoceros heads appear in the orchestra pit and on the walls of Berenger's flat the style of presentation is realistic, and this is probably the most effective way such a story can be staged, for the bizarre nature of the material gains by contrast with the commonplace surroundings, as in *The Birthday Party*. The stage directions calling for essentially expressionist elements late in the play seem to be a switch in style that is hard to justify artistically.

Plausibility

In a fantastic tale such as this the behavior of the characters must be judged entirely within the framework of the premise. Once we accept the proposition that the pressure to conform can turn men into beasts (literally, for the sake of the symbolism), then we can decide whether the actions are valid in accordance with the characterizations. *Rhinoceros* is consistent here.

ROBERT BOLT

A Man for All Seasons

1961

This is an episodic play of many scenes, in structure reminiscent of Shakespeare's historical works. The solemnity of the drama of Sir Thomas More is enlivened not only by More's own wit, but by the Brechtian figure of the Common Man and other devices usually associated with Epic Theatre. The Common Man speaks directly to the audience, bridging the gaps between episodes, serving as a sort of stage manager in charge of properties, and playing many of the minor roles himself—roles that "common men" would fill in real life. He brings a skepticism, wry humor, and plebeian point of view to the proceedings that was sorely missed in the film version of the play, which eliminated him.

Though written for the proscenium type of theatre, the play would be equally at home on a thrust stage. A single unit setting is all that is required, different locales being indicated merely by furniture, properties, changes in lighting, and so on.

A Man for All Seasons is a wonderful example of a synthesis of styles: Elizabethan, realistic, and epic. Quite aside from its literary merit, it is a completely successful theatre piece and a very moving experience.

Premise

Sir Thomas More, a Catholic and Councilor of England, is famous, popular, respected, and vastly influential throughout the kingdom and in Europe. Catholic England needs an heir, which Henry's Queen Catherine has been unable to provide, but only the pope can grant the king a divorce.

Synopsis

The play is in two acts, and except for one intermission is played without interruption. For convenience here the episodes have been numbered. They are not numbered in the text. The action flows continuously from one scene to the next.

ACT ONE

[] *Episode One*

The Common Man introduces himself, and assumes the role of the steward in the home of Sir Thomas More. Then he introduces Sir Thomas. A silver cup has been sent to More as a bribe by a woman bringing a lawsuit in his court, and More, who won't keep the cup, gives it to Richard Rich, a vastly ambitious but frustrated young man who is plainly trying to use More's friendship to advance his own career.

We now meet More's wife, Alice, and daughter, Margaret, and his other dinner guest, his friend the Duke of Norfolk. There is a reference to Thomas Cromwell, whom Rich is also cultivating, and More learns to his shocked surprise that Cromwell has been made secretary to Cardinal Wolsey. A message arrives from Wolsey asking More to call on him at once, in spite of the late hour.

[] *Episode Two*

The Common Man rearranges properties, and we are in Wolsey's office.

Wolsey urges More, as Councilor of England, to support his efforts to persuade the pope to grant the king a divorce. Queen Catherine has not borne the king an heir, and Wolsey is afraid of civil war if Henry should die without one. As a matter of conscience More cannot support the request for a divorce. Wolsey is angry as More leaves.

[]   *Episode Three*

The Common Man assumes the identity of a boatman, and the scene is a bankside on the Thames. More engages the boatman to take him home. Thomas Cromwell comes out of the shadows, on his way to Wolsey's office. He and More are frostily polite, and More hints that he has not agreed to Wolsey's request. As Cromwell leaves, Chapuys, the Spanish ambassador, appears. Chapuys is concerned lest More support the divorce, for Catherine is an aunt of the king of Spain. Though More tries to be noncommittal, Chapuys infers that he will oppose Wolsey in the matter. More leaves for home, and the Common Man becomes the steward again.

[]   *Episode Four*

More finds Will Roper and his daughter waiting for him. Roper wants to marry Margaret, but More, though he likes Roper, refuses because the young man has embraced Lutheranism. After Roper leaves, Alice appears and tells her husband that Norfolk has spoken of him as chancellor of England. More says there will be no new chancellors while Wolsey lives.

[]   *Episode Five*

The Common Man informs the audience of Wolsey's death and More's appointment as chancellor. We are now at Hampton Court, where the king is in residence. In a brief scene between Cromwell and Rich we learn that the former is in service to the king, while Rich has become Norfolk's librarian. Chapuys arrives, and Cromwell explains his own function at court. Quite simply, when the king wants something done, he does it.

Cromwell tells them that Henry will pilot a boat down the river himself to the home of Sir Thomas More, and that there they will talk about the divorce, for the king hopes to persuade More to change his mind. Chapuys is dismayed.

In a subsequent interlude with the Common Man as More's steward, Cromwell, Chapuys, and Rich each in turn try to bribe him into revealing what he may know about More's present attitude. The steward accepts the coins but gives very little information in return.

[] *Episode Six*

This takes place in More's garden. The king is expected momentarily. There is a pretence that the visit is to be a surprise, but the More family and Norfolk, who is also present, are awaiting him, and a sumptuous dinner has been prepared. As the king approaches, More cannot be ·found, and there is a moment of panic. But he appears— he has been at vespers. Henry enters, and Alice and Margaret are introduced to the king in a delightful scene in which, among other things, Margaret's Latin turns out to be better than her monarch's.

Alone with More, Henry brings up the subject of the divorce, and learns that More has not changed his mind. More gently reminds the king that when he became chancellor it was agreed that he was not to be pressed on this matter. But Henry does pursue it— he needs More's support because of his influence and his reputation for honesty. When More refuses to be moved, the king warns him that he will tolerate no active opposition. On the transparent excuse that he must catch the tide, Henry leaves without staying for dinner.

Alice, returning, is deeply concerned, and begs her husband to be ruled by the king's wishes and to remain friends with him. More chides that he is not the stuff of which martyrs are made.

Margaret and Roper enter. Roper has modified the religious views that made him unacceptable to More as a son-in-law.

Rich arrives with word that Cromwell is collecting information about More, and that the steward is one of his sources. None of this surprises More. Rich begs More to employ him. After he leaves, Roper and Alice advise More to have Rich arrested. He is a dangerous man. But More reminds them that Rich has broken no law, and there follows an eloquent statement of More's faith in the law and its processes. The laws of men, which he understands so well, will protect him from trouble. More makes peace with Roper, whom he has offended, and tries to reassure the women.

[] *Episode Seven*

The Common Man sets the stage as a pub. Cromwell and Rich enter. Cromwell is now secretary to the Council, and he promises Rich the post of Collector of Revenues for York. Rich discloses, under pressure, the value of the silver cup that More had given him—the cup with which the woman litigant had tried to bribe More. Cromwell is revealed as a ruthless enemy, determined that More shall not impede the king's divorce proceedings.

[]   *In Brief*

The lines of conflict are drawn very slowly in this play. In a dramatic sense the storm that gathers about More's head is long in coming. But the little cloud can be observed at the end of the first episode, when Wolsey sends for More, and it grows darker and blacker with each succeeding scene. By the end of I-6 we know that More is depending on his observance of English law to protect him. At the end of the act we are aware that in Cromwell More has an antagonist who will, if necessary, utterly destroy him, law or no law.

ACT TWO

[]   *Episode One*

The Common Man tells the audience that two years have passed, and that Parliament and the Church of England are bending to the king's will. The scene is More's home.

Roper, once again a loyal Catholic, is married to Margaret. More hints that, if the English bishops submit, he will resign as chancellor. Chapuys arrives and urges More to dissociate himself from Henry's actions. He tells More that if he resigns the North will consider it a signal for armed rebellion against the king. They are interrupted by the arrival of Norfolk, with Roper, Margaret, and Alice following. The bishops have severed the ties with Rome. With Alice's help More gravely removes his chain of office. Norfolk, who cannot understand More's scruples, is bitter. As he leaves, More warns him that there may be rebellion in the North. Norfolk replies that Cromwell is aware of that and is prepared.

More then defends his resignation to his family, trying to explain that it is not a mere gesture—it is impossible for him to continue in office. Alice is very worried. More insists that his safety lies in silence. So long as he doesn't speak out against these developments, he will be left alone.

The servants will have to be dismissed. The steward refuses to accept a cut in wages.

[]   *Episode Two*

Norfolk is urging Cromwell to leave More alone. More, he says, is loyal and will remain silent. But Cromwell says the king needs a statement of loyalty from More. Cromwell then summons Rich and the woman who sent a silver cup to More. Norfolk, who refuses to believe that More would accept a bribe, scornfully recalls that More gave the cup to Rich immediately on learning that it *was* a bribe. Cromwell realizes that an attempt to prove More corrupt would collapse, and makes a veiled threat to Norfolk, who leaves in fury.

Cromwell tells Rich it will take a finer net to catch this fish. As the scene ends, the steward is appealing to Rich for employment.

[] *Episode Three*

The scene is More's house. Chapuys has come to deliver a letter from the king of Spain, but More will not take it, since accepting it would compromise his position, which is simple withdrawal. As Chapuys leaves, Margaret brings in a load of bracken, which they will burn to heat the house. Poverty has forced many discomforts on them. More tries to explain to Alice why he cannot accept money raised by the clergy for their relief. Roper brings word that More has been summoned to Hampton Court to answer certain charges before Cromwell.

[] *Episode Four*

More appears in Cromwell's office, and Rich transcribes the conversation. Though outwardly polite and respectful, Cromwell tries to trap More on a couple of incidents of the past, but More is not to be intimidated. Finally Cromwell quotes the king, who has made known his great displeasure, and More, somewhat frightened, leaves. Cromwell hints to Rich that they may have to destroy More with manufactured evidence.

[] *Episode Five*

On the riverbank at Hampton Court, More, trying to engage a boat to take him home, is followed by Norfolk, who pleads with him to give in. But More is now a dangerous man to know, and he urges Norfolk, for his own safety, to break off their friendship. When he won't, More deliberately provokes a quarrel until Norfolk finally leaves him.

Margaret and Roper, who have been looking for him, bring word that by an act of Parliament an oath will be administered regarding the king's marriage. Until More has seen the wording of the oath, however, he doesn't know whether it will be possible for him to sign it.

[]   *Episode Six*

The Common Man sets the stage as a jail, and takes on the role of jailer. An envelope descends on a cord from above, and, reading, he tells us the ultimate end of Cromwell, Norfolk, Rich, and Cranmer, the Archbishop of Canterbury, all of whom by now are on stage.

The jailer brings More into their presence. He has refused to take the oath required by the Act of Succession, but steadfastly refuses to give his reasons, insisting that treason cannot be proved against him. Great pressure is brought against him, but he will not capitulate. He goes back to his cell. Rich asks Cromwell for the post of attorney general for Wales. Cromwell ponders whether torture would bring More to heel, concluding that the king would not permit it.

[]   *Episode Seven*

More's family is permitted to visit him at the jail. It develops that Margaret is under oath to try to persuade him to sign the act. She, Alice, and Roper all make the attempt. More, still adamant, tries to get them to leave the country. He says there will be no trial, since the state has no case against him, but that they will not be allowed to see him again. It particularly grieves More that his wife cannot understand his position, but when it becomes clear that in spite of this she still loves him deeply, he is cheered. The jailer herds the family out as their visiting time expires.

[]   *Episode Eight*

The stage is quickly transformed into a courtroom. Cromwell informs the Common Man that he is foreman of the jury, and the Common Man takes his place in the jury box, the other eleven men being represented by sticks on which hats are perched. Norfolk and Archbishop Cranmer come on, and Norfolk tells More he is charged with high treason, but the king will still show mercy if More abandons his obstinate position. More senses that the trial has been rigged, but he remains loyal to his conscience. Sir Richard Rich, resplendent in robes of office, is called as a witness. He perjures himself by attributing a treasonable statement to More. More emphatically denies the statement, but knows that his case is lost. Contemptuously he rebukes Rich for selling his soul for Wales.

The jury finds More guilty. Since he has nothing more to lose,

More at last defends and explains his position. He is condemned to death.

[] *Episode Nine*

The stage becomes the place of execution, and the Common Man the headsman. More bids farewell to Margaret. The woman who sent the cup as a bribe comes to gloat, and More avers that he would not alter his judgment. He indicates to the headsman that he welcomes being sent to God. After the beheading the Common Man draws his own moral from the tale—don't make trouble—and bids the audience good night.

[] *In Brief*

The second act begins with More's resignation as chancellor—an open break with the king. It proceeds with Cromwell trying one way after another to secure More's adherence to the Act of Succession, or to prove him treasonable. When all else fails, including a long imprisonment, Cromwell bribes Rich with a political post to give false testimony against More. Although condemned to death, More never wavers in adherence to his principles. The only way the king can deal with him is to destroy him.

Protagonist and Objective

Sir Thomas More is, obviously, the protagonist. The play does not begin, however, with a statement of objective from More. Rather, it shows the man being gradually subjected to pressure that forces him to take a stand. As More refuses to bend, the pressure increases, and the danger to him increases. Since he is characterized as a man of complete integrity as well as religious conviction, it is apparent very early in the play that political expediency will never dictate his course of action. His objective, which remains steady throughout, is to govern his actions according to his conscience. When More's life is finally at stake, he still stands firm.

The answer to the dramatic question, will More succeed in resisting the state's efforts to bend him to its will, is yes.

Obstacles

There are many obstacles. More stands alone in his convictions, and nearly every other major character in the play tries by persuasion or threats to get him to alter his stand. (The exceptions are Rich, who is a mere tool of Cromwell's, and Chapuys, whose support is politically motivated.) Wolsey, Norfolk, King Henry, Cromwell, Cranmer, and members of More's family all bring pressure on him—all without success. It is the variety of pressures and the way he reacts to the different kinds of pressure that provide the author with such rich material for characterization.

Major Crisis and Climax

These occur during the trial (II-8). The crisis is More's last opportunity to capitulate. It might be pinpointed as Cromwell's statement that even now the king will accept More's compliance. The climax is More's immediate and final refusal. However, since these attitudes are implicit throughout the trial, crisis and climax may also be said to extend over a longer period than the two speeches just referred to. But from the moment of these two speeches on, the course of events, including the guilty verdict, is ineluctable.

Theme

The play reminds us (and its theme is all the more forceful since we know that this case is based on historic fact) that a man of integrity can triumph over his adversaries regardless of what they do to him. Incidentally, it is this triumph that gives the play its mood of exhilaration, in spite of the death sentence. It is not a tragedy. More has won.

Resolution

This includes More's defense of his action after the verdict, the sentencing, and the entire final episode: his farewell to his daughter, his rebuke to the woman litigant, the execution, and the Common Man's comments to the audience.

Opening

Unlike more tightly constructed plays, Robert Bolt begins this dramatization quite early in the overall story. Although the king is already convinced that he must obtain a divorce and remarry if he is to provide the country with an heir, More himself is first presented as the highly respected Councilor of England, with no visible opposition. It should be noted, however, that the author has chosen to begin the play just before Wolsey sends for More, and that this is the first sign of trouble.

Unity

Conceivably the play could have begun much later, with More's resignation as chancellor, for example. But the play is, among other things, a penetrating character study of several different people, and the form in which it is constructed may be more advantageous to this purpose than a tighter structure would have been. Certainly there is almost nothing superfluous in the play, and More's steadfast refusal to compromise on what he believes to be a moral question gives the work a unity that is aesthetically satisfying.

Exposition

Exposition is delightfully handled, for the most part, by the Common Man, in direct address to the audience. This is one of the advantages of stepping outside the realistic form, for then such devices as this can be employed. It should be observed too that whatever the Common Man says is highly colored by his own personality and point of view. This adds enormously to our interest in the exposition.

What little exposition is required within the scenes is expertly handled. In I-5, for instance, as the sophisticated Cromwell intimidates the apprehensive and ambitious Rich, we are given the necessary facts about the relative positions of both men. In II-1 it is More's differences with his son-in-law that tell us the bishops have been in convocation, and that clarify More's position in regard to their decision. It is the disagreement between the two men that makes this material so playable.

Characterization

Sir Thomas More is an exceptionally well-rounded character. We meet him under all kinds of conditions—as a happy family man devoted to his wife and daughter, as a cautious but skillful politician, as a loyal subject unable to accede to the king's wishes, as Chancellor of England defending himself from attack, as a man of complete integrity enduring poverty, persecution, and imprisonment rather than compromise his principles, as a man fighting for his life, and finally, condemned to death, still a man of compassion, wit, and fortitude. This vast range of situation permits the author to explore in depth the many facets of More's character.

Others in the play, though not so exhaustively presented, are drawn in bold strokes and with equal skill. Consider Wolsey's pragmatism and imperious manner, Norfolk's bluff friendship and the deep hurt he feels when More breaks with him, Rich's sly opportunism, the ruthlessness of Cromwell, and one of the finest characterizations of all—that of Alice, who cannot understand why her husband must act as he does, who bitterly resents it, but whose love and loyalty are beyond question. The Common Man, always playing it safe and looking out for himself, is another fascinating figure. These are all people the author has obviously considered long and carefully before committing them to paper.

Development

Most of the scenes are built in the conventional way. As an example, consider I-2. Wolsey is the protagonist; his objective: to obtain More's help in securing the divorce; obstacle: More's conscience; climax: More's refusal to help; resolution: Wolsey's anger. I-6 is almost identical in construction, with Henry instead of Wolsey as the protagonist. The resolution is Alice's concern for her husband. This scene, in the structural sense, ends at this point, and another one begins with the entrance of Roper.

The trial scene (II-8) is, in structure, a miniature of the entire play, with the climax of the scene being, of course, the climax of the play as well.

Dramatic Irony

The device of dramatic irony is not employed to any great extent. We do learn, in I-7, that Cromwell is plotting against More and if possible will use Rich as a weapon. This knowledge, not shared by More, makes us apprehensive for him. Some later scenes with Cromwell have the same effect.

Preparation

Very few plants are required. More giving Rich the cup in I-1 is a plant (as well as a piece of exposition). Rich's asking Cromwell for the post of attorney general for Wales in II-6 prepares us for More's scornful rebuke of Rich at the trial.

Activity

There are a few bits of realistic stage business that reinforce the significance of the dialogue. In I-1 we see More giving away the cup with which an attempt had been made to bribe him; in II-1 his resignation as chancellor is made vivid and emphatic when he removes the chain of office; and in II-3 his refusal even to accept a letter from the king of Spain indicates the care he is taking not to compromise his position.

Dialogue

The dialogue, which manages to give the flavor of the period while still avoiding archaisms, flows effortlessly, due in large part to the constantly shifting conflicts within the scenes. It is also, of course, "heightened" speech, in that it is far more eloquent than these conversations probably were in real life. We accept the dialogue as realistic speech, however, partly because of theatrical convention, partly because the people in the play would seem naturally to be more articulate than the average.

Effects

The Brechtian influence is apparent chiefly in the character of the Common Man, who continually returns to destroy any illusion of reality that might be building up. Not only does he change the properties from scene to scene before our eyes, commenting directly to the audience, but he changes costume and takes many of the minor roles himself.

In II-6 an envelope descends from the flies. He opens it and, reading, tells us how and when each of the characters on stage died, and how he himself died. As foreman of the jury he sits with eleven upright poles, each topped by a hat. This is theatre that frankly declares itself as theatre.

Plausibility

We know, naturally, that the real Sir Thomas More was executed. But if the character had been fictitious More's end would still seem inevitable. The playwright has drawn his people in such a way that, given the conflict in which they find themselves involved, there could have been no other ending. This is a high achievement.

PETER WEISS
Marat/Sade

(*The Persecution and Assassination of Jean-Paul Marat
as Performed by the Inmates of the Asylum of Charenton
Under the Direction of the Marquis de Sade*)

1964

This play-within-a-play explores an ideological conflict—in itself rather unpromising dramatic material—by employing a startling theatrical concept and a host of devices drawn from the Brecht-Piscator Epic Theatre. Without the concept of madmen as actors and the endless epic devices the work would have a hard time holding audience interest in performance. When skillfully staged, however, it comes brilliantly alive, although it may be questioned whether we aren't more interested in the bizarre happenings on stage than in the real heart of the matter—the philosophical differences between Sade and Marat.

The play is considered an example of the Theatre of Cruelty. It was written for the proscenium theatre.

Premise

The Marquis de Sade is a patient in the asylum at Charenton in the year 1808, and he is permitted to write and stage a play, to be performed by other patients. The Parisian public, with which the actual audience is identified, is permitted to attend the performance. (Cf. *The Miracle*, *Waiting for Lefty*.)

Synopsis

For convenience the portions of *Marat/Sade* that deal with Sade's staging of the work he has composed are referred to as the "outer play." (This includes his relationship with his actors, for example, and with Coulmier, the director of the asylum.) The discussion-drama itself that Sade is presumed to have written is referred to as the "inner play."

The scene is the bath hall of the asylum. The entire work is in two acts, and the action is continuous.

ACT ONE

Coulmier, director of the asylum, in direct address, welcomes the audience to a play written and staged by one of his patients, the Marquis de Sade. The Herald, also in direct address to the audience, identifies the principal characters: Marat, sitting in his bath to relieve his skin disease, played by a paranoiac; Charlotte Corday, played by a girl suffering from sleeping sickness; Duperret, a conservative patriot, played by an erotomaniac; the former priest Jacques Roux, a revolutionary perfectionist and rabble rouser, played by a violent patient in a strait jacket; a chorus of four singers who will comment on the action; and finally Sade himself, standing at one side, cool and detached, ready to coach and prompt the actors and oversee the performance.

So far we are in the outer play, presumably taking place in 1808. Now the inner play begins, and the time is 1793. The chorus and various patients sing homage to Marat for his revolutionary fervor, his writings, and his leadership. Encouraged by Roux, however, they voice dissatisfaction with current conditions and exploitation. Coulmier, alarmed by the radical tone of some of the statements, warns Sade to keep the production under control.

The Herald calls our attention to Corday, who says that, because Marat's terroristic methods arouse people to looting and murder, she is going to kill him. She tries to gain admittance to his home but is turned away. Sade reminds the actress that she has to come to Marat's door three times.

A kind of interlude follows, celebrating the arrival in Paris of Corday, the simple country girl from Caen. In mime we see her purchase the dagger with which she will stab Marat.

The executions at the guillotine are enacted by some of the

patients, and there is a dance of death. Marat justifies the bloodshed. Coulmier protests to Sade that the patients are becoming disturbed. The Herald defends the action on the grounds that they must show what actually occurred.

Marat and Sade now begin the ideological debate that is the chief substance of the work (Sade moving from the framework of the outer play into the inner play). The subtlety and richness of this debate cannot be conveyed in this brief outline, but, as we are for the moment more concerned with form than substance, perhaps it will suffice to say that it is, on the one hand, a confrontation between a familiar radical position that leads, in the words of the author, in a direct line to Marxism and, on the other hand, an individualism carried to extreme lengths—a political nihilism represented by Sade. The argument is not resolved, nor is it ever, with the audience being left to draw its own conclusions.

Marat, in a liturgy, attacks the Church as an accomplice of the exploiters of the poor, and Coulmier again protests to Sade, the presumed author of Marat's lines. A patient prays to Satan, to Coulmier's distress. The argument between Sade and Marat is resumed, and the singers, chorus, and Herald comment upon it.

The meeting between Corday and Duperret is presented next. As a patient Duperret has to be constantly restrained in his erotic advances toward Corday. As a character in Sade's play he expresses a conservative point of view and predicts the collapse of Marat's movement. Sade shouts his scorn of patriotism, and there is a splintering of viewpoints among the singers and patients. A further assertion of Sade's individualism is followed by Marat's argument that the Revolution has merely placed the *bourgeoisie* in the position of the former rulers. The singers agree.

Roux urges rebellion, and demands a socialistic program and an end to war. Coulmier again protests. Roux begs Marat to lead the people.

Sade now tells how, during his imprisonment, he examined the wickedness within himself so that he could better understand the times. He asks Corday to whip him, and, as she does so, he talks about his own attitude toward the Revolution, which he had at first supported. Now he sees it as the creation of a state that imposes uniformity and is without meaningful contact with individuals.

The singers tell us of the persecution of Marat, and beg him to help the people secure their rights.

Duperret and Corday dream of the perfect state, in which there is universal individual responsibility and freedom. Marat deems this impossible of attainment, for the Revolution will be betrayed.

Sade asserts the inequality of human beings, and Marat the need for destroying the old order before starting to build the new. Again the four singers comment.

Corday tries a second time to see Marat, and is turned away. Sade scoffs that the Revolution is not bringing the people what they want.

Now several grotesque figures appear, characterizing Marat and summarizing his career. They represent his parents, a schoolmaster, a soldier, a scientist, a newly rich man, Voltaire (who actually detested Marat's philosophical writings), and Lavoisier (who rejected Marat's scientific theories).

Roux cries that the pioneers, the innovators, are always mocked and persecuted, and proclaims that Marat realized that without fundamental changes in the social structure all other endeavors must fail. These statements agitate Coulmier. The Herald announces an intermission.

[] *In Brief*

As is apparent even in this outline, we are in the nonillusionistic theatre with a vengeance. Not for an instant are we permitted to lose ourselves in the inner play, for not only is it being performed ostensibly by lunatics, with unrealistic business and properties, but the action of the inner play is constantly being interrupted by comments from Coulmier, the singers, the Herald, and Sade himself. Perhaps we can identify with Sade and Coulmier and accept the asylum as real, and to the extent that we do the more terrifying the play becomes.

There are different levels of responsibility for the various speeches. Marat's words, for instance, are first of all presumed to represent his own point of view. But they have been written for him by Sade, haven't they? Actually they were written by the author, Peter Weiss. Or were they? Weiss says they are Marat's own words, which he has appropriated for the play.

There is almost no forward action in the first act. The framework of the outer play is set up, the inner play is begun, but about the only development that can be considered "story" is Corday's arrival in Paris for the purpose of assassinating Marat. The rest of the act is given over to defining the positions of the various characters. It is the form and the intellectual content that must hold our interest. That they do is a tribute to the ingenuity of the author and the director.

ACT TWO

In several eloquent speeches Marat attacks the exploiters and the military, provoking mixed reactions among the singers and vehement protests from Coulmier and Duperret. Marat appeals for a leader at the same time that he denounces dictatorship but justifies violence. Disorder breaks out among the patients but is repressed by hospital attendants. The singers remind us that Marat's hours are numbered.

Sade advises Marat to abandon his efforts, says that nothing is accomplished by writing. Marat recalls his enormous output of words and the reactions whenever one of his works was published. Sade maintains that Marat's efforts have been in vain.

The patient playing Corday is wakened and brought to Marat's door. Duperret tries to persuade her to abandon her cares and give herself up to pleasure, but she is not to be moved from her purpose. She knocks.

Sade approaches Marat and asks what are his writings and speeches compared to the pleasures of the flesh. A mime of copulation begins among the singers. Sade continues that the body is all, the Revolution meaningless.

Corday is admitted to Marat's presence. As she names his opponents who have gathered at Caen, she raises the dagger to strike. The Herald stops the action and the players relax.

During this interlude the four singers summarize the events that followed the assassination of Marat, from 1793 to 1808, with Napoleon triumphant. At the conclusion of this recital Corday plunges the dagger into Marat.

There is one more episode, designated in the text as an epilogue. Coulmier voices the optimism of the times, which he says is free of oppressors and violent crime. He further states that victory for Napoleon is certain. The singers ironically note the social progress that has been made in the fifteen years since Marat's death. Meanwhile, rebellion and violence break out among the patients, threatening the safety of Coulmier and his family. There is fierce fighting and hysterical dancing. Sade laughs triumphantly.

[]   *In Brief*

The second act continues the ideological debate of the inner play, with Marat demanding and justifying violence in the cause of revolution and Sade arguing the futility of action that ignores the stubborn fact of corruption in human nature. A growing restlessness among the patients foreshadows their revolt at the end. The inner play culminates with the assassination, while the outer play, with the patients out of control, appears to confirm Sade's point of view.

Protagonist and Objective

Since we are dealing with two plays, one inside the other, there must be a protagonist for each. But in fact it happens to be the same person in each case—Sade. We might say that in the outer play his objective is to stage a play for the Paris public, setting forth his ideological views. In this he is successful. In the inner play his objective is to prove the validity of those views when measured against the revolutionary philosophy of Marat. Here the audience must decide for itself between the opposing viewpoints, although the revolt of the patients and Sade's reaction to the revolt suggests that it is he who has won. (It might be supposed at first that Marat is the protagonist of the inner play, but he is too static a figure. He does not act; he is only acted upon.)

Obstacles and Climax

There are few obstacles, and this is one reason that, in spite of its setting and its remarkable characters, the play is not especially dramatic. A debate can be enlivened, as this one has been; but, until our sympathies have been engaged by events resulting from actions of the characters (in other words, by a story), we are more likely to be intellectually than emotionally interested.

Sade's only opposition in the outer play is an occasional protest from Coulmier, but Coulmier never stops the performance. It goes right on uncensored. At the end the stage directions indicate that Coulmier is congratulating Sade. The outer play proceeds without an appreciable obstacle, and is seen to be no more than a frame for the inner one.

Since the core of the inner play is a debate, presumably intended to influence the thinking of the spectators, Marat can be regarded as the opposition to Sade. But Sade's arguments do not overwhelm Marat. Marat is destroyed by a character with whom Sade has had nothing to do. His destruction (almost at the hands of a *deus ex machina*) must serve as the climax of the inner play. It is obvious that we are here departing very far from traditional construction.

Theme

The meaning of the play is ambivalent. The destruction of Marat suggests that his point of view cannot survive, and that Sade's will prevail. But the unresolved uprising of the patients at the end of the play may be interpreted as a revolt against authoritarianism. We may infer too that revolutions, however idealistically inspired, ultimately generate more violence and new oppressions. Weiss clearly intends to have us think and decide for ourselves about the questions raised.

Resolution

The section marked "epilogue" is the resolution. In it the over-stimulated patients rebel, Coulmier succumbs to panic, and Sade reacts with knowing laughter.

Opening

The outer play begins just before the start of Sade's production at the asylum. Given the form of the work, there is hardly any other point in the larger story that could be used. Nothing would be gained by going back to Sade's imprisonment or any other event in his life before this moment.

The inner play, since it uses Marat's death as its culminating point, starts just before the assassination.

Unity

The unities of time and place are observed in both the outer and inner plays. A unity of mood is achieved, not by a strict adherence to the subject matter and the elimination of extraneous elements, but by the form and style of the work.

Exposition

At the start exposition is handled in direct address to the audience, principally by Coulmier and the Herald. Later we find exposition contained in argument, soliloquy, and in the comments of the chorus. The action of the play is stopped, for example, just before the stabbing of Marat, while the four singers relate the events of the fifteen intervening years.

Characterization

Characterization is extremely rich and varied. Participants in the inner play are doubly characterized—as lunatics and in the roles they perform. At no time is Sade, however, pictured as mad. Coulmier and the Herald are also developed only on the level of sanity.

Development

The inner play moves on a framework of the pending assassination, but the ideological arguments and comments follow an intellectual rather than a dramatic pattern. Unless one excepts the encounter between Corday and Marat that precedes the assassination, it can hardly be said that there are any "scenes" in the conventional sense. The total effect makes the work seem more like a debate than a play.

Dramatic Irony

Beyond the fact that the audience knows that Corday intends to kill Marat and that she ultimately succeeds, no use is made of dramatic irony.

Preparation

No plants are required, unless Corday's purchase of the dagger and the repeated reminders that she is to kill Marat may be so regarded.

Activity

The play offers seemingly endless opportunities for significant business. In the Royal Shakespeare Company's production, when the executions at the guillotine were mimed, buckets of paint were poured into a drain—bright red for the common people, blue for the aristocrats. In the same staging the whipping of Sade was accomplished by having Corday lash his bare back with her long hair. Other striking bits were the mime of copulation and Roux's playing his entire role while struggling to get out of a strait jacket.

Dialogue

The lines in the published English version are in many spots quite banal, which may be deliberate. Much of the dialogue is in rhymed couplets that are, to say the least, uninspired. Skilled actors can to some degree disguise the clumsiness of the verse, but one wonders whether the effect of the play wouldn't be more forceful if the lines didn't limp so painfully.

Effects

The play is most effective in performance when it appears that the audience is actually seated in the bath hall. Entrances can then be made through the auditorium, and a degree of intimacy achieved that a curtain and formal separation of actors and spectators tend to dissipate. The rebellion of the patients at the end thus seems to threaten the actual audience.

And Finally

Marat/Sade appears to demonstrate that many of the precepts of tested dramatic construction can be ignored, but only if other elements of exceptional strength and interest are employed to compensate for the lack of a sturdier skeleton. Though acknowledged as an extremely significant and influential work, it will probably never achieve a broadly based popularity. Only time will tell how widely such unconventional plays as this will be embraced by the general public.

APPENDICES

Realism and Its Predecessors

Realism

The form of theatre most familiar to us, and the form used preponderantly by the movies and television, is the so-called "realistic" form, which purports to represent life substantially as we experience it outside the theatre. It asks us to believe that the canvas wall is made of wood and plaster, that the papier-mâché tree is a real one, that the people are speaking and behaving as they would if they were experiencing the situation in real life.

Actually their speech and behavior are no more true to reality than the canvas wall and the papier-mâché tree. Their movements on the stage are governed by the fact that an audience must be able to see every significant thing they do, often through what in reality would be another wall, and their position must be such that attention is focused on the right character at the proper time. Their dialogue, even at its most "naturalistic," has little resemblance to the speech of people in ordinary conversation. It is not only considerably louder than it would be in life, but, more important, it has all been prearranged to carry a story forward, to reveal character, to furnish insights into people's behavior. The task of the director and actors in staging a representational play is to make the speech and movement as natural as possible (that is, to disguise the fact that this speech and behavior is not truly lifelike), just as it is the scene designer's job to make the tree look like a real tree, and the electrician's job to make the coming of night and the rising of the moon seem real. None of this is easy, under the circumstances. It requires great skill on the part of everyone concerned, including the playwright.

The realistic form is, in the long history of the theatre, a rather recent development. Throughout long centuries plays were written in a manner that frankly admitted to the spectators that they were in a theatre, that the actors were performing for their pleasure and benefit (precisely as they would at a concert, a circus, or a vaudeville show). Up until the advent of the realistic form actors recognized the presence of the audience, often addressed it in asides and spoke in soliloquies. Actors in a realistic play pretend that the audience isn't there.

No one seems to have imagined a play or performance that would give the illusion of reality until well into the nineteenth century. The stage itself, far from being a simulation of the environment in which the story was presumed to be taking place, was no more than a platform for the actors. Scenery, such as it was, provided a background that was sometimes, but not always, suggestive of the locale of the play. In 1836 Nikolai Gogol wrote *The Inspector General,* and in 1849 Turgenev gave us *A Month in the Country,* both plays demanding a more naturalistic style of acting than was then customary. Later in the century the two great Scandinavian dramatists, Ibsen and Strindberg, and Zola in France, as a theorist, began the development of the realistic form as we know it today. Realistic plays required, so far as possible, productions that literally reflected everyday life. With the improvement in stage lighting, and the introduction on stage of real furniture and properties, and of settings that looked something like the places they represented, actors began to subdue their declamatory tones and gestures, and the movement toward realism gained irresistible momentum. Stanislavsky, at the Moscow Art Theatre, developed the style to an extraordinary degree of perfection. The movement toward realism was so successful that within a few years it came close to sweeping the earlier forms from the Western theatre. It is this tradition that the films have inherited.

Motion pictures handle the form somewhat better than the stage, for obvious reasons. The walls are solid and the trees are real. The actors speak in tones they would normally use—soft or loud, as the scene requires—and the uniform amplification of their voices keeps the total effect in balance. They move with greater naturalness in their surroundings; for, instead of the actor's having to place himself so that the audience can see just what he's doing, the camera can be placed in the most advantageous position and bring the audience this optimum view. The camera can also pick out the single character on whom the director and scenarist wish us to concentrate. Gestures and facial expressions can be subtler, for they can be shown to us in close-up.

In fact, the films are equipped to handle the realistic form so much better than the stage that many contemporary playwrights have abandoned realism entirely, or, like O'Neill, O'Casey, Miller, Williams, Anouilh, Bolt, Albee, and many others, have combined realism with other forms. The theatre still seems to be the superior medium for the various presentational or—perhaps a better term—theatricalist forms.

But, whatever term we use—and let us say theatricalist—it covers so many different acting and production styles, extending back in time to the ancient Greeks and in distance to the traditional styles of the Orient, that the only way to become truly informed is to study the plays and whenever possible to see the performances. Theatricalist forms that preceded the advent of realism are reviewed here simply as a reminder of earlier methods and styles from which we can still learn, and which in all probability still have a contribution to make in fashioning our modern Western drama. It is, of course, a vast and complex subject. But here, at the risk of our seeming to go through the Louvre on a motorcycle, are a few of the major manifestations of theatre in other times and places.

Ancient Greece and Rome

The classic theatre of Greece offered very tightly constructed plays, written for presentation by male actors in large outdoor amphitheatres. The acting area consisted of a circular space for dancing called the *orchestra*. Beyond this was a low platform, the *proskenion*, backed by a permanent architectural structure, the *skene*, with three doors. The *proskenion* was flanked by two wings, the *paraskenia*, which could serve to indicate two other buildings. The *orchestra* was occupied by the chorus; the principal actors performed mainly on the *proskenion*, although they could also use the roof of the *skene* or go into the *orchestra*. Scenic effects, if any, were limited and formal, probably no more than moveable decorative panels or revolving prisms. The audience sat in semicircular, banked rows of seats around the *orchestra*. The productions featured music and singing, dancing and choral chanting. The subject matter ranged from the most exalted tragedy to knockabout topical satire and farce, and the dialogue from exquisite poetry to vulgar common speech.

Following is a list of some of the finest plays of the period: Aeschylus' *Prometheus Bound* (465 B.C.), *Agamemnon, The Choephori,* and *The Eumenides* (the *Oresteia* trilogy—458 B.C.); Sophocles' *Antigone* (442 B.C.), *Oedipus the King* (427 B.C.), and *Electra* (414 B.C.); Euripides' *Medea* (431 B.C.), *Hippolytus* (428 B.C.), and *The Trojan*

Women (415 B.C.); Aristophanes' *The Acharnians* (425 B.C.), *Peace* (421 B.C.), and *Lysistrata* (411 B.C.).

The Roman amphitheatres resembled half of a huge bowl, the seats being built up steeply around a flat semicircle (a remnant of the Greek *orchestra*), with the stage cutting straight across the bowl from one side to the other. The background behind the acting platform was built to the same height as the last row of seats. There were doors for the actors' entrances, and the entire background was covered with elaborate architectural and sculptural detail. Representative Roman plays include Plautus' *The Menaechmi* (215 B.C.) and *The Merchant* (214 B.C.); Terence's *Phormio* (161 B.C.) and *The Brothers* (160 B.C.).

Japan

The Japanese theatre's plays dealt with traditional subject matter in a highly formalized style. Actors developed a vocabulary of gesture that bore little resemblance to the actual emotions they were intended to convey, but which were nevertheless understood by the audience. Singers and instrumentalists at one side of the stage provided a constant obligato to the performances. The actors wore magnificent costumes, and either masks or very heavy make-up. The Kabuki Theatre of modern Japan still observes the ancient traditions, and is occasionally to be seen on tour in Western capitals. Their theatre employs a runway leading from the rear of the auditorium to the stage on which the actors, all male, make highly effective entrances and exits. The scenery is complicated and elaborate, but usually more decorative than realistic. Other traditional Oriental drama, such as Chinese, Indian, and Persian, though differing in many respects from the Japanese, was similarly stylized.

Miracle Plays

These were religious dramas performed in Europe during the Middle Ages. At first the actors were priests, who spoke in Latin. Later the laity performed the plays in the vernacular. They were often presented on portable stages set up in a public square, there being several such platforms arranged to represent anything from heaven itself to the mouth of hell, with the action moving from one stage to another. Some multiscened plays used a series of wagons for stages, each being set with the appropriate background and moved into place for each episode. In this way the production could be taken to various parts of the city to accommodate different audiences.

Commedia dell' Arte

This was a form of improvisational theatre extremely popular in Italy in the fifteenth and sixteenth centuries. Strolling troupes of players appeared on curtained platform stages set up outdoors. There were no scripts; the actors worked from scenarios only. (These were not notable for their delicacy.) The dialogue and stage business were left to the skill, wit, and inventiveness of the individual performers. The stock characters, such as Pantalone, Arlecchino, and Brighella, wore traditional masks and costumes. Some of the figures are traceable back to Roman comedy. The troupes toured extensively, even into France, Spain, and Bavaria. They were generally regarded as vagabonds, although a few were invited to perform for the nobility and were greatly honored. The *Commedia dell' Arte* was theatre reduced to bare essentials—a platform, actors, and a story.

Tudor and Stuart Theatre

The plays of this period were generally rather loosely constructed and episodic. They were written for a platform stage that thrust forward into a galleried courtyard, the audience surrounding the performance on three sides. A balcony over the main entrance at the rear of the stage gave the actors a second level on which to perform; but, aside from a few properties such as chairs, banners, and so on, the stage was bare of scenic effects. Costumes for the all-male cast were apparently rather elaborate. The stage plan permitted extreme flexibility in the arrangement of scenes, which followed one another without interruption, the audience inferring from the dialogue where and when the current action was taking place. Even today, Shakespearean productions seem to work best when performed in a simple unit setting that permits the scenes to flow easily in the order and manner their author intended. Elaborate realistic settings are not only unnecessary but inappropriate.

In addition to Shakespeare's plays, all of which should be familiar to every aspiring playwright, representative dramas of the time include Marlowe's *Doctor Faustus* (1588) and *Edward the Second* (1592), Dekker's *The Shoemaker's Holiday* (1599), Jonson's *Volpone*

(1606) and *Bartholomew Fair* (1614), and Webster's *The Duchess of Malfi* (1613).

The Renaissance

The court theatres of the Renaissance were a combination of indoor theatre and ballroom. They were used for the presentation of revivals of the classic Roman plays and contemporary pageants or spectacles of great opulence but little dramatic interest. Machiavelli's *La Mandragola* (1524) is one of the few original plays of the period to have survived even as a museum piece. Audiences, standing or seated, faced the stage from the flat ballroom floor, and, while some of the pageantry was undoubtedly carried down among the spectators by means of ramps, the scenic effects, which were very elaborate, were contained behind a large "picture frame" at one end of the room. The first true proscenium theatre was built at Parma in 1618–19. The stage occupied one end of a long hall, and was curtained off from a bank of seats arranged in a U-shaped pattern. The painted scenery, consisting of backdrop and wings, could be changed behind the curtain. Here we have, of course, the prototype of thousands of theatres across Europe and America that have been built in the last three hundred years. The curtain survives even in cinema houses, where it serves no sensible purpose at all. (The proscenium arch was actually an architectural enlargement of the actors' main up-center entrance, or palace doorway, of the classic Roman theatres. But, instead of playing in front of the arch, the actors now tended to confine their activities behind it.) This basic Italian plan quickly spread to the various court theatres of Europe, ultimately to England, and indirectly to America. It has influenced, well into our own century, not only the architectural design of theatres all over the Western world, but also the style of plays to be presented therein.

Theatre of the French Court

The French theatres of the early seventeenth century had moved indoors, but they were uncomfortably housed, often being no more than converted tennis courts. Scenery, if any, was crude, and candles supplied the illumination. Costumes, however, were elaborate. The players shared their "shelf for acting" with fops and gallants who sat or strolled about on the stage, commenting audibly and leaving barely enough room for the performance. (It was Voltaire who finally succeeded in banishing the spectators from the stage.) Cardinal Richelieu, minister to Louis XIII, who had playwriting ambitions himself, had an elaborate proscenium stage built into his ballroom in 1641, complete with Italian scenery and effects. Gradually other proscenium theatres came into being. Meanwhile, there developed strict rules, derived in part from Aristotle and the Greek classics, for the composition of French tragedy. Plays had to be in five acts; only exalted themes and illustrious characters were acceptable; violent action must take place off stage; there could be no comedy or subplots; the three unities—time, place, and action—had to be observed; and the text was composed in Alexandrine verse, a six-foot line rhymed in couplets. Two great dramatists, Corneille and Racine, composed many fine plays within these limitations. Their contemporary, Molière, an actor-manager and one of the greatest dramatists of all time, worked in a much freer form. His imperishable comedies, which often ignore the unities and employ prose as well as verse, brought the theatre a little bit closer to realism.

Significant plays of this period include Corneille's *The Cid* (1636), Molière's *The School for Husbands* (1661), *The School for Wives* (1662), *Tartuffe* (1664), *The Doctor in Spite of Himself* (1666), *The Misanthrope* (1666), and *The Would-be Gentleman* (1670), Racine's *Iphigenia* (1674) and *Phaedra* (1677). The last-named is a reworking of Euripides' play *Hippolytus*. Racine's introduction to the work, and the comparison to the earlier play, make a fascinating study in dramaturgy.

The Restoration

British theatres of the Restoration period and for many years thereafter affected a kind of compromise between the Italian proscenium plan and the Elizabethan thrust stage, which survived in the form of an apron extending far out in front of the curtain. Entrances for the players were also provided on either side of the forestage, and boxes adjoining the proscenium arch for the benefit of those spectators who preferred to be seen rather than to see. Playing far downstage on the apron, the actors were in virtually the same relationship to the audience as they were in Shakespeare's day. It is true that various painted settings were on view, appropriate to each scene, but these were mere backgrounds, in no way an environment in which the actors could achieve any sense of verisimilitude to real life. The plays, which reflected the insouciance and moral laxity of the times, were contrived in plot, and, though the dialogue was often brilliantly witty, it was highly artificial in tone. Asides and soliloquies were still in use, for no effort was being made to create an illusion of reality. The acting style, needless to say, was flamboyant in the extreme. By now women were playing the female roles.

Outstanding plays of the period are Wycherly's *The Country Wife* (1672) and *The Plain Dealer* (1674), Congreve's *Love for Love* (1695) and *The Way of the World* (1700), Vanbrugh's *The Relapse* (1696) and *The Provok'd Wife* (1697), and Farquhar's *The Recruiting Officer* (1706) and *The Beaux' Stratagem* (1707).

Eighteenth and Nineteenth Centuries

The horseshoe-shaped auditorium, with the proscenium arch and a forestage of varying depth, remained the norm of European and American theatre design until late in the nineteenth century. Lighting was inadequate (at least by today's standards), the painted scenery was anything but illusional, and the acting under these conditions was broad and declamatory. The actor was less a character in a play than a performer. (In this he somewhat resembled his cousin, the opera singer.) With the functional shape of the playhouse substantially fixed for more than two centuries, it isn't surprising that plays written during the same period show less variety in approach and form than plays written for the widely disparate theatres of earlier times.

England produced a few delightful comedies in the eighteenth century. They include John Gay's novel musical play *The Beggar's Opera* (1728), Goldsmith's *She Stoops To Conquer* (1774), Sheridan's *The Rivals* (1775) and *The School for Scandal* (1777). After this the quality of British plays plunged disastrously. The chief characteristic of British playwriting until nearly the end of the nineteenth century was sentimental melodrama. An exception must be made of the Gilbert and Sullivan operettas, with their lilting tunes and their satiric and witty lyrics, but these were well outside the contemporary norm. The renaissance began in the late eighties and early nineties with the influence of the realist Ibsen and the arrival on the scene of Bernard Shaw.

On the continent we find the drama manifesting itself in nearly every form that could be contained within the theatres of the time. In France there were the romantic dramas of Victor Hugo (*Hernani*—1830) and the elder Dumas (*The Tower of Nesle*—1832) and the "well-made plays" of Scribe (*Adrienne Lecouvreur*—1849) and Sardou (*A Scrap of Paper*—1860), as predictable in plotting as a geometric theorem. Italy, in the eighteenth century, gave us Carlo Goldoni, who, building on the nearly defunct tradition of the *Commedia dell' Arte,* fashioned a series of graceful and charming comedies. Perhaps the two finest are *The Servant of Two Masters* (1740) and *The Mistress of the Inn* (1751). Germany, somewhat later, produced three towering figures—the socially aware critic and playwright Gotthold Lessing (*Nathan the Wise—*1779), the romantic poet Schiller (*Maria Stuart—*1800, *Wilhelm Tell—*1804) and the mighty Goethe (*Faust—*1808–1831). In Russia Gogol and Turgenev, as has already been noted, wrote plays that foreshadowed the realistic form and helped to pave the way for Gorki and the great Anton Chekov. But it was in Scandinavia that the real dramatic revolution was brewing, and with the advent of Ibsen's and Strindberg's realistic plays in the 1870's and 1880's we have arrived at the turning point of modern theatre.

There are so many hundreds of fine plays in the realistic mode that it is impossible to give anything like a comprehensive list. Most of Bernard Shaw's and Anton Chekov's plays are written in this style. Following are some of their representative works: Shaw's *Mrs. Warren's Profession* (1894), *Candida* (1894), *You Never Can Tell* (1896), *The Devil's Disciple* (1897), *Caesar and Cleopatra* (1898), *Man and Superman* (1901), *Major Barbara* (1905), *The Doctor's Dilemma* (1906), *Pygmalion* (1913), and *Heartbreak House* (1919). *Saint Joan* (1923), perhaps Shaw's finest play, is realistic in treatment except for the epilogue. Chekov's best-known plays are *The Sea Gull* (1895), *Uncle Vanya* (1897), *The Three Sisters* (1900), and *The Cherry Orchard* (1903). All are identified with the Moscow Art Theatre.

Among other well-known and influential examples of the realistic style are Ibsen's *A Doll's House* (1879), *Ghosts* (1881), and *Hedda Gabler* (1890); Becque's *The Vultures* (1881); Hauptmann's *The Weavers* (1893) and *Rose Bernd* (1903); Strindberg's *The Father* (1887) and *Miss Julie* (1888); Pinero's *The Second Mrs. Tanqueray* (1893); Schnitzler's *Reigen* (1897); Gorki's *The Lower Depths* (1902); Galsworthy's *Justice* (1916); O'Neill's *Anna Christie* (1921), *Ah, Wilderness!* (1933), *The Iceman Cometh* (1939), and *Long Day's Journey Into Night* (prod. 1956); Anderson and Stalling's *What Price Glory* (1924); O'Casey's *The Plough and the Stars* (1926); Sheriff's *Journey's End* (1929); Rice's *Street Scene* (1929); Kirkland and Caldwell's *Tobacco Road* (1933); Kingsley's *Dead End* (1935); Hellman's *The Little Foxes* (1939); Barry's *The Philadelphia Story* (1939); Sherwood's *There Shall Be No Night* (1939); Rattigan's *The Winslow Boy* (1946); Miller's *All My Sons* (1947) and *The Crucible* (1953); Anderson's *Tea and Sympathy* (1953); Osborne's *Look Back in Anger* (1956); and Gibson's *The Miracle Worker* (1959). A majority of today's popular Broadway and West End comedies are also realistic in style.

Perhaps the foregoing outline, brief as it is, will indicate to the serious student of playwriting how a knowledge of the dramas of the past and the theatres in which they were performed can help him to determine the direction he should follow. The entries under "Drama" and "Theatre" in the *Encyclopedia Britannica* are both excellent as a start. There are several fine books on the subject, including *History of the Theatre,* by Freedley and Reeves, and Gassner's *Masters of the Drama.*

Grand opera has purposely been omitted from this discussion, not only because it would extend the essay beyond its desired limits, but because opera as it is composed and produced today is primarily a musical expression, not a dramatic one. With a somewhat different approach on the part of composer, librettist, producer, and director, opera could become an enormously effective theatrical medium without diminishing its musical values. The Moscow Art Theatre Musical Studio's productions of *Lysistrata* and *Carmencita and the Soldier* pointed the way many years ago.

The Revolt Against Realism

Theatricalism

Further consideration of the realistic form need not detain us here. It has already been touched on at the beginning of Appendix A; in any case we are all quite familiar with it—on the stage as well as in films and television. But few beginning playwrights are aware of the various forms in which today's dramatists are working. These diverse styles are all worth study, they are all available to everyone who can use them, and still newer forms wait to be created and developed.

Since the creation of an illusion of actuality had never been the aim of the playwright or the actor before the 1870's, all theatre till then was frankly conventional, making no pretense of reproducing "real life." The drama never asked the spectator, under the spell of its magic, to forget that he was watching a performance on a stage. It was all "theatrical."

But with the coming of a different kind of playwriting, and play-houses capable of offering a certain verisimilitude of environment for the actor, the theatricalism of twenty-five centuries was for a short time nearly abandoned. (The tradition remained unbroken, however, in the music hall, musical comedy, and opera, where musical dialogue and songs directed to the audience were inconsistent with the illusion of actuality.)

Many playwrights and directors felt that the new realism was too constricting, that what they had in mind could not be contained in the confines of the form. So within a short time a number of new forms appeared—some, like romanticism, harking back to earlier forms; others, like expressionism, a modern invention.

All these nonrealistic modes, both before and after the advent of realism, can be lumped together under the term "theatricalism," * and it is these modern manifestations of theatricalism that we shall now consider.

Sometimes the various theatricalist modes were intended, as in Epic Theatre, to destroy utterly the illusion of reality, and thus to maintain the critical detachment of the audience. At other times the forms were introduced into otherwise realistic plays in order to create or reinforce some effect not possible within the more constraining form.

Theatricality has been achieved in our time and in our present-day playhouses in many ways. These include the use of music, dance, and ballet, exaggerated acting styles and gestures, asides, direct address to the audience, narration, the absence or substitution of stage proper-ties, the use of masks, and, of course, nonrealistic scenery—or, as in the case of *Our Town*, no scenery at all.

A great many modern plays have been written in the theatricalist mode, or have incorporated strong theatricalist elements. Later we shall consider more specific categories of modern theatricalism, but not all plays fit into the narrower classifications. Meanwhile, here are some of the better-known and easily accessible works that can be grouped only under the wider heading: Molnar's *Liliom* (1908); Pirandello's *Six Characters in Search of an Author* (1916) and *Henry IV* (1922); Ansky's *The Dybbuk* (1917); O'Neill's *Lazarus Laughed* (1927) and *Strange Interlude* (1928); Obey's *Noah* (1931); O'Casey's *Within the Gates* (1934); Cocteau's *The Infernal Machine* (1934); Giraudoux's *Electra* (1937), *Ondine* (1939), and *The Madwoman of Chaillot* (1943); Wilder's *Our Town* (1938) and *The Skin of Our Teeth* (1942); Saroyan's *My Heart's in the Highlands* (1939); Sartre's *The Flies* (1943); Anderson's *Joan of Lorraine* (1946); Williams' *Summer and Smoke* (1948); and the Anouilh-Fry *Ring 'Round the Moon* (1950). Then, of course, there are the innumerable musical comedies, every one of which is an example of theatricalism. Some of the best known are *Oklahoma, South Pacific, Carousel, Brigadoon, My Fair Lady, Lady*

---

* John Gassner refers to the more restrained manifestations of theatricalism as "formalism"; but, in the interest of cutting down the number of "isms" to be con-sidered, the term is not used in this book. The reader is cautioned only to remember that all the forms can be employed to a greater or lesser degree. For the same reason the word "naturalism" has been dropped. This is often used interchangeably with realism, but sometimes to indicate a more intense application of it.

in the Dark, Kiss Me, Kate, Guys and Dolls, West Side Story, Finian's Rainbow, Oliver, and *Fiddler on the Roof.*

Let us now consider some of the more specialized forms of modern theatricalism.

Symbolism

There was bound to be a reaction to the swift triumph of the realistic theatre, and it was not long in coming. The earliest rebellion was begun in the closing decade of the nineteenth century by the symbolists, led by the Belgian dramatist Maurice Maeterlinck. Holding that the new realism dealt merely with the mundane world of facts and topical problems, they maintained that drama should elevate itself to reflect spiritual reality and eternal truths. To this end their plays employed a frequently obscure and misty kind of poetry, and often dealt with magic and mysticism in an attempt to achieve universality. The creation of mood was considered far more important than narrative storytelling, and suspense was virtually eliminated. Dramatically the plays today seem very static. Scenery and lighting were extremely important in their productions, and this led to a healthy simplification of settings. Gordon Craig and Adolph Appia were the two great theorists in the movement toward more evocative scenery and lighting, and the American Robert Edmond Jones was one of the finest designers to come under the symbolist influence.

With a few exceptions, most of which are short plays, not many symbolist works have stood the test of time. The best are Maeterlinck's *The Intruder* and *The Blind* (both 1890) and Synge's *Riders to the Sea* (1904), all one-act plays. Other representative examples include Maeterlinck's *Péléas and Mélisande* (1892), Hofmannsthal's *Death and the Fool* (1893), Hauptmann's *The Sunken Bell* (1896), Yeats' *The Hour Glass* (1903), Claudel's *The Tidings Brought to Mary* (1910), and Andreyev's *He Who Gets Slapped* (1915). Chekov, no symbolist himself in spite of some superficial similarities, parodied the movement in his play-within-a-play in *The Sea Gull.* In the American theatre both O'Neill and Williams at times show the symbolist influence.

Romanticism

Romantic verse drama was not a new movement in the theatre, but a revival of earlier styles, such as those of Hugo and Schiller. The popularity of many of the plays written in this mode is proof that realism didn't entirely take over the Western theatre, even when it seemed most pervasive.

There is a significant distinction to be made between romanticism and symbolism. The former is objective, clear in motivation and action. Symbolism is subjective, metaphorical, and often elusive.

Well-known examples of modern romantic drama include Rostand's *Cyrano de Bergerac* (1897), Stephen Phillips' *Paolo and Francesca* (1899), D'Annunzio's *Francesca da Rimini* (1902), Maxwell Anderson's *Elizabeth the Queen* (1930) and *Mary of Scotland* (1933), and Christopher Fry's *The Lady's Not for Burning* (1948).

Verse Drama

In addition to the use of verse dialogue in the romantic type of play already mentioned, several playwrights continued to employ it in works where the use of "realistic" prose might at first glance seem more appropriate. Verse, by its very nature, brings a kind of eloquence and richness of texture to dialogue, though the prose-poetry of such masters as O'Casey, Giraudoux, and Tennessee Williams shows that it is not necessary to turn to formal verse to achieve such effects.

García Lorca's *Blood Wedding* (1933) and *Yerma* (1934), Anderson's *Winterset* (1935), Eliot's *The Cocktail Party* (1949), and Alfred's *Hogan's Goat* (1965) all employ verse in what otherwise might be considered realistic drama.

Expressionism

Oddly, one of the originators of theatrical realism was also among the first to turn against the form. Of his expressionist fantasy *The Dream Play* (1902) Strindberg explained that he had tried to imitate the disconnected but seemingly logical form of a dream, that the patterns in the play were a medley of memories, experiences, free fantasies, absurdities, and improvisations.

The expressionist's approach to his subject matter was subjective. (This is the basic difference between expressionism and Epic Theatre, which is completely objective, although there are some superficial similarities between the two.) Characteristic of the form was the depersonalization of the individual, who was often nameless, appearing merely as Man or Woman, or else as a symbol. Dialogue, dispensing with everything regarded as superfluous, was frequently distorted and enigmatic. Speed, exaggeration, extravagant color, movement, and sound were all enlisted in the evocation of a state of mind on the part of one of the characters, to emphasize a particular plot situation or, if it extended throughout the play, to express the author's interpretation of reality.

Although expressionism was substantially dead as a theatre movement by 1925, it had a profound and widespread influence on later drama—more, perhaps, than any other form except the epic. Besides *The Dream Play,* another early expressionist play of Strindberg's was *The Ghost Sonata* (1907). Other examples are Kaiser's *From Morn to Midnight* (1916) and *Gas* (1918–20), Toller's *Man and the Masses* (1920), and Rice's *The Adding Machine* (1923). O'Neill's *The Emperor Jones* (1920) and *The Hairy Ape* (1922) show strong expressionist influence, as does Kaufman and Connelly's *Beggar on Horseback* (1924), O'Casey's *The Silver Tassie* (1929), and Miller's *Death of a Salesman* (1949).

Surrealism

The surrealist movement carried its rejection of realistic writing and staging even further than expressionism, maintaining that only by the total destruction of actuality's façade could the theatre explore the mind's unconscious, our obsessions and anxieties, the primitive desires that lie at the roots of human behavior.

As may be imagined, logical narrative was lost in a welter of inconsistencies, anachronisms, and puzzling juxtapositions. The response of the spectator was quite unpredictable.

The so-called Theatre of Cruelty found even surrealist forms inadequate in its exploration of the dark recesses of the human mind. The word "cruelty" may be somewhat misleading, for *le théâtre de la cruauté* is not an exhibition of sadistic acts. Basically it was an attempt to create a metaphysical experience that would be shared by all the participants, actors and spectators alike. Its principal theorist was Antonin Artaud, a poet associated with the surrealist movement in Paris in the 1920's. Less a mode of playwriting than a method of production, it emphasized violent, startling, and ludicrous action, fantastic decor, grotesquely masked and costumed figures, extravagant gesture and color, and intense light and sound. It was strongly influenced by the Kabuki Theatre of Japan and by Balinese dancing. The play's text was a subordinate factor, Artaud holding that the dramatic experience should be created in the theatre itself, on a playing area that extended not only across the stage but among and around the spectators on ramps, aisles, and catwalks. He wanted to reach the audience through their nerves and senses rather than their minds. Words became "objects," of value for their shape and sound more than for their meaning.

The best-known surrealist plays are Jarry's *Ubu Roi* (1896), Apollinaire's *The Breasts of Teresias* (1903), Cocteau's *Orpheus* (1926), Cummings' *him* (1927), and García Lorca's *The Love of Don Perlimpín and Belisa in His Garden* (1931). The British director Peter Brook has successfully experimented with the Theatre of Cruelty form, the most notable example being the Royal Shakespeare Company's production of *Marat/Sade*. Artaud's theories also hold considerable interest for a number of *avant-garde* groups in the United States, whose experiments have met with divided reactions.

Epic Theatre

Similar in some respects to the traditional Chinese theatre, the style known as "epic" was devised by the German playwright Bertolt Brecht and the director Erwin Piscator. Committed to a social viewpoint and frankly aiming at instruction and the furtherance of an ideology, it turned its back on realism entirely, employing theatricalism in an extreme form. It aimed to circumvent undue emotional involvement on the part of the spectators. This so-called "alienation" was thought essential if the audience was to maintain a properly detached and critical attitude toward the subject matter.

To this end, epic productions are characterized by a great number of highly theatrical devices. Scenes are interrupted by songs, dances, narration, and lectures, and the acting is often stylized, with a particular emphasis on gesture. Moving or revolving platforms, treadmills, charts, and cartoons, as well as film and slide projections, may all make their appearance. No one is permitted to forget that he is in a theatre, watching actors perform a play. (There remains a question as to whether the hortatory effect of such a work as *The Diary of Anne Frank*, for example, would be rendered more powerful by epic instead of realistic treatment.) But Epic Theatre has had enormous influence on contemporary drama.

Examples of the style include Brecht's own vast body of work, some of the best known of his plays being *The Three-Penny Opera*

(1928), *Galileo* (1937), *The Good Woman of Setzuan* (1938), *Mother Courage* (1939), *The Caucasian Chalk Circle* (1944), and *The Private Life of the Master Race* (1945). The Federal Theatre's "Living Newspaper" plays, *Power* (1937) and *One-third of a Nation* (1938), as well as Paul Green's *Johnny Johnson* (1936), should also be included. The epic influence may be felt in Patrick's *The Teahouse of the August Moon* (1953) and Bolt's *A Man for All Seasons* (1961).

Theatre of the Absurd

The term "Theatre of the Absurd" was coined by the critic Martin Esslin and used as the title of a book in which he discussed the work of a number of leading contemporary dramatists who seemed to share a certain philosophical position—that of bewilderment and dismay at the apparent meaninglessness of man's place in the universe, a lack filled in former times, more or less, by various systems of metaphysical and religious beliefs. The word "absurd," then, is used in the sense of "purposeless," "useless," "lost," and the Theatre of the Absurd reflects the irrationality of life. To this end, plays of this school often abandon narrative techniques in favor of poetic images; conventional structure frequently gives way to inconsistent and illogical—even chaotic—presentation. The plays nearly always require a subjective approach on the part of the audience, and are difficult of rational analysis. Though often very effective on stage, they can sometimes be extremely puzzling too. No doubt they will seem less so as we become more familiar with this type of writing. And the Theatre of the Absurd, like Epic Theatre, will undoubtedly influence more conventional forms.

Notable and successful examples of the school include Ghelderode's *Pantagleize* (1929); Genet's *The Maids* (1947), *The Balcony* (1956), and *The Blacks* (1957); Ionesco's *The Bald Soprano* (1948), *The Chairs* (1951), and *Rhinoceros* (1959); Beckett's *Waiting for Godot* (1952) and *Endgame* (1957); Pinter's *The Birthday Party* (1958), *The Caretaker* (1960), and *Homecoming* (1965); Arrabal's *The Automobile Graveyard* (1958); Albee's *The Zoo Story* (1959) and *The American Dream* (1961); Simpson's *One Way Pendulum* (1959); Grass's *The Wicked Cooks* (1962); and Stoppard's *Rosencrantz and Guildenstern Are Dead* (1966). Some of these writers might object, on philosophical grounds, to being classed as part of the Theatre of the Absurd. The fact remains that all the above-listed plays bear a marked similarity of approach and treatment.

Synthesis

It occurs to me that the theatres of the past that have been most at home with themselves, content under their own skins, have been theatres in which the anti-illusionistic elements have co-existed with the illusionistic ones, held in balance throughout.

We need an easygoing partnership between the real and the unreal, happy to be in the same place at the same time.

—Walter Kerr

It seems clear that increasing numbers of our foremost dramatists are finding the most expressive and congenial forms in a combination of realism with some degree of theatricalism. The realistic form survives in the popular comedies of Neil Simon, for example, and pure theatricalism may be seen not only on the musical comedy stage but in a great deal of the work of the younger experimental playwrights. But it has surely been proven that there can be a blending of forms, that realism can put a solid base under theatricalism at the same time that it is being enlivened by the latter's showmanship.

It should be obvious that any combination of styles in presentation had better begin with the playwright's conception of the work, that the blend be inherent in the written text. For a director to impose on a work a foreign style not envisioned by the author can often lead to disaster.* This is not to discourage experiment; it is merely to observe that the dramatist's intent, and the kind of theatre for which he wrote the play, should serve as guides to production. *Henry V* does not lend itself to epic treatment. Similarly, *A Man for All Seasons* suffered when it was rewritten as a realistic film play.

The co-existence of realism and theatricalism in the same plays has already led to a rich variety of styles, and more will follow. The theatre in times of change is always experimenting and developing new forms. And these are ultimately assimilated in the mainstream, with varying degrees of influence. The chapter on "Theatricalism and Crisis" in John Gassner's *Form and Idea in Modern Theatre* (also issued under the title *Directions in Modern Theatre and Drama*) is especially recommended for further discussion of this subject.

Tomorrow's drama, in a world that is changing as rapidly as

---

* Occasionally a truly brilliant director, like Peter Brook, can provide freshness and new insights to a play—as he did with *A Midsummer Night's Dream*—by drastically altering the style of presentation. Even in this case we must bear in mind that what he did was closer to the Elizabethan staging for which the play was conceived that it was to the gauze-and-tinsel, realistic tradition of the nineteenth century. The latter was the true departure from the author's intent.

ours, will alter too. But it will be the product not only of our present culture, but also, like the culture itself, of all that has gone before—a synthesis of the past, the current, and the new forms still to come. It behooves the playwrights of tomorrow to know the roots from which their work will spring.

APPENDIX C

Today's Playhouses

It must be clear that there is a strong link between the type of drama being written in any age and the physical conditions under which it could be produced. Each influences the other. Shakespeare wrote his plays for a stage that both permitted and encouraged great fluidity of form. Realistic drama and the kind of playhouse it required developed simultaneously. Today's playwrights must not only be aware of the resources available to them in today's theatres, but should be prepared for the changes that are already taking place.

We have seen how the stage platform gradually drew back toward the proscenium arch, how the proscenium itself was enlarged from a mere up-center entrance until it became a sort of elaborate picture frame, and how the auditorium with its galleries and boxes formed a *U* whose ends embraced the playing area.

It was Richard Wagner, in 1876, who first insisted (to the architect of the *Festspielhaus* at Bayreuth) that every member of the audience have a clear view of the full depth of the stage. This led to the placing of the seats in a fan shape—an arrangement that came into general use later. Sight lines in the new theatres were also improved by raking the orchestra floor more steeply. The apron stage was virtually eliminated, with all action now taking place behind the proscenium arch, and the *U*-shaped tiers of galleries and boxes gave way to one or two balconies at the rear of the house that followed the same curve as the seats below. Electricity, of course, brought an incalculable improvement in illumination (as well as safety). Altogether, this was a type of playhouse admirably adapted to the kind of play it most frequently displayed. (In fact, it is the only kind of theatre in which strictly realistic plays can be presented as their authors intended.) Certainly it is the prevailing type of legitimate commercial theatre today.

But more and more playhouses are being built that depart from the form that has been standard for many years. Probably the most versatile is the thrust stage, of which the Vivian Beaumont Theatre in New York's Lincoln Center, the Tyrone Guthrie Theatre in Minneapolis, and the Festival Theatres in Stratford, Ontario, and Chichester, England, are all splendid examples. In the relationship of actor to spectators they are somewhat like the Elizabethan theatres. The audience is normally seated in steeply raked, concentric semicircles, much as they were in the old Roman theatres. There is no proscenium or front curtain, and, if any changes of scenery are required, this is done in view of the audience. Settings are usually evocative rather than illusionistic. Obviously this type of playhouse is superbly suited to Elizabethan drama, though it also lends itself well to the production of many other forms. Even realistic plays have been successfully performed on the thrust stages, though with some loss of illusionistic detail. This has not proved a serious liability. It seems likely that many new playhouses, especially those being built for the universities and for regional repertory groups, will be of this type. Any new commercial theatres, however, in order to accommodate the standard Broadway and West End productions, are more apt to have the recessed proscenium stages.

Central staging, which employs a production method called theatre-in-the-round, or sometimes theatre-in-three-quarter-round, puts the performance in the center of the audience, with properties but without scenery, or else in an area surrounded on three sides by the spectators, with minimal scenery, if any, on the fourth. The rectangular Arena Stage in Washington, D.C., with the audience sitting on all four sides of the acting area, is a notable theatre of this type.

The advantages of arena staging are its extreme intimacy, which brings the spectator closer to the actor than even the thrust stage, and low production costs, due to the absence of scenery and a crew to handle it. A disadvantage is the fact that an actor can, of necessity, face only a portion of the spectators at a time. In order not to slight any section of the audience, the actors must frequently change their orientation on stage, which may make for a lot of meaningless and excessive movement. At best, some spectators are going to be treated to the backs of the actors' heads when they might prefer to look at their faces. Another negative factor in central staging is the large portion of the audience visible beyond the acting area—a fact which tends to destroy the illusion of actuality—if that is what is desired. This has not proven a serious drawback, however, for the spectator tends to forget his opposite numbers as the play proceeds.

It is a curious fact that no recognizable production style seems to have developed in the arena playhouses. A large proportion of the plays staged in this manner have been realistic works originally intended for proscenium theatres. But the illusion of actuality is created by having the actors ignore the presence of the audience, and by the use of realistic speech and gesture, furniture, and properties. Small productions that can use the style's intimacy to advantage work best in arena staging. The conditions are hopeless—at least in the small arenas —for anything large, noisy, and spectacular.

Now we are beginning to get a few outdoor theatres, a notable one being the Delacorte Theatre in Central Park in New York, where Joseph Papp produces free Shakespeare in the summer. This is a thrust stage without a proscenium, and the audience is seated on banked and curved rows of seats. As with the indoor thrust stages, big productions of a spectacular and highly theatricalized nature are seen to advantage under these circumstances. The only real hazards are the weather and low-flying planes. Theatres like the Delacorte are not suitable to realistic plays.

Other outdoor theatres, built specifically for the presentation of historical and regional pageants—the so-called symphonic dramas of Paul Green and Kermit Hunter—are to be found in various localities, so far mostly in the American mid-South. As is typical of pageants, they employ music, singing, dancing, bright costuming, and spectacle, and are highly theatricalized.

Still another kind of playhouse which, for want of a better term, might be called "environmental" is making its appearance. In this type of staging the action takes place around and among the spectators. An early example is Max Reinhardt's production of *The Miracle*, a religious drama. It was seen in London in 1912 and some years later in several American cities. Each of the huge auditoriums in which it was performed was treated as a Gothic cathedral, the stage being converted into transept and apse. The aisles of the theatre became those of the church, and the audience the communicants. For sheer size and spectacle the show was impressive.

In 1935 Clifford Odets wrote a totally realistic drama, *Waiting for Lefty*, that was presumed to take place in a hall where an audience of taxi drivers was being addressed by officers of their union. It is questionable whether spectators at either of these productions were persuaded that they were anything but theatregoers attending a play, or whether they wanted to be anything else.

Environmental staging derives to some degree from the theories of Antonin Artaud, which are examined briefly in Appendix B under "Surrealism," and *avant-garde* groups are experimenting with the form. So far their efforts to induce audience participation by breaking down the dividing line between performers and spectators seem to have aroused as much embarrassment as rapport.

With the various types of playhouse available, the fact remains that most modern dramatists, even those who have abandoned the realistic form entirely, are still writing with the proscenium theatre in mind (a Broadway success can be immensely profitable), hoping that their plays can be adapted to as yet less conventional types of presentation.

APPENDIX D
The Typing Formats

The following pages show the standard format for typing stage plays, television plays (live or taped), and motion picture scenarios (including filmed television).

For the stage the name of the character who is speaking is centered over the speech, which runs straight across the page. Stage directions are indented and put in parentheses. Typing is single-spaced, except between speeches, when it is double-spaced. The act, scene, and page numbers are put in the upper right corner, the pages being numbered separately for each act. Plays typed this way usually run about a minute to a page, so that a script of 120 pages may be roughly estimated to run two hours, plus intermissions.

The standard form of typing for the stage is somewhat different in England, where the name of the character speaking is put at the left, with the stage directions and speeches indented and placed on the same line as the speaker's name. As with the American format, the typing is single-spaced, double-spaced between speeches.

The live and taped television format is quite different, and with good reason. Only the left-hand side of the page is used, the right side being left entirely blank for the director's notes and camera instructions. Everything in the script that is not actually spoken dialogue—that is, names of characters, descriptions of scenes, stage directions, actors' business—is written in capital letters. This is for quick identification in the control room of audio and visual elements. The name of the character speaking is centered in the left-hand column, over the speech. And only double spacing is used throughout, never single spacing. Television plays typed in this manner average about thirty seconds to a page, less if the speeches are very short.

Obviously the quality of the writing is not going to be altered by the way it is typed, but people working in the theatre and television are used to these formats, and a script neatly typed in the standard form certainly looks more professional.

The motion picture script differs in format from both of these. Normally a film play is written first as a "treatment," which is simply a telling of the story, so far as possible in visual terms, to help the reader picture the effect of the completed film.

The shooting script is a consecutively numbered list of shots, with a brief indication, in capital letters, of the locale, time of day, and the kind of camera shot. A description of the action and other visual elements follows this, starting at the left margin and going all the way across the page. Names of the characters speaking are capitalized and centered. Dialogue is indented and centered under the speaker's name. Single spacing is used except between shots and between speeches, which are double-spaced. A sample page of film script follows, but there are so many technicalities in writing for the movie medium that it would be wise for the inexperienced writer to secure a book on film scenarios before attempting anything beyond the treatment.

Typing Format—Stage

I-3-23

Daniel
He's a lawyer, you know, employed by one of the largest Paris banks.

Perrichon
Perhaps I should show my appreciation in some tangible way.
(Taking out a large pocket watch)
Here is a watch I purchased in Geneva. It strikes the hours.
Listen--it's just eleven now.
(He holds it up, and they listen to it chime)
I bought it for myself, but under the circumstances--

Daniel
If you will permit me, Monsieur, I believe the knowledge that he
has done you a service will be, for Armand, reward enough.

Perrichon
Good. I'm glad you agree.
(He pockets the watch)
Just between ourselves, the service he has done me is not quite
so heroic as my wife and daughter would lead one to think.

Daniel
Indeed?

Perrichon
(Hastily)
Oh, so long as the heart of Perrichon beats, there will be a place--
and so on, I assure you. But the fact is that well before he caught
me, I had already picked out a little pine tree at the cliff's edge,
and this I intended to grab hold of as I was--so to speak--rolling
past.

Daniel
That showed great presence of mind, Monsieur.

Perrichon
The proprietress tells me that last year a Russian, a prince--and
an excellent horseman, too--tumbled down the same slope.

Daniel
Truly?

Perrichon
His guide caught him in time, and the Russian gave him a hundred-
franc tip.

Proprietress
(Entering with the visitors' book and pen)
You are feeling better, Monsieur?

Perrichon
In the pink, Madame.

Proprietress
Then perhaps you will be kind enough to write something in the
visitors' book?

Typing Format—Live and Taped Television

ZACHARY GLENN ENTERS THE ROOM,

DRESSED IN A RIDING HABIT. ABOUT

FIFTY, HE IS BRUSQUE, EFFICIENT,

IMPATIENT OF SLOWER MINDS, AND

BUBBLING WITH ENERGY.

    ZACH (TOSSING ASIDE

HIS RIDING CROP AND GLOVES) Where's

Julian? He ought to be up.

    BELLE

He's having his breakfast, dear.

(SHE RISES) Zach, riding in the

Park this morning! Couldn't you

see it was going to rain? (TOUCHES

HIM) You're soaked.

HE BRUSHES HER HAND AWAY IMPATIENT-

LY AND PULLS OFF HIS COAT.

    ABBY

If the horse can stand it, I guess

Zach can.

ZACH GRINS APPRECIATIVELY AT HIS

MOTHER. BELLE PULLS A BELLROPE.

    ZACH (DROPPING HIS COAT

ON THE FLOOR) You got some milk

there? (BELLE POURS A GLASS. HE

DOWNS IT) Aah! That's a great

drink. Keeps me sound as a roach.

THE FOOTMAN ENTERS, AND, AT A SIG-

NAL FROM ZACH, PULLS OFF HIS BOOTS.

Typing Format—Film

GLAD TIDINGS--Rev. 7 Aug 71

247   MED. SHOT--MAUD

                    MAUD (for once a bit nervous
               and not in full control)
    Claire, what I wanted to say is--this
    is your father, dear. Mr. Whitney.

248   CLOSE-UP--CLAIRE

249   CLOSE-UP--STEVE

250   MED. SHOT--CLAIRE

    She rises, looks at Steve.

                    CLAIRE   (after a moment)
    How do you do?

251   ANGLE SHOT--STEVE OVER CLAIRE

    Steve extends his hand.

                    STEVE
    I'm fine, thanks. How are you?

                    CLAIRE
    Very well, thank you.

252   BACK TO MAUD

                    MAUD
    Well, surely this calls for something
    besides the usual amenities. Or didn't
    you hear me correctly? I said that this
    gentleman, Steven Whitney, the disting-
    uished foreign correspondent, is your
    father.

253   BACK TO STEVE OVER CLAIRE

                    CLAIRE
    I know, Mother.

    PAN Claire as she crosses to Maud, LOSE Steve.

    And I'm very pleased.

                    MAUD
    Are you, indeed?

    She rises.

    Oh, Claire, I'm so happy, and so touched.

    They are in each other's arms.

EDWARD MABLEY, author of *Dramatic Construction*, has for many years written and directed for the theatre, radio and television. His best known play is *Glad Tidings*, a comedy that enjoyed a long run on Broadway and is still extensively performed here and abroad. With Elie Siegmeister as composer, Mr. Mabley wrote the text of both the grand opera, *The Plough and the Stars* (after O'Casey), and a shorter work employing jazz and rock forms, *The Mermaid in Lock No. 7.* Bordeaux recently saw the European première of *The Plough*, and Antwerp of *The Mermaid.* Among dozens of radio and television plays of his authorship is *Borderline of Fear*, a collaboration with actress Joanna Roos. It is published in Kaufman's *Best Television Plays* and *Vanguard*, a Scott, Foresman anthology. Mr. Mabley is also the author of *The Motor Balloon "America,"* an account of the first attempt, in 1910, to fly the Atlantic, recently published by The Stephen Greene Press. When not writing, he directs television for the major networks and teaches playwriting at the New School for Social Research in New York. He lives in a 200-year-old farmhouse in a Hudson Valley village of which he also happens to be the mayor.

M